Contents

Credits

http://create.mheducation.com

ISBN-10: 1308129572   ISBN-13: 9781308129570

Course	Management Information Systems
Course Number	**BUSA2200**
	BUSA2650
	King University
	School of Business and Economics

1
CHAPTER

Management Information Systems: Business Driven MIS

CHAPTER OUTLINE

What's in IT for me?

This chapter sets the stage for the textbook. It starts from ground zero by providing a clear description of what information is and how it fits into business operations, strategies, and systems. It provides an overview of how companies operate in competitive environments and why they must continually define and redefine their business strategies to create competitive advantages. Doing so allows them to survive and thrive. Information systems are key business enablers for successful operations in competitive environments.

You, as a business student, must understand the tight correlation between business and technology. You must first recognize information's role in daily business activities, and then understand how information supports and helps implement global business strategies and competitive advantages. After reading this chapter, you should have a solid understanding of business driven information systems and their role in managerial decision making and problem solving.

The World Is Flat: Thomas Friedman

Christopher Columbus proved in 1492 that the world is round. For centuries, sailors maneuvered the seas discovering new lands, new people, and new languages as nations began trading goods around the globe. Then Thomas Friedman, a noted columnist for *The New York Times,* published his book *The World Is Flat.*

Friedman argues that the world has become flat due to technological advances connecting people in China, India, and the United States as if we were all next-door neighbors. Physicians in India are reading X-rays for U.S. hospitals, and JetBlue Airways ticket agents take plane reservations for the company from the comfort of their Utah homes. Technology has eliminated some of the economic and cultural advantages developed countries enjoy, making the world a level playing field for all participants. Friedman calls this Globalization 3.0.

Globalization 1.0 started when Christopher Columbus discovered the world is round and the world shrank from large to medium. For the next several hundred years, countries dominated by white men controlled business. Globalization 2.0 began around 1800, during the Industrial Revolution, when the world went from medium to small. In this era international companies dominated by white men controlled business. Globalization 3.0 began in early 2000, removing distance from the business equation, and the world has gone from small to tiny. In this era, people of all colors from the four corners of the world will dominate business. Farmers in remote villages in Nepal carry an iPhone to access the world's knowledge at, say, Wikipedia or the stock market closing prices at Bloomberg.

Outsourcing, or hiring someone from another country to complete work remotely, will play an enormous role in this era. It has advantages and disadvantages. Outsourcing work to countries where labor is cheap drives down production costs and allows companies to offer lower prices to U.S. consumers. Having an accountant in China complete a U.S. tax return is just as easy as driving to the H&R Block office on the corner, and probably far cheaper. Calling an 800 number for service can connect consumers to an Indian, Canadian, or Chinese worker on the other end of the line. Of course, outsourcing also eliminates some U.S. manufacturing and labor jobs, causing pockets of unemployment. In fact, the United States has outsourced several million service and manufacturing jobs to offshore, low-cost producers.

Figure 1.1 shows Friedman's list of forces that flattened the world. They converged around the year 2000 and "created a flat world: a global, web-enabled platform for multiple forms of sharing knowledge and work, irrespective of time, distance, geography, and increasingly, language." Three powerful new economies began materializing at this time. In

FIGURE 1.1

Thomas Friedman's 10 Forces
That Flattened the World

Friedman's 10 Forces That Flattened the World	
1. Fall of the Berlin Wall	The events of November 9, 1989, tilted the worldwide balance of power toward democracies and free markets.
2. Netscape IPO	The August 9, 1995, offering sparked massive investment in fiber-optic cables.
3. Work flow software	The rise of applications from PayPal to VPNs enabled faster, closer coordination among far-flung employees.
4. Open sourcing	Self-organizing communities, such as Linux, launched a collaborative revolution.
5. Outsourcing	Migrating business functions to India saved money *and* a Third World economy.
6. Offshoring	Contract manufacturing elevated China to economic prominence.
7. Supply chaining	Robust networks of suppliers, retailers, and customers increased business efficiency.
8. In-sourcing	Logistics giants took control of customer supply chains, helping mom-and-pop shops go global.
9. Informing	Power searching allowed everyone to use the Internet as a "personal supply chain of knowledge."
10. Wireless	Wireless technologies pumped up collaboration, making it mobile and personal.

India, China, and the former Soviet Union, more than 3 billion new willing and able partici-pants walked onto the business playing field. Business students will be competing for their first jobs not only against other local students, but also against students from around the country and around the globe.[1]

section 1.1 | Business Driven MIS

1.1 Describe the information age and the differences among data, information, business intelligence, and knowledge.

1.2 Identify the different departments in a company and why they must work together to achieve success.

1.3 Explain systems thinking and how management information systems enable business communications.

COMPETING IN THE INFORMATION AGE

Did you know that . . .

LO. 1.1: Describe the information age and the differences among data, information, business intelligence, and knowledge.

- The movie *Avatar* took more than four years to create and cost $450 million.
- Lady Gaga's real name is Stefani Joanne Angelina Germanotta.
- Customers pay $2.6 million for a 30-second advertising time slot during the Super Bowl.[2]

A *fact* is the confirmation or validation of an event or object. In the past, people primarily learned facts from books. Today, by simply pushing a button people can find out anything, from anywhere, at any time. We live in the *information age,* when infinite quantities of facts are widely available to anyone who can use a computer. The impact of information technology on the global business environment is equivalent to the printing press's impact on publishing and electricity's impact on productivity. College student startups were mostly unheard of before the information age. Now, it's not at all unusual to read about a business student starting a multimillion-dollar company from his or her dorm room. Think of Mark Zuckerberg, who started Facebook from his dorm, or Michael Dell (Dell Computers) and Bill Gates (Microsoft), who both founded their legendary companies as college students.

You may think only students well versed in advanced technology can compete in the information age. This is simply not true. Many business leaders have created exceptional opportunities by coupling the power of the information age with traditional business methods. Here are just a few examples:

- Amazon is not a technology company; its original business focus was to sell books, and it now sells nearly everything.
- Netflix is not a technology company; its primary business focus is to rent videos.
- Zappos is not a technology company; its primary business focus is to sell shoes, bags, clothing, and accessories.

Amazon's founder, Jeff Bezos, at first saw an opportunity to change the way people purchase books. Using the power of the information age to tailor offerings to each customer and speed the payment process, he in effect opened millions of tiny virtual bookstores, each with a vastly larger selection and far cheaper product than traditional bookstores. The success of his original business model led him to expand Amazon to carry many other types of products. The founders of Netflix and Zappos have done the same thing for videos and shoes. All these entrepreneurs were business professionals, not technology experts. However, they understood enough about the information age to apply it to a particular business, creating innovative companies that now lead entire industries.

Students who understand business along with the power associated with the information age will create their own opportunities and perhaps even new industries, as cofounders Chris DeWolfe and Tom Anderson did with MySpace and Mark Zuckerberg did

BUSINESS DRIVEN DISCUSSION

View from a Flat World

Bill Gates, founder of Microsoft, stated that 20 years ago most people would rather have been a B student in New York City than a genius in China because the opportunities available to students in developed countries were limitless. Today, many argue that the opposite is now true due to technological advances making it easier to succeed as a genius in China than a B student in New York. As a group, discuss if you agree or disagree with Bill Gates statement.[3]

with Facebook. Our primary goal in this course is to arm you with the knowledge you need to compete in the information age. The core drivers of the information age are:

- Data
- Information
- Business intelligence
- Knowledge (see Figure 1.2)

FIGURE 1.2

The Differences among Data, Information, Business Intelligence, and Knowledge

Data

Data are raw facts that describe the characteristics of an event or object. Before the information age, managers manually collected and analyzed data, a time-consuming and complicated task without which they would have little insight into how to run their

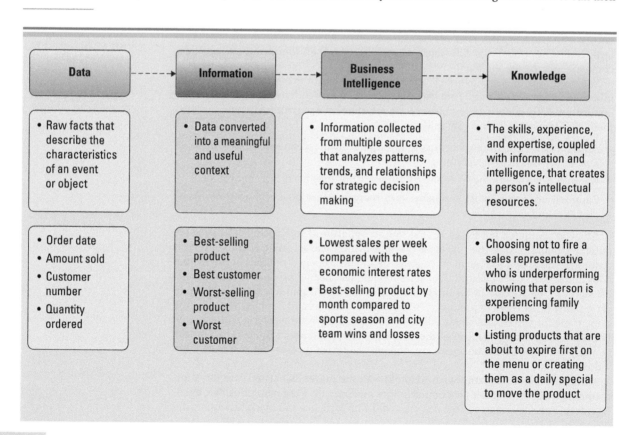

business. Lacking data, managers often found themselves making business decisions about how many products to make, how much material to order, or how many employees to hire based on intuition or gut feelings. In the information age, successful managers compile, analyze, and comprehend massive amounts of data daily, which helps them make more successful business decisions.

Figure 1.3 shows sales data for Tony's Wholesale Company, a fictitious business that supplies snacks to stores. The data highlight characteristics such as order date, customer, sales representative, product, quantity, and profit. The second line in Figure 1.3, for instance, shows that Roberta Cross sold 90 boxes of Ruffles to Walmart for $1,350, resulting in a profit of $450 (note that Profit = Sales − Costs). These data are useful for understanding individual sales; however, they do not provide us much insight into how Tony's business is performing as a whole. Tony needs to answer questions that will help him manage his day-to-day operations such as:

- Who are my best customers?
- Who are my least-profitable customers?
- What is my best-selling product?
- What is my slowest-selling product?
- Who is my strongest sales representative?
- Who is my weakest sales representative?

What Tony needs, in other words, is not data but *information.*

Information

Information is data converted into a meaningful and useful context. Having the right information at the right moment in time can be worth a fortune. Having the wrong information at the right moment; or the right information at the wrong moment can be disastrous. The truth about information is that its value is only as good as the people who use it. People using the same information can make different decisions depending on how they interpret or analyze the information. Thus information has value only insofar as the people using it do as well.

Tony can analyze his sales data and turn them into information to answer all the above questions and understand how his business is operating. Figures 1.4 and 1.5, for instance, show us that Walmart is Roberta Cross's best customer, and that Ruffles is Tony's best product measured in terms of total sales. Armed with this information, Tony can identify and then address such issues as weak products and underperforming sales representatives.

A ***variable*** is a data characteristic that stands for a value that changes or varies over time. For example, in Tony's data, price and quantity ordered can vary. Changing

FIGURE 1.3

Tony's Snack Company Data

Order Date	Customer	Sales Representative	Product	Qty	Unit Price	Total Sales	Unit Cost	Total Cost	Profit
4-Jan	Walmart	PJ Helgoth	Doritos	41	$24	$ 984	$18	$738	$246
4-Jan	Walmart	Roberta Cross	Ruffles	90	$15	$1,350	$10	$900	$450
5-Jan	Safeway	Craig Schultz	Ruffles	27	$15	$ 405	$10	$270	$135
6-Jan	Walmart	Roberta Cross	Ruffles	67	$15	$1,005	$10	$670	$335
7-Jan	7-Eleven	Craig Schultz	Pringles	79	$12	$ 948	$ 6	$474	$474
7-Jan	Walmart	Roberta Cross	Ruffles	52	$15	$ 780	$10	$520	$260
8-Jan	Kroger	Craig Schultz	Ruffles	39	$15	$ 585	$10	$390	$195
9-Jan	Walmart	Craig Schultz	Ruffles	66	$15	$ 990	$10	$660	$330
10-Jan	Target	Craig Schultz	Ruffles	40	$15	$ 600	$10	$400	$200
11-Jan	Walmart	Craig Schultz	Ruffles	71	$15	$1,065	$10	$710	$355

Order Date	Customer	Sales Representative	Product	Quantity	Unit Price	Total Sales	Unit Cost	Total Cost	Profit
26-Apr	Walmart	Roberta Cross	Fritos	86	$ 19	$ 1,634	$ 17	$ 1,462	$ 172
29-Aug	Walmart	Roberta Cross	Fritos	76	$ 19	$ 1,444	$ 17	$ 1,292	$ 152
7-Sep	Walmart	Roberta Cross	Fritos	20	$ 19	$ 380	$ 17	$ 340	$ 40
22-Nov	Walmart	Roberta Cross	Fritos	39	$ 19	$ 741	$ 17	$ 663	$ 78
30-Dec	Walmart	Roberta Cross	Fritos	68	$ 19	$ 1,292	$ 17	$ 1,156	$ 136
7-Jul	Walmart	Roberta Cross	Pringles	79	$ 18	$ 1,422	$ 8	$ 632	$ 790
6-Aug	Walmart	Roberta Cross	Pringles	21	$ 12	$ 252	$ 6	$ 126	$ 126
2-Oct	Walmart	Roberta Cross	Pringles	60	$ 18	$ 1,080	$ 8	$ 480	$ 600
15-Nov	Walmart	Roberta Cross	Pringles	32	$ 12	$ 384	$ 6	$ 192	$ 192
21-Dec	Walmart	Roberta Cross	Pringles	92	$ 12	$ 1,104	$ 6	$ 552	$ 552
28-Feb	Walmart	Roberta Cross	Ruffles	67	$ 15	$ 1,005	$ 10	$ 670	$ 335
6-Mar	Walmart	Roberta Cross	Ruffles	8	$ 15	$ 120	$ 10	$ 80	$ 40
16-Mar	Walmart	Roberta Cross	Ruffles	68	$ 15	$ 1,020	$ 10	$ 680	$ 340
23-Apr	Walmart	Roberta Cross	Ruffles	34	$ 15	$ 510	$ 10	$ 340	$ 170
4-Aug	Walmart	Roberta Cross	Ruffles	40	$ 15	$ 600	$ 10	$ 400	$ 200
18-Aug	Walmart	Roberta Cross	Ruffles	93	$ 15	$ 1,395	$ 10	$ 930	$ 465
5-Sep	Walmart	Roberta Cross	Ruffles	41	$ 15	$ 615	$ 10	$ 410	$ 205
12-Sep	Walmart	Roberta Cross	Ruffles	8	$ 15	$ 120	$ 10	$ 80	$ 40
28-Oct	Walmart	Roberta Cross	Ruffles	50	$ 15	$ 750	$ 10	$ 500	$ 250
21-Nov	Walmart	Roberta Cross	Ruffles	79	$ 15	$ 1,185	$ 10	$ 790	$ 395
29-Jan	Walmart	Roberta Cross	Sun Chips	5	$ 22	$ 110	$ 18	$ 90	$ 20
12-Apr	Walmart	Roberta Cross	Sun Chips	85	$ 22	$ 1,870	$ 18	$ 1,530	$ 340
16-Jun	Walmart	Roberta Cross	Sun Chips	55	$ 22	$ 1,210	$ 18	$ 990	$ 220
				1,206	$383	$20,243	$273	$14,385	$5,858

Sorting the data reveals the information that Roberta Cross's total sales to Walmart were $20,243 resulting in a profit of $5,858.
(Profit $5,858 = Sales $20,243 − Costs $14,385)

FIGURE 1.4

Tony's Data Sorted by Customer "Walmart" and Sales Representative "Roberta Cross"

variables allows managers to create hypothetical scenarios to study future possibilities. Tony may find it valuable to anticipate how sales or cost increases affect profitability. To estimate how a 20 percent increase in prices might improve profits, Tony simply changes the price variable for all orders, which automatically calculates the amount of new profits. To estimate how a 10 percent increase in costs hurts profits, Tony changes the cost variable for all orders, which automatically calculates the amount of lost profits. Manipulating variables is an important tool for any business.

Business Intelligence

Business intelligence (BI) is information collected from multiple sources such as suppliers, customers, competitors, partners, and industries that analyzes patterns, trends, and relationships for strategic decision making. BI manipulates multiple variables and in some cases even hundreds of variables including such items as interest rates, weather conditions, and even gas prices. Tony could use BI to analyze internal data such as company sales, along with external data about the environment such as competitors, finances, weather, holidays, and even sporting events. Both internal and external variables affect snack sales, and analyzing these variables will help Tony determine ordering levels and sales forecasts. For instance, BI can predict inventory requirements for Tony's business for the week before the Super Bowl if, say, the home team is playing, average

BUSINESS DRIVEN MIS

Manipulating the Data to Find Your Version of the Truth

How can global warming be real when there is so much snow and cold weather? That's what some people wondered after a couple of massive snowstorms buried Washington, D.C. Politicians across the capital made jokes and built igloos as they disputed the existence of climate change. Some concluded the planet simply could not be warming with all the snow on the ground.

These comments frustrated Joseph Romm, a physicist and climate expert with the Center for American Progress. He spent weeks turning data into information and graphs to educate anyone who would listen as to why this reasoning was incorrect. Climate change is all about analyzing data, turning it into information to detect trends. You cannot observe climate change by looking out the window; you have to review decades of weather data with advanced tools to really understand the trends.

Increasingly we see politicians, economists, and newscasters taking tough issues and boiling them down to simplistic arguments over what the data mean, each interpreting the data and spinning the data to support their views and agendas. You need to understand the data and turn them into useful information or else you will not understand when someone is telling the truth and when you are being lied to.

Brainstorm two or three types of data economists use to measure the economy. How do they turn the data into information? What issues do they encounter when attempting to measure the economy? As a manager, what do you need to understand when reading or listening to economic and business reports?[4]

Tony's Business Information	Name	Total Profit
Who is Tony's best customer by total sales?	Walmart	$ 560,789
Who is Tony's least-valuable customer by total sales?	Walgreens	$45,673
Who is Tony's best customer by profit?	7-Eleven	$ 324,550
Who is Tony's least-valuable customer by profit?	King Soopers	$ 23,908
What is Tony's best-selling product by total sales?	Ruffles	$ 232,500
What is Tony's weakest-selling product by total sales?	Pringles	$ 54,890
What is Tony's best-selling product by profit?	Tostitos	$ 13,050
What is Tony's weakest-selling product by profit?	Pringles	$ 23,000
Who is Tony's best sales representative by profit?	R. Cross	$1,230,980
Who is Tony's weakest sales representative by profit?	Craig Schultz	$ 98,980
What is the best sales representative's best-selling product by total profit?	Ruffles	$ 98,780
Who is the best sales representative's best customer by total profit?	Walmart	$ 345,900
What is the best sales representative's weakest-selling product by total profit?	Sun Chips	$ 45,600
Who is the best sales representative's weakest customer by total profit?	Krogers	$ 56,050

FIGURE 1.5

Information Gained after Analyzing Tony's Data

BUSINESS DRIVEN ETHICS AND SECURITY

Information Issues in the Information Age

We live in the information age where the collection, storage, and use of data are hot topics. One example of inappropriate data handling occurred at a college where the monitoring of restrooms occurred every 15 seconds to observe the use of toilets, mirrors, and sinks. Students, faculty, and staff began complaining that the data collection was an invasion of their privacy and a violation of their rights.

Another example of inappropriate data handling occurred when a professor of accounting at a college lost a flash drive containing information for more than 1,800 students, including Social Security numbers, grades, and names. Social Security numbers were included because the data went back to before 1993 when the college used Social Security numbers to identify students.

What types of student data does your college collect? What could happen if your professor lost a thumb drive with all of your personal information? What types of issues could you encounter if someone stole your personal data? What can your college do to ensure this type of data storage violation does not occur?[5]

temperature is above 80 degrees, and the stock market is performing well. This is BI at its finest, incorporating all types of internal and external variables to anticipate business performance.

Top managers use BI to define the future of the business, analyzing markets, industries, and economies to determine the strategic direction the company must follow to remain profitable. Tony will set the strategic direction for his firm, which might include introducing new flavors of potato chips or sport drinks as new product lines or schools and hospitals as new market segments.

Knowledge

Knowledge includes the skills, experience, and expertise, coupled with information and intelligence, that creates a person's intellectual resources. *Knowledge workers* are individuals valued for their ability to interpret and analyze information. Today's workers are commonly referred to as knowledge workers and they use BI along with personal experience to make decisions based on both information and intuition, a valuable resource for any company.

Imagine that Tony analyzes his data and finds his weakest sales representative for this period is Craig Schultz. If Tony considered only this information, he might conclude that firing Craig was a good business decision. However, because Tony has knowledge about how the company operates, he knows Craig has been out on medical leave for several weeks; hence, his sales numbers are low. Without this additional knowledge, Tony might have executed a bad business decision, delivered a negative message to the other employees, and sent his best sales representatives out to look for other jobs.

The key point in this scenario is that it is simply impossible to collect all the information about every situation, and yet without that, it can be easy to misunderstand the problem. Using data, information, business intelligence, *and* knowledge to make decisions and solve problems is the key to finding success in business. These core drivers of the information age are the building blocks of business systems.

THE CHALLENGE: DEPARTMENTAL COMPANIES

Companies are typically organized by department or functional area such as:

- **Accounting:** Records, measures, and reports monetary transactions.
- **Finance:** Deals with strategic financial issues including money, banking, credit, investments, and assets.
- **Human resources:** Maintains policies, plans, and procedures for the effective management of employees.
- **Marketing:** Supports sales by planning, pricing, and promoting goods or services.
- **Operations management:** Manages the process of converting or transforming or resources into goods or services.
- **Sales:** Performs the function of selling goods or services (see Figure 1.6).

Each department performs its own activities. Sales and marketing focus on moving goods or services into the hands of consumers; they maintain transactional data. Finance and accounting focus on managing the company's resources and maintain monetary data. Operations management focuses on manufacturing and maintains production data, while human resources focuses on hiring and training people and maintains employee data. Although each department has its own focus and data, none can work independently if the company is to operate as a whole. It is easy to see how a

LO 1.2: Identify the different departments in a company and why they must work together to achieve success.

FIGURE 1.6

Departments Working Independently

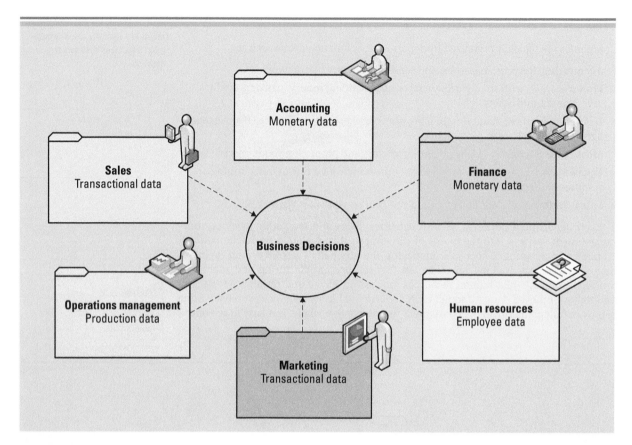

FIGURE 1.7

Departments Working Together

business decision made by one department can affect other departments. Marketing needs to analyze production and sales data to come up with product promotions and advertising strategies. Production needs to understand sales forecasts to determine the company's manufacturing needs. Sales needs to rely on information from operations to understand inventory, place orders, and forecast consumer demand. All departments need to understand the accounting and finance departments' information for budgeting. For the firm to be successful, all departments must work together as a single unit sharing common information and not operate independently or in a silo (see Figure 1.7).

LO 1.3: Explain systems thinking and how management information systems enable business communications.

THE SOLUTION: MANAGEMENT INFORMATION SYSTEMS

You probably recall the old story of three blind men attempting to describe an elephant. The first man, feeling the elephant's girth, said the elephant seemed very much like a wall. The second, feeling the elephant's trunk, declared the elephant was like a snake. The third man felt the elephant's tusks and said the elephant was like a tree or a cane. Companies that operate departmentally are seeing only one part of the elephant, a critical mistake that hinders successful operation.

Successful companies operate cross-functionally, integrating the operations of all departments. Systems are the primary enabler of cross-functional operations. A *system* is a collection of parts that link to achieve a common purpose. A car is a good example of a system, since removing a part, such as the steering wheel or accelerator, causes the entire system to stop working.

Before jumping into how systems work, it is important to have a solid understanding of the basic production process for goods and services. *Goods* are material items or products that customers will buy to satisfy a want or need. Clothing, groceries, cell phones, and cars are all examples of goods that people buy to fulfill their needs. *Services*

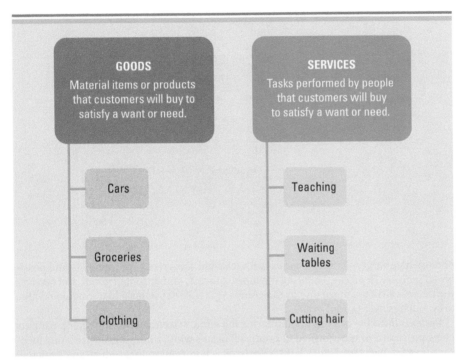

FIGURE 1.8

Different Types of Goods and Services

are tasks performed by people that customers will buy to satisfy a want or need. Waiting tables, teaching, and cutting hair are all examples of services that people pay for to fulfill their needs (see Figure 1.8).

Production is the process where a business takes raw materials and processes them or converts them into a finished product for its goods or services. Just think about making a hamburger (see Figure 1.9). First, you must gather all of the *inputs* or raw materials such as the bun, patty, lettuce, tomato, and ketchup. Second, you *process* the raw materials, so in this example you would need to cook the patty, wash and chop the lettuce and tomato, and place all of the items in the bun. Finally, you would have your *output* or finished product—your hamburger! **Productivity** is the rate at which goods and services are produced based upon total output given total inputs. Given our previous example, if a business could produce the same hamburger with less expensive inputs

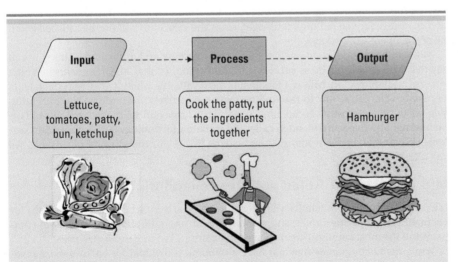

FIGURE 1.9

Input, Process, Output Example

FIGURE 1.10

Overview of Systems Thinking

or more hamburgers with the same inputs it would see a rise in productivity and possibly an increase in profits. Ensuring the input, process, and output of goods and services work across all of the departments of a company is where systems add tremendous value to overall business productivity.

Systems thinking is a way of monitoring the entire system by viewing multiple inputs being processed or transformed to produce outputs while continuously gathering feedback on each part (see Figure 1.10). *Feedback* is information that returns to its original transmitter (input, transform, or output) and modifies the transmitter's actions. Feedback helps the system maintain stability. For example, a car's system continuously monitors the fuel level and turns on a warning light if the gas level is too low. Systems thinking provides an end-to-end view of how operations work together to create a product or service. Business students who understand systems thinking are valuable resources because they can implement solutions that consider the entire process, not just a single component.

Management information systems (MIS) is a business function, like accounting and human resources, which moves information about people, products, and processes across the company to facilitate decision making and problem solving. MIS incorporates systems thinking to help companies operate cross-functionally. For example, to fulfill product orders, an MIS for sales moves a single customer order across all functional areas including sales, order fulfillment, shipping, billing, and finally customer service. Although different functional areas handle different parts of the sale, thanks to MIS, to the customer the sale is one continuous process. If one part of the company is experiencing problems, however, then, like the car without a steering wheel, the entire system fails. If order fulfillment packages the wrong product, it will not matter that shipping, billing, and customer service did their jobs right, since the customer will not be satisfied when he or she opens the package.

MIS can be an important enabler of business success and innovation. This is not to say that MIS *equals* business success and innovation, or that MIS *represents* business success and innovation. MIS is a tool that is most valuable when it leverages the talents of people who know how to use and manage it effectively. To perform the MIS function effectively, almost all companies, particularly large and medium-sized ones, have an internal MIS department, often called information technology (IT), information systems (IS), or management information systems (MIS). For the purpose of this text, we will refer to it as MIS.

MIS Department Roles and Responsibilities

MIS as a department is a relatively new functional area, having been around formally for about 40 years. Job titles, roles, and responsibilities often differ from company to company, but the most common are displayed in Figure 1.11.

While many companies may not have a different individual for each of these positions, they must have top managers who take responsibility for all these areas.

Chief security officer (CSO)

Responsible for ensuring the security of business systems and developing strategies and safeguards against attacks by hackers and viruses.

Chief knowledge officer (CKO)

Responsible for collecting, maintaining, and distributing company knowledge.

Chief technology officer (CTO)

Responsible for ensuring the speed, accuracy, availability, and reliability of the MIS.

Chief information officer (CIO)

Responsible for (1) overseeing all uses of MIS and (2) ensuring that MIS strategically aligns with business goals and objectives.

MIS Department Roles and Responsibilities

Chief privacy officer (CPO)

Responsible for ensuring the ethical and legal use of information within a company.

FIGURE 1.11

The Roles and Responsibilities of MIS

section 1.2 | Business Strategy

LEARNING OUTCOMES

1.4 Explain why competitive advantages are temporary.

1.5 Describe Porter's Five Forces Model and explain each of the five forces.

1.6 Compare Porter's three generic strategies.

1.7 Demonstrate how a company can add value by using Porter's value chain analysis.

IDENTIFYING COMPETITIVE ADVANTAGES

LO 1.4: **Explain why competitive advantages are temporary.**

Running a company today is similar to leading an army; the top manager or leader ensures all participants are heading in the right direction and completing their goals and objectives. Companies lacking leadership quickly implode as employees head in different directions attempting to achieve conflicting goals. To combat these challenges, leaders communicate and execute business strategies (from the Greek word *stratus* for army and *ago* for leading). A **business strategy** is a leadership plan that achieves a specific set of goals or objectives as displayed in Figure 1.12.

Good leaders also anticipate unexpected misfortunes, from strikes and economic recessions to natural disasters. Their business strategies build in buffers or slack,

FIGURE 1.12

Examples of Business
Strategies

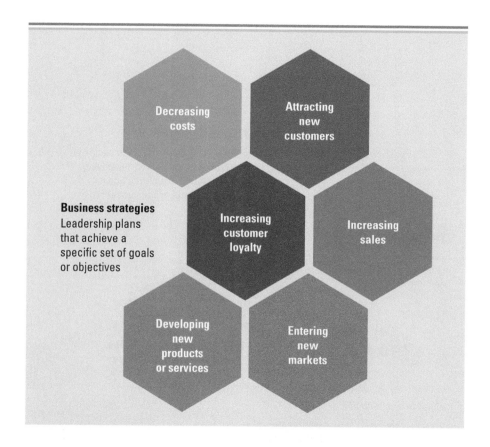

allowing the company the ability to ride out any storm and defend against competitive or environmental threats. Of course, updating business strategies is a continuous undertaking as internal and external environments rapidly change. Business strategies that match core company competencies to opportunities result in competitive advantages, a key to success!

A *competitive advantage* is a feature of a product or service on which customers place a greater value than they do on similar offerings from competitors. Competitive advantages provide the same product or service either at a lower price or with additional value that can fetch premium prices. Unfortunately, competitive advantages are typically temporary, because competitors often quickly seek ways to duplicate them. In turn, organizations must develop a strategy based on a new competitive advantage. Ways that companies duplicate competitive advantages include acquiring the new technology, copying the business operations, and hiring away key employees. The introduction of Apple's iPod and iTunes, a brilliant merger of technology, business, and entertainment, offers an excellent example.

In early 2000, Steve Jobs was fixated on developing video editing software when he suddenly realized that millions of people were using computers to listen to music, a new trend in the industry catapulted by illegal online services such as Napster. Jobs was worried that he was looking in the wrong direction and had missed the opportunity to jump on the online music bandwagon. He moved fast, however, and within four months he had developed the first version of iTunes for the Mac. Jobs' next challenge was to make a portable iTunes player that could hold thousands of songs and be completely transportable. Within nine months the iPod was born. With the combination of iTunes and iPod, Apple created a significant competitive advantage in the marketplace. Many firms began following Apple's lead by creating portable music players to compete with the iPod. In addition, Apple continues to create new and exciting products to gain competitive advantages, such as its iPad, a larger version of the iPod that functions more as a computer than a music player.[6]

BUSINESS DRIVEN GLOBALIZATION

According to the Economic Policy Institute, over the past decade the United States has lost an estimated 2.4 million factory jobs to China. Factories in South Korea, Taiwan, and China are producing toys, toothpaste, running shoes, computers, appliances, and cars. For a long time U.S. firms did not recognize these products as competition; they regarded Asia's high-tech products as second-rate knockoffs and believed Asian countries maintained a "factory culture"—they could imitate but not innovate.

In hindsight, it is obvious that once these countries did begin designing and creating high-end products, they would have obvious competitive advantages, with high-value research and development coupled with low-cost manufacturing of unbeatable goods and services. Asia is now on the rise in all industries from wind turbines to high-speed bullet trains. According to *Bloomberg Businessweek*'s ranking of the most innovative companies, 15 of the top 50 are Asian, up from just 5 in 2006. In fact, for the first time, the majority of the top 25 are based outside the United States.

How do you, as a business student, view these statistics? What type of global business climate will you be competing in when you graduate? If you wanted to gather competitive intelligence about the job market, where would you look and what types of data would you want to analyze? What can you do to create personal competitive advantages to differentiate yourself when searching for a job?[7]

The Competitive Landscape for Students

When a company is the first to market with a competitive advantage, it gains a particular benefit, such as Apple did with its iPod. This *first-mover advantage* occurs when a company can significantly increase its market share by being first with a new competitive advantage. FedEx created a first-mover advantage by developing its customer self-service software, which allows people to request parcel pickups, print mailing slips, and track parcels online. Other parcel delivery companies quickly began creating their own online services. Today, customer self-service on the Internet is a standard feature of the parcel delivery business.

Competitive intelligence is the process of gathering information about the competitive environment, including competitors' plans, activities, and products, to improve a company's ability to succeed. It means understanding and learning as much as possible as soon as possible about what is occurring outside the company to remain competitive. Frito-Lay, a premier provider of snack foods such as Cracker Jacks and Cheetos, does not send its sales representatives into grocery stores just to stock shelves; they carry handheld computers and record the product offerings, inventory, and even product locations of competitors. Frito-Lay uses this information to gain competitive intelligence on everything from how well competing products are selling to the strategic placement of its own products.[8]

Managers use three common tools to analyze competitive intelligence and develop competitive advantages including:

1. The Five Forces Model (for evaluating industry attractiveness).
2. The three generic strategies (for choosing a business focus).
3. Value chain analysis (for executing business strategies).

THE FIVE FORCES MODEL — EVALUATING INDUSTRY ATTRACTIVENESS

Michael Porter, a university professor at Harvard Business School, identified the following pressures that can hurt potential sales:

- Knowledgeable customers can force down prices by pitting rivals against each other.
- Influential suppliers can drive down profits by charging higher prices for supplies.
- Competition can steal customers.
- New market entrants can steal potential investment capital.
- Substitute products can steal customers.

Formally defined, ***Porter's Five Forces Model*** analyzes the competitive forces within the environment in which a company operates to assess the potential for profitability in an industry. Its purpose is to combat these competitive forces by identifying opportunities, competitive advantages, and competitive intelligence. If the forces are strong, they increase competition; if the forces are weak, they decrease competition. This section details each of the forces and its associated MIS business strategy (see Figure 1.13).[9]

Buyer Power

Buyer power is the ability of buyers to affect the price they must pay for an item. Factors used to assess buyer power include number of customers, their sensitivity to price, size of orders, differences between competitors, and availability of substitute products. If buyer power is high, customers can force a company and its competitors to compete on price, which typically drives prices down.

One way to reduce buyer power is by manipulating ***switching costs***, costs that make customers reluctant to switch to another product or service. Switching costs include financial as well as intangible values. The cost of switching doctors, for instance, includes the powerful intangible components of having to build relationships with the new doctor and nurses, as well as transferring all your medical history. With MIS, however, patients can store their medical records on DVDs or thumb drives, allowing easy transferability. The Internet also lets patients review websites for physician referrals, which takes some of the fear out of trying someone new.[10]

FIGURE 1.13

Porter's Five Forces Model

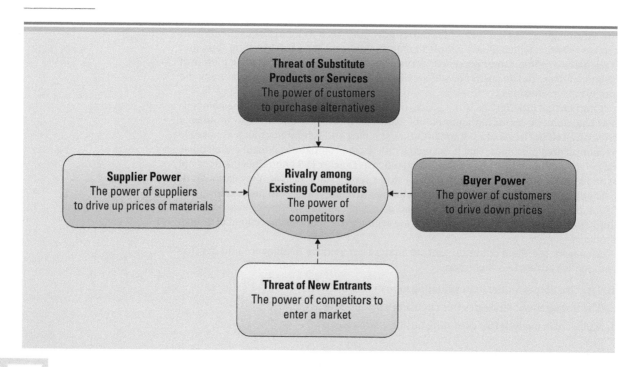

Companies can also reduce buyer power with **loyalty programs,** which reward customers based on their spending. The airline industry is famous for its frequent-flyer programs, for instance. Because of the rewards travelers receive (free airline tickets, upgrades, or hotel stays), they are more likely to be loyal to or give most of their business to a single company. Keeping track of the activities and accounts of many thousands or millions of customers covered by loyalty programs is not practical without large-scale business systems, however. Loyalty programs are thus a good example of using MIS to reduce buyer power.[11]

Supplier Power

A **supply chain** consists of all parties involved, directly or indirectly, in obtaining raw materials or a product. In a typical supply chain, a company will be both a supplier (to customers) and a customer (of other suppliers), as illustrated in Figure 1.14. **Supplier power** is the suppliers' ability to influence the prices they charge for supplies (including materials, labor, and services). Factors used to appraise supplier power include number of suppliers, size of suppliers, uniqueness of services, and availability of substitute products. If supplier power is high, the supplier can influence the industry by:

- Charging higher prices.
- Limiting quality or services.
- Shifting costs to industry participants.[12]

Typically, when a supplier raises prices, the buyers will pass on the increase to their customers by raising prices on the end product. When supplier power is high, buyers lose revenue because they cannot pass on the raw material price increase to their customers. Some powerful suppliers, such as pharmaceutical companies, can exert a threat over an entire industry when substitutes are limited and the product is critical to the buyers. Patient who need to purchase cancer-fighting drugs have no power over price and must pay whatever the drug company asks because there are few available alternatives.

Using MIS to find alternative products is one way of decreasing supplier power. Cancer patients can now use the Internet to research alternative medications and practices, something that was next to impossible just a few decades ago. Buyers can also use MIS to form groups or collaborate with other buyers, increasing the size of the buyer group and reducing supplier power. For a hypothetical example, the collective group of 30,000 students from a university has far more power over price when purchasing laptops than a single student.[13]

Threat of Substitute Products or Services

The **threat of substitute products or services** is high when there are many alternatives to a product or service and low when there are few alternatives from which to choose. For example, travelers have numerous substitutes for airline transportation including automobiles, trains, and boats. Technology even makes videoconferencing and virtual meetings possible, eliminating the need for some business travel. Ideally, a company would like to be in a market in which there are few substitutes for the products or services it offers.

Polaroid had this unique competitive advantage for many years until it forgot to observe competitive intelligence. Then the firm went bankrupt when people began taking digital pictures with everything from video cameras to cell phones.

A company can reduce the threat of substitutes by offering additional value through wider product distribution. Soft-drink manufacturers distribute their products through

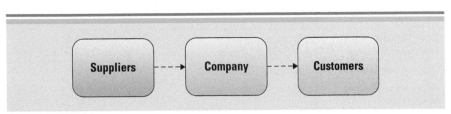

FIGURE 1.14

Traditional Supply Chain

vending machines, gas stations, and convenience stores, increasing the availability of soft drinks relative to other beverages. Companies can also offer various add-on services, making the substitute product less of a threat. For example, iPhones include capabilities for games, videos, and music, making a traditional cell phone less of a substitute.[14]

Threat of New Entrants

The ***threat of new entrants*** is high when it is easy for new competitors to enter a market and low when there are significant entry barriers to joining a market. An ***entry barrier*** is a feature of a product or service that customers have come to expect and entering competitors must offer the same for survival. For example, a new bank must offer its customers an array of MIS-enabled services, including ATMs, online bill paying, and online account monitoring. These are significant barriers to new firms entering the banking market. At one time, the first bank to offer such services gained a valuable first-mover advantage, but only temporarily, as other banking competitors developed their own MIS services.[15]

Rivalry among Existing Competitors

Rivalry among existing competitors is high when competition is fierce in a market and low when competitors are more complacent. Although competition is always more intense in some industries than in others, the overall trend is toward increased competition in almost every industry. The retail grocery industry is intensively competitive. Kroger, Safeway, and Albertsons in the United States compete in many different ways, essentially trying to beat or match each other on price. Most supermarket chains have implemented loyalty programs to provide customers special discounts while gathering valuable information about their purchasing habits. In the future, expect to see grocery stores using wireless technologies that track customer movements throughout the store to determine purchasing sequences.

   Product differentiation occurs when a company develops unique differences in its products or services with the intent to influence demand. Companies can use differentiation to reduce rivalry. For example, while many companies sell books and videos on the Internet, Amazon differentiates itself by using customer profiling. When a customer visits Amazon.com repeatedly, Amazon begins to offer products tailored to that particular customer based on his or her profile. In this way, Amazon has reduced its rivals' power by offering its customers a differentiated service.

   To review, the Five Forces Model helps managers set business strategy by identifying the competitive structure and economic environment of an industry. If the forces are strong, they increase competition; if the forces are weak, they decrease it (see Figure 1.15).[16]

Analyzing the Airline Industry

Let us bring Porter's five forces together to look at the competitive forces shaping an industry and highlight business strategies to help it remain competitive. Assume a shipping company is deciding whether to enter the commercial airline industry. If

FIGURE 1.15

Strong and Weak Examples of Porter's Five Forces

	Weak Force: Decreases Competition or Few Competitors	Strong Force: Increases Competition or Lots of Competitors
Buyer Power	An international hotel chain purchasing milk	A single consumer purchasing milk
Supplier Power	A company that makes airline engines	A company that makes pencils
Threat of Substitute Products or Services	Cancer drugs from a pharmaceutical company	Coffee from McDonald's
Threat of New Entrants	A professional hockey team	A dog walking business
Rivalry among Existing Competitors	Department of Motor Vehicles	A coffee shop

BUSINESS DRIVEN INNOVATION

Fixing the Post Office

Is there anything more frustrating than waiting in line at the post office? Not only are those lines frustrating, but they are also unprofitable. The U.S. Postal Service has faced multibillion-dollar losses every year for the past few years, making for one of the greatest challenges in its history.

What is killing the post office? Perhaps it is Stamps.com, a website that allows you to customize and print your own stamps 24 hours a day. Getting married? Place a photo of the happy couple right on the stamp for the invitations. Starting a business? Place your business logo on your stamps. Stamps.com even keeps track of a customer's postal spending and can recommend optimal delivery methods. Plus, Stamps.com gives you postage discounts you can't get at the post office or with a postage meter.

Evaluate the U.S. Postal Service using Porter's Five Forces Model. How could the Postal Service create new products and services to help grow its business? What types of competitive advantages can you identify for the Postal Service?[18]

performed correctly, an analysis of the five forces should determine that this is a highly risky business strategy because all five forces are strong. It will thus be difficult to generate a profit.

- **Buyer power:** Buyer power is high because customers have many airlines to choose from and typically make purchases based on price, not carrier.
- **Supplier power:** Supplier power is high since there are limited plane and engine manufacturers to choose from, and unionized workforces (suppliers of labor) restrict airline profits.
- **Threat of substitute products or services:** The threat of substitute products is high from many transportation alternatives including automobiles, trains, and boats, and from transportation substitutes such as videoconferencing and virtual meetings.
- **Threat of new entrants:** The threat of new entrants is high because new airlines are continuously entering the market, including sky taxies offering low-cost on-demand air taxi service.
- **Rivalry among existing competitors:** Rivalry in the airline industry is high, and websites such as Travelocity.com force them to compete on price (see Figure 1.16).[17]

	Strong (High) Force: Increases Competition or Lots of Competitors
Buyer Power	Many airlines for buyers to choose from forcing competition based on price
Supplier Power	Limited number of plane and engine manufacturers to choose from along with unionized workers
Threat of Substitute Products or Services	Many substitutes including cars, trains, and busses. Even substitutes to travel such as video conferencing and virtual meetings.
Threat of New Entrants	Many new airlines entering the market all the time including the latest sky taxis.
Rivalry among Existing Competitors	Intense competition—many rivals.

FIGURE 1.16

Five Forces Model in the Airline Industry

THE THREE GENERIC STRATEGIES—CHOOSING A BUSINESS FOCUS

Once top management has determined the relative attractiveness of an industry and decided to enter it, the firm must formulate a strategy for doing so. If our sample company decided to join the airline industry, it could compete as a low-cost, no-frills airline or as a luxury airline providing outstanding service and first-class comfort. Both options offer different ways of achieving competitive advantages in a crowded marketplace. The low-cost operator saves on expenses and passes the savings along to customers in the form of low prices. The luxury airline spends on high-end service and first-class comforts and passes the costs on to the customer in the form of high prices.

Porter has identified three generic business strategies for entering a new market: (1) broad cost leadership, (2) broad differentiation, and (3) focused strategy. Broad strategies reach a large market segment, while focused strategies target a niche or unique market with either cost leadership or differentiation. Trying to be all things to all people is a recipe for disaster, since doing so makes it difficult to project a consistent image to the entire marketplace. For this reason, Porter suggests adopting only one of the three generic strategies illustrated in Figure 1.17.[19]

Figure 1.18 applies the three strategies to real companies, demonstrating the relationships among strategies (cost leadership versus differentiation) and market segmentation (broad versus focused).

- **Broad market and low cost:** Walmart competes by offering a broad range of products at low prices. Its business strategy is to be the low-cost provider of goods for the cost-conscious consumer.

- **Broad market and high cost:** Neiman Marcus competes by offering a broad range of differentiated products at high prices. Its business strategy offers a variety of specialty and upscale products to affluent consumers.

FIGURE 1.17

Porter's Three Generic Strategies

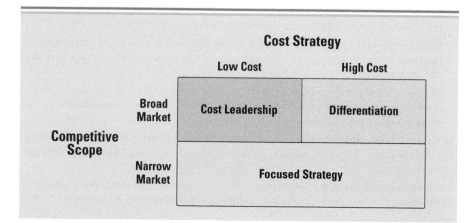

FIGURE 1.18

Examples of Porter's Three Generic Strategies

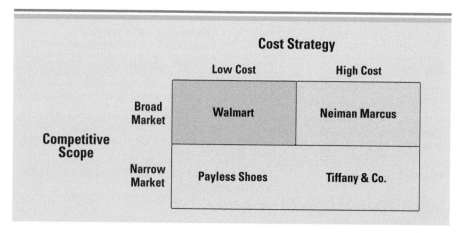

BUSINESS DRIVEN DEBATE

Apple sold 300,000 units of its highly anticipated iPad in the first 15 hours it was available for sale. Hundreds of thousands of Apple devotees flocked to stores during Passover and Easter to be the first to obtain the new device, even though it is neither a phone nor a laptop computer and many people are still wondering what it's for.

The controversy over the usefulness of Apple's portable tablet began as soon as Apple announced the device was heading to market. At first glance, the iPad is little more than a touch screen the size of a slim book, with a few control buttons along the edges and a home button at the bottom. Shrink it, and it would look like an iPod Touch. What is the value of this device? That's the question everyone wants to answer.

The iPad's modest features might represent an entirely new way of consuming media—video, web pages, music, pictures, and even books. Break into groups and review the current value of the iPad for business. Find three examples of the ways businesses are using, or could use, the iPad. Do you consider it the next revolutionary device or just an overpriced music player?[20]

The iPad— Greatest Product in History or Just Another Gadget?

- **Narrow market and low cost:** Payless competes by offering a specific product, shoes, at low prices. Its business strategy is to be the low-cost provider of shoes. Payless competes with Walmart, which also sells low-cost shoes, by offering a far bigger selection of sizes and styles.
- **Narrow market and high cost:** Tiffany & Co. competes by offering a differentiated product, jewelry, at high prices. Its business strategy allows it to be a high-cost provider of premier designer jewelry to affluent consumers.

VALUE CHAIN ANALYSIS—EXECUTING BUSINESS STRATEGIES

LO 1.7 Demonstrate how a company can add value by using Porter's value chain analysis.

Firms make profits by taking raw inputs and applying a business process to turn them into a product or service that customers find valuable. A *business process* is a standardized set of activities that accomplish a specific task, such as processing a customer's order. Once a firm identifies the industry it wants to enter and the generic strategy it will focus on, it must then choose the business processes required to create its products or services. Of course, the firm will want to ensure the processes add value and create competitive advantages. To identify these competitive advantages, Michael Porter created *value chain analysis*, which views a firm as a series of business processes that each add value to the product or service.

Value chain analysis is a useful tool for determining how to create the greatest possible value for customers (see Figure 1.19). The goal of value chain analysis is to identify processes in which the firm can add value for the customer and create a competitive advantage for itself, with a cost advantage or product differentiation.

The *value chain* groups a firm's activities into two categories, primary value activities, and support value activities. *Primary value activities*, shown at the bottom of the value chain in Figure 1.19, acquire raw materials and manufacture, deliver, market, sell, and provide after-sales services.

1. **Inbound logistics:** acquires raw materials and resources and distributes to manufacturing as required.
2. **Operations:** transforms raw materials or inputs into goods and services.
3. **Outbound logistics:** distributes goods and services to customers.

FIGURE 1.19

The Value Chain

4. **Marketing and sales:** promotes, prices, and sells products to customers.

5. **Service:** Provides customer support after the sale of goods and services.[21]

Support value activities, along the top of the value chain in Figure 1.19, include firm infrastructure, human resource management, technology development, and procurement. Not surprisingly, these support the primary value activities.

- **Firm infrastructure:** includes the company format or departmental structures, environment, and systems.

- **Human resource management:** provides employee training, hiring, and compensation.

- **Technology development:** applies MIS to processes to add value.

- **Procurement:** purchases inputs such as raw materials, resources, equipment, and supplies.

It is easy to understand how a typical manufacturing firm takes raw materials such as wood pulp and transforms it into paper. Adding value in this example might include using high-quality raw materials or offering next-day free shipping on any order. How, though, might a typical service firm take raw inputs such as time, knowledge, and MIS and transform them into valuable customer service knowledge? A hotel might use MIS to track customer reservations and then inform front-desk employees when a loyal customer is checking in so the employee can call the guest by name and offer additional services, gift baskets, or upgraded rooms. Examining the firm as a value chain allows managers to identify the important business processes that add value for customers and then find MIS solutions that support them.

When performing a value chain analysis, a firm could survey customers about the extent to which they believe each activity adds value to the product or service. This step generates responses the firm can measure, shown as percentages in Figure 1.20, to describe how each activity adds (or reduces) value. Then the competitive advantage decision for the firm is whether to (1) target high value-adding activities to further enhance their value, (2) target low value-adding activities to increase their value, or (3) perform some combination of the two.

MIS adds value to both primary and support value activities. One example of a primary value activity facilitated by MIS is the development of a marketing campaign management system that could target marketing campaigns more efficiently, thereby reducing marketing costs. The system would also help the firm better pinpoint target market needs, thereby increasing sales. One example of a support value activity facilitated by MIS is the development of a human resources system that could more efficiently reward employees based on performance. The system could also identify

BUSINESS DRIVEN START-UP

Derek Johnson, a student at the University of Houston, was having lunch with his friend who happened to be the communications director for her sorority. During lunch Derek's friend was telling him how hard it was to communicate with all of her sisters in the sorority. She had to send out important announcements about meetings, charitable events, and even dues. She had tried everything including Facebook, email, and message boards, but so far nothing was working. As Derek pondered his friend's dilemma, he came up with a solution: mass text messaging.

Johnson began researching mass text messaging products and was surprised to find that none existed for the average consumer. Spotting an entrepreneurial opportunity, Derek quickly began working on a product. Within a few months he launched his website, Tatango, and began offering group text messaging at a reasonable price. Now, a few years later, Tatango offers customers subscription plans starting under $20 a month that allows groups to send text messages to all members at once—whether 10 or 10,000—from any device.

In a group, brainstorm a list of problems you are currently experiencing. Decide whether any present potential new business opportunities, and if so, analyze the potential using the tools introduced in this chapter. Be prepared to present your new business to the class.[22]

Want to Start Your Own Business? Just Find a Problem to Solve

---

employees who are at risk of quitting, allowing manager's time to find additional challenges or opportunities that would help retain these employees and thus reduce turnover costs.

FIGURE 1.20

The Value Chain and Porter's Five Forces Model

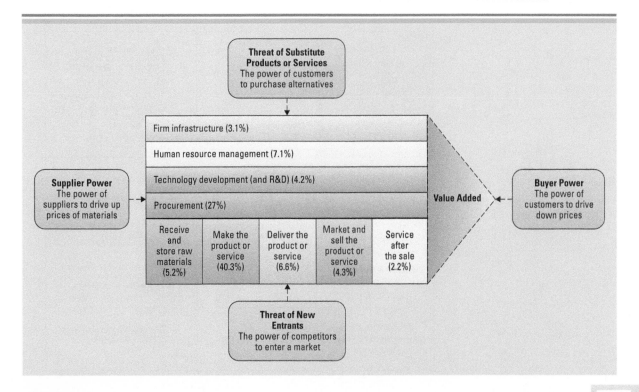

FIGURE 1.21

Overview of *Business Driven Information Systems*

MODULE 1: BUSINESS DRIVEN MIS	Business Strategy	MIS Topics
Chapter 1: Management Information Systems	Understanding Business Driven MIS	Data Information Business Intelligence Knowledge Systems Thinking Porter's Business Strategies
Chapter 2: Decisions and Processes	Creating Value Driven Businesses	Transaction Processing Systems Decision Support Systems Executive Information Systems Artificial Intelligence Business Process Reengineering
Chapter 3: Ebusiness	Finding Electronic Business Value	eBusiness eBusiness Models Social Networking Knowledge Management Collaboration
Chapter 4: Ethics and Information Security	Identifying MIS Business Concerns	Information Security Policies Authentication and Authorization Prevention and Resistance Detection and Response

MODULE 2: TECHNICAL FOUNDATIONS OF MIS	Business Strategy	MIS Topics
Chapter 5: Infrastructures	Deploying Organizational MIS	Grid Computing Cloud Computing Virtualization Sustainable MIS Infrastructures
Chapter 6: Data	Uncovering Business Intelligence	Database Data Management Systems Data Warehousing Data Mining
Chapter 7: Networks	Supporting Mobile Business	Business Networks Web 1.0, Web 2.0, Web 3.0 Mobile MIS Wireless MIS GPS, GIS, and LBS

MODULE 3: ENTERPRISE MIS	Business Strategy	MIS Topics
Chapter 8: Enterprise Applications	Enhancing Business Communications	Customer Relationship Management Supply Chain Management Enterprise Resource Planning
Chapter 9: Systems Development and Project Management	Leading MIS Projects	MIS Development Methodologies Project Management Outsourcing

Value chain analysis is a highly useful tool that provides hard and fast numbers for evaluating the activities that add value to products and services. Managers can find additional value by analyzing and constructing the value chain in terms of Porter's Five Forces Model (see Figure 1.20). For example, if the goal is to decrease buyer power, a company can construct its value chain activity of "service after the sale" by offering high levels of customer service. This will increase customers' switching costs and reduce their power. Analyzing and constructing support value activities can help decrease the threat of new entrants. Analyzing and constructing primary value activities can help decrease the threat of substitute products or services.[23]

Revising Porter's three business strategies is critical. Firms must continually adapt to their competitive environments, which can cause business strategy to shift. In the remainder of this text we discuss how managers can formulate business strategies using MIS to create competitive advantages. Figure 1.21 gives an overview of the remaining chapters, along with the relevant business strategy and associated MIS topics.

LEARNING OUTCOME REVIEW

Learning Outcome 1.1: Describe the information age and the differences among data, information, business intelligence, and knowledge.

We live in the information age, when infinite quantities of facts are widely available to anyone who can use a computer. The core drivers of the information age include data, information, business intelligence, and knowledge. Data are raw facts that describe the characteristics of an event or object. Information is data converted into a meaningful and useful context. Business intelligence (BI) is information collected from multiple sources such as suppliers, customers, competitors, partners, and industries that analyzes patterns, trends, and relationships for strategic decision making. Knowledge includes the skills, experience, and expertise, coupled with information and intelligence, that creates a person's intellectual resources. As you move from data to knowledge you include more and more variables for analysis resulting in better, more precise support for decision making and problem solving.

Learning Outcome 1.2: Identify the different departments in a company and why they must work together to achieve success.

Companies are typically organized by department or functional area such as accounting, finance, human resources, marketing, operations management, and sales. Although each department has its own focus and its own data, none can work independently if the company is to operate as a whole. It is easy to see how a business decision made by one department can affect other departments. Functional areas are anything but independent in a business. In fact, functional areas are interdependent. Sales must rely on information from operations to understand inventory, place orders, calculate transportation costs, and gain insight into product availability based on production schedules. For an organization to succeed, every department or functional area must work together sharing common information and not be a "silo." Information technology can enable departments to more efficiently and effectively perform their business operations.

Learning Outcome 1.3: Explain systems thinking and how management information systems enable business communications.

A system is a collection of parts that link to achieve a common purpose. Systems thinking is a way of monitoring the entire system by viewing multiple inputs being processed or transformed to produce outputs while continuously gathering feedback on each part. Feedback is information that returns to its original transmitter (input, transform, or output) and modifies the transmitter's actions. Feedback helps the system maintain stability. Management information systems (MIS) is a business function, like accounting and human resources, which moves information about people, products, and processes across the company to facilitate decision making and problem solving. MIS incorporates systems thinking to help companies operate cross-functionally. For example, to fulfill product orders, an MIS for sales moves a single customer order across all functional areas including sales, order fulfillment, shipping, billing, and finally customer service. Although different functional areas handle different parts of the sale, thanks to MIS, to the customer the sale is one continuous process.

Learning Outcome 1.4: Explain why competitive advantages are temporary.

A competitive advantage is a feature of a product or service on which customers place a greater value than they do on similar offerings from competitors. Competitive advantages provide the same product or service either at a lower price or with additional value that can fetch premium prices. Unfortunately, competitive advantages are typically temporary, because competitors often quickly seek ways to duplicate them. In turn, organizations must develop a strategy based on a new competitive advantage. Ways that companies duplicate competitive advantages include acquiring the new technology, copying business processes, and hiring away employees.

Learning Outcome 1.5: Describe Porter's Five Forces Model and explain each of the five forces.

Porter's Five Forces Model analyzes the competitive forces within the environment in which a company operates, to assess the potential for profitability in an industry.

- Buyer power is the ability of buyers to affect the price they must pay for an item.
- Supplier power is the suppliers' ability to influence the prices they charge for supplies (including materials, labor, and services).
- Threat of substitute products or services is high when there are many alternatives to a product or service and low when there are few alternatives from which to choose.
- Threat of new entrants is high when it is easy for new competitors to enter a market and low when there are significant entry barriers to entering a market.
- Rivalry among existing competitors is high when competition is fierce in a market and low when competition is more complacent.

Learning Outcome 1.6: Compare Porter's three generic strategies.

Organizations typically follow one of Porter's three generic strategies when entering a new market: (1) broad cost leadership, (2) broad differentiation, (3) focused strategy. Broad strategies reach a large market segment. Focused strategies target a niche market. Focused strategies concentrate on either cost leadership or differentiation.

Learning Outcome 1.7: Demonstrate how a company can add value by using Porter's value chain analysis.

To identify competitive advantages, Michael Porter created value chain analysis, which views a firm as a series of business processes that each add value to the product or service. The goal of value chain analysis is to identify processes in which the firm can add value for the customer and create a competitive advantage for itself, with a cost advantage or product differentiation. The value chain groups a firm's activities into two categories—primary value activities and support value activities. Primary value activities acquire raw materials and manufacture, deliver, market, sell, and provide after-sales services. Support value activities, along the top of the value chain in the figure, include firm infrastructure, human resource management, technology development, and procurement. Not surprisingly, these support the primary value activities.

OPENING CASE QUESTIONS

1. **Knowledge:** Define Globalization 1.0, 2.0, and 3.0 and provide a sample of the type of business data managers collected during each era.

2. **Comprehension:** Explain Friedman's flat world and the reasons it is important for all businesses, small or large, to understand.

3. **Application:** Demonstrate how students competing for jobs in a "flat world" can create competitive advantages to differentiate themselves in the marketplace.

4. **Analysis:** Analyze the current business environment and identify a new flattener not mentioned on Friedman's list.

5. **Synthesis:** Propose a plan for how a start-up company can use any of Porter's strategies to combat competition in a global world.

6. **Evaluate:** Argue for or against the following statement: "The world is not flat (in Friedman's sense of the term) because many undeveloped countries are not connected electronically."

KEY TERMS

Business intelligence (BI), 8
Business process, 23
Business strategy, 15
Buyer power, 18
Chief information officer (CIO), 15
Chief knowledge officer (CKO), 15
Chief privacy officer (CPO), 15
Chief security officer (CSO), 15
Chief technology officer (CTO), 15
Competitive advantage, 16
Competitive intelligence, 17
Data, 6
Entry barrier, 20

Fact, 5
Feedback, 14
First-mover advantage, 17
Goods, 12
Information, 7
Information age, 5
Knowledge, 10
Knowledge worker, 10
Loyalty program, 19
Management information systems (MIS), 14
Porter's Five Forces Model, 18
Primary value activities, 23
Production, 13
Productivity, 13

Product differentiation, 20
Rivalry among existing competitors, 20
Services, 12
Supplier power, 19
Supply chain, 19
Support value activities, 24
Switching costs, 18
System, 12
Systems thinking, 14
Threat of new entrants, 20
Threat of substitute products or services, 19
Value chain analysis, 23
Variable, 7

REVIEW QUESTIONS

1. What is data and why is it important to a business?

2. How can a manager turn data into information?

3. What is the relationship between data, information, business intelligence, and knowledge?

4. Why is it important for a company to operate cross-functionally?

5. Why would a company want to have a CIO, CPO, and CSO?

6. Explain MIS and the role it plays in a company and global business.

7. Do you agree that MIS is essential for businesses operating in the information age? Why or why not?

8. Why is it important for a business major to understand MIS?

9. What type of career are you planning to pursue? How will your specific career use data, information, business intelligence, and knowledge?

10. Explain systems thinking and how it supports business operations.

11. What business strategies would you use if you were developing a competitive advantage for a company?

12. Explain Porter's Five Forces Model and the role it plays in decision making.

13. How could a company use loyalty programs to influence buyer power? How could a company use switching costs to lock in customers and suppliers?

14. What are Porter's three generic strategies and why would a company want to follow only one?

15. How can a company use Porter's value chain analysis to measure customer satisfaction?

CLOSING CASE ONE

Apple—Merging Technology, Business, and Entertainment

This might sound hard to believe, but a bit more than a decade ago, Apple was on the brink of bankruptcy. Apple Computer Inc., now back from near oblivion, is blazing a trail through the digital world with innovation and creativity that has been missing from the company for the past 20 years. The unique feature of Apple's competitive advantages is that they come from customers and users, not Apple employees. That's right; the company welcomes products created by consumers to sell to consumers, a trend new to business.

Capitalizing on the iPod

With millions of iPods in the hands of consumers, many people are finding ways to capitalize on the product. John Lin created a prototype of a remote control for the iPod and took his prototype to *Macworld,* where he found success. A few months later, Lin's company had Apple's blessing and a commitment for shelf space in its retail stores. "This is how Apple supports the iPod economy," Lin said.

In the iPod-dominated market, hundreds of companies have been inspired to develop more than 500 accessories—everything from rechargers for the car to $1,500 Fendi bags. Eric Tong, vice president at Belkin, a cable and peripheral manufacturer, believes that 75 percent of all iPod owners purchase at least one accessory—selling over 30 million accessories to date. With most of the products priced between $10 and $200, that puts the iPod economy well over $300 million and perhaps as high as $6 billion. Popular iPod accessories include:

- Altec Lansing Technologies—iPod speakers and recharger dock ($150).
- Belkin—TuneCast mobile FM transmitter ($40).
- Etymotic Research—high-end earphones ($150).
- Griffin Technology—iTrip FM transmitter ($35).
- Kate Spade—Geneva faux-croc mini iPod holder ($55).
- Apple—socks set in six colors: green, purple, blue, orange, pink, and gray ($29).
- Apple—digital camera connector ($29).

Capitalizing on the iPhone

Looking at someone using an iPhone is an interesting experience because there is a good chance they are not making a phone call. They could be doing a number of things from playing a game to trading stocks, watching a TV show, or even conducting business with a mobile version of salesforce.com's customer-management software. In a brilliant strategic move, Apple let outsiders offer software for the iPhone and in less than six months, more than 10,000 applications had been created. In fact, more than 15,000 applications are available at its app store section of iTunes, and they have been downloaded a total of 500 million times. Now, many of the iPhone apps are available for the iPad.

The iPhone and iPad app store market is getting so huge relative to other smartphone markets that some developers argue there is little point adapting applications for Google's Android or any other iPhone competitor. According to Jeff Holden, CEO of Pelago Inc., when he created his social networking company he fully intended to follow the conventional wisdom for how to build a sizable, fast-growing software company: Get your programs on as many platforms and devices as possible. But when he crunched the numbers he came to an interesting business conclusion: The 13 million iPhone owners had already downloaded more applications than the 1.1 billion other cell phone owners! To entrepreneurs, developing a program for the iPhone automatically provides a significantly larger market—almost 94 times larger than its competitors. "Why would I ever build for anything but the iPhone?" Holden asked.

Capitalizing on the iPad

Apple's latest release, the iPad, is a lightweight, portable, tablet computer, similar to the iPhone, that allows customers to download applications, check email, and play music all at the touch of a button. Both the iPhone and the iPad can multitask, allowing customers to read a web page while downloading email in the background over wireless networks. The arrival of the iPad brought a simultaneous expansion of the network of accessories. Because the iPad was designed with an exposed screen and without a camera, separate keyboard, memory card slots, or expansion ports, one might say it was specifically built for accessories. Many owners will modify it in some way, whether for mere decoration or hard-core protection. A few of the new accessories include:

- iPad Clear Armor screen protector—$35.
- iPad Antique book case cover—$40.
- iPad wireless keyboard—$99.
- iPad overcoat sleeve—$35.
- iPad Joule luxury stand—$130.

Apple has consistently outperformed its key rivals through the development of its MP3 player, the iPod, and continues to make its products smaller and less expensive, while providing complementary features such as games and applications. For the iPhone, Apple developed a unique application called Siri, a voice-activation system that is capable of recognizing voice commands. Siri can perform all kinds of functions from dialing a contact and creating an email to location services such as "Find my Phone," ensuring lost phones are found quickly.

Apple's latest offering is a new service called the iCloud. The iCloud has the ability to collect all of the content, including videos, photos, songs, books, etc., from customer devices such as iPods, iPads, and iPhones in one secure location in "the cloud." Apple customers no longer have to worry about backing up their applications or data because everything is automatically uploaded and stored in the iCloud when using an Apple device. In a fast-paced, technology-driven sector, with competitors quickly following suit, Apple is constantly pressured to develop new products and product extensions. Luckily Apple stays ahead of the pack by focusing on the following key competitive advantages:

- **Customer focus:** Apple is driven by customer satisfaction and ensures customers are deeply involved in product development and application development.
- **Resources and capabilities:** Apple continues to invest heavily in research and development to take advantage of new technologies, improved facilities, and cloud infrastructures.
- **Strategic vision:** Apple has a clear alignment of its vision, mission, and business leadership and goals.
- **Branding:** Apple is the leader in brand loyalty as it has achieved cult status with its authentic product image.
- **Quality focus:** Apple has an outstanding commitment to quality.[24]

Customer Focus — Resources and Capabilities — Strategic Vision — Branding — Quality Focus

Questions

1. Do you agree or disagree that Apple's iTunes, iPhone apps, and iPad apps give the company a competitive advantage? Be sure to justify your answer.
2. Why are data, information, business intelligence, and knowledge important to Apple? Give an example of each type in relation to the iPad.
3. Analyze Apple using Porter's Five Forces Model.
4. Which of the three generic strategies is Apple following?
5. Which of Porter's five forces did Apple address through its introduction of the iPhone?
6. Which of Porter's five forces did Apple address through its customer-developed applications?

CLOSING CASE TWO

Best of the Best of the Best—Under 25

Bloomberg Businessweek runs a yearly article featuring the top five American entrepreneurs under 25 years old. With between 200 and 300 applications each year, choosing 5 is difficult. To help ensure fair competition, the magazine narrows it down to 25 and then asks its readers to decide which 5 have the greatest potential. Below are the top five winners from 2011.

1: SCOREASCORE

Founder: Jordan Passman, 24
Revenue: $250,000

Growing up in Los Angeles, Jordan Passman knew the ins and outs of the music business where his father worked as a high-profile music attorney. Passman, wanting to follow in his father's footsteps, was working for the American Society of Composers when he noticed an unmet need in the marketplace—music buyers in the film, commercial, and television market looking for music composers. An idea was born and Passman began working on a website that connected music buyers with music composers. "People were still scrounging Craigslist for composers, and I knew there were so many composers out there that didn't have representation," says Passman. ScoreAscore links music buyers who are looking for scores for film, commercials, video games, or other productions with 100 select professional music composers represented by Passman, who charges 20 to 40 percent as a fee for each transaction. Passman aspires to be the go-to for YouTube filmmakers!

2: THINKLITE

Founders: Dinesh Wadhwani, 21; Enrico Palmerino, 22
Revenue: $3,500,000

In 2009, Babson College students Dinesh Wadhwani and Enrico Palmerino were reading an article about energy-efficient lightbulbs when their own lightbulbs went off! The roommates began collaborating on how they could build a business with the primary competitive advantage of saving money with energy-efficient lights, instead of focusing solely on saving the environment as most of the current manufacturers in the market were focusing on as their product niche. ThinkLite's mission is to help companies reduce electric bills through energy-efficient lighting. The pair began ThinkLite by licensing technologies from private companies in Germany, coupled with parts from Korea, and designs from Boston, with final production occurring in China. Clients, such as AT&T and Kodak, boast lighting bill reductions ranging from 50 percent to 80 percent, a significant savings for big business! ThinkLite now has over 100 clients and is looking to expand into smaller markets such as restaurants and stores.

3: DELTA PRODUCE

Founders: Kosta Dionisopoulos, 24; Christos Marafatsos, 24
Revenue: $2,600,000

The supply chain of food distribution is a tough business, and getting the right perishable goods to the correct location at the perfect time is more an art form than analytics and logistics. Kosta Dionisopoulos was driving a van delivering produce while attending the University of Maryland when Christos Marafatsos saw an opportunity to start a unique produce delivery business. Delta Produce not only delivers food, but also provides online marketing, allowing customers to reduce costs by buying in bulk or in groups. Delta Produce now has 18 employees and its customers include restaurants, grocery stores, and wholesalers. "Both my partner and I are young, so interacting online is something we're accustomed to doing," says Marafatsos.

4: APPLETON LEARNING

Founder: Glenn Clayton, 25
Revenue: $4,200,000

Glenn Clayton found himself looking for ways to earn extra money while attending the University of Alabama, so he began tutoring local high school students. Clayton soon recognized a need in the market and launched Appleton Learning, which matches college tutors with high school students. Clayton began hiring friends to help meet the tutoring needs, and by the end of his sophomore year he was spending over 60 hours each week managing Appleton Learning. "I realized if people were leaving big name tutoring companies to come to some college kid working out of a broom closet, there was a need in the market not being met," Clayton says. Appleton Learning has found sales doubling yearly, and Clayton has built a unique website that matches students with tutors based on their individual learning needs and styles. Appleton Learning has over 1,000 tutors, including college students, professionals, and retirees, serving over 6,000 high school students. Appleton Learning is looking to expand opening 20 new branches across the Southeast over the next few years.

5: DESMOS

Founder: Eli Luberoff, 24
Revenue: $200,000

While taking a year off from Yale, Eli Luberoff noticed a problem in the education arena—software compatibility issues. Luberoff decided to create software that would overcome these issues and allow teachers and students to collaborate regardless of the systems they were using or their location. Luberoff launched his company, Desmos, by testing software from several large publishers, including McGraw-Hill, Houghton Mifflin Harcourt, and Pearson just to name a few. Luberoff's strategy for making money is to provide the software for free while charging licensing fees to publishers.[25]

Questions

1. If you had $1 million to invest in one of the five above-mentioned start-ups, which one would you choose and why? Be sure to justify your answer using Porter's Five Forces Model and three generic strategies analysis.

2. Choose one of the above businesses and explain why data, information, business intelligence, and knowledge are important to successfully running the business over the next few years. Be sure to list examples of the different types of data, information, business intelligence, and knowledge you might find in this company.

3. Review *Bloomberg Businessweek*'s most current top five under 25. Choose one of the companies and perform a detailed analysis of the company using the strategies discussed in this chapter. Determine a few ways the company can improve its business by creating competitive advantages using the ideas and methods discussed throughout this chapter.

CRITICAL BUSINESS THINKING

1. **Focusing on Friedman**

   Thomas Friedman's newest book is titled *Hot, Flat, and Crowded: Why We Need a Green Revolution— And How It Can Renew America*. Research the Internet to find out as much information as you can about this text. Why would a business manager be interested in reading this text? How will this text impact global business? Do you think *Hot, Flat, and Crowded* will have as great an impact on society as *The World Is Flat* had on business? Why or why not?[26]

2. **Pursuing Porter**

   There is no doubt that Michael Porter is one of the more influential business strategists of the 21st century. Research Michael Porter on the Internet for interviews, additional articles, and new or updated business strategies. Create a summary of your findings to share with your class. How can learning about people such as Thomas Friedman and Michael Porter help prepare you for a career in business? Name three additional business professionals you should follow to help prepare for your career in business.

3. **Renting Movies**

   The video rental industry is fiercely competitive. Customers have their choice of renting a movie by driving to a store (Blockbuster), ordering through the mail (Netflix), or watching directly from their television (pay-per-view or Netflix). Using Porter's Five Forces Model (buyer power, supplier power, threat of new entrants, threat of substitute products, and competition), evaluate the attractiveness of entering the movie rental business. Be sure to include product differentiation, switching costs, and loyalty programs in your analysis.

4. **Working for the Best**

   Each year, *Fortune* magazine creates a list of the top 100 companies to work for. Find the most recent list. What types of data do you think *Fortune* analyzed to determine the company ranking? What issues could occur if the analysis of the data was inaccurate? What types of information can you gain by analyzing the list? Create five questions a student performing a job search could answer by analyzing this list.

5. **Salary Surveys**

   Salary surveys offer great tools for highlighting the opportunities associated with an MIS major. The starting annual salaries in the MIS field range from $50,000 to $85,000 and many are rising. Figure 1.22 displays a *Computerworld* salary survey. Research the Internet for a current MIS salary survey. Which types of jobs are on the rise? If there are any jobs you are unfamiliar with, research

Job Description	Compensation
Business intelligence analyst	$ 81,866
Communications specialist	$ 85,938
Database architect	$ 98,995
Ebusiness specialist	$ 71,717
Information security specialist	$ 83,693
IT / IS technology / business systems analyst	$ 78,305
Network architect	$ 96,302
Programmer / analyst	$ 75,995
Project leader	$ 87,922
Senior systems analyst	$ 89,987
Software developer	$ 85,684
Software engineer	$ 93,726
Storage architect / engineer	$111,077
Systems programmer	$ 89,472
Web developer	$ 66,347

FIGURE 1.22

Computerworld Salary Survey

the Internet to determine the job characteristics. List the top three jobs you would want if you were to pursue a career in MIS. What do you find interesting about these jobs? What skills can you build to help you prepare for these jobs?[27]

6. **Starting your own Business**

Josh James recently sold his web analytics company, Omniture, to Adobe for $1.8 billion. Yes, James started Omniture from his dorm room! Have you begun to recognize the unbelievable opportunities available to those students who understand the power of MIS, regardless of their major? Answer the following questions.[28]

a. Why is it so easy today for students to create start-ups while still in college?
b. What would it take for you to start a business from your dorm room?
c. How will this course help you prepare to start your own business?
d. Research the Internet and find three examples of college student start-ups.
e. What's stopping you from starting your own business today? You are living in the information age and with the power of MIS, it is easier than ever to jump into the business game with very little capital investment. Why not start your own business today?

7. **The Five Forces Model at Work**

Your team is working for a small investment company that specializes in technology investments. A new company, Geyser, has just released an operating system that plans to compete with Microsoft's operating systems. Your company has a significant amount of capital invested in Microsoft. Your boss, Kellee Lazarus, has asked you to compile a Porter's Five Forces analysis for Microsoft to ensure that your company's Microsoft investment is not at risk.

8. **Competitive Analysis**

Cheryl O'Connell is the owner of a small, high-end retailer of women's clothing called Excelus. Excelus's business has been successful for many years, largely because of O'Connell's ability to anticipate the needs and wants of her loyal customer base and provide them with personalized service. O'Connell does not see any value in IT and does not want to invest any capital in something that will not directly affect her bottom line. Develop a proposal describing the potential IT-enabled competitive opportunities or threats O'Connell might be missing by not embracing IT. Be sure to include a Porter's Five Forces analysis and discuss which one of the three generic strategies O'Connell should pursue.

9. **Applying the Three Generic Strategies**

This chapter discussed several examples of companies that pursue differentiated strategies so that they are not forced into positions where they must compete solely based on price. In a team, choose an industry and find and compare two companies, one that is competing based on price and another that is pursuing a differentiated strategy enabled by the creative use of IT. Some industries you may want to consider are clothing retailers, grocery stores, airlines, and personal computers. Prepare a presentation for the class on the ways that the company is using IT to help it differentiate and compete against the low-cost provider. Before you begin, spend some class time to make sure each team selects a different industry.

10. **10 Best Things You Will Say to Your Grandchildren**

Wired magazine recently posted the top 10 things you will say to your grandchildren. For each expression below try to identify what it is referring to and why it will be considered outdated.[29]

1. Back in my day, we only needed 140 characters.

2. There used to be so much snow up here, you could strap a board to your feet and slide all the way down.

3. Televised contests gave cash prizes to whoever could store the most data in their head.

4. Well, the screens were bigger, but they only showed the movies at certain times of day.

5. We all had one, but nobody actually used it. Come to think of it, I bet my LinkedIn profile is still out there on the web somewhere.

6. Translation: "English used to be the dominant language. Crazy, huh?"

7. Our bodies were made of meat and supported by little sticks of calcium.

8. You used to keep files right on your computer, and you had to go back to that same computer to access them!

9. Is that the new iPhone 27G? Got multitasking yet?

10. I just can't get used to this darn vat-grown steak. Texture ain't right.

ENTREPRENEURIAL CHALLENGE

BUILD YOUR OWN BUSINESS

You have recently inherited your grandfather's business, which is conveniently located in your city's downtown. The business offers many different kinds of specialized products and services and was first opened in 1952 and was a local hot spot for many years. Unfortunately, business has been steadily declining over the past few years. The business runs without any computers and all ordering takes place manually. Your grandfather had a terrific memory and knew all of his customers and suppliers by name, but unfortunately, none of this information is located anywhere in the store. The operational information required to run the business, such as sales trends, vendor information, promotional information, and so on, is all located in your grandfather's memory. Inventory is tracked in a notepad, along with employee payroll, and marketing coupons. The business does not have a website, uses very little marketing except word of mouth, and essentially still operates the same as it did in 1952.

Throughout this course you will own and operate your grandfather's business, and by taking advantage of business practices discussed in this text, you will attempt to increase profits, decrease expenses, and bring the business into the 21st century. For the purpose of this case, please choose the business you wish to operate and create a name for the business. For example, the business could be a coffee shop called The Broadway Café, an extreme sports store called Cutting Edge Sports, or even a movie store called The Silver Screen. Try to pick a business you are genuinely interested in running and that aligns with your overall career goals.

Project Focus: Competitive Advantage

1. Identify the business you are going to build throughout this course and choose a name for your business.

2. Write an analysis of buyer power and supplier power for your business using Porter's Five Forces Model. Be sure to discuss how you could combat the competition with strategies such as switching costs and loyalty programs.

3. Write an analysis of rivalry, entry barriers, and the threat of substitute products for your business using Porter's Five Forces Model. Be sure to discuss how you could combat the competition with strategies such as product differentiation.

4. Describe which of Porter's three generic strategies you would use for your business. Be sure to describe the details of how you will implement this strategy and how it will help you create a competitive advantage in your industry.

APPLY YOUR KNOWLEDGE BUSINESS PROJECTS

PROJECT I Capitalizing on Your Career

Business leaders need to be comfortable with management information systems (MIS) for the following (primary) reasons:

- The sheer magnitude of the dollars spent on MIS must be managed to ensure business value.

- Research has consistently shown that when top managers are active in supporting MIS, they realize a number of benefits, such as gaining a competitive advantage, streamlining business processes, and even transforming entire industries.

- When business leaders are not involved in MIS, systems fail, revenue is lost, and entire companies can even fail because of poorly managed systems.

How do companies get managers involved in MIS? One of the biggest positive factors is managers' personal experience with MIS and MIS education, including university classes and executive seminars. Once managers understand MIS through experience and education, they are more likely to lead their companies in achieving business success through MIS.

1. Search the Internet for examples of the types of technologies currently used in the field or industry that you plan to pursue. For example, if you are planning a career in accounting or finance, you should become familiar with financial systems such as Oracle Financials. For a career in logistics or distribution, research supply chain management systems. If marketing appeals to you, research customer relationship management systems, blogs, emarketing, and social networking.

2. As a competitive tool, MIS can differentiate products, services, and prices from competitors' offerings by improving product quality, shortening product development or delivery time, creating new MIS-based products and services, and improving customer service before, during, and after a transaction. Search the Internet for examples of companies in the industry where you plan to work that have achieved a competitive advantage through MIS.

3. Create a brief report of your findings; include an overview of the type of technologies you found and how companies are using them to achieve a competitive advantage.

PROJECT II   Achieving Alignment

Most companies would like to be in the market-leading position of JetBlue, Dell, or Walmart, all of which have used management information systems to secure their respective spots in the market-place. These companies are relentless about keeping the cost of technology down by combining the best of MIS and business leadership.

The future belongs to those organizations perceptive enough to grasp the significance of MIS and resourceful enough to coordinate their business and management information systems.

1. Use any resource to answer the question, "Why is it challenging for businesses to align MIS and their other operations?" Use the following questions to begin your analysis:

    a. How do companies monitor competitive intelligence and create competitive advantages?
    b. What are some of the greatest MIS challenges for most firms?
    c. What drives MIS decisions?
    d. Who or what is the moving force behind MIS decisions for most companies?

PROJECT III   Market Dissection

To illustrate the use of the three generic strategies, consider Figure 1.23. The matrix shown demonstrates the relationships among strategies (cost leadership versus differentiation) and market segmentation (broad versus focused).

- Hyundai is following a broad cost leadership strategy. It offers low-cost vehicles, in each particular model stratification, that appeal to a large audience.

- Audi is pursuing a broad differentiation strategy with its Quattro models available at several price points. Audi's differentiation is safety, and it prices its models higher than Hyundai's to reach a large, stratified audience.

- Kia has a more focused cost leadership strategy. Kia mainly offers low-cost vehicles in the lower levels of model stratification.

- Hummer offers the most focused differentiation strategy of any in the industry (including Mercedes-Benz).

FIGURE 1.23

Porter's Three Generic Strategies

	Cost leadership strategy	Differentiation strategy
Broad market	Hyundai	Audi
Focused market	Kia	Hummer

Create a similar graph displaying each strategy for a product of your choice. The strategy must include an example of the product in each of the following markets: (1) cost leadership, broad market; (2) differentiation, broad market; (3) cost leadership, focused market; and (4) differentiation, focused market. Potential products include cereal, dog food, soft drinks, computers, shampoo, snack foods, jeans, sneakers, sandals, mountain bikes, TV shows, movies.

PROJECT IV   Porter's Five Forces

Setting strategic direction for a business is a challenge for even seasoned professionals. The good news is there are many tools available you can use to help you find competitive advantages, including Porter's Five Forces. Porter's Five Forces Model analyzes the competitive forces within the environment in which a company operates to assess the potential for profitability in an industry. Its purpose is to combat these competitive forces by identifying opportunities, competitive advantages, and competitive intelligence. If the forces are strong, they increase competition; if the forces are weak, they decrease competition.

Porter's Five Forces Model is a good framework for understanding market forces. Break into groups and choose a comparison from the list below to perform a Porter's Five Forces analysis.

- Notebook computer and laptop computer.
- PDA and laptop computer.
- iPhone and cell phone.
- iPod and CD player.
- GPS device and a road atlas.
- Digital books and printed books.

PROJECT V   Adding Value

To identify these competitive advantages, Michael Porter created value chain analysis, which views a firm as a series of business processes that each add value to the product or service. Value chain analysis is a useful tool for determining how to create the greatest possible value for customers. The goal of value chain analysis is to identify processes in which the firm can add value for the customer and create a competitive advantage for itself, with a cost advantage or product differentiation.

Starbucks has hired you after your graduation for a temporary position that could turn into a full-time opportunity. With new cafés and juice shops popping up on every corner, coupled with the global recession, Starbucks is worried about losing market share to competitors. Your boss, Heather Sweitzer, is out of ideas for ways to improve the company's profitability. You decide that one of the most useful tools for identifying competitive advantages is Porter's value chain analysis. Of course, you do not yet have the detailed knowledge to complete all of the elements required, but you know enough to get started and plan to take your draft to Sweitzer next week. Using your knowledge of Starbucks, create a value chain analysis. Feel free to make assumptions about operations; just be sure to list any that you make. Also, be sure to write an overview of the tool and its potential value so Sweitzer can understand how it works.

PROJECT VI   Flat Competition

"When I was growing up in Minneapolis, my parents always said, 'Tom, finish your dinner. There are people starving in China and India.' Today I tell my girls, 'Finish your homework, because people in China and India are starving for your jobs.' And in a flat world, they can have them, because there's no such thing as an American job anymore." Thomas Friedman.

In his book, *The World Is Flat,* Thomas Friedman describes the unplanned cascade of techno-logical and social shifts that effectively leveled the economic world, and "accidentally made Beijing, Bangalore, and Bethesda next-door neighbors." The video of Thomas Friedman's lecture at MIT discussing the flat world is available at http://mitworld.mit.edu/video/266. If you want to be prepared to compete in a flat world you must watch this video and answer the following questions:

- Do you agree or disagree with Friedman's assessment that the world is flat?
- What are the potential impacts of a flat world for a student performing a job search?
- What can students do to prepare themselves for competing in a flat world?[30]

PROJECT VII   Wikiblunders

According to *PC World* these false facts all appeared on Wikipedia:

1. Robbie Williams eats domestic pets in pubs for money.
2. David Beckham was a Chinese goalkeeper in the 18th century.
3. Paul Reiser's dead. (Reiser is an actor).
4. Sinbad's dead. (Sinbad is an actor).
5. Sergey Brin's sexy, dating Jimmy Wales, and dead. (Brin founded Google and Wales founded Wikipedia).
6. Tony Blair worships Hitler. (Blair was the former prime minister of the United Kingdom).
7. The Duchess of Cornwall's Christian name is Cow-miller.
8. Robert Byrd's dead. (Byrd is a U.S. senator from West Virginia).
9. John Seigenthaler helped assassinate John and Robert Kennedy. (Seigenthaler is a journalist).
10. Conan O'Brien assaults sea turtles while canoeing.[31]

We know that people use information technology to work with information. Knowing this, how could these types of errors occur? What could happen if you decided to use Wikipedia to collect business intelligence for a research paper? What could Wikipedia do to help prevent these types of errors?

PROJECT VIII   What's Wrong with This Bathroom?

If you were the CEO of a global financial company that was experiencing a financial crisis, would you invest $1 million to renovate your office? Probably not and you are possibly wondering if this is a fabricated story from *The Onion*. Guess what, this is a true story! John Thain, the former CEO of Merrill Lynch, decided to spend $1.2 million refurbishing his office—well after Merrill Lynch posted huge financial losses. Thain personally signed off on all of the following:

- Area rug: $87,784
- Mahogany pedestal table: $25,713
- 19th century credenza: $68,179
- Pendant light furniture: $19,751
- 4 pairs of curtains: $28,091
- Pair of guest chairs: $87,784
- George IV chair: $18,468
- 6 wall sconces: $2,741
- Parchment waste can: $1,405 (yes, for a trash can!!)
- Roman shade fabric: $10,967
- Roman shades: $7,315
- Coffee table: $5,852
- Commode on legs: $35,115[32]

It takes years of education and work experience for people to build the skills necessary to take on the role of CEO. Obviously, a company like Merril Lynch would only hire a highly qualified person for the job. What do you think happened to John Thain? Why would he spend an obscene amount of money redecorating his office when his company was having financial trouble? What happens to a company whose executives are not aligned with company goals? How can you ensure that your company's executives are not making monumental mistakes, such as million dollar bathroom renovations?

PROJECT IX   I Love TED!

A small nonprofit started in 1984, TED (Technology, Entertainment, Design) hosts conferences for Ideas Worth Spreading. TED brings people from all over the globe to share award-winning talks covering the most innovative, informative, and exciting speeches ever given in 20 minutes. You can find TED talks by Al Gore, Bill Gates, Steve Jobs, Douglas Adams, Steven Levitt, Seth Godin, Malcolm Gladwell, and so on.[33]

Visit www.ted.com and peruse the thousands of videos that are available then answer the following:

- Review the TED website and find three talks you would want to watch. Why did you pick these three and will you make time outside of class to watch them?
- How can you gain a competitive advantage by watching TED?
- How can you find innovative ideas for a start-up by watching TED?
- How can you find competitive intelligence by watching TED?

AYK APPLICATION PROJECTS

If you are looking for Excel projects to incorporate into your class, try any of the following after reading this chapter.

Project Number	Project Name	Project Type	Plug-In Focus Area	Project Level	Skill Set	Page Number
1	Financial Destiny	Excel	T2	Personal Budget	Introductory Formulas	AYK.4
2	Cash Flow	Excel	T2	Cash Flow	Introductory Formulas	AYK.4
3	Technology Budget	Excel	T1, T2	Hardware and Software	Introductory Formulas	AYK.4
4	Tracking Donations	Excel	T2	Employee Relationships	Introductory Formulas	AYK.4
5	Convert Currency	Excel	T2	Global Commerce	Introductory Formulas	AYK.5
6	Cost Comparison	Excel	T2	Total Cost of Ownership	Introductory Formulas	AYK.5
7	Time Management	Excel or Project	T12 Project Management	Introductory	Gantt Charts	AYK.6

What's in IT for me?

Working faster and smarter has become a necessity for companies. A firm's value chain is directly affected by how well it designs and coordinates its business processes. Business processes offer competitive advantages if they enable a firm to lower operating costs, differentiate, or compete in a niche market. They can also be huge burdens if they are outdated, which impedes operations, efficiency, and effectiveness. Thus, the ability of management information systems to improve business processes is a key advantage.

The goal of Chapter 2 is to provide an overview of specific MIS tools managers can use to support the strategies discussed in Chapter 1. After reading this chapter, you, the business student, should have detailed knowledge of the types of information systems that exist to support decision making and business process reengineering, which in turn can improve organization efficiency and effectiveness and help an organization create and maintain competitive advantages.

Action Finally—Actionly

Data are all over the Internet! Tons and tons and tons of data! For example, over 152 million blogs are created each year, along with 100 million Twitter accounts resulting in 25 billion Tweets, 107 trillion emails are sent, and 730 billion hours of YouTube videos are watched. Known as the social media sector, this arena is by far one of the fastest growing and most influential sectors in business. Companies are struggling to understand how the social media sector impacts it both financially and strategically.

Data are valuable to any company and the data on the Internet are unique because the information comes directly from customers, suppliers, competitors, and even employees. As the social media sector takes off, companies are finding themselves at a disadvantage when attempting to keep up with all of the "online chatter" about their goods and services on the many different social media websites, including Facebook, Twitter, MySpace, Flickr, LinkedIn, Yelp, Google, blogs, etc.

Any time there is a problem there is a potential business solution, and Actionly.com chooses to capitalize on the data glut problem. Actionly monitors multiple social media channels through one tracking service looking for specific keywords for industries, brands, companies, and trends. Actionly customers choose a keyword to monitor—such as a brand, product names, industry terms, or competitors—and then Actionly constantly collects the data from these social channels and pulls that data into a cohesive digital dashboard. The digital dashboard tracks the desired information, such as marketplace trends, specific companies, competitive brands, entire industries (for example, clean technology), by simultaneously searching Twitter, Facebook, Google, YouTube, Flickr, and blogs. After completing a search, Actionly.com uses Google Analytics to create graphs and charts indicating how frequently each keyword was found throughout the various channels. Additionally, it links each respective channel to the dashboard and filters them with "positive" and "negative" connections, allowing users to respond to any comments.

Actionly.com's business model sets it up for success in this emerging industry. Actionly has a first-mover advantage because it was the first online brand management company offering this service to customers. And the company benefits by using its own services to ensure its brand stays number one on all social media websites. Actionly uses Google Analytics to help transform the data it collects from the various social media websites into valuable business intelligence. Its digital dashboard monitors several key metrics, including:

- **Reputation Management:** Actionly's easy to use digital dashboard allows customers to observe and analyze trends and track mentions about brands based on historical data as well as continuously updated data. For example, a customer can view graphs that highlight key trends across 30 days for specific brands, products, or companies.

- **Social ROI:** By connecting to Google Analytics from Actionly, a customer can analyze its campaign performance for individual tweets or Facebook posts to determine which are successful and which are failing. Actionly analyzes every post and click to track page views, visitor information, goal completions, and so on, through its digital dashboard, allowing users to customize reports tracking the performance of daily posts.

- **Twitter Analytics:** After adding Twitter accounts to the dashboard, a user can drill down into the data to view graphs of followers, mentions, and retweets. This eliminates the need to manually track a number of Twitter accounts, and a user can view the data in graphs or export the data in Excel for further analysis.

- **Marketing Campaign Tracking:** If a company is launching a big promotion or contest, it can post messages across multiple Facebook or Twitter accounts; all the user has to do is select which Twitter or Facebook accounts it wants to use and when. Actionly's Campaign Tracking helps a user view which posts are resonating well with customers and measure metrics such as page views, signups, conversions, and revenue by post. Actionly even segments the data by post, account, campaign, or channel, allowing users to measure performance over time.

- **Click Performance:** Actionly tracks performance by hour and day of week, allowing customers to view which clicks are getting the most attention. Actionly's algorithm automatically assigns a sentiment to tweets, allowing the customer to immediately filter positive or negative or neutral posts to react to information quickly.

- **Sentiment Analysis:** Reviewing positive and negative feedback helps gauge how a brand is doing over time, allowing the client to try to increase the positive sentiment. However, no sentiment scoring is 100 percent accurate due to the complexities of interpretation, culture, sarcasm, and other language nuances. For example, if Actionly is incorrectly tracking a metric, it can change it, allowing users to assign their unique sentiments directly to their tweets. A user can also select to have positive or negative alerts for keywords emailed as soon as the keyword is posted to help manage online brand and company reputations.

- **Competitive Analysis:** Actionly tracks competitor intelligence by watching new-product releases, acquisitions, or customer feedback, allowing a company to stay on top of market entrants, market-related blogs, news, or industry-related seminars/webinars.

- **Find Influencers:** Actionly's digital dashboard allows a user to engage directly with key influencers or people who are driving the online chatter about goods and services. Actionly identifies influencers and determines their relevance to the company, brand, or product. It then compiles a list of influencers based on users with the most followers and who have been most active for the specific searches in the past 30 days.[1]

section 2.1 | Decision Support Systems

LEARNING OUTCOMES

2.1 Explain the importance of decision making for managers at each of the three primary organization levels along with the associated decision characteristics.

2.2 Define critical success factors (CSFs) and key performance indicators (KPIs), and explain how managers use them to measure the success of MIS projects.

2.3 Classify the different operational support systems, managerial support systems, and strategic support systems, and explain how managers can use these systems to make decisions and gain competitive advantages.

2.4 Describe artificial intelligence, and identify its five main types.

MAKING BUSINESS DECISIONS

Porter's strategies outlined in Chapter 1 suggest entering markets with a competitive advantage in either overall cost leadership, differentiation, or focus. To achieve these results, managers must be able to make decisions and forecast future business needs and requirements. The most important and most challenging question confronting managers today is how to lay the foundation for tomorrow's success while competing to win in today's business environment. A company will not have a future if it is not cultivating strategies for tomorrow. The goal of this section is to expand on Porter's Five Forces Model, three generic strategies, and value chain analysis to demonstrate how managers can learn the concepts and practices of business decision making to add value. It will also highlight how companies heading into the 21st century are taking advantage of advanced MIS capable of generating significant competitive advantages across the value chain.

As we discussed in Chapter 1, decision making is one of the most important and challenging aspects of management. Decisions range from routine choices, such as how many items to order or how many people to hire, to unexpected ones such as what to do if a key employee suddenly quits or needed materials do not arrive. Today, with massive volumes of information available, managers are challenged to make highly complex decisions—some involving far more information than the human brain can comprehend—in increasingly shorter time frames. Figure 2.1 displays the three primary challenges managers face when making decisions.

LO. 2.1: Explain the importance of decision making for managers at each of the three primary organization levels along with the associated decision characteristics.

FIGURE 2.1

Managerial Decision-Making Challenges

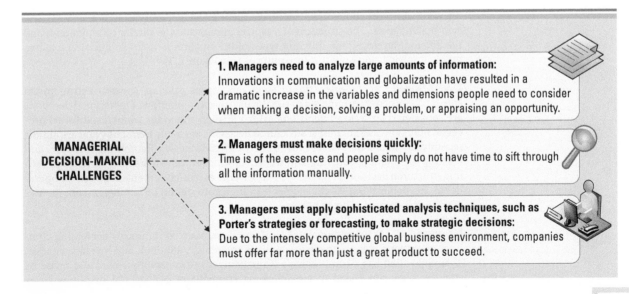

MANAGERIAL DECISION-MAKING CHALLENGES

1. Managers need to analyze large amounts of information:
Innovations in communication and globalization have resulted in a dramatic increase in the variables and dimensions people need to consider when making a decision, solving a problem, or appraising an opportunity.

2. Managers must make decisions quickly:
Time is of the essence and people simply do not have time to sift through all the information manually.

3. Managers must apply sophisticated analysis techniques, such as Porter's strategies or forecasting, to make strategic decisions:
Due to the intensely competitive global business environment, companies must offer far more than just a great product to succeed.

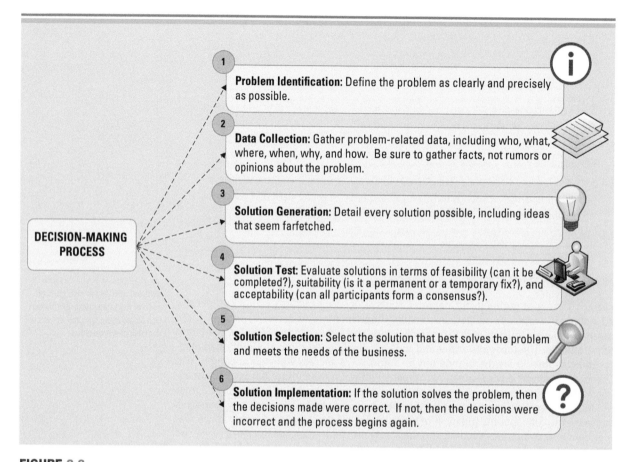

FIGURE 2.2

The Six-Step Decision-Making Process

The Decision-Making Process

The process of making decisions plays a crucial role in communication and leadership for operational, managerial, and strategic projects. **Analytics** is the science of fact-based decision making. There are numerous academic decision-making models; Figure 2.2 presents just one example.[2]

Decision-Making Essentials

A few key concepts about organizational structure will help our discussion of MIS decision-making tools. The structure of a typical organization is similar to a pyramid, and the different levels require different types of information to assist in decision making, problem solving, and opportunity capturing (see Figure 2.3).

Operational   At the **operational level**, employees develop, control, and maintain core business activities required to run the day-to-day operations. Operational decisions are considered **structured decisions**, which arise in situations where established processes offer potential solutions. Structured decisions are made frequently and are almost repetitive in nature; they affect short-term business strategies. Reordering inventory and creating the employee staffing and weekly production schedules are examples of routine structured decisions. Figure 2.4 highlights the essential elements required for operational decision making. All the elements in the figure should be familiar, except metrics which are discussed in detail below.

Managerial   At the **managerial level**, employees are continuously evaluating company operations to hone the firm's abilities to identify, adapt to, and leverage change. A company that has a competitive advantage needs to constantly adjust and revise its strategy to remain ahead of fast-following competitors. Managerial decisions cover

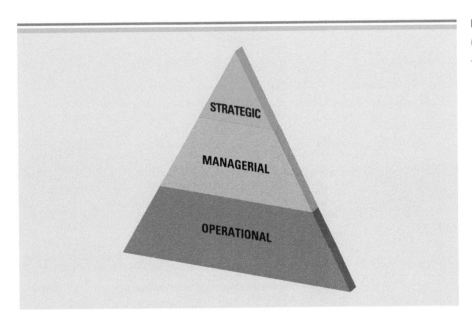

FIGURE 2.3

Common Company Structure

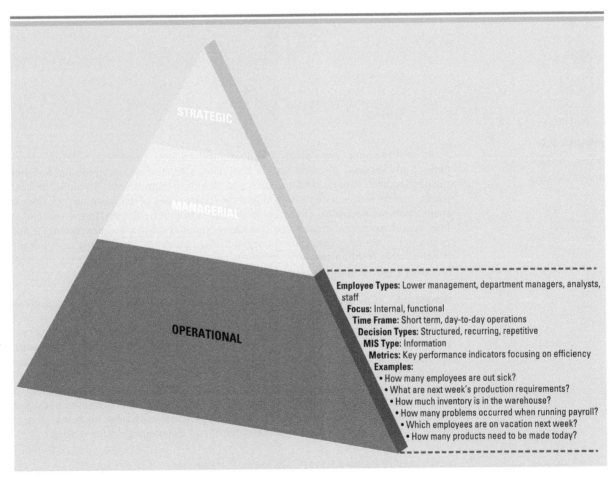

Employee Types: Lower management, department managers, analysts, staff
Focus: Internal, functional
Time Frame: Short term, day-to-day operations
Decision Types: Structured, recurring, repetitive
MIS Type: Information
Metrics: Key performance indicators focusing on efficiency
Examples:
- How many employees are out sick?
- What are next week's production requirements?
- How much inventory is in the warehouse?
- How many problems occurred when running payroll?
- Which employees are on vacation next week?
- How many products need to be made today?

FIGURE 2.4

Overview of Operational
Decision Making

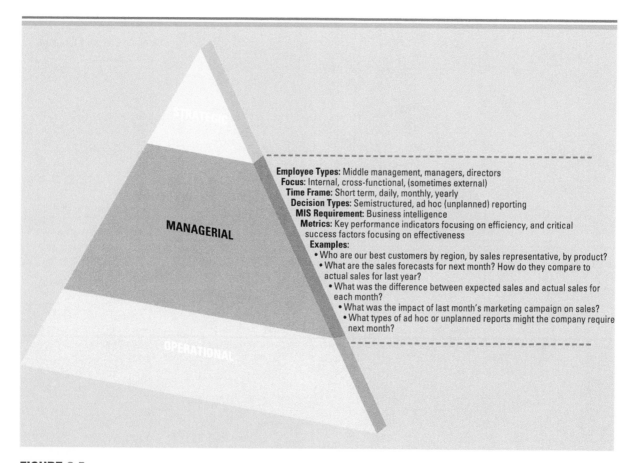

Employee Types: Middle management, managers, directors
Focus: Internal, cross-functional, (sometimes external)
Time Frame: Short term, daily, monthly, yearly
Decision Types: Semistructured, ad hoc (unplanned) reporting
MIS Requirement: Business intelligence
Metrics: Key performance indicators focusing on efficiency, and critical success factors focusing on effectiveness
Examples:
• Who are our best customers by region, by sales representative, by product?
• What are the sales forecasts for next month? How do they compare to actual sales for last year?
• What was the difference between expected sales and actual sales for each month?
• What was the impact of last month's marketing campaign on sales?
• What types of ad hoc or unplanned reports might the company require next month?

FIGURE 2.5

Overview of Managerial
Decision Making

short- and medium-range plans, schedules, and budgets along with policies, procedures, and business objectives for the firm. They also allocate resources and monitor the performance of organizational subunits, including departments, divisions, process teams, project teams, and other work groups. These types of decisions are considered ***semistructured decisions;*** they occur in situations in which a few established processes help to evaluate potential solutions, but not enough to lead to a definite recommended decision. For example, decisions about producing new products or changing employee benefits range from unstructured to semistructured. Figure 2.5 highlights the essential elements required for managerial decision making.

Strategic   At the ***strategic level***, managers develop overall business strategies, goals, and objectives as part of the company's strategic plan. They also monitor the strategic performance of the organization and its overall direction in the political, economic, and competitive business environment. Strategic decisions are highly ***unstructured decisions***, occurring in situations in which no procedures or rules exist to guide decision makers toward the correct choice. They are infrequent, extremely important, and typically related to long-term business strategy. Examples include the decision to enter a new market or even a new industry over, say, the next three years. In these types of decisions, managers rely on many sources of information, along with personal knowledge, to find solutions. Figure 2.6 highlights the essential elements required for strategic decision making.

LO 2.2: Define critical success factors (CSFs) and key performance indicators (KPIs), and explain how managers use them to measure the success of MIS projects.

METRICS: MEASURING SUCCESS

A ***project*** is a temporary activity a company undertakes to create a unique product, service, or result. For example, the construction of a new subway station is a project, as is a movie theater chain's adoption of a software program to allow online ticketing. Peter Drucker, a famous management writer, once said that if you cannot measure

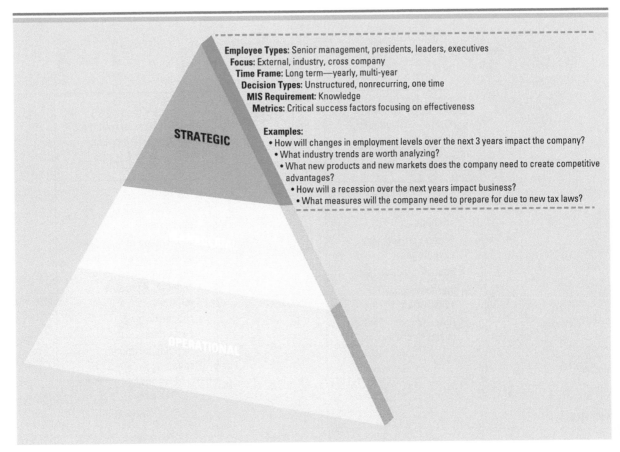

Employee Types: Senior management, presidents, leaders, executives
Focus: External, industry, cross company
Time Frame: Long term—yearly, multi-year
Decision Types: Unstructured, nonrecurring, one time
MIS Requirement: Knowledge
Metrics: Critical success factors focusing on effectiveness

STRATEGIC

Examples:
- How will changes in employment levels over the next 3 years impact the company?
- What industry trends are worth analyzing?
- What new products and new markets does the company need to create competitive advantages?
- How will a recession over the next years impact business?
- What measures will the company need to prepare for due to new tax laws?

OPERATIONAL

FIGURE 2.6

Overview of Strategic
Decision Making

something, you cannot manage it. How do managers measure the progress of a complex business project?

Metrics are measurements that evaluate results to determine whether a project is meeting its goals. Two core metrics are critical success factors and key performance indicators. *Critical success factors (CSFs)* are the crucial steps companies perform to achieve their goals and objectives and implement their strategies (see Figure 2.7). *Key performance indicators (KPIs)* are the quantifiable metrics a company uses to evaluate progress toward critical success factors. KPIs are far more specific than CSFs.

It is important to understand the relationship between critical success factors and key performance indicators. CSFs are elements crucial for a business strategy's success. KPIs measure the progress of CSFs with quantifiable measurements, and one CSF can have several KPIs. Of course, both categories will vary by company and industry. Imagine *improve graduation rates* as a CSF for a college. The KPIs to measure this CSF can include:

- Average grades by course and gender.
- Student dropout rates by gender and major.
- Average graduation rate by gender and major.
- Time spent in tutoring by gender and major.

KPIs can focus on external and internal measurements. A common external KPI is *market share*, or the proportion of the market that a firm captures. We calculate it by dividing the firm's sales by the total market sales for the entire industry. Market share measures a firm's external performance relative to that of its competitors. For example, if a firm's total sales (revenues) are $2 million and sales for the entire industry are $10 million, the firm has captured 20 percent of the total market (2/10 = 20%) or a 20 percent market share.

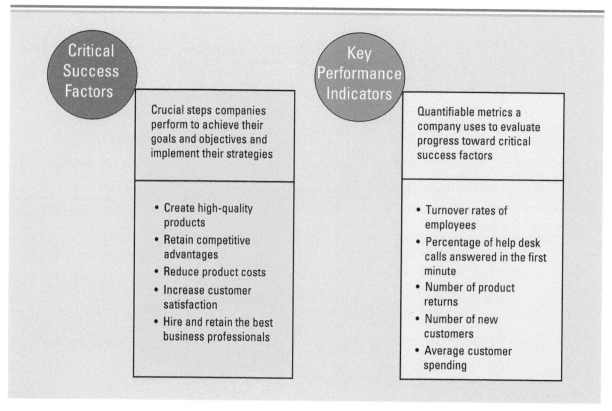

FIGURE 2.7

CSF and KPI Metrics

A common internal KPI is ***return on investment (ROI)***, which indicates the earning power of a project. We measure it by dividing the profitability of a project by the costs. This sounds easy, and for many departments where the projects are tangible and self-contained it is; however, for projects that are intangible and cross departmental lines (such as MIS projects), ROI is challenging to measure. Imagine attempting to calculate the ROI of a fire extinguisher. If the fire extinguisher is never used, its ROI is low. If the fire extinguisher puts out a fire that could have destroyed the entire building, its ROI is astronomically high.

Creating KPIs to measure the success of an MIS project offers similar challenges. Think about a firm's email system. How could managers track departmental costs and profits associated with company email? Measuring by volume does not account for profitability, because one sales email could land a million-dollar deal while 300 others might not generate any revenue. Non-revenue-generating departments such as human resources and legal require email but will not be using it to generate profits. For this reason, many managers turn to higher-level metrics, such as efficiency and effectiveness, to measure MIS projects. ***Best practices*** are the most successful solutions or problem-solving methods that have been developed by a specific organization or industry. Measuring MIS projects helps determine the best practices for an industry.

Efficiency and Effectiveness Metrics

Efficiency MIS metrics measure the performance of MIS itself, such as throughput, transaction speed, and system availability. ***Effectiveness MIS metrics*** measure the impact MIS has on business processes and activities, including customer satisfaction and customer conversion rates. Efficiency focuses on the extent to which a firm is using its resources in an optimal way, while effectiveness focuses on how well a firm is achieving its goals and objectives. Peter Drucker offers a helpful distinction between efficiency and effectiveness: Doing things right addresses efficiency—getting the most from each resource.

BUSINESS DRIVEN DISCUSSION

Driving Decisions

How do people make decisions? Almost daily you can read about someone who makes a decision most people would find mind-boggling. Here are a few examples:

- A woman in Ohio was charged with child endangerment after police said she admitted to breast-feeding her child and talking on a cell phone while driving her other children to school.

- A woman in South Florida was caught driving while talking on a cell phone on her left shoulder and eating from a cup of soup in her left hand. The woman would take her right hand off the wheel to spoon soup, driving with no hands while she continued to talk on the phone.

- A man in California was cited for driving while carrying a swimming pool. He drove with one hand while he held his new swimming pool on the roof of his car with the other. His three children were leaning out of the car windows, not wearing seat belts, to help hold onto the pool.

- A woman in Baltimore was charged with diapering her child in the front seat of the car while driving at 65 miles per hour down the highway.[3]

Find an example of a company that found itself in trouble because its employees made bad decisions. What could the company have done to protect itself from these types of employee blunders?

Doing the right things addresses effectiveness—setting the right goals and objectives and ensuring they are accomplished. Figure 2.8 describes a few of the common types of efficiency and effectiveness MIS metrics. KPIs that measure MIS projects include both efficiency and effectiveness metrics. Of course, these metrics are not as concrete as market share or ROI, but they do offer valuable insight into project performance.[4]

Large increases in productivity typically result from increases in effectiveness, which focus on CSFs. Efficiency MIS metrics are far easier to measure, however, so most managers tend to focus on them, often incorrectly, to measure the success of MIS projects. Consider measuring the success of automated teller machines (ATMs). Thinking in terms of MIS efficiency metrics, a manager would measure the number of daily transactions, the average amount per transaction, and the average speed per transaction to determine the success of the ATM. Although these offer solid metrics on how well the system is performing, they miss many of the intangible or value-added benefits associated with ATM effectiveness. Effectiveness MIS metrics might measure how many new customers joined the bank due to its ATM locations or the ATMs' ease of use. They can also measure increases in customer satisfaction due to reduced ATM fees or additional ATM services such as the sale of stamps and movie tickets, significant time savers and value-added features for customers. Being a great manager means taking the added viewpoint offered by effectiveness MIS metrics to analyze all benefits associated with an MIS project.

The Interrelationship Between Efficiency and Effectiveness MIS Metrics

Efficiency and effectiveness are definitely related. However, success in one area does not necessarily imply success in the other. Efficiency MIS metrics focus on the technology itself. While these efficiency MIS metrics are important to monitor, they do not always guarantee effectiveness. Effectiveness MIS metrics are determined according

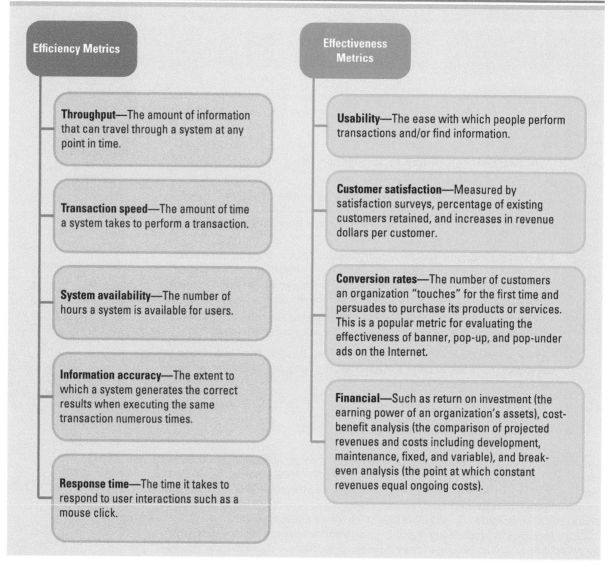

FIGURE 2.8

Common Types of Efficiency
and Effectiveness Metrics

to an organization's goals, strategies, and objectives. Here, it becomes important to consider a company's CSFs, such as a broad cost leadership strategy (Walmart, for example), as well as KPIs such as increasing new customers by 10 percent or reducing new-product development cycle times to six months. In the private sector, eBay continuously benchmarks its MIS projects for efficiency and effectiveness. Maintaining constant website availability and optimal throughput performance are CSFs for eBay.

Figure 2.9 depicts the interrelationships between efficiency and effectiveness. Ideally, a firm wants to operate in the upper right-hand corner of the graph, realizing both significant increases in efficiency and effectiveness. However, operating in the upper left-hand corner (minimal effectiveness with increased efficiency) or the lower right-hand corner (significant effectiveness with minimal efficiency) may be in line with an organization's particular strategies. In general, operating in the lower left-hand corner (minimal efficiency and minimal effectiveness) is not ideal for the operation of any organization.

Benchmarks   Regardless of what process is measured, how it is measured, and whether it is performed for the sake of efficiency or effectiveness, managers must set *benchmarks*, or baseline values the system seeks to attain. *Benchmarking* is a process of continuously measuring system results, comparing those results to optimal system

BUSINESS DRIVEN GLOBALIZATION

It is late at night and you are working on your final exam when your computer crashes. As your blood pressure climbs and your stress level skyrockets, you call your computer manufacturer's technical support number. Of course that person tells you the problem has nothing to do with the computer and must have a different source. What are you going to do?

iYogi.net is a 24/7 online support service that allows technicians to take remote control of your computer from Gurgaon, India, and try to fix what ails it. iYogi provides technical support for all Walmart computer customers and sells its services through Walmart.com and Amazon.com. If the thought of turning control over to someone you never met half a world away fills you with terror, it shouldn't. All iYogi technicians are Microsoft, Cisco, and Hewlett-Packard certified.[5]

Describe the types of decisions iYogi technicians are required to make when helping a customer with a computer problem. What would potential CSFs and KPIs for iYogi be? What types of metrics would managers track so they could control operations?

iYogi Help Desk Support

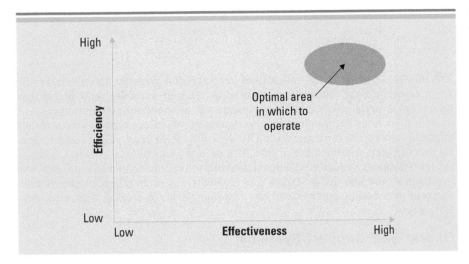

FIGURE 2.9

The Interrelationships Between Efficiency and Effectiveness

performance (benchmark values), and identifying steps and procedures to improve system performance. Benchmarks help assess how an MIS project performs over time. For instance, if a system held a benchmark for response time of 15 seconds, the manager would want to ensure response time continued to decrease until it reached that point. If response time suddenly increased to 1 minute, the manager would know the system was not functioning correctly and could start looking into potential problems. Continuously measuring MIS projects against benchmarks provides feedback so managers can control the system.

SUPPORT: ENHANCING DECISION MAKING WITH MIS

Now that we've reviewed the essentials of decision making, we are ready to understand the powerful benefits associated with using MIS to support managers making decisions.

LO 2.3: Classify the different operational support systems, managerial support systems, and strategic support systems, and explain how managers can use these systems to make decisions and gain competitive advantages.

FIGURE 2.10

Primary Types of MIS Systems
for Decision Making

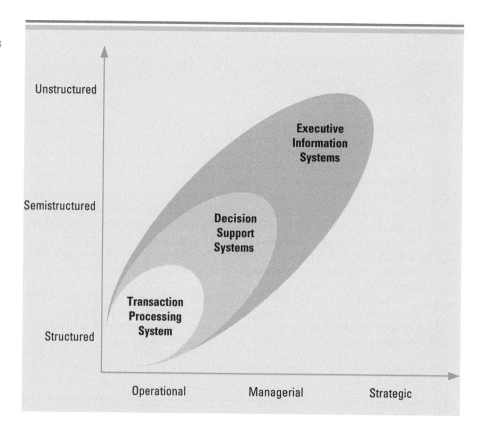

A *model* is a simplified representation or abstraction of reality. Models help managers calculate risks, understand uncertainty, change variables, and manipulate time to make decisions. MIS support systems rely on models for computational and analytical routines that mathematically express relationships among variables. For example, a spreadsheet program, such as Microsoft Office Excel, might contain models that calculate market share or ROI. MIS have the capability and functionality to express far more complex modeling relationships that provide information, business intelligence, and knowledge. Figure 2.10 highlights the three primary types of management information systems available to support decision making across the company levels.

Operational Support Systems

Transactional information encompasses all the information contained within a single business process or unit of work, and its primary purpose is to support the performance of daily operational or structured decisions. Transactional information is created, for example, when customers are purchasing stocks, making an airline reservation, or withdrawing cash from an ATM. Managers use transactional information when making structured decisions at the operational level, such as when analyzing daily sales reports to determine how much inventory to carry.

Online transaction processing (OLTP) is the capture of transaction and event information using technology to (1) process the information according to defined business rules, (2) store the information, and (3) update existing information to reflect the new information. During OLTP, the organization must capture every detail of transactions and events. A *transaction processing system (TPS)* is the basic business system that serves the operational level (analysts) and assists in making structured decisions. The most common example of a TPS is an operational accounting system such as a payroll system or an order-entry system.

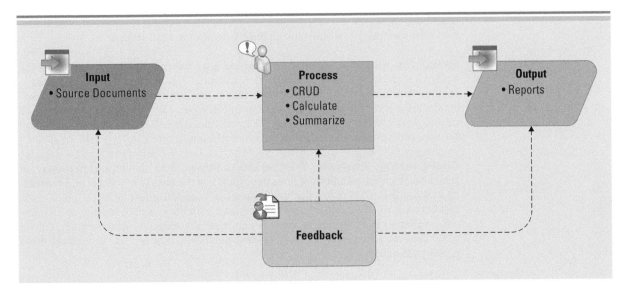

FIGURE 2.11

Systems Thinking Example
of a TPS

Using systems thinking, we can see that the inputs for a TPS are *source documents*, the original transaction record. Source documents for a payroll system can include time sheets, wage rates, and employee benefit reports. Transformation includes common procedures such as creating, reading, updating, and deleting (commonly referred to as CRUD) employee records, along with calculating the payroll and summarizing benefits. The output includes cutting the paychecks and generating payroll reports. Figure 2.11 demonstrates the systems thinking view of a TPS.[6]

Managerial Support Systems

Analytical information encompasses all organizational information, and its primary purpose is to support the performance of managerial analysis or semistructured decisions. Analytical information includes transactional information along with other information such as market and industry information. Examples of analytical information are trends, sales, product statistics, and future growth projections. Managers use analytical information when making important semistructured decisions, such as whether the organization should build a new manufacturing plant or hire additional sales reps.

Online analytical processing (OLAP) is the manipulation of information to create business intelligence in support of strategic decision making. *Decision support systems (DSSs)* model information using OLAP, which provides assistance in evaluating and choosing among different courses of action. DSSs enable high-level managers to examine and manipulate large amounts of detailed data from different internal and external sources. Analyzing complex relationships among thousands or even millions of data items to discover patterns, trends, and exception conditions is one of the key uses associated with a DSS. For example, doctors may enter symptoms into a decision support system so it can help diagnose and treat patients. Insurance companies also use a DSS to gauge the risk of providing insurance to drivers who have imperfect driving records. One company found that married women who are homeowners with one speeding ticket are rarely cited for speeding again. Armed with this business intelligence, the company achieved a cost advantage by lowering insurance rates to this specific group of customers. The following are common DSS analysis techniques.

What-If Analysis *What-if analysis* checks the impact of a change in a variable or assumption on the model. For example, "What will happen to the supply chain if a hurricane in South Carolina reduces holding inventory from 30 percent to 10 percent?" A user would be able to observe and evaluate any changes that occurred to the values in the model, especially to a variable such as profits. Users repeat this analysis with different variables until they understand all the effects of various situations.

Sensitivity Analysis   *Sensitivity analysis*, a special case of what-if analysis, is the study of the impact on other variables when one variable is changed repeatedly. Sensitivity analysis is useful when users are uncertain about the assumptions made in estimating the value of certain key variables. For example, repeatedly changing revenue in small increments to determine its effects on other variables would help a manager understand the impact of various revenue levels on other decision factors.

Goal-Seeking Analysis   *Goal-seeking analysis* finds the inputs necessary to achieve a goal such as a desired level of output. It is the reverse of what-if and sensitivity analysis. Instead of observing how changes in a variable affect other variables, goal-seeking analysis sets a target value (a goal) for a variable and then repeatedly changes other variables until the target value is achieved. For example, goal-seeking analysis could determine how many customers must purchase a new product to increase gross profits to $5 million.

Optimization Analysis   *Optimization analysis*, an extension of goal-seeking analysis, finds the optimum value for a target variable by repeatedly changing other variables, subject to specified constraints. By changing revenue and cost variables in an optimization analysis, managers can calculate the highest potential profits. Constraints on revenue and cost variables can be taken into consideration, such as limits on the amount of raw materials the company can afford to purchase and limits on employees available to meet production needs.

Figure 2.12 shows the common systems view of a DSS. Figure 2.13 shows how TPSs supply transactional data to a DSS. The DSS then summarizes and aggregates the information from the different TPSs, which assist managers in making semistructured decision.

Strategic Support Systems

Decision making at the strategic level requires both business intelligence and knowledge to support the uncertainty and complexity associated with business strategies. An ***executive information system (EIS)*** is a specialized DSS that supports senior-level executives and unstructured, long-term, nonroutine decisions requiring judgment, evaluation, and insight. These decisions do not have a right or wrong answer, only efficient and

FIGURE 2.12

Systems Thinking Example
of a DSS

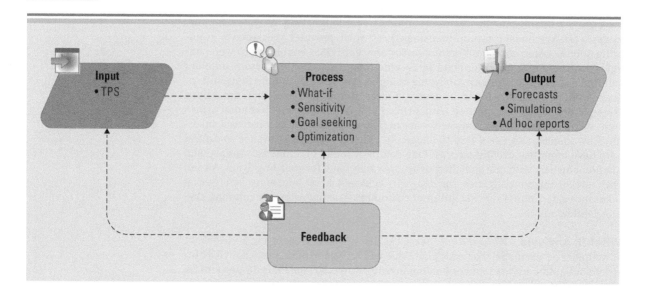

BUSINESS DRIVEN ETHICS AND SECURITY

What if the person sitting in the cubicle next to you was running a scam that cost your company $7 billion? An employee at a French bank allegedly used his inside knowledge of business processes to bypass the system and place roughly $73 billion in bogus trades that cost the bank more than $7 billion to unwind.

Findings from the U.S. Secret Service's examination of 23 incidents conducted by 26 insiders determined that 70 percent of the time, insiders took advantage of failures in business process rules and authorization mechanisms to steal from their company. These insiders were authorized and active computer users 78 percent of the time, and a surprising 43 percent used their own user name and passwords to commit their crimes.[7]

This is a daunting reminder that every employee has the potential to become a knowledgeable insider and, if started on a criminal path, to do tremendous damage to your company. Many DSSs and EISs contain the business intelligence your company needs to operate effectively, and you need to protect these assets. What types of sensitive information is housed in a company's TPS, DSS, and EIS? What problems could you encounter if one of your employees decided to steal the information housed in your DSS? How could you protect your EIS from unethical users? What would you do if you thought the person sharing your cube was a rogue insider?

The Criminal in the Cube Next Door

FIGURE 2.13

Interaction Between TPS and DSS to Support Semistructured Decisions

effective answers. Moving up through the organizational pyramid, managers deal less with the details ("finer" information) and more with meaningful aggregations of information ("coarser" information). **Granularity** refers to the level of detail in the model or the decision-making process. The greater the granularity, the deeper the level of detail or fineness of data (see Figure 2.14).

BUSINESS DRIVEN START-UP

Digital Dashboard for Tracking Junk

Do you enjoy kidnapping your rivals' team mascots or toilet-papering their frat houses? If so, you might find your ideal career at College Hunks Hauling Junk. The company hires college students and recent grads to pick up junk and take it away. The founder, Nick Friedman, had a goal of capturing that friendly rivalry so often associated with college life and turning it into profits. When the company launched in 2005, the haulers from Virginia found their truck had been lathered in shaving cream and draped with a University of Maryland flag. The Virginia haulers retaliated, and soon after dead fish were found on the seats of Maryland's truck. Friedman decided to use this energy as an incentive instead of condemning the unorthodox behavior. "We wanted to harness that competitive, prankster enthusiasm and channel it for good," he says.

Freidman made a bold move and decided that instead of tracking typical key performance indicators such as revenue, average job size, and customer loyalty, he would set up his dashboard to track volume of junk collected and amount donated or recycled. The winning team gains such things as bragging rights and banners, modest monetary prizes, and the right to eat first at the annual company meeting. Most employees check the dashboard daily to view their own and rivals' latest standings.[8]

Why do you think competition is helping College Hunks Hauling Junk exceed its revenue goals? If you were to build a team competition dashboard for your school or your work, what types of metrics would you track? What types of motivators would you use to ensure your team is always in the green? What types of external information would you want tracked in your dashboard? Could an unethical person use the information from your dashboard to hurt your team or your organization? What can you do to mitigate these risks?

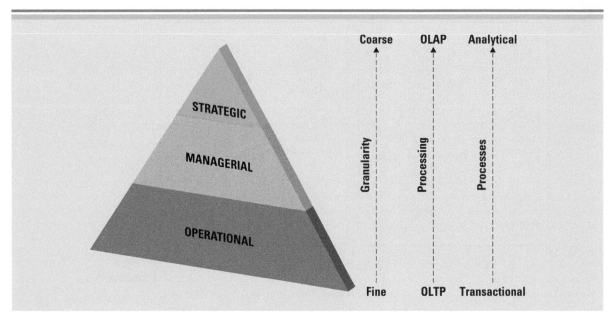

FIGURE 2.14

Information Levels Throughout an Organization

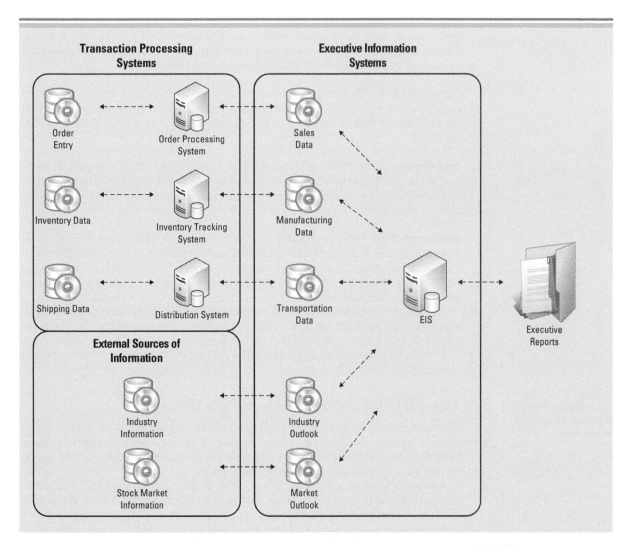

FIGURE 2.15

Interaction Between
a TPS and EIS

A DSS differs from an EIS in that an EIS requires data from external sources to support unstructured decisions (see Figure 2.15). This is not to say that DSSs never use data from external sources, but typically DSS semistructured decisions rely on internal data only.

Visualization produces graphical displays of patterns and complex relationships in large amounts of data. Executive information systems use visualization to deliver specific key information to top managers at a glance, with little or no interaction with the system. A common tool that supports visualization is a ***digital dashboard***, which tracks KPIs and CSFs by compiling information from multiple sources and tailoring it to meet user needs. Following is a list of potential features included in a dashboard designed for a manufacturing team:

- A hot list of key performance indicators, refreshed every 15 minutes.
- A running line graph of planned versus actual production for the past 24 hours.
- A table showing actual versus forecasted product prices and inventories.
- A list of outstanding alerts and their resolution status.
- A graph of stock market prices.

Digital dashboards, whether basic or comprehensive, deliver results quickly. As they become easier to use, more employees can perform their own analyses without inundating MIS staff with questions and requests for reports. Digital dashboards enable employees to move beyond reporting to using information to directly increase business performance. With them, employees can react to information as soon as it becomes available and make decisions, solve problems, and change strategies daily instead of monthly. Digital dashboards offer the following capabilities:

Consolidation *Consolidation* is the aggregation of data from simple roll-ups to complex groupings of interrelated information. For example, data for different sales representatives can then be rolled up to an office level, then a state level, then a regional sales level.

Drill-Down *Drill-down* enables users to view details, and details of details, of information. This is the reverse of consolidation; a user can view regional sales data and then drill down all the way to each sales representative's data at each office. Drill-down capability lets managers view monthly, weekly, daily, or even hourly information.

Slice-and-Dice *Slice-and-dice* is the ability to look at information from different perspectives. One slice of information could display all product sales during a given promotion. Another slice could display a single product's sales for all promotions. Slicing and dicing is often performed along a time axis to analyze trends and find time-based patterns in the information.

One thing to remember when making decisions is the old saying, "Garbage in, garbage out." If the transactional data used in the support system are wrong, then the managerial analysis will be wrong and the DSS will simply assist in making a wrong decision faster. Managers should also ask, "What is the DSS *not* telling me before I make my final decision?"

LO 2.4: Describe artificial intelligence, and identify its five main types.

THE FUTURE: ARTIFICIAL INTELLIGENCE

Executive information systems are starting to take advantage of artificial intelligence to facilitate unstructured strategic decision making. *Artificial intelligence (AI)* simulates human thinking and behavior, such as the ability to reason and learn. Its ultimate goal is to build a system that can mimic human intelligence.

Intelligent systems are various commercial applications of artificial intelligence. They include sensors, software, and devices that emulate and enhance human capabilities, learn or understand from experience, make sense of ambiguous or contradictory information, and even use reasoning to solve problems and make decisions effectively. Intelligent systems perform such tasks as boosting productivity in factories by monitoring equipment and signaling when preventive maintenance is required. They are beginning to show up everywhere:

- At Manchester Airport in England, the Hefner AI Robot Cleaner alerts passengers to security and nonsmoking rules while it scrubs up to 65,600 square feet of floor per day. Laser scanners and ultrasonic detectors keep it from colliding with passengers.
- Shell Oil's SmartPump keeps drivers in their cars on cold, wet winter days. It can service any automobile built after 1987 that has been fitted with a special gas cap and a windshield-mounted transponder that tells the robot where to insert the pump.
- Matsushita's courier robot navigates hospital hallways, delivering patient files, X-ray films, and medical supplies.
- The FireFighter AI Robot can extinguish flames at chemical plants and nuclear reactors with water, foam, powder, or inert gas. The robot puts distance between human operators and the fire.[9]

AI systems increase the speed and consistency of decision making, solve problems with incomplete information, and resolve complicated issues that cannot be solved by conventional computing. There are many categories of AI systems; five of the most familiar are (1) expert systems, (2) neural networks, (3) genetic algorithms, (4) intelligent agents, and (5) virtual reality (see Figure 2.16).

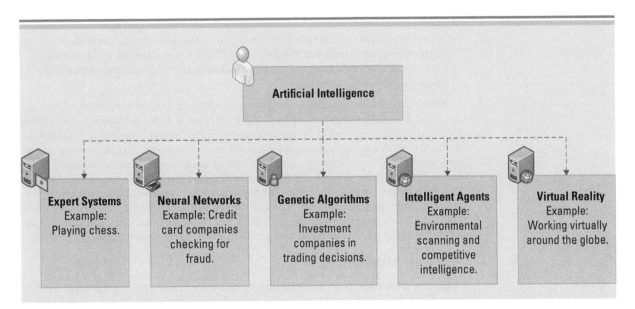

FIGURE 2.16

Examples of Artificial Intelligence

Expert Systems

Expert systems are computerized advisory programs that imitate the reasoning processes of experts in solving difficult problems. Typically, they include a knowledge base containing various accumulated experience and a set of rules for applying the knowledge base to each particular situation. Expert systems are the most common form of AI in the business arena because they fill the gap when human experts are difficult to find or retain or are too expensive. The best-known systems play chess and assist in medical diagnosis.

Neural Networks

A *neural network*, also called an artificial neural network, is a category of AI that attempts to emulate the way the human brain works. Neural networks analyze large quantities of information to establish patterns and characteristics in situations where the logic or rules are unknown. Neural networks' many features include:

- Learning and adjusting to new circumstances on their own.
- Lending themselves to massive parallel processing.
- Functioning without complete or well-structured information.
- Coping with huge volumes of information with many dependent variables.
- Analyzing nonlinear relationships in information (they have been called fancy regression analysis systems).

The finance industry is a veteran in the use of neural network technology and has been relying on various forms for over two decades. It uses neural networks to review loan applications and create patterns or profiles of applications that fall into two categories—approved or denied. Here are some examples of neural networks in finance:

- Citibank uses neural networks to find opportunities in financial markets. By carefully examining historical stock market data with neural network software, Citibank financial managers learn of interesting coincidences or small anomalies (called market inefficiencies). For example, it could be that whenever IBM stock goes up, so does Unisys stock, or that a U.S. Treasury note is selling for 1 cent less in Japan than in the United States. These snippets of information can make a big difference to Citibank's bottom line in a very competitive financial market.

- Visa, MasterCard, and many other credit card companies use a neural network to spot peculiarities in individual accounts and follow up by checking for fraud. MasterCard estimates neural networks save it $50 million annually.

- Insurance companies along with state compensation funds and other carriers use neural network software to identify fraud. The system searches for patterns in billing charges, laboratory tests, and frequency of office visits. A claim for which the diagnosis was a sprained ankle but treatment included an electrocardiogram would be flagged for the account manager.[10]

Fuzzy logic is a mathematical method of handling imprecise or subjective information. The basic approach is to assign values between 0 and 1 to vague or ambiguous information. Zero represents information not included, while 1 represents inclusion or membership. For example, fuzzy logic is used in washing machines that determine by themselves how much water to use or how long to wash (they continue washing until the water is clean). In accounting and finance, fuzzy logic allows people to analyze information with subjective financial values (intangibles such as goodwill) that are very important considerations in economic analysis. Fuzzy logic and neural networks are often combined to express complicated and subjective concepts in a form that makes it possible to simplify the problem and apply rules that are executed with a level of certainty.

Genetic Algorithms

A *genetic algorithm* is an artificial intelligence system that mimics the evolutionary, survival-of-the-fittest process to generate increasingly better solutions to a problem. A genetic algorithm is essentially an optimizing system: It finds the combination of inputs that gives the best outputs. *Mutation* is the process within a genetic algorithm of randomly trying combinations and evaluating the success (or failure) of the outcome.

Genetic algorithms are best suited to decision-making environments in which thousands, or perhaps millions, of solutions are possible. Genetic algorithms can find and evaluate solutions with many more possibilities, faster and more thoroughly than a human. Organizations face decision-making environments for all types of problems that require optimization techniques, such as the following:

- Business executives use genetic algorithms to help them decide which combination of projects a firm should invest in, taking complicated tax considerations into account.
- Investment companies use genetic algorithms to help in trading decisions.
- Telecommunication companies use genetic algorithms to determine the optimal configuration of fiber-optic cable in a network that may include as many as 100,000 connection points. The genetic algorithm evaluates millions of cable configurations and selects the one that uses the least amount of cable.

Intelligent Agents

An *intelligent agent* is a special-purpose knowledge-based information system that accomplishes specific tasks on behalf of its users. Intelligent agents usually have a graphical representation, such as "Sherlock Holmes" for an information search agent.

One of the simplest examples of an intelligent agent is a shopping bot. A *shopping bot* is software that will search several retailer websites and provide a comparison of each retailer's offerings including price and availability. Increasingly, intelligent agents handle the majority of a company's Internet buying and selling and complete such processes as finding products, bargaining over prices, and executing transactions. Intelligent agents also have the capability to handle all supply chain buying and selling.

Another application for intelligent agents is in environmental scanning and competitive intelligence. For instance, an intelligent agent can learn the types of competitor information users want to track, continuously scan the web for it, and alert users when a significant event occurs.

Multiagent Systems and Agent-Based Modeling What do cargo transport systems, book distribution centers, the video game market, and a flu epidemic have in common with an ant colony? They are all complex adaptive systems. By observing parts of Earth's ecosystem, like ant colonies, artificial intelligence scientists can use hardware and software models that incorporate insect characteristics and behavior to (1) learn

BUSINESS DRIVEN INNOVATION

Building Robots

Humans are not permitted inside Staples' Denver distribution center. Who is filling all the orders, you ask? Robots! This 100,000-square-foot space belongs to 150 orange robots that resemble overstuffed ottomans and race around with uncanny accuracy. They're making Staples employees more than twice as productive. The robots, or bots, are built by Kiva Systems, a company with a single critical success factor: Replace the labyrinth of conveyor belts and humans that most distributors rely on to pack items in the online mail-order business. Companies using Kiva bots include Walgreens, Zappos, The Gap, and Amazon.

Robots have captured people's attention for years. From the quirky droids in *Star Wars* to the powerful fighting machines in *Transformers*, they seem to fascinate everyone. Assume your professor has asked you to participate in The Robot Challenge, and you must design a robot that will enhance business operations. It must contain a digital dashboard and provide decision support capabilities for its owners. Be sure to describe your robot, its functions, how the digital dashboard works and supports users, and why customers would purchase your robot. Feel free to include a picture or diagram of how your robot works.[11]

how people-based systems behave, (2) predict how they will behave under a given set of circumstances, and (3) improve human systems to make them more efficient and effective. This process of learning from ecosystems and adapting their characteristics to human and organizational situations is called biomimicry.

In the past few years, AI research has made much progress in modeling complex organizations as a whole with the help of multiagent systems. In a multiagent system, groups of intelligent agents have the ability to work independently and to interact with each other. Agent-based modeling is a way of simulating human organizations using multiple intelligent agents, each of which follows a set of simple rules and can adapt to changing conditions.

Agent-based modeling systems are being used to model stock market fluctuations, predict the escape routes people seek in a burning building, estimate the effects of interest rates on consumers with different types of debt, and anticipate how changes in conditions will affect the supply chain, to name just a few.

Virtual Reality

Virtual reality is a computer-simulated environment that can be a simulation of the real world or an imaginary world. Virtual reality is a fast-growing area of artificial intelligence that had its origins in efforts to build more natural, realistic, multisensory human-computer interfaces. Virtual reality enables telepresence where users can be anywhere in the world and use virtual reality systems to work alone or together at a remote site. Typically, this involves using a virtual reality system to enhance the sight and touch of a human who is remotely manipulating equipment to accomplish a task. Examples range from virtual surgery, where surgeon and patient may be on opposite sides of the globe, to the remote use of equipment in hazardous environments such as chemical plants and nuclear reactors. *Augmented reality* is the viewing of the physical world with computer-generated layers of information added to it.

Virtual Workforce At Microsoft's headquarters in Redmond, Washington, traffic congestion occurs daily for the 35,000 commuters. To alleviate the congestion Microsoft is offering its employees the ability to work virtually from home. Over 42 percent of IBM's

330,000 employees work virtually, saving over $100 million per year in real estate-related expenses. Working virtually offers several advantages such as fewer cars on the road, increases in worker productive, and decreased real estate expenses. Drawbacks include the fear among workers that they will jeopardize their careers by working from home, and some workers need a busy environment to stay productive. Virtual workers also tend to feel alone, secluded, and deprived of vital training and mentoring.

section 2.2 | Business Processes

LEARNING OUTCOMES

2.5 Explain the value of business processes for a company, and differentiate between customer-facing and business-facing processes.

2.6 Demonstrate the value of business process modeling, and compare As-Is and To-Be models.

2.7 Differentiate among automation, streamlining, and reengineering.

2.8 Describe business process management and its value to an organization.

LO 2.5: Explain the value of business processes for a company, and differentiate between customer-facing and business-facing processes.

EVALUATING BUSINESS PROCESSES

Most companies pride themselves on providing breakthrough products and services for customers. But if customers do not receive what they want quickly, accurately, and hassle-free, even fantastic offerings will not prevent a company from annoying customers and ultimately eroding its own financial performance. To avoid this pitfall and protect its competitive advantage, a company must continually evaluate all the business processes in its value chain. Recall from Chapter 1 that a *business process* is a standardized set of activities that accomplish a specific task, such as processing a customer's order. Business processes transform a set of inputs into a set of outputs—goods or services—for another person or process by using people and tools. Understanding business processes helps a manager envision how the entire company operates.

Improving the efficiency and effectiveness of its business processes will improve the firm's value chain. The goal of this section is to expand on Porter's value chain analysis by detailing the powerful value-adding relationships between business strategies and core business processes. Figure 2.17 illustrates several common business processes.

The processes outlined in Figure 2.17 reflect functional thinking. Some processes, such as a programming process, may be contained wholly within a single department. However, most, such as ordering a product, are cross-functional or cross-departmental processes and span the entire organization. The process of "order to delivery" focuses on the entire customer order process across functional departments (see Figure 2.18). Another example is "product realization," which includes not only the way a product is developed, but also the way it is marketed and serviced. Some other cross-functional business processes are taking a product from concept to market, acquiring customers, loan processing, providing post-sales service, claim processing, and reservation handling.

Customer-facing processes, also called front-office processes, result in a product or service received by an organization's external customer. They include fulfilling orders, communicating with customers, and sending out bills and marketing information. *Business-facing processes*, also called back-office processes, are invisible to the external customer but essential to the effective management of the business; they include goal setting, day-to-day planning, giving performance feedback and rewards, and allocating resources. Figure 2.19 displays the different categories of customer-facing and business-facing processes along with an example of each.[12]

A company's strategic vision should provide guidance on which business processes are core, that is, which are directly linked to the firm's critical success factors. Mapping these core business processes to the value chain reveals where the processes touch the customers and affect their perceptions of value. This type of map conceptualizes the

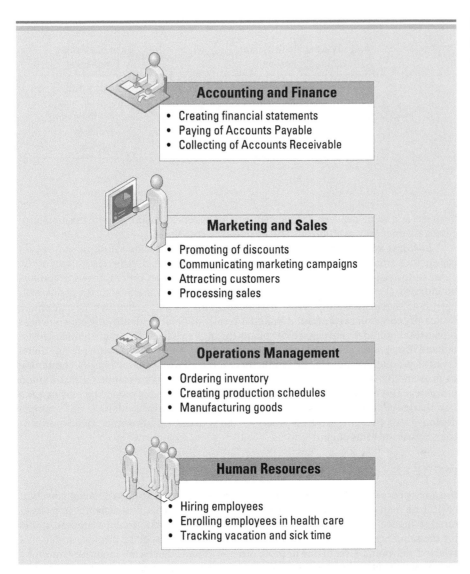

FIGURE 2.17

Sample Business Processes

FIGURE 2.18

Five Steps in the Order-to-
Delivery Business Process

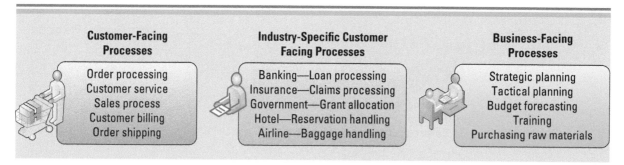

FIGURE 2.19

Customer-Facing, Industry-Specific, and Business-Facing Processes

business as a value delivery system, allowing managers to ensure all core business processes are operating as efficiently and effectively as possible.

A ***business process patent*** is a patent that protects a specific set of procedures for conducting a particular business activity. A firm can create a value chain map of the entire industry to extend critical success factors and business process views beyond its boundaries. ***Core processes*** are business processes, such as manufacturing goods, selling products, and providing service, that make up the primary activities in a value chain. Evaluating core processes allowed National Semiconductor to identify the core business processes required to move assembly plants to Southeast Asia. The map identified logistics and distribution as critical to the success of the move. Thus, to ensure reliable delivery of its products, National Semiconductor contracted with Federal Express, combining its outstanding manufacturing process and Federal Express's exceptional distribution processes. The move allowed National Semiconductor to save money by closing nine warehouses while maintaining excellence in logistics and distribution. As this example demonstrates, changing business processes can generate significant competitive advantages across the value chain.[13]

LO 2.6: Demonstrate the value of business process modeling, and compare As-Is and To-Be models.

MODELS: MEASURING PERFORMANCE

Business process modeling, or ***mapping***, is the activity of creating a detailed flowchart or process map of a work process that shows its inputs, tasks, and activities in a structured sequence. A ***business process model*** is a graphic description of a process, showing the sequence of process tasks, which is developed for a specific purpose and from a selected viewpoint. A set of one or more process models details the many functions of a system or subject area with graphics and text, and its purpose is to:

■ Expose process detail gradually and in a controlled manner.

■ Encourage conciseness and accuracy in describing the process model.

■ Focus attention on the process model interfaces.

■ Provide a powerful process analysis and consistent design vocabulary. (Figures 2.20 through Figure 2.23 provide examples of business process modeling.)[14]

Business process modeling usually begins with a functional process representation of *what* the process problem is, or an As-Is process model. ***As-Is process models*** represent the current state of the operation that has been mapped, without any specific improvements or changes to existing processes. The next step is to build a To-Be process model that displays *how* the process problem will be solved or implemented. ***To-Be process models*** show the results of applying change improvement opportunities to the current (As-Is) process model. This approach ensures that the process is fully and clearly understood before the details of a process solution are decided upon. The To-Be process model shows *how* the *what* is to be realized. Figure 2.24 displays the As-Is and To-Be process models for ordering a hamburger.

FIGURE 2.20

Online Sales Process Model

FIGURE 2.21

Online Banking Process Model

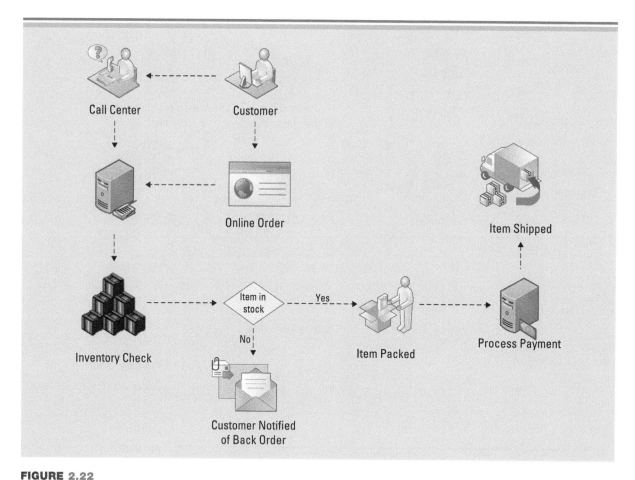

FIGURE 2.22

Order Fulfillment Process Model

As-Is and To-Be process models are both integral in business process reengineering projects, since these diagrams are very powerful in visualizing the activities, processes, and data flow of an organization. Figure 2.25 illustrates an As-Is process model of the order to delivery process using swim lanes to represent the relevant departments. The *swim lane* layout arranges the steps of a business process into a set of rows depicting the various elements.

You need to be careful not to become inundated in excessive detail when creating an As-Is process model. The primary goal is to simplify, eliminate, and improve the To-Be processes. Process improvement efforts focus on defining the most efficient and effective process identifying all of the illogical, missing, or irrelevant processes.

Investigating business processes can help an organization find bottlenecks, remove redundant tasks, and recognize smooth-running processes. For example, a florist might have a key success factor of reducing delivery time. A florist that has an inefficient ordering process or a difficult distribution process will be unable to achieve this goal. Taking down inaccurate orders, incorrect addresses, or shipping delays can cause errors in the delivery process. Improving order entry, production, or scheduling processes can improve the delivery process.

Business processes should drive MIS choices and should be based on business strategies and goals (see Figure 2.26). Only after determining the most efficient and effective business process should an organization choose the MIS that supports that business process. Of course, this does not always happen, and managers may find themselves in the difficult position of changing a business process because the system cannot support the ideal solution (see Figure 2.26). Managers who make MIS choices and only then determine how their business processes should perform typically fail.

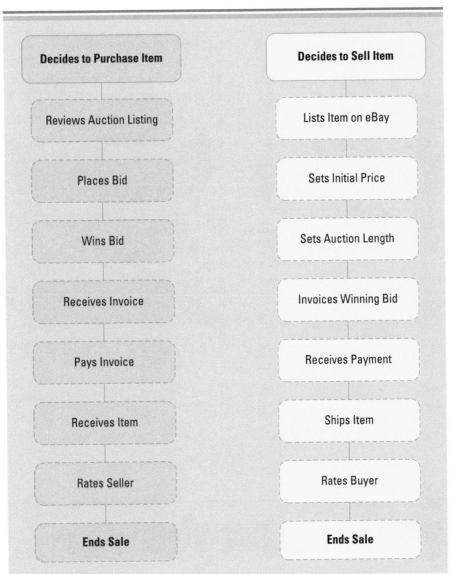

FIGURE 2.23

Purchasing an Item on eBay
and Selling an Item on eBay
Process Model

FIGURE 2.24

As-Is and To-Be Process
Model for Ordering
a Hamburger

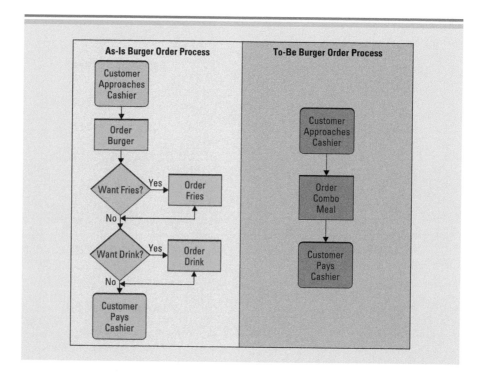

FIGURE 2.25

As-Is Process Model for Order
Fulfillment

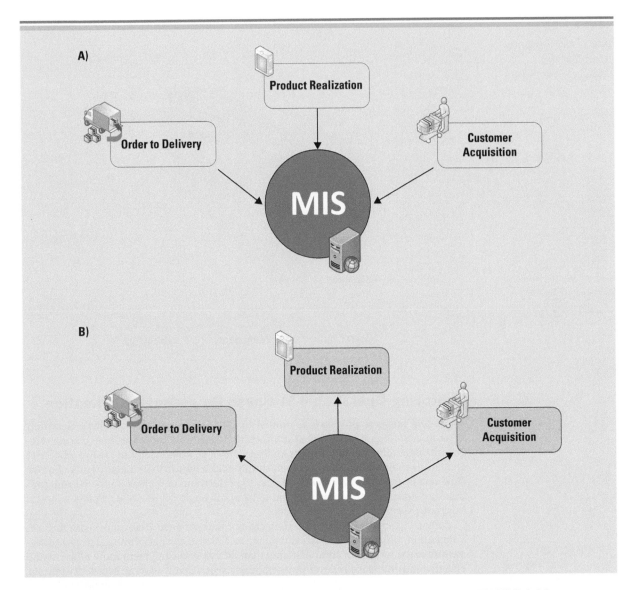

SUPPORT: ENHANCING BUSINESS PROCESSES WITH MIS

FIGURE 2.26

For Best Results, Business Processes Should Drive MIS Choices

Workflow includes the tasks, activities, and responsibilities required to execute each step in a business process. Understanding workflow, customers' expectations, and the competitive environment provides managers with the necessary ingredients to design and evaluate alternative business processes in order to maintain competitive advantages when internal or external circumstances change.

Alternative business process should be effective (they deliver the intended results) and efficient (they consume the least amount of resources for the intended value). They should also be adaptable or flexible and support change as customers, market forces, and technology shift. Figure 2.27 shows the three primary types of business process change available to firms and the business areas in which they are most often effective. How does a company know whether it needs to undertake the giant step of changing core business processes? Three conditions indicate the time is right to initiate a business process change:

LO 2.7: Differentiate among automation, streamlining, and reengineering.

1. There has been a pronounced shift in the market the process was designed to serve.

2. The company is markedly below industry benchmarks on its core processes.

3. To regain competitive advantage, the company must leapfrog competition on key dimensions.[15]

FIGURE 2.27

Primary Types of Business
Process Change

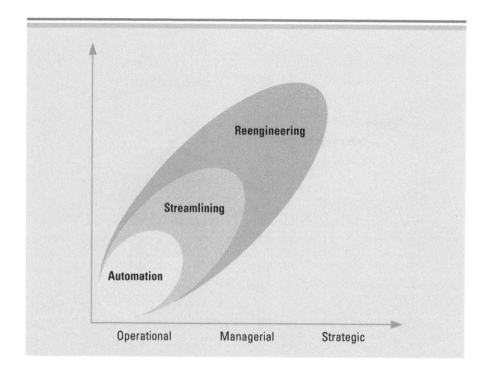

Improving Operational Business Processes—Automation

Improving business processes is critical to staying competitive in today's electronic marketplace. Organizations must improve their business processes because customers are demanding better products and services; if customers do not receive what they want from one supplier, often they can simply click a mouse to find many other choices. ***Business process improvement*** attempts to understand and measure the current process and make performance improvements accordingly. Figure 2.28 displays a typical business process improvement model.[16]

Early adopters of MIS recognized that they could enhance their value chain through automation, which reduces costs and increases the speed of performing activities. ***Automation*** is the process of computerizing manual tasks, making them more efficient and effective and dramatically lowering operational costs. Payroll offers an excellent example. Calculating and tracking payroll for 5,000 employees is a highly labor-intensive process requiring 30 full-time employees. Every two weeks accounting employees must gather everyone's hours worked, cross-check with wage rates, and then calculate the amount due, minus taxes and other withholding such as pension contributions and insurance premiums, to create the paychecks. They also track benefits, sick time, and vacation time. If the payroll process is automated, however, one employee can easily calculate payroll, track withholding and deductions, and create paychecks for 5,000 people in a few hours, since everything is performed by the system. Automation improves efficiency and effectiveness and reduces head count, lowering overall operational costs. Transaction processing systems (TPS) are primarily used to automate business processes.

Figure 2.29 illustrates the basic steps for business process improvement. Organizations begin by documenting what they currently do, then they establish a way to measure the process, follow the process, measure the performance, and finally identify improvement opportunities based on the collected information. The next step is to implement process improvements and measure the performance of the new improved process. The loop repeats over and over again as it is continuously improved.[17]

This method of improving business processes is effective for obtaining gradual, incremental improvement. However, several factors have accelerated the need to radically improve business processes. The most obvious is technology. New technologies (such as wireless Internet access) rapidly bring new capabilities to businesses, thereby raising the

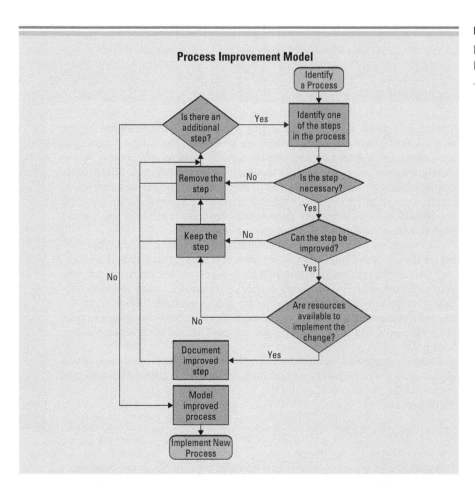

FIGURE 2.28

Business Process
Improvement Model

FIGURE 2.29

Steps in Business
Process Improvement

competitive bar and the need to improve business processes dramatically. For example, Amazon.com reinvented the supply chain for selling books online. After gaining from automation, companies began to look for new ways to use MIS to improve operations, and managers recognized the benefits of pairing MIS with business processes by streamlining. We look at this improvement method next.

Improving Managerial Business Processes—Streamlining

Streamlining improves business process efficiencies by simplifying or eliminating unnecessary steps. *Bottlenecks* occur when resources reach full capacity and cannot handle any additional demands; they limit throughput and impede operations. A computer working at its maximum capacity will be unable to handle increased demand and will become a bottleneck in the process. Streamlining removes bottlenecks, an important step if the efficiency and capacity of a business process are being increased. It also eliminates redundancy. *Redundancy* occurs when a task or activity is unnecessarily repeated, for example, if both the sales department and the accounting department check customer credit.

BUSINESS DRIVEN MIS

Streamlining Your Email

The biggest problem with email is that it interferes with workflow. Many employees stop what they are working on and begin checking new email as soon as it arrives. If they do not have the time or capacity to answer it immediately, however, they leave it in the in-box, creating a bottleneck. This process continues all day, and eventually the in-box is overflowing with hundreds of emails, most of which require a response or action. Employees begin dreading email and feel stressed because their workflow process is off track, and they do not know which tasks need to be completed and when.

To streamline workflow, you can designate certain times for email processing (at the top of the hour, or for 30 minutes at three set times a day, for example). Turning off email notification also ensures you are not interrupted during your workflow. When you do begin to check your emails, review them one at a time from top to bottom, and deal with each one immediately. Either reply, put a note on your to-do list, forward the email, or delete it. Now you are working far more efficiently and effectively, and you are less stressed because your in-box is empty.[18]

Choose a process in your life that is inefficient or ineffective and causing you stress. Using the principles of streamlining, remove the bottlenecks and reduce redundancies. Be sure to diagram the As-Is process and your newly created To-Be process.

Automating a business process that contains bottlenecks or redundancies will magnify or amplify these problems if they are not corrected first. Here's an example based on a common source of tension in an organization. Increasing orders is a standard KPI for most marketing/sales departments. To meet this KPI, the sales department tends to say yes to any customer request, such as for rush or custom orders. Reducing *cycle time*, the time required to process an order, is a common KPI for operations management. Rush and custom orders tend to create bottlenecks, causing operations to fall below its benchmarked cycle time. Removing these bottlenecks, however, can create master streamlined business processes that deliver both standard and custom orders reliably and profitably. The goal of streamlining is not only to automate but also to improve by monitoring, controlling, and changing the business process.

FedEx streamlined every business process to provide a CSF of speedy and reliable delivery of packages. It created one central hub in Memphis, Tennessee, that processed all its orders. It purchased its own planes to be sure it could achieve the desired level of service. FedEx combined MIS and traditional distribution and logistics processes to create a competitive advantage. FedEx soon identified another market segment of customers who cared a little less about speed and were willing to trade off early-morning delivery for delivery any time *within* the next day at a significantly lower price. The firm had to reevaluate its strategy and realign its business processes to capture this market segment. Had Federal Express focused only on improving its traditional delivery process to handle increased volume faster and more reliably, it could have missed an entire customer segment.[19]

Improving Strategic Business Processes—Reengineering

The flat world (see Chapter 1) is bringing more companies and more customers into the marketplace, greatly increasing competition. Wine wholesalers in the United States must now compete globally, for instance, because customers can just as easily order a bottle of wine from a winery in France as from them. Companies need breakthrough performance and business process changes just to stay in the game. As the rate of change increases, companies looking for rapid change and dramatic improvement are turning to **business process reengineering (BPR)**, the analysis and redesign of workflow within and between enterprises. Figure 2.30 highlights an analogy to process improvement by explaining the different means of traveling along the same route. A company could improve the way it travels by changing from foot to horse and then from horse to car. With a BPR mind-set, however, it would look beyond automating and streamlining to find a completely different approach. It would ignore the road and travel by air to get from point A to point B. Companies often follow the same indirect path for doing business, not realizing there might be a different, faster, and more direct way.

An organization can reengineer its cross-departmental business processes or an individual department's business processes to help meet its CSFs and KPIs. When selecting a business process to reengineer, wise managers focus on those core processes that are critical to performance, rather than marginal processes that have little impact. The effort to reengineer a business process as a strategic activity requires a different mind-set than that required in continuous business process improvement programs. Because companies have tended to overlook the powerful contribution that processes can make to strategy, they often undertake process improvement efforts using their current processes as the starting point. Managers focusing on reengineering can instead use several criteria to identify opportunities:

- Is the process broken?
- Is it feasible that reengineering of this process will succeed?
- Does it have a high impact on the agency's strategic direction?
- Does it significantly impact customer satisfaction?
- Is it antiquated?
- Does it fall far below best-in-class?
- Is it crucial for productivity improvement?
- Will savings from automation be clearly visible?
- Is the return on investment from implementation high and preferably immediate?

BPR relies on a different school of thought than business process improvement. *In the extreme,* BPR assumes the current process is irrelevant, does not work, or is broken and must be overhauled from scratch. Starting from such a clean slate enables business process designers to disassociate themselves from today's process and focus on a new process. It is as if they are projecting themselves into the future and asking: What should the process look like? What do customers want it to look like? What do other employees want it to look like? How do best-in-class companies do it? How can new technology facilitate the process?

Figure 2.31 displays the basic steps in a business process reengineering effort. It begins with defining the scope and objectives of the reengineering project and then takes the process designers through a learning process with customers, employees, competitors, and new technology. Given this knowledge base, the designers can create a plan of action based on the gap between current processes, technologies, and structures and

FIGURE 2.30

Different Ways to Travel the Same Route

Better, Faster, Cheaper

FIGURE 2.31

Business Process
Reengineering Model

their vision of the processes of the future. It is then top management's job to implement the chosen solution.[20]

System thinking plays a big role in BPR. Automation and streamlining operate departmentally, whereas BPR occurs at the systems level or companywide level and the end-to-end view of a process.

Creating value for the customer is the leading reason for instituting BPR, and MIS often plays an important enabling role. Fundamentally new business processes enabled Progressive Insurance to slash its claims settlement time from 31 days to four hours, for instance. Typically, car insurance companies follow this standard claims resolution process: The customer gets into an accident, has the car towed, and finds a ride home. The customer then calls the insurance company to begin the claims process, which includes an evaluation of the damage, assignment of fault, and an estimate of the cost of repairs, and which usually takes about a month (see Figure 2.32). Progressive Insurance's innovation was to offer a mobile claims process. When a customer has a car accident, he or she calls in the claim on the spot. The Progressive claims adjuster comes to the accident site, surveying the scene and taking digital photographs. The adjuster then offers the customer on-site payment, towing services, and a ride home. A true BPR effort does more for a company than simply improve a process by performing it better, faster, and cheaper. Progressive Insurance's BPR effort redefined best practices for an entire industry.[21]

The Business Process Systems View   Leveraging business processes has enormous implications for the business system as a whole. It requires recognition that any meaningful change within the organization affects the entire organization. Without a systems view, the identification of business process flaws and implementation of proposed solutions will often fix only symptoms. Many times what can make one process effective is what makes another process ineffective. Therefore, the redesign of any process within an integrated system requires appreciating the impact of the redesign on other processes. For example, operations management often wants to wait until a truck is full before sending it out for deliveries because the department's KPI measures cost-per-mile-transported. Conversely, the customer satisfaction KPIs measure the ability to make the order-to-delivery cycle time as short as possible, requiring the truck to leave as soon as the product is available, whether it is full or not. Changing business processes to

FIGURE 2.32

Auto Insurance Claims
Processes

BUSINESS DRIVEN DEBATE

Trina Thompson, a New York City resident, is filing a lawsuit against Monroe College stating that she is unable to find employment after graduating with her bachelor's degree. Thompson is seeking tuition reimbursement of $70,000 and states that she has been unable to find gainful employment since graduating because the school's Office of Career Advancement failed to provide her with the leads and career advice it promised. Monroe College spokesman Gary Axelbank says Thompson's lawsuit is completely without merit and insists it helps its graduates find jobs.[22]

Do you agree that students should be allowed to hold their academic institutions liable for their inability to find a job after graduation? Design the current (As-Is) business process at your school from the time a student begins his or her program until graduation. How could your school reengineer the process to ensure it does not end up in litigation over an individual's expectation of automatically receiving a job after graduation?

Education Processes

meet operations management KPIs will thus reduce customer satisfaction KPIs. Changing business processes to meet customer satisfaction KPIs will lower operations management KPIs. A systems view, on the other hand, will allow managers to understand the impact business processes have across the entire organization, so both can be improved.

THE FUTURE: BUSINESS PROCESS MANAGEMENT

LO 2.8: Describe business process management and its value to an organization.

Creating a company that can quickly adapt to market, industry, and economic changes to create a competitive advantage requires a new set of operating rules based on achieving speed, performance, and improved delivery. Until recently, business process improvement initiatives focused on improving workflow or document-based processes that were completed by hand. Now, however, *business process management (BPM) systems* focus on evaluating and improving processes that include both person-to-person workflow and system-to-system communications. BPM systems include advanced features such as enhanced process modeling, simulation, execution, and monitoring, providing a high level of flexibility while reducing costs. Think of BPM as a way to build, implement, and monitor automated processes that span organizational boundaries—a kind of next-generation workflow. BPM not only allows a business process to be executed more efficiently, but it also provides the tools to measure performance and identify opportunities for improvement, as well as to easily capture opportunities such as:

- Bringing processes, people, and information together.
- Breaking down the barriers between business areas and finding "owners" for the processes.
- Managing front-office and back-office business processes.

BPM uniquely offers two types of systems: (1) Customer-facing or front-office BPM focuses on person-to-person workflow and (2) business-facing or back-office BPM focuses on system-to-system workflow. With BPM the two systems function as one, allowing continual improvements to many business processes simultaneously and in real time. BPM's unified environment encourages people to observe, think, and provide feedback, harnessing the power of ideas and insight and promoting systems thinking throughout the organization. Providing the flexibility for quick BPM change drives efficiency and effectiveness, creating optimal business processes. This ability is the foundation for creating an operation that gives a company competitive advantage.

LEARNING OUTCOME REVIEW

Learning Outcome 2.1: Explain the importance of decision making for managers at each of the three primary organization levels along with the associated decision characteristics.

Decision-making skills are essential for all business professionals, at every company level, who make decisions that run the business. At the operational level, employees develop, control, and maintain core business activities required to run the day-to-day operations. Operational decisions are considered structured decisions, which arise in situations where established processes offer potential solutions. Structured decisions are made frequently and are almost repetitive in nature; they affect short-term business strategies.

At the managerial level, employees are continuously evaluating company operations to hone the firm's abilities to identify, adapt to, and leverage change. Managerial decisions cover short- and medium-range plans, schedules, and budgets along with policies, procedures, and business objectives for the firm. These types of decisions are considered semistructured decisions; they occur in situations in which a few established processes help to evaluate potential solutions, but not enough to lead to a definite recommended decision.

At the strategic level, managers develop overall business strategies, goals, and objectives as part of the company's strategic plan. They also monitor the strategic performance of the organization and its overall direction in the political, economic, and competitive business environment. Strategic decisions are highly unstructured decisions, occurring in situations in which no procedures or rules exist to guide decision makers toward the correct choice. They are infrequent, extremely important, and typically related to long-term business strategy.

Learning Outcome 2.2: Define critical success factors (CSFs) and key performance indicators (KPIs), and explain how managers use them to measure the success of MIS projects.

Metrics are measurements that evaluate results to determine whether a project is meeting its goals. Two core metrics are critical success factors and key performance indicators. CSFs are the crucial steps companies perform to achieve their goals and objectives and implement their strategies and include creating high-quality products, retaining competitive advantages, and reducing product costs. KPIs are the quantifiable metrics a company uses to evaluate progress toward critical success factors. KPIs are far more specific than CSFs; examples include turnover rates of employees, percentage of help-desk calls answered in the first minute, and number of products returned.

It is important to understand the relationship between critical success factors and key performance indicators. CSFs are elements crucial for a business strategy's success. KPIs measure the progress of CSFs with quantifiable measurements, and one CSF can have several KPIs. Of course, both categories will vary by company and industry. Imagine improved graduation rates as a CSF for a college.

Learning Outcome 2.3: Classify the different operational support systems, managerial support systems, and strategic support systems, and explain how managers can use these systems to make decisions and gain competitive advantages.

Being able to sort, calculate, analyze, and slice-and-dice information is critical to an organization's success. Without knowing what is occurring throughout the organization there is no way that managers and executives can make solid decisions to support the business. The different operational, managerial, and strategic support systems include:

- Operational: A transaction processing system (TPS) is the basic business system that serves the operational level (analysts) in an organization. The most common example of a TPS is an operational accounting system such as a payroll system or an order-entry system.

■ Managerial: A decision support system (DSS) models information to support managers and business professionals during the decision-making process.

■ Strategic: An executive information system (EIS) is a specialized DSS that supports senior-level executives within the organization.

Learning Outcome 2.4: Describe artificial intelligence, and identify its five main types.

Artificial intelligence (AI) simulates human thinking and behavior, such as the ability to reason and learn. The five most common categories of AI are:

1. Expert systems—computerized advisory programs that imitate the reasoning processes of experts in solving difficult problems.
2. Neural networks—attempts to emulate the way the human brain works.
3. Genetic algorithm—a system that mimics the evolutionary, survival-of-the-fittest process to generate increasingly better solutions to a problem.
4. Intelligent agents—a special-purpose knowledge-based information system that accomplishes specific tasks on behalf of its users.
5. Virtual reality—a computer-simulated environment that can be a simulation of the real world or an imaginary world.

Learning Outcome 2.5: Explain the value of business processes for a company, and differentiate between customer-facing and business-facing process.

A business process is a standardized set of activities that accomplish a specific task, such as processing a customer's order. Business processes transform a set of inputs into a set of outputs (goods or services) for another person or process by using people and tools. Without processes, organizations would not be able to complete activities. Customer-facing processes result in a product or service that is received by an organization's external customer. Business-facing processes are invisible to the external customer but essential to the effective management of the business.

Learning Outcome 2.6: Demonstrate the value of business process modeling, and compare As-Is and To-Be models.

Business process modeling (or mapping) is the activity of creating a detailed flowchart or process map of a work process showing its inputs, tasks, and activities, in a structured sequence. A business process model is a graphic description of a process, showing the sequence of process tasks, which is developed for a specific purpose and from a selected viewpoint.

Business process modeling usually begins with a functional process representation of what the process problem is, or an As-Is process model. As-Is process models represent the current state of the operation that has been mapped, without any specific improvements or changes to existing processes. The next step is to build a To-Be process model that displays how the process problem will be solved or implemented. To-Be process models show the results of applying change improvement opportunities to the current (As-Is) process model. This approach ensures that the process is fully and clearly understood before the details of a process solution are decided upon.

Learning Outcome 2.7: Differentiate among automation, streamlining, and reengineering.

Business process improvement attempts to understand and measure the current process and make performance improvements accordingly. Automation is the process of computerizing manual tasks, making them more efficient and effective and dramatically lowering operational costs. Streamlining improves business process efficiencies by simplifying or eliminating unnecessary steps. Bottlenecks occur when resources reach full capacity and cannot handle any additional demands; they limit throughput and impede operations. Streamlining removes bottlenecks, an important step if the efficiency and capacity of a business process are being increased. Business process reengineering (BPR) is the analysis and redesign of workflow within and between enterprises and occurs at the systems level or companywide level and the end-to-end view of a process.

Learning Outcome 2.8: Describe business process management and its value to an organization.

Business process management (BPM) systems focus on evaluating and improving processes that include both person-to-person workflow and system-to-system communications. BPM systems include advanced features such as enhanced process modeling, simulation, execution, and monitoring, providing a high level of flexibility while reducing costs.

OPENING CASE QUESTIONS

1. **Knowledge:** Define the three primary types of decision-making systems, and explain how a customer of Actionly might use them to find business intelligence.

2. **Comprehension:** Describe the difference between transactional and analytical information, and determine which types Actionly uses to create a customer's digital dashboard.

3. **Application:** Illustrate the business process model used by a customer of Actionly following Twitter tweets.

4. **Analysis:** Explain business process reengineering and how Actionly used it to create its unique business model.

5. **Synthesis:** Formulate different metrics Actionly uses to measure the success of a customer's marketing campaign.

6. **Evaluation:** Argue for or against the following statement: Actionly invades consumer privacy by taking data from different websites such as Twitter and Flickr without the consent of the customer that posted the information.

KEY TERMS

Analytical information, 55
Analytics, 46
Artificial intelligence (AI), 60
As-Is process model, 66
Augmented reality, 63
Automation, 72
Benchmarking, 52
Benchmarks, 52
Best practices, 50
Bottlenecks, 73
Business-facing process, 64
Business process
    improvement, 72
Business process management
    (BPM) system, 77
Business process model, 66
Business process modeling
    (or mapping), 66
Business process patent, 66
Business process reengineering
    (BPR), 75
Consolidation, 60
Core processes, 66
Critical success factors (CSFs), 49
Customer-facing process, 64

Cycle time, 74
Decision support system (DSS), 55
Digital dashboard, 59
Drill-down, 60
Effectiveness MIS metrics, 50
Efficiency MIS metrics, 50
Executive information system
    (EIS), 56
Expert system, 61
Fuzzy logic, 62
Genetic algorithm, 62
Goal-seeking analysis, 56
Granularity, 57
Intelligent agent, 62
Intelligent system, 60
Key performance indicators
    (KPIs), 49
Managerial level, 46
Market share, 49
Metrics, 49
Model, 54
Mutation, 62
Neural network, 61
Online analytical processing
    (OLAP), 55

Online transaction processing
    (OLTP), 54
Operational level, 46
Optimization analysis, 56
Project, 48
Redundancy, 73
Return on investment (ROI), 50
Semistructured decision, 48
Sensitivity analysis, 56
Shopping bot, 62
Slice-and-dice, 60
Source document, 55
Strategic level, 48
Streamlining, 73
Structured decision, 46
Swim lane, 68
To-Be process model, 66
Transaction processing system
    (TPS), 54
Transactional information, 54
Unstructured decision, 48
Virtual reality, 63
Visualization, 59
What-if analysis, 55
Workflow, 71

REVIEW QUESTIONS

1. Why must business professionals understand how MIS supports decision making and problem solving?

2. What is the relationship between critical success factors and key performance indicators? How can a manager use them to understand business operations?

3. What are the three different levels found in a company? What types of decisions are made at each level?

4. Define transaction processing systems and describe the role they play in a business.

5. Define decision support systems and describe the role they play in a business.

6. Define expert systems and describe the role they play in a business.

7. What are the capabilities associated with digital dashboards?

8. What are the common DSS analysis techniques?

9. How does an electronic spreadsheet program, such as Excel, provide decision support capabilities?

10. What is the difference between the ability of a manager to retrieve information instantly on demand using an MIS and the capabilities provided by a DSS?

11. What is artificial intelligence? What are the five types of AI systems? What applications of AI offer the greatest business value?

12. What is a business process and what role does it play in an organization?

13. Why do managers need to understand business processes? Can you make a correlation between systems thinking and business processes?

14. Why would a manager need to review an As-Is and To-Be process model?

15. How can a manager use automation, streamlining, and business process reengineering to gain operational efficiency and effectiveness?

16. Explain the difference between customer-facing processes and business-facing processes. Which one is more important to an organization?

17. Explain how finding different ways to travel the same road relates to automation, streamlining, and business process reengineering.

CLOSING CASE ONE

Political Micro-Targeting: What Decision Support Systems Did for Barack Obama

On the day he took the oath of office in 2009, President Barack Obama spoke a word rarely heard in inaugural addresses—*data*—referencing indicators of economic and other crises. His use of the word is perhaps not so surprising. Capturing and analyzing data were crucial to Obama's rise to power. Throughout his historic campaign he not only used the Internet for networking and fundraising, but he also relied on decision support systems to identify potential swing voters. Obama's team carefully monitored contested states and congressional districts, where as few as 2,000 voters could prove decisive—a tiny fraction of the voting public. Both presidential candidates hired technology wizards to help sift through mountains of consumer and demographic details to recognize these important voters.

10 "Tribes"

Spotlight Analysis, a Democratic consultancy, used political micro-targeting to analyze neighborhood details, family sizes, and spending patterns to categorize every person of voting age—all 175 million—into 10 "values" tribes. Individual tribe members do not necessarily share the same race, religion, or income bracket, but they have common mind-sets about political issues: God, community, responsibility, and opportunity. Spotlight Analysis predicted the influence of a particular morally guided (but not necessarily religious) tribe of some 14 million voters, dubbed Barn Raisers. Barn Raisers are of many races, religions, and ethnicities; about 40 percent favor Democrats and 27 percent Republicans. Barn Raisers are slightly less likely to have a college education than Spotlight's other swing groups. They are active in community organizations, ambivalent about government, and deeply concerned about "playing by the rules" and "keeping promises," to use Spotlight's definitions. Spotlight believed the Barn Raisers held the key to the race between Obama and his Republican challenger, Arizona Senator John McCain.

Political micro-targeting, which depends on MIS to support decision making, is turning government segments into sophisticated, intelligent, methodical political machines. In nanoseconds, decision support systems sort 175 million voters into segments and quickly calculate the potential for each individual voter to swing from red or purple to blue.

For some, political micro-targeting signals the dehumanization of politics. For others, this type of sophisticated analysis is a highly efficient way of pinpointing potential voters. For example, the analysis of a voter in Richmond, Virginia, simply identifies the number of his or her school-age children, type of car, zip code, magazine subscriptions, and mortgage balance. Data could even indicate whether the voter has dogs or cats. (Cat owners lean slightly for Democrats, dog owners trend Republican.) After the analysis, the voter is placed into a political tribe, and analysts can draw conclusions about the issues that matter to him or her and make campaign decisions accordingly. Is this a bad thing?

Behavioral Grouping

For generations, governments lacked the means to study individual behaviors and simply placed all citizens into enormous groupings such as Hispanics, Catholics, union members, hunters, soccer moms, and so on. With the use of sophisticated MIS analysis techniques, companies such as Spotlight Analysis can group individuals based more on specific behavior and choices, and less on the names, colors, and clans that mark us from birth.

When Spotlight first embarked on its research, it interviewed thousands of voters the old-fashioned way. The Barn Raisers did not seem significant; the tribe represented about 9 percent of the electorate. However, when Spotlight's analysts drilled down or dug deeper, they discovered that Barn Raisers stood at the epicenter of a political swing. In 2004, 90 percent of them voted for President Bush, but then the group's political leanings shifted, with 64 percent saying they voted for Democrats in the 2006 election. Spotlight surveys showed that Republican political scandals, tax-funded boondoggles such as Alaska's "bridge to nowhere," and the botched recovery job after Hurricane Katrina sent them packing.

Suddenly, Spotlight had identified millions of potential swing voters. The challenge then was to locate them by state. For this, the company analyzed the demographics and buying patterns of the Barn Raisers it had surveyed personally. Then it began correlating its data with commercially available data to match profiles. By Spotlight's count, this approach nailed Barn Raisers three times out of four. So Democrats could bet that at least three-quarters of them would be likely to welcome an election appeal stressing honesty and fair play.

Still Swing Voters

Spotlight has not correlated the Barn Raisers to their actual votes, so it's not clear how well the company's strategy worked. However, it is reasonable to presume that amid that sea of humanity stretched out before the newly inaugurated Obama on the National Mall, at least some were moved by micro-targeted appeals. And if Obama and his team fail to honor their mathematically honed vows, the Barn Raisers may abandon them in droves. They are swing voters, after all.[23]

Questions

1. Define the three primary types of decision-making systems, and explain how Obama's campaign team used them to win votes.
2. Describe the difference between transactional and analytical information, and determine which types Spotlight Analysis used to identify its 10 tribes.
3. Illustrate the business process model used to identify the 10 tribes.
4. Explain business process reengineering and how Obama's team used it to develop political micro-targeting.
5. Formulate different metrics the Obama team used to measure the success of political micro-targeting.
6. Argue for or against the following statement: Political micro-targeting signals the dehumanization of politics.

CLOSING CASE TWO

Second Life: Succeeding in Virtual Times

Second Life is a virtual world built and owned by its residents. It is inhabited by millions of residents from around the world. The three main parts to Second Life are:

- **The World:** The world of Second Life is constantly changing and growing. It is filled with hundreds of games, from multiplayer role-playing games to puzzles and grid-wide contests. There are also dance clubs, shopping malls, space stations, vampire castles, and movie theaters. To find something to do at any time of the day or night, residents simply open the Search menu and click on Events for a listing of discussions, sports, entertainment, games, pageants, education, arts and culture, and charity/support groups.

- **The Creations:** Second Life is dedicated to creativity. Everything in Second Life is resident-created, from the strobe lights in the nightclubs to the cars (or spaceships) in driveways. Imagine tinkering with the steering and handling program of a motorcycle while a friend tweaks the shape of the fuel tank and gives it a wicked flame paint job, in-world and in real-time, before taking it for a spin down a newly created road to look for land to buy. Have you ever wondered what it would be like to have a pair of black leather wings? Build them and give it a go.

- **The Marketplace:** The Marketplace currently supports millions of U.S. dollars in monthly transactions. This commerce is transacted with the in-world unit of trade, the Linden dollar, which can be converted to U.S. dollars at several thriving online Linden dollar exchanges or at LindeX, the official exchange. Users can make real money in a virtual world because Second Life has a fully integrated economy designed to reward risk, innovation, and craftsmanship. Residents create their own virtual goods and services, retain the intellectual property rights of their creations, and sell them at various in-world venues. Businesses succeed on the ingenuity, artistic ability, entrepreneurial acumen, and good reputation of their owners.

Businesses on Second Life

Second Life is an exciting venue for collaboration, business ventures, distance learning, new media studies, and marketing. Business possibilities there are endless; a few examples include:

- Holding a virtual meeting with sales managers located in Europe and Asia.
- Presenting new sales initiatives and discussing them with the team real-time.
- Allowing Second Life residents to interact with company products or services and test new designs and concepts before they are introduced to the real world.

▪ Selling products and services in Second Life by creating an event to promote the product: a concert, a class, a famous speaker, a party, a contest. Many companies are excited about the numerous ways they can use Second Life to support their business.[24] A few companies paving the way on Second Life include the following:

1-800-flowers.com	H&R Block	Sony
Adidas	IBM	Sprint
Amazon	Intel	Student Travel Association
American Apparel	Kraft Food	Starwood Hotels
American Cancer Society	Lacoste	Sundance Channel
BBC Radio 1	Major League Baseball	Toyota
Best Buy Co. Inc.	Mazda	Universal Motown Records
BMW	Mercedes-Benz	Visa
Calvin Klein	Microsoft	Warner Bros. Music
Circuit City	MTV	Weather Channel
Cisco	NASA	*Wired* magazine
Coca-Cola	National Basketball	Xerox
Coldwell Banker	Association	Yahoo
Comcast	NBC	Yankee Stadium
Crayola	Nissan	
Dell	NPR	

Questions

1. How could financial companies use neural networks in Second Life to help their businesses?

2. How could a company such as Nike use decision support systems on Second Life to help its business?

3. How could an apparel company use Second Life to build a digital dashboard to monitor virtual operations?

4. How could a company use Second Life to revamp its customer service process?

5. How could a company use Second Life to revamp its order-entry process?

6. How could a company use Second Life to reinvent its relationships with customers, partners, and employees?

CRITICAL BUSINESS THINKING

1. Modeling a Business Process

Do you hate waiting in line at the grocery store? Do you find it frustrating when you go to the video rental store and cannot find the movie you wanted? Do you get annoyed when the pizza delivery person brings you the wrong order? This is your chance to reengineer the process that drives you crazy. Choose a problem you are currently experiencing and reengineer the process to make it more efficient. Be sure to provide an As-Is and To-Be process model.

2. Revamping Accounts

The accounting department at your company deals with the processing of critical documents that include invoices, purchase orders, statements, purchase requisitions, financial statements, sales orders, and price quotes. These documents must arrive at their intended destination in a secure and efficient manner.

Processing is currently done manually, which causes a negative ripple effect. Documents tend to be misplaced or delayed, becoming vulnerable to unauthorized changes or exposure of confidential information. In addition, the accounting department incurs costs such as for preprinted forms, inefficient distribution, and storage. Explain automation, streamlining, and business process reengineering and how they can be used to revamp the accounting department.

3. What Type of System Would You Use?

You have been assigned as senior director for a large manufacturing company. Your first assignment is to decide which type of MIS can best support your decision-making needs. For all of the following, determine which type of system you would use to help solve the business problem or make a business decision.

a. You need to analyze daily sales transactions for each region.

b. You need to analyze staffing requirements for each plant.

c. You need to determine which customers are at risk of defaulting on their bills.

d. You need to analyze your competition including prices, discounts, goods, and services.

e. You need to analyze critical success factors and key performance indicators for status on operations.

f. You need to produce a graphical display of patterns and complex relationships for large amounts of data.

4. Unstructured Communications

You have just received a job as a business analyst for a large sports marketing company. Your boss, Sandy Fiero, wants you to evaluate and improve the current corporate communication process. With the current process, employees receive a great deal of unstructured information in the form of emails, including corporate policies, corporate announcements, and human resource information. You quickly realize that using an email system for communication is causing a great deal of issues including inaccessible information for any new hires, lost productivity as employees search through hundreds of emails to find information, and miscommunication as global divisions of your organization send out regional human resource policies.

To begin analyzing the processes, create a list of issues you might encounter by using email as a primary communication tool for corporate information. What are the redundancies associated with an email communication process? What are the bottlenecks with an email communication process? Document the As-Is process for sending email communications to employees. Then, reengineer the process and document your suggestions for improving the process and the To-Be communication process.

5. IGoogle Digital Dashboard

Executives find information from a variety of sources coming across their computers every day. The digital dashboard containing this information might include their calendar, email, issues such as production delays or accounts past due, and even financial and industry information. Although it would be impossible to fit all of an organization's information into a single screen, it can summarize the data in ways tailored to meet the executive's needs.

IGoogle is a type of digital dashboard you can create for your own personal view of the world through Google. IGoogle allows users to create personalized home pages containing Google search along with a number of Google gadgets that provide access to activities and information from all over the Internet. If you want one location where you can view Gmail messages, peruse Google news, review weather forecasts, stock quotes, and movie showtimes, iGoogle is for you. Visit iGoogle and determine how you could customize your Google home page as a digital dashboard for your computer.

6. Bot Shopping

For those of us who love (or hate) shopping, a shopping bot can become your best friend. Regardless of whether you are shopping in a store or online you still have to research products, compare prices, select a seller, and find the safest way to pay. Shopping in the information age is easier than ever, especially with the help of a shopping bot. Shopping bots are price comparison websites that automatically search the inventory of different vendors to find the lowest possible price, saving you time and money. Shopping bots will rank the product you are looking for by price and link you directly to the vendor's website. Popular shopping bots include mysimon.com, Gomez. com, Bizrate.com, shopzilla.com, and Google's shopping bot at www.google.com/products.

Choose a product you are interested in purchasing and use three of the different shopping bots to compare prices. Did the different shopping bots return the same information and prices? Which shopping bot was the easiest to use? Will you continue using shopping bots? What are the advantages and disadvantages for a company using shopping bots to purchase office supplies or raw materials?

7. Networking Neural

Neural networks are a category of AI that attempts to emulate the way the human brain works. A neural network could be a great asset for any college student. If a neural network could scan each brain for all of the students in your course, what types of information would it acquire? How could you use the student neural network to improve your grades? How could you use the student neural network to identify trends and new market segments? What would be the risks of using this neural network for academic improvement? What types of confidentiality and privacy issues would be encountered with this neural network?

8. Driving Your Business

You have recently opened your own business—choose the business of your dreams and assume you have it up and running. What types of decision will you need to make to operate your business? How can you use MIS to support your decision-making efforts? What types of processes will you find throughout your business? How can you use MIS to revamp your business process for efficiency and effectiveness? Overall, how dependent will your business be on MIS? Do you think you could be just as successful running your business without MIS? Can you name a business that can operate efficiently and effectively without MIS?

ENTREPRENEURIAL CHALLENGE

BUILD YOUR OWN BUSINESS

1. You realize that you need a digital dashboard to help you operate your business. Create a list of all of the components you would want to track in your digital dashboard that would help you run your business. Be sure to justify how each component would help you gain insight into the operations of your business and flag potential issues that could ruin your business. (Be sure to identify your business and the name of your company as you defined it in Chapter 1.)

2. Explain three customer-facing processes and three business-facing process associated with your business. Be sure to detail why the process is customer facing or business facing.

3. Your friends have asked you to review the customer ordering process for their restaurant, The Broadway Café. To make the café as efficient and effective as possible, you want to redesign processes to remove bottlenecks, reduce redundancies, and streamline workflow. Review The Broadway Café's customer ordering process highlighted in the accompanying image and reengineer it for improvements in efficiency and effectiveness. If you are looking for a real challenge, create your As-Is and To-Be process diagrams using PowerPoint or Visio.

After revamping the ordering process for your friends, you decide to create a To-Be process model of the most important business processes required for your startup to find success. Create the To-Be process model for your most critical business process to ensure you know how to operate your startup in the most efficient and effective manner.

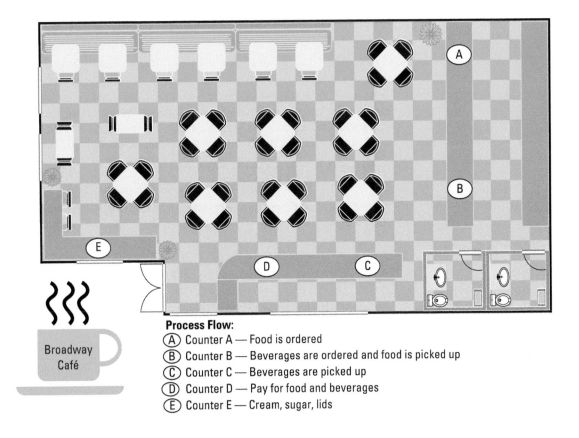

Process Flow:
- (A) Counter A — Food is ordered
- (B) Counter B — Beverages are ordered and food is picked up
- (C) Counter C — Beverages are picked up
- (D) Counter D — Pay for food and beverages
- (E) Counter E — Cream, sugar, lids

Broadway Café

APPLY YOUR KNOWLEDGE BUSINESS PROJECTS

PROJECT I   Making Business Decisions

You are the vice president of human resources for a large consulting company. You are compiling a list of questions that you want each job interviewee to answer. The first question on your list is, "How can MIS enhance your ability to make decisions at our organization?" Prepare a one-page report to answer this question.

PROJECT II   DSS and EIS

Dr. Rosen runs a large dental conglomerate—Teeth Doctors—that employs more than 700 dentists in six states. Dr. Rosen is interested in purchasing a competitor called Dentix that has 150 dentists in three additional states. Before deciding whether to purchase Dentix, Dr. Rosen must consider several issues:

- The cost of purchasing Dentix.
- The location of the Dentix offices.
- The current number of customers per dentist, per office, and per state.
- The merger between the two companies.
- The professional reputation of Dentix.
- Other competitors.

Explain how Dr. Rosen and Teeth Doctors can benefit from the use of information systems to make an accurate business decision about whether to purchase Dentix.

PROJECT III   Finding Information on Decision Support Systems

You are working on the sales team for a small catering company that maintains 75 employees and generates $1 million in revenues per year. The owner, Pam Hetz, wants to understand how she can use decision support systems to help expand her business. Hetz has an initial understanding of DSS and is interested in learning more about what types are available, how they can be used in a small business, and the costs associated. In a group, research the website www.dssresources.com and compile a presentation that discusses DSSs in detail. Be sure to answer all Hetz's questions on DSS in your presentation.

PROJECT IV   Discovering Reengineering Opportunities

In an effort to increase efficiency, your college has hired you to analyze its current business processes for registering for classes. Analyze the current process and determine which steps are:

- Broken
- Redundant
- Antiquated

Be sure to define how you would reengineer the processes for efficiency.

PROJECT V   Dashboard Design

Digital dashboards offer an effective and efficient way to view enterprisewide information at near real time. According to Nucleus Research, there is a direct correlation between use of digital dashboards and a company's return on investment (ROI); hence, all executives should be using or pushing the development of digital dashboards to monitor and analyze organizational operations.

Design a digital dashboard for a customer tracking and enterprise operations system. Be sure to address at least four of the following indicators by showing how you would measure it, such as red, yellow, green status; percentage complete status; and so on.

Customer Tracking System	Enterprise Operations
Customers	Accounting
Marketing	Finance
Order entry	Logistics
Collections	Production
Sales	Distribution
Customer service	Manufacturing
Billing	Human resources
Credit limits	Sales
Transportation	Total profit

PROJECT VI   Defense Advanced Research Projects Agency (DARPA) Grand Challenge

The goal of the DARPA Grand Challenge is to save lives by making one-third of ground military forces autonomous or driverless vehicles by 2015. Created in response to a congressional and U.S. Department of Defense (DoD) mandate, the DARPA Grand Challenge brings together individuals and organizations from industry, the research and development (R&D) community, government, the armed services, and academia and includes students, backyard inventors, and automotive enthusiasts.

The DARPA Grand Challenge 2004 field test of autonomous ground vehicles ran from Barstow, California, to Primm, Nevada, and offered a $1 million prize. From the qualifying round at the California Speedway, 15 finalists emerged to attempt the Grand Challenge. However, the prize went unclaimed when no vehicles were able to complete the difficult desert route.

The DARPA Grand Challenge 2005 was held in the Mojave Desert and offered a $2 million prize to the team that completed the 132-mile course in the shortest time under 10 hours. The race, over desert terrain, included narrow tunnels, sharp turns, and a winding mountain pass with a sheer drop-off on one side and a rock face on the other. Five teams completed the course, and "Stanley," the Stanford Racing Team's car, won the $2 million prize with a time of 6 hours, 53 minutes.

The third DARPA Grand Challenge was an urban challenge on the site of the now-closed George Air Force Base in Victorville, California. It offered a $2 million prize to the autonomous vehicle that could cover the 60-mile course in less than 6 hours. The vehicles had to obey stop lights, navigate around other vehicles, and even merge into heavy traffic. Tartan Racing, a collaborative effort by Carnegie Mellon University and General Motors Corporation, won the prize with "Boss," a Chevy Tahoe. The Stanford Racing Team's "Junior," a 2006 Volkswagen Passat, won second prize of $1 million. "Victor Tango," a 2005 Ford Escape hybrid from Virginia Tech, won third place along with a $500,000 prize.[25]

1. How is the DoD using AI to improve its operations and save lives?

2. Why would the DoD use an event like the DARPA Grand Challenge to further technological innovation?

3. Describe how autonomous vehicles could be used by organizations around the world to improve business efficiency and effectiveness.

4. The Ansari X is another technological innovation competition focusing on spacecraft. To win the $10 million Ansari X Prize, a private spacecraft had to be the first to carry the weight equivalent of three people to an altitude of 62.14 miles twice within two weeks. SpaceShipOne, a privately built spacecraft, won on October 4, 2004. Describe the potential business impacts of the Ansari X competition.

AYK APPLICATION PROJECTS

If you are looking for Excel projects to incorporate into your class, try any of the following after reading this chapter.

Project Number	Project Name	Project Type	Plug-In Focus Area	Project Focus	Project Skill Set	Page Number
1	Financial Destiny	Excel	T2	Personal Budget	Introductory Formulas	AYK.4
2	Cash Flow	Excel	T2	Cash Flow	Introductory Formulas	AYK.4
3	Technology Budget	Excel	T1, T2	Hardware and Software	Introductory Formulas	AYK.4
4	Tracking Donations	Excel	T2	Employee Relationships	Introductory Formulas	AYK.4
5	Convert Currency	Excel	T2	Global Commerce	Introductory Formulas	AYK.5
6	Cost Comparison	Excel	T2	Total Cost of Ownership	Introductory Formulas	AYK.5
7	Time Management	Excel or Project	T2 or T12	Project Management	Introductory Gantt Charts	AYK.6
8	Maximize Profit	Excel	T2, T4	Strategic Analysis	Intermediate Formulas or Solver	AYK.6
9	Security Analysis	Excel	T3	Filtering Data	Intermediate Conditional Formatting, Autofilter, Subtotal	AYK.7
10	Gathering Data	Excel	T3	Data Analysis	Intermediate Conditional Formatting, PivotTable	AYK.8
11	Scanner System	Excel	T2	Strategic Analysis	Intermediate	AYK.8
12	Competitive Pricing	Excel	T2	Profit Maximization	Intermediate	AYK.9
13	Adequate Acquisitions	Excel	T2	Break-Even Analysis	Intermediate	AYK.9

4

CHAPTER

Ethics and Information Security: MIS Business Concerns

CHAPTER OUTLINE

What's in IT for me?

This chapter concerns itself with protecting information from potential misuse. Organizations must ensure they collect, capture, store, and use information in an ethical manner. This means any type of information they collect and utilize, including about customers, partners, and employees. Companies must ensure that personal information collected about someone remains private. This is not just a nice thing to do. The law requires it. Perhaps more important, information must be kept physically secure to prevent access and possible dissemination and use by unauthorized sources.

You, the business student, must understand ethics and security because they are the top concerns voiced by customers today. The way they are handled directly influences a customer's likelihood of embracing electronic technologies and conducting business over the web—and thus the company's bottom line. You can find evidence in recent news reports about how the stock price of organizations falls dramatically when information privacy and security breaches are made known. Further, organizations face potential litigation if they fail to meet their ethical, privacy, and security obligations in the handling of information.

To Share—Or Not to Share

People love social networks! Social networks are everywhere and a perfect way to share vacation photos, family events, and birthday parties with family, friends, and co-workers. About 40 percent of adults use at least one social media website, and 51 percent of those use more than one website. The majority of users are between the ages of 18 and 24. The Pew Research Center found that 89 percent of social network users primarily use the websites to update friends and family, while 57 percent use the websites to make plans with friends, and 49 percent use the websites to make new friends.

Facebook, MySpace, LinkedIn, Friendster, Urban Chat, and Black Planet are just a few of more than 100 websites connecting people around the world who are eager to share everything from photos to thoughts and feelings. But we need to remember that sometimes you can share too much; there can be too much information. Choosing who you share with and what you share is something you want to think about for your personal social networks and corporate social networks. According to Pew Research, more than 40 percent of users allow open access to their social networking profiles, which allows anyone from anywhere to view all of their personal information. The remaining 60 percent restrict access to friends, family, and co-workers. The following are the top 10 things you should consider before posting information to your social networks.

1: If You Don't Want to Share It – Don't Post It

You can select all the privacy settings you want on social networking sites, but the fact is, if you post it, it has the potential to be seen by someone you don't want seeing it. You know all those fun Facebook applications, quizzes, and polls you can't help but fill out? A study performed by the University of Virginia found that of the top 150 applications on Facebook, 90 percent were given access to information they didn't need in order for the application to function. So when you sign up to find out what sitcom star you most identify with, the makers of that poll now have access to your personal information. It's anybody's guess where it goes from there. Social networking is all about sharing, so something you think is in confidence can easily be shared and then shared again, and before you know it, someone you don't even know has access to something private. "When in doubt, leave it out" is a good motto to follow. And always remember that anything you share has the potential to be leaked in some way.

2: Never Give Out Your Password Hints

Most websites that contain secure personal information require a password and also have at least one password hint in case you forget. It typically goes like this: You sign up for something such as online banking and you get a log-in and password and then choose a security question for when you forget your password. What's the name of your first pet? What's your mother's maiden name? What was your high school mascot? What's the name of the first street you lived on? Including any of these details on a Facebook wall or status update may not seem like a big deal, but it could provide an identity thief with the last piece of the puzzle needed to hack into your bank account. Think before you post anything that could compromise this information.

3: Never Give Out Your Password

This one really seems like a no-brainer, but if it didn't happen, then Facebook probably wouldn't feel the need to list it in the No. 1 slot on its list of things you shouldn't share. Even sharing the password with a friend so he or she can log on and check something for you can be a risk. This is especially true with couples who feel like there's enough trust to share these kinds of things. Here's another scenario for you: You give your boyfriend your Facebook password because he wants to help you upload some vacation photos. A couple of months later, the relationship sours, he turns into a not-so-nice guy, and then there's a person out there who doesn't like you and has your log-in information. Time to cancel your account and get a new one. If you'd kept that information private, you could simply move on with your life. Now you have a compromised profile, and if you link to other sites or profiles, all that information is at risk as well. Keep your password to yourself, no matter what, and you never have to worry about it.

4: Never Provide Personal Financial Information

You would think that nobody would share things like where they do their banking or what their stock portfolio looks like, but it happens. It's easy for an innocent Facebook comment to reveal too much about your personal finances. Consider this scenario: You're posting to a long thread on a friend's wall about the bank crisis. You say something along the lines of, "We don't need to worry because we bank with a teacher's credit union," or even, "We put all our money into blue chip stocks and plan to ride it out." Again, if you're one of the 40 percent who allow open access to your profile, then suddenly identity thieves know where you bank and where you have the bulk of your investments. It's easy to forget that what may seem like a harmless comment on a Facebook wall could reveal a great deal about your personal finances. It's best to avoid that kind of talk.

5: Never Give Out Your Address or Phone Numbers

File this one under security risk. If you share your address and phone number on a social networking site, you open yourself up to threats of identity theft and other personal dangers such as burglaries. If you post that you're going on vacation and you have your address posted, then everyone knows you have an empty house. Identity thieves could pay a visit to your mailbox and open up a credit card in your name. Burglars could rid your home of anything of value. Even just posting your phone number gives people with Internet savvy easy access to your address. Reverse lookup services can supply anyone with your home address in possession of your phone number.

6: Never Share Photos of Your Children

Social networking sites are a common place for people to share pictures of their families, but if you're one of the 40 percent of users who don't restrict access to your profile, then those pictures are there for everyone to see. It's a sad fact, but a lot of predators use the Internet to stalk their prey. If you post pictures of your family and combine that with information like, "My husband is out of town this weekend" or "Little Johnny is old enough to stay at home by himself now," then your children's safety could be at risk. Nobody ever thinks it will happen to them until it does, so safety first is a good default mode when using social networking sites. Just like with other private matters, send family photos only to a select group of trusted friends and colleagues who you know won't share them.

7: Never Provide Company Information

You may be dying to tell the world about your new work promotion, but if it's news that could be advantageous to one of your company's competitors, then it's not something you should share. News of a planned expansion or a big project role and anything else about your workplace should be kept private. Sophos, a security software company, found that 63 percent of companies were afraid of what their employees were choosing to share on social networking sites. If you want to message it out, be selective and send private emails. Many companies are so serious about not being included in social networking sites that they forbid employees from using sites like Facebook at work. Some IT departments even filter the URLs and block access to these sites so employees aren't tempted to log on.

8: Never Give Links to Websites

With 51 percent of social network users taking advantage of more than one site, there's bound to be some crossover, especially if you have the sites linked. You may post something you find innocuous on Facebook, but then it's linked to your LinkedIn work profile and you've put your job at risk. If you link your various profiles, be aware that what you post in one world is available to the others. In 2009, a case of an employee caught lying on Facebook hit the news. The employee asked off for a weekend shift because he was ill and then posted pictures on his Facebook profile of himself at a party that same weekend. The news got back to his employer easily enough and he was fired. So if you choose to link your profiles, it's no longer a "personal life" and "work life" scenario.

9: Keep Your Social Plans to Yourself

Sharing your social plans for everybody to see isn't a good idea. Unless you're planning a big party and inviting all the users you're connected to, it will only make your other friends feel left out. There are also some security issues at stake here. Imagine a scenario where a jealous ex-boyfriend knows that you're meeting a new date out that night. What's to keep the ex from showing up and causing a scene or even potentially getting upset or violent? Nothing. If you're planning a party or an outing with a group of friends, send a personal "e-vite" for their eyes only and nobody is the wiser. If you're trying to cast a wide net by throwing out an idea for a social outing, just remember that anyone who has access to your profile sees it.

10. Do Not Share Personal Conversations

On Facebook, users can send personal messages or post notes, images, or videos to another user's wall. The wall is there for all to see, while messages are between the sender and the receiver, just like an email. Personal and private matters should never be shared on your wall. You wouldn't go around with a bullhorn announcing a private issue to the world, and the same thing goes on the Internet. This falls under the nebulous world of social networking etiquette. There is no official handbook for this sort of thing, but use your best judgment. If it's not something you'd feel comfortable sharing in person with extended family, acquaintances, work colleagues, or strangers, then you shouldn't share it on your Facebook wall.[1]

section 4.1 | Ethics

LEARNING OUTCOMES

4.1 Explain the ethical issues in the use of information technology.

4.2 Identify the six epolicies organizations should implement to protect themselves.

INFORMATION ETHICS

LO 4.1: Explain the ethical issues in the use of information technology.

Ethics and security are two fundamental building blocks for all organizations. In recent years, enormous business scandals along with 9/11 have shed new light on the meaning of ethics and security. When the behavior of a few individuals can destroy billion-dollar organizations, the value of ethics and security should be evident.

Copyright is the legal protection afforded an expression of an idea, such as a song, book, or video game. *Intellectual property* is intangible creative work that is embodied in physical form and includes copyrights, trademarks, and patents. A *patent* is an exclusive right to make, use, and sell an invention and is granted by a government to the inventor. As it becomes easier for people to copy everything from words and data to music and video, the ethical issues surrounding copyright infringement and the violation of intellectual property rights are consuming the ebusiness world. Technology poses new challenges for our *ethics*—the principles and standards that guide our behavior toward other people.

The protection of customers' privacy is one of the largest, and murkiest, ethical issues facing organizations today. *Privacy* is the right to be left alone when you want to be, to have control over your personal possessions, and not to be observed without your consent. Privacy is related to *confidentiality,* which is the assurance that messages and information remain available only to those authorized to view them. Each time employees make a decision about a privacy issue, the outcome could sink the company.

Trust among companies, customers, partners, and suppliers is the support structure of ebusiness. Privacy is one of its main ingredients. Consumers' concerns that their privacy will be violated because of their interactions on the web continue to be one of the primary barriers to the growth of ebusiness.

Information ethics govern the ethical and moral issues arising from the development and use of information technologies, as well as the creation, collection, duplication, distribution, and processing of information itself (with or without the aid of computer technologies). Ethical dilemmas in this area usually arise not as simple, clear-cut situations but as clashes among competing goals, responsibilities, and loyalties. Inevitably, there will be more than one socially acceptable or "correct" decision. The two primary areas concerning software include pirated software and counterfeit software. *Pirated software* is the unauthorized use, duplication, distribution, or sale of copyrighted software. *Counterfeit software* is software that is manufactured to look like the real thing and sold as such. *Digital rights management* is a technological solution that allows publishers to control their digital media to discourage, limit, or prevent illegal copying and distribution. Figure 4.1 contains examples of ethically questionable or unacceptable uses of information technology.[2]

Individuals copy, use, and distribute software.
Employees search organizational databases for sensitive corporate and personal information.
Organizations collect, buy, and use information without checking the validity or accuracy of the information.
Individuals create and spread viruses that cause trouble for those using and maintaining IT systems.
Individuals hack into computer systems to steal proprietary information.
Employees destroy or steal proprietary organization information such as schematics, sketches, customer lists, and reports.

FIGURE 4.1

Ethically Questionable or Unacceptable Information Technology Use

BUSINESS DRIVEN DISCUSSION

Information— Does It Have Ethics?

A high school principal decided it was a good idea to hold a confidential conversation about teachers, salaries, and student test scores on his cellular phone in a local Starbucks. Not realizing that one of the student's parents was sitting next to him, the principal accidentally divulged sensitive information about his employees and students. The irate parent soon notified the school board about the principal's inappropriate behavior and a committee was formed to decide how to handle the situation.[3]

With the new wave of collaboration tools, electronic business, and the Internet, employees are finding themselves working outside the office and beyond traditional office hours. Advantages associated with remote workers include increased productivity, decreased expenses, and boosts in morale as employees are given greater flexibility to choose their work location and hours. Unfortunately, disadvantages associated with remote workers include new forms of ethical challenges and information security risks.

In a group, discuss the following statement: Information does not have any ethics. If you were elected to the committee to investigate the principal's inappropriate Starbucks phone conversation, what types of questions would you want answered? What type of punishment, if any, would you enforce on the principal? What types of policies would you implement across the school district to ensure this scenario is never repeated? Be sure to highlight how remote workers impact business along with any potential ethical challenges and information security issues.

Unfortunately, few hard and fast rules exist for always determining what is ethical. Many people can either justify or condemn the actions in Figure 4.1, for example. Knowing the law is important but that knowledge will not always help, because what is legal might not always be ethical, and what might be ethical is not always legal. For example, Joe Reidenberg received an offer for AT&T cell phone service. AT&T used Equifax, a credit reporting agency, to identify potential customers such as Joe Reidenberg. Overall, this seemed like a good business opportunity between Equifax and AT&T wireless. Unfortunately, the Fair Credit Reporting Act (FCRA) forbids repurposing credit information except when the information is used for "a firm offer of credit or insurance." In other words, the only product that can be sold based on credit information is credit. A representative for Equifax stated, "As long as AT&T Wireless (or any company for that matter) is offering the cell phone service on a credit basis, such as allowing the use of the service before the consumer has to pay, it is in compliance with the FCRA." However, the question remains—is it ethical?[4]

Figure 4.2 shows the four quadrants where ethical and legal behaviors intersect. The goal for most businesses is to make decisions within quadrant I that are both legal and ethical. There are times when a business will find itself in the position of making a decision in quadrant III, such as hiring child labor in foreign countries, or in quadrant II where a business might pay a foreigner who is in the process of getting her immigration status approved because the company is in the process of hiring the person. A business should never find itself operating in quadrant IV. Ethics are critical to operating a successful business today.

BUSINESS DRIVEN ETHICS AND SECURITY

Is IT Really Worth the Risk?

Ethics. It's just one tiny word, but it has monumental impact on every area of business. From the magazines, blogs, and newspapers you read to the courses you take, you will encounter ethics as it is a hot topic in today's electronic world. Technology has provided so many incredible opportunities, but it has also provided those same opportunities to unethical people. Discuss the ethical issues surrounding each of the following situations (yes, these are true stories):

■ A student raises her hand in class and states, "I can legally copy any DVD I get from Netflix because Netflix purchased the DVD and the copyright only applies to the company who purchased the product."

■ A student stands up the first day of class before the professor arrives and announces that his fraternity scans textbooks and he has the textbook for this course on his thumb drive, which he will gladly sell for $20. Several students pay on the spot and upload the scanned textbook to their PCs. One student takes down the student information and contacts the publisher about the incident.

■ A senior marketing manager is asked to monitor his employee's email because there is a rumor that the employee is looking for another job.

■ A vice president of sales asks her employee to burn all of the customer data onto an external hard drive because she made a deal to provide customer information to a strategic partner.

■ A senior manager is asked to monitor his employee's email to discover if she is sexually harassing another employee.

■ An employee is looking at the shared network drive and discovers his boss's entire hard drive, including his email backup, has been copied to the network and is visible to all.

■ An employee is accidently copied on an email listing the targets for the next round of layoffs.

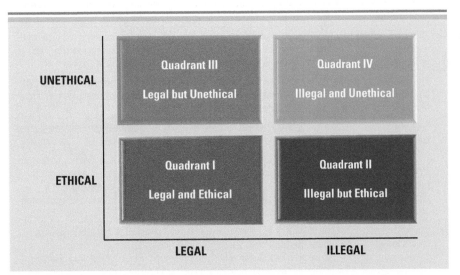

FIGURE 4.2

Acting Ethically and Acting Legally Are Not Always the Same Thing

Information Does Not Have Ethics, People Do

Information itself has no ethics. It does not care how it is used. It will not stop itself from spamming customers, sharing itself if it is sensitive or personal, or revealing details to third parties. Information cannot delete or preserve itself. Therefore, it falls to those who own the information to develop ethical guidelines about how to manage it. **Information management** examines the organizational resource of information and regulates its definitions, uses, value, and distribution ensuring it has the types of data/information required to function and grow effectively. **Information governance** is a method or system of government for information management or control. **Information compliance** is the act of conforming, acquiescing, or yielding information. **Information property** is an ethical issue that focuses on who owns information about individuals and how information can be sold and exchanged. A few years ago the ideas of information management, governance, and

FIGURE 4.3

Established Information-Related Laws

Established Information-Related Laws	
Privacy Act—1974	Restricts what information the federal government can collect; allows people to access and correct information on themselves; requires procedures to protect the security of personal information; and forbids the disclosure of name-linked information without permission.
Family Education Rights and Privacy Act—1974	Regulates access to personal education records by government agencies and other third parties and ensures the right of students to see their own records.
Cable Communications Act—1984	Requires written or electronic consent from viewers before cable TV providers can release viewing choices or other personally identifiable information.
Electronic Communications Privacy Act—1986	Allows the reading of communications by a firm and says that employees have no right to privacy when using their companies' computers.
Computer Fraud and Abuse Act—1986	Prohibits unauthorized access to computers used for financial institutions, the U.S. government, or interstate and international trade.
The Bork Bill (officially known as the Video Privacy Protection Act, 1988)	Prohibits the use of video rental information on customers for any purpose other than that of marketing goods and services directly to the customer.
Communications Assistance for Law Enforcement Act—1994	Requires that telecommunications equipment be designed so that authorized government agents are able to intercept all wired and wireless communications being sent or received by any subscriber. The act also requires that subscriber call-identifying information be transmitted to a government when and if required.
Freedom of Information Act—1967, 1975, 1994, and 1998	Allows any person to examine government records unless it would cause an invasion of privacy. It was amended in 1974 to apply to the FBI, and again in 1994 to allow citizens to monitor government activities and information gathering, and once again in 1998 to access government information on the Internet.
Health Insurance Portability and Accountability Act (HIPAA)—1996	Requires that the health care industry formulate and implement regulations to keep patient information confidential.
Identity Theft and Assumption Deterrence Act—1998	Strengthened the criminal laws governing identity theft making it a federal crime to use or transfer identification belonging to another. It also established a central federal service for victims.
USA Patriot Act—2001 and 2003	Allows law enforcement to get access to almost any information, including library records, video rentals, bookstore purchases, and business records when investigating any act of terrorist or clandestine intelligence activities. In 2003, Patriot II broadened the original law.
Homeland Security Act—2002	Provided new authority to government agencies to mine data on individuals and groups including emails and website visits; put limits on the information available under the Freedom of Information Act; and gave new powers to government agencies to declare national health emergencies.
Sarbanes-Oxley Act—2002	Sought to protect investors by improving the accuracy and reliability of corporate disclosures and requires companies to (1) implement extensive and detailed policies to prevent illegal activity within the company, and (2) to respond in a timely manner to investigate illegal activity.
Fair and Accurate Credit Transactions Act—2003	Included provisions for the prevention of identity theft including consumers' right to get a credit report free each year, requiring merchants to leave all but the last five digits of a credit card number off a receipt, and requiring lenders and credit agencies to take action even before a victim knows a crime has occurred when they notice any circumstances that might indicate identity theft.
CAN-Spam Act—2003	Sought to regulate interstate commerce by imposing limitations and penalties on businesses sending unsolicited email to consumers. The law forbids deceptive subject lines, headers, return addresses, etc., as well as the harvesting of email addresses from websites. It requires businesses that send spam to maintain a do-not-spam list and to include a postal mailing address in the message.

compliance were relatively obscure. Today, these concepts are a must for virtually every company, both domestic and global, primarily due to the role digital information plays in corporate legal proceedings or litigation. Frequently, digital information serves as key evidence in legal proceedings and it is far easier to search, organize, and filter than paper documents. Digital information is also extremely difficult to destroy, especially if it is on a corporate network or sent via email. In fact, the only reliable way to truly obliterate digital information is to destroy the hard drives where the file was stored. **Ediscovery** (or **electronic discovery**) refers to the ability of a company to identify, search, gather, seize, or export digital information in responding to a litigation, audit, investigation, or information inquiry. As the importance of ediscovery grows, so does information governance and information compliance. The **Child Online Protection Act (COPA)** was passed to protect minors from accessing inappropriate material on the Internet. Figure 4.3 provides an overview of some of the important laws individuals and firms must follow in managing and protecting information.[5]

DEVELOPING INFORMATION MANAGEMENT POLICIES

LO 4.2: Identify the six epolicies organizations should implement to protect themselves.

Treating sensitive corporate information as a valuable resource is good management. Building a corporate culture based on ethical principles that employees can understand and implement is responsible management. Organizations should develop written policies establishing employee guidelines, employee procedures, and organizational rules for information. These policies set employee expectations about the organization's practices and standards and protect the organization from misuse of computer systems and IT resources. If an organization's employees use computers at work, the organization should, at a minimum, implement epolicies. **Epolicies** are policies and procedures that address information management along with the ethical use of computers and the Internet in the business environment. Figure 4.4 displays the epolicies a firm should implement to set employee expectations.

Ethical Computer Use Policy

In a case that illustrates the perils of online betting, a leading Internet poker site reported that a hacker exploited a security flaw to gain an insurmountable edge in high-stakes, no-limit Texas hold-'em tournaments—the ability to see his opponents' hole cards. The cheater, whose illegitimate winnings were estimated at between $400,000 and $700,000 by one victim, was an employee of AbsolutePoker.com and hacked the system to show that it could be done. Regardless of what business a company operates—even one that many view as unethical—the company must protect itself from unethical employee behavior.[6] **Cyberbulling** includes threats, negative remarks, or defamatory comments transmitted via the Internet or posted on the website. A **threat** is an act or object that poses a danger to assets. **Click-fraud** is the abuse of pay-per-click, pay-per-call, and pay-per-conversion revenue models by repeatedly clicking on a link to increase charges or costs for the advertiser. **Competitive click-fraud** is a computer crime where a competitor or disgruntled employee increases a company's search advertising costs by repeatedly clicking on the advertiser's link.

FIGURE 4.4

Overview of Epolicies

Cyberbullying and click-fraud are just a few examples of the many types of unethical computer use found today.

One essential step in creating an ethical corporate culture is establishing an ethical computer use policy. An **ethical computer use policy** contains general principles to guide computer user behavior. For example, it might explicitly state that users should refrain from playing computer games during working hours. This policy ensures the users know how to behave at work and the organization has a published standard to deal with infractions. For example, after appropriate warnings, the company may terminate an employee who spends significant amounts of time playing computer games at work.

Organizations can legitimately vary in how they expect employees to use computers, but in any approach to controlling such use, the overriding principle should be informed consent. The users should be *informed* of the rules and, by agreeing to use the system on that basis, *consent* to abide by them.

Managers should make a conscientious effort to ensure all users are aware of the policy through formal training and other means. If an organization were to have only one epolicy, it should be an ethical computer use policy because that is the starting point and the umbrella for any other policies the organization might establish.

Information Privacy Policy

An organization that wants to protect its information should develop an **information privacy policy**, which contains general principles regarding information privacy. Visa created Inovant to handle all its information systems including its coveted customer information, which details how people are spending their money, in which stores, on which days, and even at what time of day. Just imagine what a sales and marketing department could do if it gained access to this information. For this reason, Inovant bans the use of Visa's customer information for anything outside its intended purpose—billing. Innovant's privacy specialists developed a strict credit card information privacy policy, which it follows.

Now Inovant is being asked if it can guarantee that unethical use of credit card information will never occur. In a large majority of cases, the unethical use of information happens not through the malicious scheming of a rogue marketer, but rather unintentionally. For instance, information is collected and stored for some purpose, such as record keeping or billing. Then, a sales or marketing professional figures out another way to use it internally, share it with partners, or sell it to a trusted third party. The information is "unintentionally" used for new purposes. The classic example of this type of unintentional information reuse is the Social Security number, which started simply as a way to identify government retirement benefits and then was used as a sort of universal personal ID, found on everything from drivers' licenses to savings accounts.

Acceptable Use Policy

An **acceptable use policy (AUP)** requires a user to agree to follow it to be provided access to corporate email, information systems, and the Internet. **Nonrepudiation** is a contractual stipulation to ensure that ebusiness participants do not deny (repudiate) their online actions. A nonrepudiation clause is typically contained in an acceptable use policy. Many businesses and educational facilities require employees or students to sign an acceptable use policy before gaining network access. When signing up with an email provider, each customer is typically presented with an AUP, which states the user agrees to adhere to certain stipulations. Users agree to the following in a typical acceptable use policy:

- Not using the service as part of violating any law.
- Not attempting to break the security of any computer network or user.
- Not posting commercial messages to groups without prior permission.
- Not performing any nonrepudiation.

Some organizations go so far as to create a unique information management policy focusing solely on Internet use. An **Internet use policy** contains general principles to guide the proper use of the Internet. Because of the large amounts of computing resources that Internet users can expend, it is essential that such use be legitimate. In addition, the Internet contains numerous materials that some believe are offensive, making regulation in the

BUSINESS DRIVEN GLOBALIZATION

Censoring Google

The Google debate over operations in China is an excellent example of types of global ethical and security issues U.S. companies face as they expand operations around the world. Google's systems were targeted by highly sophisticated hacker attacks aimed at obtaining proprietary information including personal data belonging to Chinese human rights activists who use Google's Gmail service. Google, which originally agreed to filter search results based on Chinese government censorship rules, decided to unfilter search results after what it called an infiltration of its technology and the email accounts of Chinese human-rights activists. China called Google's plan to defy government censorship rules unfriendly and irresponsible and demanded Google shut down all operations in China.

Why would China want to filer search results? Do you agree or disagree with China's censorship rules? Do you think Google was acting ethically when it agreed to implement China's censorship rules? Why do companies operating abroad need to be aware of the different ethical perspective found in other cultures?[7]

workplace a requirement. **Cybervandalism** is the electronic defacing of an existing website. **Typosquatting** is a problem that occurs when someone registers purposely misspelled variations of well-known domain names. These variants sometimes lure consumers who make typographical errors when entering a URL. **Website name stealing** is the theft of a website's name that occurs when someone, posing as a site's administrator, changes the ownership of the domain name assigned to the website to another website owner. These are all examples of unacceptable Internet use. **Internet censorship** is government attempts to control Internet traffic, thus preventing some material from being viewed by a country's citizens. Generally, an Internet use policy:

- Describes the Internet services available to users.
- Defines the organization's position on the purpose of Internet access and what restrictions, if any, are placed on that access.
- Describes user responsibility for citing sources, properly handling offensive material, and protecting the organization's good name.
- States the ramifications if the policy is violated.

Email Privacy Policy

An **email privacy policy** details the extent to which email messages may be read by others. Email is so pervasive in organizations that it requires its own specific policy. Most working professionals use email as their preferred means of corporate communications. While email and instant messaging are common business communication tools, there are risks associated with using them. For instance, a sent email is stored on at least three or four computers (see Figure 4.5). Simply deleting an email from one computer does not delete it from the others. Companies can mitigate many of the risks of using electronic messaging systems by implementing and adhering to an email privacy policy.

One major problem with email is the user's expectations of privacy. To a large extent, this expectation is based on the false assumption that email privacy protection exists somehow analogous to that of U.S. first-class mail. Generally, the organization that owns the email system can operate the system as openly or as privately as it wishes. Surveys indicate that the majority of large firms regularly read and analyze employees' email looking for confidential data leaks such as unannounced financial results or the sharing

FIGURE 4.5

Email Is Stored on Multiple
Computers

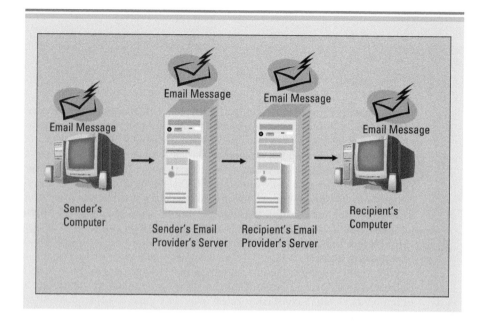

Email Message

Email Message

Email Message

Email Message

Sender's
Computer

Sender's Email
Provider's Server

Recipient's Email
Provider's Server

Recipient's
Computer

of trade secrets that result in the violation of an email privacy policy and eventual termination of the employee. That means that if the organization wants to read everyone's email, it can do so. Basically, using work email for anything other than work is not a good idea. A typical email privacy policy:

- Defines legitimate email users and explains what happens to accounts after a person leaves the organization.
- Explains backup procedure so users will know that at some point, even if a message is deleted from their computer, it is still stored by the company.
- Describes the legitimate grounds for reading email and the process required before such action is performed.
- Discourages sending junk email or spam to anyone who does not want to receive it.
- Prohibits attempting to mail bomb a site. A *mail bomb* sends a massive amount of email to a specific person or system that can cause that user's server to stop functioning.
- Informs users that the organization has no control over email once it has been transmitted outside the organization.

Spam is unsolicited email. It plagues employees at all levels within an organization, from receptionist to CEO, and clogs email systems and siphons MIS resources away from legitimate business projects. An *anti-spam policy* simply states that email users will not send unsolicited emails (or spam). It is difficult to write anti-spam policies, laws, or software because there is no such thing as a universal litmus test for spam. One person's spam is another person's newsletter. End users have to decide what spam is, because it can vary widely not just from one company to the next, but from one person to the next. A user can *opt out* of receiving emails by choosing to deny permission to incoming emails.

Teergrubing is an antispamming approach where the receiving computer launches a return attack against the spammer, sending email messages back to the computer that originated the suspected spam.

Social Media Policy

Did you see the YouTube video showing two Domino's Pizza employees violating health codes while preparing food by passing gas on sandwiches? Millions of people did and the company took notice when disgusted customers began posting negative comments all over Twitter. Not having a Twitter account, corporate executives at Domino's did not know about the damaging tweets until it was too late. The use of social media can

BUSINESS DRIVEN MIS

The Canadian Broadcasting Company (CBC) has issued a social networking policy directing journalists to avoid adding sources or contacts as friends on social networking sites such as Facebook or LinkedIn. Basic rules state that reporters never allow one source to view what another source says and reporters want to ensure private conversations with sources remain private. Adding sources as "friends" can compromise a journalist's work by allowing friends to view other friends in the network. It may also not be in a journalist's best interest to become a "friend" in a source's network. The CBC also discourages posting any political preferences in personal profiles, commenting on bulletin boards or people's "Facebook wall."

This might seem like common sense, but for employees who do not spend countless hours on the Internet, using social networking sites can be confusing and overwhelming. Why is it critical for any new hire to research and review all policies, especially social media policies? Research three companies you would like to work for upon graduation, and detail the types of social media policies that the company currently has or should implement.[9]

Sources Are Not Friends

contribute many benefits to an organization, and implemented correctly it can become a huge opportunity for employees to build brands. But there are also tremendous risks as a few employees representing an entire company can cause tremendous brand damage. Defining a set of guidelines implemented in a social media policy can help mitigate that risk. Companies can protect themselves by implementing a ***social media policy*** outlining the corporate guidelines or principles governing employee online communications. Having a single social media policy might not be enough to ensure the company's online reputation is protected. Additional, more specific, social media policies a company might choose to implement include:[8]

- Employee online communication policy detailing brand communication.
- Employee blog and personal blog policies.
- Employee social network and personal social network policies.
- Employee Twitter, corporate Twitter, and personal Twitter policies.
- Employee LinkedIn policy.
- Employee Facebook usage and brand usage policy.
- Corporate YouTube policy.

Organizations must protect their online reputations and continuously monitor blogs, message boards, social networking sites, and media sharing sites. However, monitoring the hundreds of different social media sites can quickly become overwhelming. To combat these issues, a number of companies specialize in online social media monitoring; for example, Trackur.com creates digital dashboards allowing executives to view at a glance the date published, source, title, and summary of every item tracked. The dashboard not only highlights what's being said, but also the influence of the particular person, blog, or social media site.

Workplace Monitoring Policy

Increasingly, employee monitoring is not a choice; it is a risk-management obligation. Michael Soden, CEO of the Bank of Ireland, issued a mandate stating that company employees could not surf illicit websites with company equipment. Next, he hired

Hewlett-Packard to run the MIS department and illicit websites were discovered on Soden's own computer, forcing Soden to resign. Monitoring employees is one of the biggest challenges CIOs face when developing information management policies.[10]

Physical security is tangible protection such as alarms, guards, fireproof doors, fences, and vaults. New technologies make it possible for employers to monitor many aspects of their employees' jobs, especially on telephones, computer terminals, through electronic and voice mail, and when employees are using the Internet. Such monitoring is virtually unregulated. Therefore, unless company policy specifically states otherwise (and even this is not assured), your employer may listen, watch, and read most of your workplace communications. **Workplace MIS monitoring** tracks people's activities by such measures as number of keystrokes, error rate, and number of transactions processed (see Figure 4.6 for an overview). The best path for an organization planning to engage in employee monitoring is open communication including an **employee monitoring policy** stating explicitly how, when, and where the company monitors its employees. Several common stipulations an organization can follow when creating an employee monitoring policy include:

- Be as specific as possible stating when and what (email, IM, Internet, network activity, etc.) will be monitored.
- Expressly communicate that the company reserves the right to monitor all employees.
- State the consequences of violating the policy.
- Always enforce the policy the same for everyone.

Many employees use their company's high-speed Internet access to shop, browse, and surf the web. Most managers do not want their employees conducting personal business during working hours, and they implement a Big Brother approach to employee monitoring. Many management gurus advocate that organizations whose corporate cultures are based on trust are more successful than those whose corporate cultures are based on mistrust. Before an organization implements monitoring technology, it should ask itself, "What does this say about how we feel about our employees?" If the organization really does not trust its employees, then perhaps it should find new ones. If an organization does trust its employees, then it might want to treat them accordingly. An organization that follows its employees' every keystroke might be unwittingly undermining the relationships with its employees, and it might find the effects of employee monitoring are often worse than lost productivity from employee web surfing.

FIGURE 4.6

Internet Monitoring Technologies

Common Internet Monitoring Technologies	
Key logger, or key trapper, software	A program that records every keystroke and mouse click.
Hardware key logger	A hardware device that captures keystrokes on their journey from the keyboard to the motherboard.
Cookie	A small file deposited on a hard drive by a website containing information about customers and their web activities. Cookies allow websites to record the comings and goings of customers, usually without their knowledge or consent.
Adware	Software that generates ads that install themselves on a computer when a person downloads some other program from the Internet.
Spyware (sneakware or stealthware)	Software that comes hidden in free downloadable software and tracks online movements, mines the information stored on a computer, or uses a computer's CPU and storage for some task the user knows nothing about.
Web log	Consists of one line of information for every visitor to a website and is usually stored on a web server.
Clickstream	Records information about a customer during a web surfing session such as what websites were visited, how long the visit was, what ads were viewed, and what was purchased.

BUSINESS DRIVEN DEBATE

New technologies make it possible for employers to monitor many aspects of their employees' jobs, especially on telephones, computer terminals, through electronic and voice mail, and when employees are using the Internet. Such monitoring is virtually unregulated. Therefore, unless company policy specifically states otherwise (and even this is not assured), your employer may listen, watch, and read most of your workplace communications.

Employers are taking monitoring activity a step further and monitoring employees, and employees' spouses, at home and on weekends. Yes, you read that correctly. Numerous employees have been fired for smoking cigarettes on the weekend in the privacy of their own home. As health care costs escalate, employers are increasingly seeking to regulate employee behavior—at home as well as in the workplace. Weyco, an insurance benefits administrator in Michigan, initiated a program requiring mandatory breath tests to detect for nicotine, and any employee testing positive would be sent home without pay for one month. If the employee failed the nicotine test a second time, that person would be fired—no matter how long the employee had been with the company. Weyco's smoking prohibition does not stop with employees but extends to spouses also who must pass monthly nicotine tests. A positive test means the employee must pay a monthly fee of $80 until the spouse takes a smoking-cessation program and tests nicotine-free.[11]

Do you agree that companies have the right to hold employees accountable for actions they perform on weekends in the privacy of their own homes? If you were the CEO of Weyco, what would be your argument supporting its smoking prohibition policies? Do you think Weyco's monitoring practices are ethical? Do you think Weyco's monitoring practices are legal?

Fired for Smoking on the Weekend

---

section 4.2 | Information Security

LEARNING OUTCOMES

4.3 Describe the relationships and differences between hackers and viruses.

4.4 Describe the relationship between information security policies and an information security plan.

4.5 Provide an example of each of the three primary information security areas: (1) authentication and authorization, (2) prevention and resistance, and (3) detection and response.

PROTECTING INTELLECTUAL ASSETS

To accurately reflect the crucial interdependence between MIS and business processes, we should update the old business axiom "Time is money" to say "Uptime is money." **Downtime** refers to a period of time when a system is unavailable. Unplanned downtime can strike at any time for any number of reasons, from tornadoes to sink overflows to network failures to power outages (see Figure 4.7). Although natural disasters may appear to be the most devastating causes of MIS outages, they are hardly the most frequent or most expensive. Figure 4.8 demonstrates that the costs of downtime are not only associated

LO 4.3: Describe the relationships and differences between hackers and viruses.

FIGURE 4.7

Sources of Unplanned
Downtime

Sources of Unplanned Downtime		
Bomb threat	Frozen pipe	Snowstorm
Burst pipe	Hacker	Sprinkler malfunction
Chemical spill	Hail	Static electricity
Construction	Hurricane	Strike
Corrupted data	Ice storm	Terrorism
Earthquake	Insects	Theft
Electrical short	Lightning	Tornado
Epidemic	Network failure	Train derailment
Equipment failure	Plane crash	Smoke damage
Evacuation	Power outage	Vandalism
Explosion	Power surge	Vehicle crash
Fire	Rodents	Virus
Flood	Sabotage	Water damage (various)
Fraud	Shredded data	Wind

FIGURE 4.8

The Cost of Downtime

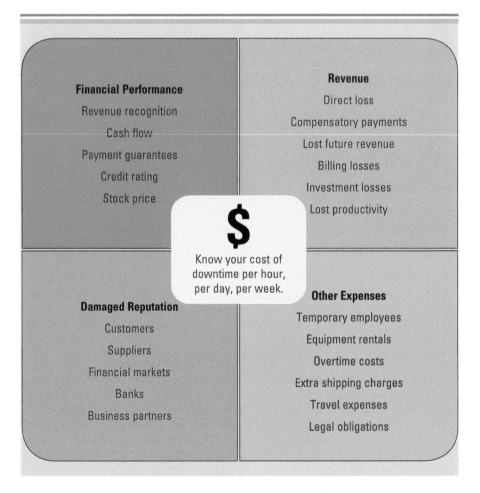

Financial Performance
Revenue recognition
Cash flow
Payment guarantees
Credit rating
Stock price

Revenue
Direct loss
Compensatory payments
Lost future revenue
Billing losses
Investment losses
Lost productivity

$
Know your cost of
downtime per hour,
per day, per week.

Damaged Reputation
Customers
Suppliers
Financial markets
Banks
Business partners

Other Expenses
Temporary employees
Equipment rentals
Overtime costs
Extra shipping charges
Travel expenses
Legal obligations

with lost revenues, but also with financial performance, damage to reputations, and even travel or legal expenses. A few questions managers should ask when determining the cost of downtime are:[12]

- How many transactions can the company afford to lose without significantly harming business?

- Does the company depend upon one or more mission-critical applications to conduct business?

- How much revenue will the company lose for every hour a critical application is unavailable?

- What is the productivity cost associated with each hour of downtime?

- How will collaborative business processes with partners, suppliers, and customers be affected by an unexpected IT outage?

- What is the total cost of lost productivity and lost revenue during unplanned downtime?

The reliability and resilience of IT systems have never been more essential for success as businesses cope with the forces of globalization, 24/7 operations, government and trade regulations, global recession, and overextended IT budgets and resources. Any unexpected downtime in today's business environment has the potential to cause both short- and long-term costs with far-reaching consequences.

Information security is a broad term encompassing the protection of information from accidental or intentional misuse by persons inside or outside an organization. Information security is the primary tool an organization can use to combat the threats associated with downtime. Understanding how to secure information systems is critical to keeping downtime to a minimum and uptime to a maximum. Hackers and viruses are two of the hottest issues currently facing information security.

Security Threats Caused by Hackers and Viruses

Hackers are experts in technology who use their knowledge to break into computers and computer networks, either for profit or just motivated by the challenge. Smoking is not just bad for a person's health; it seems it is also bad for company security as hackers regularly use smoking entrances to gain building access. Once inside they pose as employees from the MIS department and either ask for permission to use an employee's computer to access the corporate network, or find a conference room where they simply plug-in their own laptop. *Drive-by hacking* is a computer attack where an attacker accesses a wireless computer network, intercepts data, uses network services, and/or sends attack instructions without entering the office or organization that owns the network. Figure 4.9 lists the various types of hackers for organizations to be aware of, and Figure 4.10 shows how a virus is spread.

One of the most common forms of computer vulnerabilities is a virus. A *virus* is software written with malicious intent to cause annoyance or damage. Some hackers create and leave viruses causing massive computer damage. Figure 4.11 provides an overview of the most common types of viruses. Two additional computer vulnerabilities include adware and spyware. *Adware* is software that, while purporting to serve some useful

FIGURE 4.9

Types of Hackers

Common Types of Hackers
▪ *Black-hat hackers* break into other people's computer systems and may just look around or may steal and destroy information.
▪ *Crackers* have criminal intent when hacking.
▪ *Cyberterrorists* seek to cause harm to people or to destroy critical systems or information and use the Internet as a weapon of mass destruction.
▪ *Hactivists* have philosophical and political reasons for breaking into systems and will often deface the website as a protest.
▪ *Script kiddies* or *script bunnies* find hacking code on the Internet and click-and-point their way into systems to cause damage or spread viruses.
▪ *White-hat hackers* work at the request of the system owners to find system vulnerabilities and plug the holes.

FIGURE 4.10

How Computer Viruses Spread

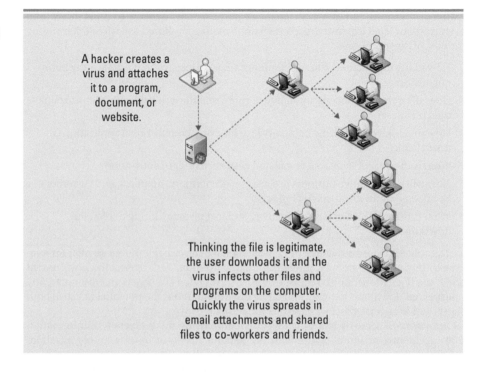

A hacker creates a virus and attaches it to a program, document, or website.

Thinking the file is legitimate, the user downloads it and the virus infects other files and programs on the computer. Quickly the virus spreads in email attachments and shared files to co-workers and friends.

FIGURE 4.11

Common Forms of Viruses

Backdoor programs open a way into the network for future attacks.
Denial-of-service attack (DoS) floods a website with so many requests for service that it slows down or crashes the site.
Distributed denial-of-service attack (DDoS) attacks from multiple computers that flood a website with so many requests for service that it slows down or crashes. A common type is the Ping of Death, in which thousands of computers try to access a website at the same time, overloading it and shutting it down.
Polymorphic viruses and worms change their form as they propagate.
Trojan-horse virus hides inside other software, usually as an attachment or a downloadable file.
Worm spreads itself, not only from file to file, but also from computer to computer. The primary difference between a virus and a worm is that a virus must attach to something, such as an executable file, to spread. Worms do not need to attach to anything to spread and can tunnel themselves into computers.

function and often fulfilling that function, also allows Internet advertisers to display advertisements without the consent of the computer user. **Spyware** is a special class of adware that collects data about the user and transmits it over the Internet without the user's knowledge or permission. Spyware programs collect specific data about the user, ranging from general demographics such as name, address, and browsing habits to credit card numbers, Social Security numbers, and user names and passwords. Not all adware programs are spyware and used correctly it can generate revenue for a company allowing users to receive free products. Spyware is a clear threat to privacy. Figure 4.12 displays a few additional weapons hackers use for launching attacks.[13]

Organizational information is intellectual capital. Just as organizations protect their tangible assets—keeping their money in an insured bank or providing a safe working environment for employees—they must also protect their intellectual capital, everything from patents to transactional and analytical information. With security breaches and viruses on the rise and computer hackers everywhere, an organization must put in place strong security measures to survive.

Elevation of privilege is a process by which a user misleads a system into granting unauthorized rights, usually for the purpose of compromising or destroying the system. For example, an attacker might log onto a network by using a guest account and then exploit a weakness in the software that lets the attacker change the guest privileges to administrative privileges.

Hoaxes attack computer systems by transmitting a virus hoax, with a real virus attached. By masking the attack in a seemingly legitimate message, unsuspecting users more readily distribute the message and send the attack on to their co-workers and friends, infecting many users along the way.

Malicious code includes a variety of threats such as viruses, worms, and Trojan horses.

Packet tampering consists of altering the contents of packets as they travel over the Internet or altering data on computer disks after penetrating a network. For example, an attacker might place a tap on a network line to intercept packets as they leave the computer. The attacker could eavesdrop or alter the information as it leaves the network.

A **sniffer** is a program or device that can monitor data traveling over a network. Sniffers can show all the data being transmitted over a network, including passwords and sensitive information. Sniffers tend to be a favorite weapon in the hacker's arsenal.

Spoofing is the forging of the return address on an email so that the message appears to come from someone other than the actual sender. This is not a virus but rather a way by which virus authors conceal their identities as they send out viruses.

Splogs (spam blogs) are fake blogs created solely to raise the search engine rank of affiliated websites. Even blogs that are legitimate are plagued by spam, with spammers taking advantage of the Comment feature of most blogs to comments with links to spam sites.

Spyware is software that comes hidden in free downloadable software and tracks online movements, mines the information stored on a computer, or uses a computer's CPU and storage for some task the user knows nothing about.

FIGURE 4.12

Hacker Weapons

THE FIRST LINE OF DEFENSE—PEOPLE

LO 4.4: Describe the relationship between information security policies and an information security plan.

Organizations today are able to mine valuable information such as the identity of the top 20 percent of their customers, who usually produce 80 percent of revenues. Most organizations view this type of information as intellectual capital and implement security measures to prevent it from walking out the door or falling into the wrong hands. At the same time, they must enable employees, customers, and partners to access needed information electronically. Organizations address security risks through two lines of defense; the first is people, the second technology.

Surprisingly, the biggest problem is people as the majority of information security breaches result from people misusing organizational information. *Insiders* are legitimate users who purposely or accidentally misuse their access to the environment and cause some kind of business-affecting incident. For example, many individuals freely give up their passwords or write them on sticky notes next to their computers, leaving the door wide open for hackers. Through *social engineering,* hackers use their social skills to trick people into revealing access credentials or other valuable information. *Dumpster diving,* or looking through people's trash, is another way hackers obtain information.

Information security policies identify the rules required to maintain information security, such as requiring users to log off before leaving for lunch or meetings, never sharing passwords with anyone, and changing passwords every 30 days. An *information security plan* details how an organization will implement the information security policies. The best way a company can safeguard itself from people is by implementing and communicating its information security plan. This becomes even more important with Web 2.0 and as the use of mobile devices, remote workforce, and contractors are growing. A few details managers should consider surrounding people and information security policies include defining the best practices for[14]

- Applications allowed to be placed on the corporate network, especially various file sharing applications (Kazaz), IM software, and entertainment or freeware created by unknown sources (iPhone applications).
- Corporate computer equipment used for personal reason on personal networks.
- Password creation and maintenance including minimum password length, characters to be included while choosing passwords, and frequency for password changes.
- Personal computer equipment allowed to connect to the corporate network.

- Virus protection including how often the system should be scanned and how frequently the software should be updated. This could also include if downloading attachments is allowed and practices for safe downloading from trusted and untrustworthy sources.

LO 4.5: Provide an example of each of the three primary information security areas: (1) authentication and authorization, (2) prevention and resistance, and (3) detection and response.

THE SECOND LINE OF DEFENSE—TECHNOLOGY

Once an organization has protected its intellectual capital by arming its people with a detailed information security plan, it can begin to focus on deploying technology to help combat attackers. **Destructive agents** are malicious agents designed by spammers and other Internet attackers to farm email addresses off websites or deposit spyware on machines. Figure 4.13 displays the three areas where technology can aid in the defense against attacks.

People: Authentication and Authorization

Identity theft is the forging of someone's identity for the purpose of fraud. The fraud is often financial, because thieves apply for and use credit cards or loans in the victim's name. Two means of stealing an identity are phishing and pharming. **Information secrecy** is the category of computer security that addresses the protection of data from unauthorized disclosure and confirmation of data source authenticity. **Phishing** is a technique to gain personal information for the purpose of identity theft, usually by means of fraudulent emails that look as though they came from legitimate businesses. The messages appear to be genuine, with official-looking formats and logos, and typically ask for verification of important information such as passwords and account numbers, ostensibly for accounting or auditing purposes. Since the emails look authentic, up to one in five recipients responds with the information and subsequently becomes a victim of identity theft and other fraud. Figure 4.14 displays a phishing scam attempting to gain information for Bank of America; you should never click on emails asking you to verify your identity as companies will never contact you directly asking for your user name or password.[15] **Phishing expedition** is a masquerading attack that combines spam with spoofing. The perpetrator sends millions of spam emails that appear to be from a respectable company. The emails contain a link to a website that is designed to look exactly like the company's website. The victim is encouraged to enter his or her username, password, and sometimes credit card information. **Spear phishing** is a phishing expedition in which the emails are carefully designed to target a particular person or organization. **Vishing (or voice phishing)** is a

FIGURE 4.13

Three Areas of Information Security

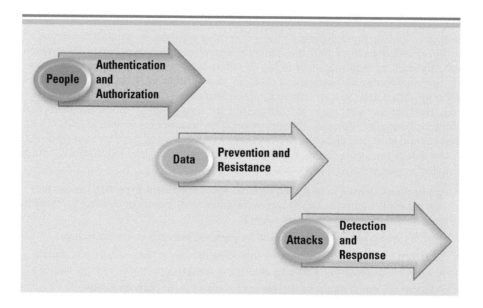

FIGURE 4.14

Bank of America Phishing Scam

| From: | Bank of America Online [ealert@replies.em.bankofamerica.com] |
| Subject: | Customer Alert: Your Account was been Attended |

Bank of America 🏦 **Higher Standards**

The sooner you sign in to Online Banking,
the simpler your life will get.

Important Notification

Dear **Valued Customer**,

As part of Bank of America Online commitment to provide you with exceptional service, Bank of America Online is taking additional steps to ensure that your account data is secure.

Therefore, we are sending you this e-mail as a security precaution to confirm to you the Inability to accurately verify your account information due to an internal error within server

You are required to confirm your account information to forestall a re-occurrence of any future attention with your online banking.

However, failure to update your account information might result in your account being suspended. Click below to get started.

Get Started

Thank you,
Bank of America Online Banking.

----

* Please do not respond to this email as your reply will not be received.

Bank of America Email, 8th Floor, 101 South Tryon St., Charlotte, NC 28255-0001

phone scam that attempts to defraud people by asking them to call a bogus telephone number to "confirm" their account information.

Pharming reroutes requests for legitimate websites to false websites. For example, if you were to type in the URL to your bank, pharming could redirect to a fake site that collects your information. A *zombie* is a program that secretly takes over another computer for the purpose of launching attacks on other computers. Zombie attacks are almost impossible to trace back to the attacker. A *zombie farm* is a group of computers on which a hacker has planted zombie programs. A *pharming attack* uses a zombie farm, often by an organized crime association, to launch a massive phishing attack.

Authentication and authorization technologies can prevent identity theft, phishing, and pharming scams. *Authentication* is a method for confirming users' identities. Once a system determines the authentication of a user, it can then determine the access privileges (or authorization) for that user. *Authorization* is the process of providing a user with permission including access levels and abilities such as file access, hours of access, and amount of allocated storage space. Authentication and authorization techniques fall into three categories; the most secure procedures combine all three:

1. Something the user knows, such as a user ID and password.
2. Something the user has, such as a smart card or token.
3. Something that is part of the user, such as a fingerprint or voice signature.

BUSINESS DRIVEN INNOVATION

Doodling Passwords

As our online world continues to explode, people are finding the number of user names and passwords they need to remember growing exponentially. For this reason many users will assign the same password for every log-on, choose easy to remember names and dates, or simply write down their passwords on sticky notes and attach them to their computers. Great for the person who needs to remember 72 different passwords, but not so great for system security.

Of course the obvious answer is to deploy biometrics across the board, but once you start reviewing the costs associated with biometrics you quickly realize that this is not feasible. What is coming to the rescue to help with the password nightmare we have created? The doodle. Background Draw-a-Secret (BDAS) is a new program created by scientists at Newcastle University in England. BDAS begins by recording the number of strokes it takes a user to draw a doodle and when the user wants to gain access to the system he simply redraws the doodle on a touchpad and it is matched against the stored prototype. If the doodle matches, the user is granted access. Doodles are even described as being far more anonymous, therefore offering greater security, than biometrics.

You are probably thinking that you'll end up right back in the same position having to remember all 72 of your password doodles. The good news is that with doodle passwords you don't have to remember a thing. The doodle password can be displayed to users, and they simply have to redraw it since the system analyzes how the user draws or the user's unique hand strokes, not the actual doodle (similar to handwriting recognition technologies).[16]

If you were going to deploy doodle passwords to your organization, what issues and concerns do you think might occur? Do you agree that doodles are easier to remember than text passwords? Do you agree that doodles offer the most effective way to manage authentication and authorization, even greater than biometrics? What types of unethical issues do you think you might encounter with doodle passwords?

Something the User Knows Such as a User ID and Password   The first type of authentication, using something the user knows, is the most common way to identify individual users and typically consists of a unique user ID and password. However, this is actually one of the most *ineffective* ways for determining authentication because passwords are not secure. All it typically takes to crack one is enough time. More than 50 percent of help-desk calls are password related, which can cost an organization significant money, and a social engineer can coax a password from almost anybody.

Something the User Has Such as a Smart Card or Token   The second type of authentication, using something the user has, offers a much more effective way to identify individuals than a user ID and password. Tokens and smart cards are two of the primary forms of this type of authentication. *Tokens* are small electronic devices that change user passwords automatically. The user enters his or her user ID and token-displayed password to gain access to the network. A *smart card* is a device about the size of a credit card, containing embedded technologies that can store information and small amounts of software to perform some limited processing. Smart cards can act as identification instruments, a form of digital cash, or a data storage device with the ability to store an entire medical record.

Something That Is Part of the User Such as a Fingerprint or Voice Signature The third kind of authentication, something that is part of the user, is by far the best and most effective way to manage authentication. *Biometrics* (narrowly defined) is the identification of a user based on a physical characteristic, such as a fingerprint, iris, face, voice, or handwriting. Unfortunately, biometric authentication can be costly and intrusive.

Data: Prevention and Resistance

Prevention and resistance technologies stop intruders from accessing and reading data by means of content filtering, encryption, and firewalls. *Time bombs* are computer viruses that wait for a specific date before executing their instructions. *Content filtering* occurs when organizations use software that filters content, such as emails, to prevent the accidental or malicious transmission of unauthorized information. Organizations can use content filtering technologies to filter email and prevent emails containing sensitive information from transmitting, whether the transmission was malicious or accidental. It can also filter emails and prevent any suspicious files from transmitting such as potential virus-infected files. Email content filtering can also filter for spam, a form of unsolicited email.

Encryption scrambles information into an alternative form that requires a key or password to decrypt. If there were a security breach and the stolen information were encrypted, the thief would be unable to read it. Encryption can switch the order of characters, replace characters with other characters, insert or remove characters, or use a mathematical formula to convert the information into a code. Companies that transmit sensitive customer information over the Internet, such as credit card numbers, frequently use encryption. To *decrypt* information is to decode it and is the opposite of *encrypt*. *Cryptography* is the science that studies encryption, which is the hiding of messages so that only the sender and receiver can read them. The National Institute of Standards and Technology (NIST) introduced an *advanced encryption standard (AES)* designed to keep government information secure.

Some encryption technologies use multiple keys. *Public key encryption (PKE)* uses two keys: a public key that everyone can have and a private key for only the recipient (see Figure 4.15). The organization provides the public key to all customers, whether end consumers or other businesses, who use that key to encrypt their information and send it via the Internet. When it arrives at its destination, the organization uses the private key to unscramble it.

Public keys are becoming popular to use for authentication techniques consisting of digital objects in which a trusted third party confirms correlation between the user and the public key. A *certificate authority* is a trusted third party, such as VeriSign, that validates user identities by means of digital certificates. A *digital certificate* is a

FIGURE 4.15

Public Key Encryption (PKE)

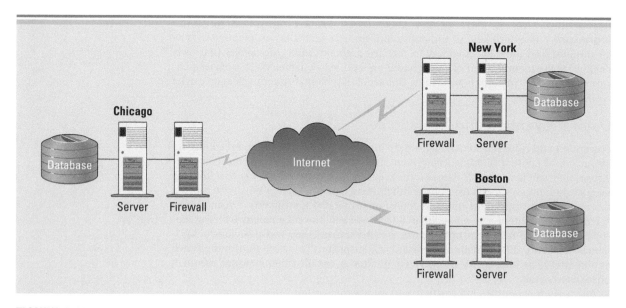

FIGURE 4.16

Sample Firewall Architecture
Connecting Systems Located in
Chicago, New York, and Boston

data file that identifies individuals or organizations online and is comparable to a digital signature.

A *firewall* is hardware and/or software that guard a private network by analyzing incoming and outgoing information for the correct markings. If they are missing, the firewall prevents the information from entering the network. Firewalls can even detect computers communicating with the Internet without approval. As Figure 4.16 illustrates, organizations typically place a firewall between a server and the Internet. Think of a firewall as a gatekeeper that protects computer networks from intrusion by providing a filter and safe transfer points for access to and from the Internet and other networks. It screens all network traffic for proper passwords or other security codes and allows only authorized transmissions in and out of the network.

Firewalls do not guarantee complete protection, and users should enlist additional security technologies such as antivirus software and antispyware software. *Antivirus software* scans and searches hard drives to prevent, detect, and remove known viruses, adware, and spyware. Antivirus software must be frequently updated to protect against newly created viruses.

Attack: Detection and Response

Cyberwar is an organized attempt by a country's military to disrupt or destroy information and communication systems for another country. *Cyberterrorism* is the use of computer and networking technologies against persons or property to intimidate or coerce governments, individuals, or any segment of society to attain political, religious, or ideological goals. With so many intruders planning computer attacks, it is critical that all computer systems are protected. The presence of an intruder can be detected by watching for suspicious network events such as bad passwords, the removal of highly classified data files, or unauthorized user attempts. *Intrusion detection software (IDS)* features full-time monitoring tools that search for patterns in network traffic to identify intruders. IDS protects against suspicious network traffic and attempts to access files and data. If a suspicious event or unauthorized traffic is identified, the IDS will generate an alarm and can even be customized to shut down a particularly sensitive part of a network. After identifying an attack, an MIS department can implement response tactics to mitigate the damage. Response tactics outline procedures such as how long a system under attack will remain plugged in and connected to the corporate network,

BUSINESS DRIVEN START-UP

Have you ever seen a LifeLock advertisement? If so, you know the Social Security number of LifeLock CEO Todd Davis because he posts it in all ads daring hackers to try to steal his identity. Davis has been a victim of identity theft at least 13 times. The first theft occurred when someone used his identity to secure a $500 loan from a check-cashing company. Davis discovered the crime only after the company called his wife's cell phone to recover the unpaid debt.[17]

If you were starting an identity theft prevention company, do you think it would be a good idea to post your Social Security number in advertisements? Why or why not? What do you think happened that caused Davis' identity to be stolen? What types of information security measure should LifeLock implement to ensure Davis' Social Security number is not stolen again? If you were LifeLock's CEO, what type of marketing campaign would you launch next?

LifeLock: Keeping Your Identity Safe

when to shut down a compromised system, and how quickly a backup system will be up and running.

Guaranteeing the safety of organization information is achieved by implementing the two lines of defense: people and technology. To protect information through people, firms should develop information security policies and plans that provide employees with specific precautions they should take in creating, working with, and transmitting the organization's information assets. Technology-based lines of defense fall into three categories: authentication and authorization; prevention and resistance; and detection and response.

LEARNING OUTCOME REVIEW

Learning Outcome 4.1: Explain the ethical issues in the use of information technology.

Information ethics govern the ethical and moral issues arising from the development and use of information technologies, as well as the creation, collection, duplication, distribution, and processing of information itself (with or without the aid of computer technologies). Ethical dilemmas in this area usually arise not as simple, clear-cut situations but as clashes between competing goals, responsibilities, and loyalties. Inevitably, there will be more than one socially acceptable or "correct" decision. For this reason, acting ethically and legally are not always the same.

Learning Outcome 4.2: Identify the six epolicies organizations should implement to protect themselves.

1. An ethical computer use policy contains general principles to guide computer user behavior. For example, it might explicitly state that users should refrain from playing computer games during working hours.

2. An information privacy policy contains general principles regarding information privacy.

3. An acceptable use policy (AUP) is a policy that a user must agree to follow in order to be provided access to corporate email, information systems, and to the Internet.

4. An email privacy policy details the extent to which email messages may be read by others.

5. A social media policy outlines the corporate guidelines or principles governing employee online communications.

6. An employee monitoring policy states explicitly how, when, and where the company monitors its employees.

Learning Outcome 4.3: Describe the relationships and differences between hackers and viruses.

Hackers are experts in technology who use their knowledge to break into computers and computer networks, either for profit or just motivated by the challenge. A virus is software written with malicious intent to cause annoyance or damage. Some hackers create and leave viruses causing massive computer damage.

Learning Outcome 4.4: Describe the relationship between information security policies and an information security plan.

Information security policies identify the rules required to maintain information security, such as requiring users to log off before leaving for lunch or meetings, never sharing passwords with anyone, and changing passwords every 30 days. An information security plan details how an organization will implement the information security policies. The best way a company can safeguard itself from people is by implementing and communicating its information security plan.

Learning Outcome 4.5: Provide an example of each of the three primary information security areas: (1) authentication and authorization, (2) prevention and resistance, and (3) detection and response.

Authentication and authorization: Authentication is a method for confirming users' identities. Once a system determines the authentication of a user, it can then determine the access privileges (or authorization) for that user. Authorization is the process of providing a user with permission including access levels and abilities such as file access, hours of access, and amount of allocated storage space.

Prevention and resistance: Content filtering occurs when organizations use software that filters content, such as emails, to prevent the accidental or malicious transmission of unauthorized information. Encryption scrambles information into an alternative form that requires a key or password to decrypt. In a security breach, a thief is unable to read encrypted information. A firewall is hardware and/or software that guard a private network by analyzing incoming and outgoing information for the correct markings.

Detection and response: Intrusion detection software (IDS) features full-time monitoring tools that search for patterns in network traffic to identify intruders.

OPENING CASE QUESTIONS

1. **Knowledge:** Define information ethics and information security and explain why each is critical to any business.

2. **Comprehension:** Identify two epolicies that a business could implement to ensure the protection of sensitive corporate data.

3. **Application:** Demonstrate how a business can use authentication and authorization technologies to prevent information theft.

4. **Analysis:** Analyze how a business can use prevention and resistance technologies to safeguard its employees from hackers and viruses.

5. **Synthesis:** Propose a plan to implement information security plans to ensure your critical information is safe and protected.

6. **Evaluate:** Evaluate the information security issues facing a business and identify its three biggest concerns.

KEY TERMS

Acceptable use policy (AUP), 146
Adware, 153
Advanced encryption standard (AES), 159
Anti-spam policy, 148
Antivirus software, 160
Authentication, 157
Authorization, 157
Biometrics, 159
Black-hat hackers, 153
Certificate authority, 159
Child Online Protection Act (COPA), 145
Click-fraud, 145
Competitive click-fraud, 145
Confidentiality, 141
Content filtering, 159
Copyright, 141
Counterfeit software, 141
Cracker, 153
Cryptography, 159
Cyberterrorists, 153
Cyberbullying, 145
Cybervandalism, 147
Cyberterrorism, 160
Cyberwar, 160
Decrypt, 159
Destructive agents, 157
Digital certificate, 159
Digital rights management, 141
Downtime, 151

Drive-by hacking, 153
Dumpster diving, 155
Ediscovery (or electronic discovery), 145
Email privacy policy, 147
Employee monitoring policy, 150
Encryption, 159
Epolicies, 145
Ethical computer use policy, 146
Ethics, 141
Firewall, 160
Hackers, 153
Hactivists, 153
Identity theft, 156
Information compliance, 144
Information ethics, 141
Information governance, 144
Information management, 144
Information property, 144
Information secrecy, 156
Information privacy policy, 146
Information security, 153
Information security plan, 155
Information security policies, 155
Insiders, 155
Intellectual property, 141
Internet censorship, 147
Internet use policy, 146
Intrusion detection software (IDS), 160
Mail bomb, 148

Nonrepudiation, 146
Opt out, 148
Patent, 141
Pharming, 157
Pharming attack, 157
Phishing, 156
Phishing expedition, 156
Physical security, 150
Pirated software, 141
Privacy, 141
Public key encryption (PKE), 159
Script kiddies or script bunnies, 153
Smart card, 158
Spear phishing, 156
Social engineering, 155
Social media policy, 149
Spam, 148
Spyware, 154
Teergrubing, 148
Threat, 142
Time bomb, 159
Tokens, 158
Typosquatting, 147
Virus, 153
Vishing (voice phishing), 156
Website name stealing, 147
White-hat hackers, 153
Workplace MIS monitoring, 150
Zombie, 157
Zombie farm, 157

REVIEW QUESTIONS

1. What are ethics and why are they important to a company?
2. What is the relationship between information management, governance, and compliance?
3. Why are epolicies important to a company?
4. What is the correlation between privacy and confidentiality?
5. What is the relationship between adware and spyware?
6. What are the positive and negative effects associated with monitoring employees?
7. What is the relationship between hackers and viruses?
8. Why is security a business issue, not just a technology issue?
9. What are the growing issues related to employee communication methods and what can a company do to protect itself?
10. How can a company participating in ebusiness keep its information secure?
11. What technologies can a company use to safeguard information?
12. Why is ediscovery important to a company?
13. What are the reasons a company experiences downtime?
14. What are the costs associated with downtime?

CLOSING CASE ONE

E-Espionage

BusinessWeek magazine probed the rising attacks on America's most sensitive computer networks, uncovering startling security gaps. The email message addressed to a Booz Allen Hamilton executive from the Pentagon was mundane—a shopping list of weaponry India wanted to buy. But the missive was a brilliant fake. Lurking beneath the description of aircraft, engines, and radar equipment was an insidious piece of computer code, known as Poison Ivy, designed to suck sensitive data out of the $4 billion consulting firm's computer network.

The Pentagon had not sent the email. Its origin is unknown, but the message traveled through Korea on its way to Booz Allen. Its authors knew enough about the "sender" and "recipient" to craft a message unlikely to arouse suspicion. Had the Booz Allen executive clicked on the attachment, his every keystroke would have been reported back to a mysterious master at the Internet address cybersyndrome.3322.org, which is registered through an obscure company headquartered on the banks of China's Yangtze River.

The email aimed at Booz Allen paints a vivid picture of the alarming new capabilities of America's cyberenemies. The email message was sent to John F. "Jack" Mulhern, vice president for international military assistance programs at Booz Allen. In the high-tech world of weapons sales, Mulhern's specialty, the email looked authentic enough. "Integrate U.S., Russian, and Indian weapons and avionics," the email noted, describing the Indian government's expectations for its fighter jets. "Source code given to India for indigenous computer upgrade capability." Such lingo could easily be understood by Mulhern. The 62-year-old former U.S. Naval officer and 33-year veteran of Booz Allen's military consulting business is an expert in helping to sell U.S. weapons to foreign governments.

The email was more convincing because of its apparent sender: Stephen J. Moree, a civilian who worked for a group that reported to the office of then-Air Force Secretary Michael W. Wynne. Among its duties, Moree's unit evaluated the security of selling U.S. military aircraft to other countries. There would be little reason to suspect anything seriously amiss in Moree passing along the highly technical document with "India MRCA Request for Proposal" in the subject line. The Indian government had just released the request a week earlier, on August 28, and the language in the email closely tracked the request. Making the message appear more credible still, it referred to upcoming Air Force communiqués and a "Team Meeting" to discuss the deal.

But the correspondence from Moree to Jack Mulhern was a fake. An analysis of the email's path and attachment, conducted for *BusinessWeek* by three cybersecurity specialists, shows it was sent by an unknown attacker, bounced through an Internet address in South Korea, relayed through a Yahoo! server in New York, and finally made its way to Mulhern's Booz Allen in-box. The analysis also shows the code—known as malware, for malicious software—tracks keystrokes on the computers of people who open it. A separate program disables security measures such as password protection on Microsoft Access database files, a program often used by large organizations such as the U.S. defense industry to manage big batches of data.

Global Threats

The U.S. government and its sprawl of defense contractors have been the victims of an unprecedented rash of similar attacks, say current and former U.S. government officials. "It's espionage on a massive scale," said Paul B. Kurtz, a former high-ranking national security official. Government agencies reported 12,986 cybersecurity incidents to the U.S. Homeland Security Department in one fiscal year, triple the number from two years earlier. Incursions on the military's networks were up 55 percent, said Lieutenant General Charles E. Croom, head of the Pentagon's Joint Task Force for Global Network Operations. Private targets such as Booz Allen are just as vulnerable and pose just as much potential security risk. "They have our information on their networks. They're building our weapon systems. You wouldn't want that in enemy hands," Croom said. Cyber attackers "are not denying, disrupting, or destroying operations—yet. But that doesn't mean they don't have the capability."

Poison Ivy

Commercial computer security firms have dubbed the malicious code hidden inside the email attachment Poison Ivy, and it has a devious—and worrisome—capability known as a RAT, a remote administration tool. RAT gives the attacker control over the host PC, capturing screen shots and perusing files. It lurks in the background of Microsoft Internet Explorer browsers while users surf the web. Then it phones home to its "master" at an Internet address currently registered under the name cybersyndrome.3322.org.

The digital trail to cybersyndrome.3322.org, followed by analysts at *BusinessWeek*'s request, leads to one of China's largest free domain-name-registration and email services. Called 3322.org, it is registered to a company called Bentium in the city of Changzhou, an industrial hub outside Shanghai. A range of security experts say that 3322.org provides names for computers and servers that act as the command and control centers for more than 10,000 pieces of malicious code launched at government and corporate networks in recent years. Many of those PCs are in China; the rest could be anywhere.

The founder of 3322.org, a 37-year-old technology entrepreneur named Peng Yong, says his company merely allows users to register domain names. "As for what our users do, we cannot completely control it," Peng said. The bottom line: If Poison Ivy infected Jack Mulhern's computer at Booz Allen, any secrets inside could be seen in China. And if it spread to other computers, as malware often does, the infection opens windows on potentially sensitive information there, too.

Many security experts worry the Internet has become too unwieldy to be tamed. New threats appear every day, each seemingly more sophisticated than the previous one. The Defense Department, whose Advanced Research Projects Agency (DARPA) developed the Internet in the 1960s, is beginning to think it created a monster. "You don't need an Army, a Navy, an Air Force to beat the U.S.," said General William T. Lord, commander of the Air Force Cyber Command, a unit formed to upgrade Air Force computer defenses. "You can be a peer force for the price of the PC on my desk."[18]

Questions

1. Define information ethics and information security and explain why each is critical to any government operation.

2. Identify two epolicies the government should implement to help combat cyberterrorism.

3. Demonstrate how the government can use authentication and authorization technologies to prevent information theft.

4. Analyze how the government can use prevention and resistance technologies to safeguard its employees from hackers and viruses.

5. Propose a plan for how the government can implement information security plans to ensure its critical information is safe and protects.

6. Evaluate the information security issues facing the government and identify its three biggest concerns.

CLOSING CASE TWO

Hacker Hunters

Hacker hunters are the new breed of crime fighter. They employ the same methodology used to fight organized crime in the 1980s—informants and the cyberworld equivalent of wiretaps. Daniel Larking, a 20-year veteran who runs the FBI's Internet Crime Complaint Center, taps online service providers to help track down criminal hackers. Leads supplied by the FBI and eBay helped Romanian police round up 11 members of a gang that set up fake eBay accounts and auctioned off cell phones, laptops, and cameras they never intended to deliver.

The FBI unleashed Operation Firewall, targeting the ShadowCrew, a gang whose members were schooled in identity theft, bank account pillage, and selling illegal goods on the Internet. ShadowCrew's 4,000 gang members lived in a dozen countries and across the United States. For months, agents had been watching their every move through a clandestine gateway into their website, shadowcrew. com. One member turned informant and called a group meeting, ensuring the members would be at home on their computers during a certain time, when the Secret Service issued orders to move in on the gang. The move was synchronized around the globe to prevent gang members from warning each other via instant messages. Twenty-eight gang members in eight states and six countries were arrested, most still at their computers. Authorities seized dozens of computers and found 1.7 million credit card numbers and more than 18 million email accounts.

ShadowCrew's Operations

The alleged ringleaders of ShadowCrew included Andres Mantovani, 23, a part-time community college student in Arizona, and David Appleyard, 45, a former New Jersey mortgage broker. Mantovani and Appleyard allegedly were administrators in charge of running the website and recruiting members. The site created a marketplace for more than 4,000 gang members who bought and sold hot information and merchandise. The website was open for business 24 hours a day, but since most of the members held jobs, the busiest time was from 10 p.m. to 2 a.m. on Sundays. Hundreds of gang members would meet online to trade credit card information, passports, and even equipment to make fake identity documents. Platinum credit cards cost more than gold ones, and discounts were offered for package deals. One member known as "Scarface" sold 115,695 stolen credit card numbers in a single trade. Overall, the gang made more than $4 million in credit card purchases over two years. ShadowCrew was equivalent to an eBay for the underworld. The site even posted crime tips on how to use stolen credit cards and fake IDs at big retailers.

The gang stole credit card numbers and other valuable information through clever tricks. One of the favorites was sending millions of phishing emails—messages that appeared to be from legitimate companies such as Yahoo!—designed to steal passwords and credit card numbers. The gang also hacked into corporate databases to steal account data. According to sources familiar with the investigation, the gang cracked the networks of 12 unidentified companies that were not even aware their systems had been breached.

Police Operations

Brian Nagel, an assistant director at the Secret Service, coordinated the effort to track the ShadowCrew. Allies included Britain's national high-tech crimes unit, the Royal Canadian Mounted Police, and the Bulgarian Interior Ministry. Authorities turned one of the high-ranking members of the gang into a snitch and had the man help the Secret Service set up a new electronic doorway for ShadowCrew members to enter their website. The snitch spread the word that the new gateway was a more secure way to the website. It was the first-ever tap of a private computer network. "We became shadowcrew. com," Nagel said. Mantovani and Appleyard were slated for trial. Authorities anticipated making additional arrests.[19]

Questions

1. What types of technology could big retailers use to prevent identity thieves from purchasing merchandise?
2. What can organizations do to protect themselves from hackers looking to steal account data?
3. Authorities frequently tap online service providers to track down hackers. Do you think it is ethical for authorities to tap an online service provider and read people's email? Why or why not?
4. Do you think it was ethical for authorities to use one of the high-ranking officials to trap other gang members? Why or why not?
5. In a team, research the Internet and find the best ways to protect yourself from identity theft.

CRITICAL BUSINESS THINKING

1. Cheerleader Charged $27,750 for File Sharing 37 Songs

A federal appeals court is ordering a university student to pay the Recording Industry Association of America $27,750—$750 a track—for file sharing 37 songs when she was a high school cheerleader. Have you ever illegally copied or downloaded a song or movie? If you have and you were forced to pay $750 per track, how much would you owe? What is the difference between file sharing and Internet radio streaming? Do you agree or disagree with the federal appeals decision? Why or why not? Why is claiming a lack of copyright knowledge not a good defense against illegally sharing movies or music? If you do not have a good understanding of information laws, what can you do to ensure you are never placed in a federal lawsuit for violating information laws?[20]

2. Police Records Found in Old Copy Machine

Copy machines made after 2002 all contain a hard drive that stores a copy of every document the machine has ever scanned, printed, copied, or faxed. If the hard drive is not erased or scrubbed when the copy machine is resold, all of that digital information is still maintained inside the machine. The Buffalo, New York, Police Sex Crimes Division recently sold several copy machines without scrubbing the hard drives. The hard drives yielded detailed domestic violence complaints and a list of wanted sex offenders. A machine from the Buffalo Police Narcotics Unit contained targets in a major drug raid, and a copier once used by a New York construction company stored 95 pages of pay stubs with names, addresses, and Social Security numbers.[21]

Who do you think should be held responsible for the information issues caused at the Buffalo police department? What types of ethical issues and information security issues are being violated? What types of epolicies could a company implement to ensure these situations do not occur? What forms of information security could a company implement to ensure these situations do not occur? How does this case support the primary reason why ediscovery is so important to litigation?

3. Firewall Decisions

You are the CEO of Inverness Investments, a medium-size venture capital firm that specializes in investing in high-tech companies. The company receives more than 30,000 email messages per year. On average, there are two viruses and three successful hackings against the company each year, which result in losses to the company of about $250,000. Currently, the company has antivirus software installed but does not have any firewalls.

Your CIO is suggesting implementing 10 firewalls for a total cost of $80,000. The estimated life of each firewall is about three years. The chances of hackers breaking into the system with the firewalls installed are about 3 percent. Annual maintenance costs on the firewalls are estimated around $15,000. Create an argument for or against supporting your CIO's recommendation to purchase the firewalls. Are there any considerations in addition to finances?

4. Preventing Identity Theft

The FBI states that identity theft is one of the fastest-growing crimes. If you are a victim of identity theft, your financial reputation can be ruined, making it impossible for you to cash a check or receive a bank loan. Learning how to avoid identity theft can be a valuable activity. Using the Internet, research the most current ways the government recommends for you to to prevent identity theft.

5. Discussing the Three Areas of Information Security

Great Granola Inc. is a small business operating out of northern California. The company specializes in selling homemade granola, and its primary sales vehicle is through its website. The company is growing exponentially and expects its revenues to triple this year to $12 million.

The company also expects to hire 60 additional employees to support its growth. Joan Martin, the CEO, is aware that if her competitors discover the recipe for her granola, or who her primary customers are, it could easily ruin her business. Martin has hired you to draft a document discussing the different areas of information security, along with your recommendations for providing a secure ebusiness environment.

6. **Spying on Email**

Technology advances now allow individuals to monitor computers that they do not even have physical access to. New types of software can capture an individual's incoming and outgoing email and then immediately forward that email to another person. For example, if you are at work and your child is home from school and she receives an email from John at 3:00 p.m., at 3:01 p.m. you can receive a copy of that email sent to your email address. If she replies to John's email, within seconds you will again receive a copy of what she sent to John. Describe two scenarios (other than those described here) for the use of this type of software: one in which the use would be ethical and one in which it would be unethical.

7. **Stealing Software**

The software industry fights against pirated software on a daily basis. The major centers of software piracy are in places such as Russia and China where salaries and disposable income are comparatively low. People in developing and economically depressed countries will fall behind the industrialized world technologically if they cannot afford access to new generations of software. Considering this, is it reasonable to blame someone for using pirated software when it could cost him or her two months' salary to purchase a legal copy? Create an argument for or against the following statement: Individuals who are economically less fortunate should be allowed access to software free of charge in order to ensure that they are provided with an equal technological advantage.

ENTREPRENEURIAL CHALLENGE

BUILD YOUR OWN BUSINESS

1. Providing employees with computer access is one of the perks offered by your business. Employees enjoy checking their personal email and surfing the Internet on their breaks. So far, computer access has been a cherished employee benefit. When you came into work this morning you found the following anonymous letter from one of your employees on your desk. "I received a highly inappropriate joke from a fellow employee that I found extremely offensive. The employee who sent the joke was Debbie Fernandez and I believe she should be reprimanded for her inappropriate actions. Signed—a disturbed employee." What would you do? What could you have done to ensure situations such as these would be easily handled if they did arise? What could you do to ensure such situations do not happen in the future and if they do all employees are aware of the ramifications of inappropriate emails? (Be sure to identify your business and the name of your company.)

2. The local community has always been a big part of your grandfather's business and he knew almost everyone in the community. Your grandfather attended all types of community events and would spend hours talking with friends and neighbors soliciting feedback and ideas on his business. As you know, data are important to any business. In fact, data are an essential business asset. You have decided to start tracking detailed customer information for all business events from fund-raising to promotions. Since you took over the business you have been collecting more and more event data to help you run marketing campaigns across events and optimize the event schedules. One day, a sophisticated businessman walks into your business and asks to speak

to the owner. He introduces himself as Lance Smith and says that he would like to talk to you in private. Smith is retiring and is closing his business that was located just down the street, and he wants to sell you his detailed customer information. Smith would like a large sum of money to sell you his confidential customer contact information and sales reports for the past 20 years. He says he has more than 10,000 customers in his unique database. What do you do?

3. Yesterday you had an interesting conversation with one of your loyal customers, Dan Martello. He asked you the following question: "If I find a digital camera on the street is it OK to look at the contents, or am I invading the owner's privacy?" You have a lengthy debate and decided that in some scenarios it is an invasion of privacy to be looking at someone else's photos and is similar to looking in their windows. In other scenarios, it is not an invasion of privacy if you do not know the person and it is the primary way to identify the owner to return the camera, similar to looking in a wallet. As you are cleaning your business, you find a 30 gigabyte thumb drive and you know that it probably belongs to one of your valuable customers and contains their sensitive information. What do you do? What security concerns are associated with the thumb drive? How could information security policies or an information security plan help your business with this type of situation?

APPLY YOUR KNOWLEDGE BUSINESS PROJECTS

PROJECT I   Grading Security

Making The Grade is a nonprofit organization that helps students learn how to achieve better grades in school. The organization has 40 offices in 25 states and more than 2,000 employees. The company wants to build a website to offer its services online. Making The Grade's online services will provide parents seven key pieces of advice for communicating with their children to help them achieve academic success. The website will offer information on how to maintain open lines of communication, set goals, organize academics, regularly track progress, identify trouble spots, get to know their child's teacher, and celebrate their children's successes.

You and your team work for the director of information security. Your team's assignment is to develop a document discussing the importance of creating information security polices and an information security plan. Be sure to include the following:

- The importance of educating employees on information security.
- A few samples of employee information security policies specifically for Making The Grade.
- Other major areas the information security plan should address.
- Signs the company should look for to determine if the website is being hacked.
- The major types of attacks the company should expect to experience.

PROJECT II   Eyes Everywhere

The movie *Minority Report* chronicled a futuristic world where people are uniquely identifiable by their eyes. A scan of each person's eyes gives or denies them access to rooms, computers, and anything else with restrictions. The movie portrayed a black market in new eyeballs to help people hide from the authorities. (Why did they not just change the database entry instead? That would have been much easier, but a lot less dramatic.)

The idea of using a biological signature is entirely plausible because biometrics is currently being used and is expected to gain wider acceptance in the near future because forging documents has become much easier with the advances in computer graphics programs and color printers. The next time you get a new passport, it may incorporate a chip that has your biometric information encoded on it. Office of Special Investigations agents with fake documents found that it was relatively easy to enter the United States from Canada, Mexico, and Jamaica, by land, sea, and air.

The task of policing the borders is daunting. Some 500 million foreigners enter the country every year and go through identity checkpoints. More than 13 million permanent-resident and border-crossing cards have been issued by the U.S. government. Also, citizens of 27 countries do not need visas to enter this country. They are expected to have passports that comply with U.S. specifications that will also be readable at the border.

In the post-9/11 atmosphere of tightened security, unrestricted border crossing is not acceptable. The Department of Homeland Security is charged with securing the nation's borders, and as part of this plan, new entry/exit procedures were instituted at the beginning of 2003. An integrated system, using biometrics, will be used to identify foreign visitors to the United States and reduce the likelihood of terrorists entering the country.

Early in 2003, after 6 million biometric border-crossing cards had been issued, a pilot test conducted at the Canadian border detected more than 250 imposters. The testing started with two biometric identifiers: photographs for facial recognition and fingerprint scans. As people enter and leave the country, their actual fingerprints and facial features are compared to the data on the biometric chip in the passport.

In a group, discuss the following:

a. How do you feel about having your fingerprints, facial features, and perhaps more of your biometric features encoded in documents such as your passport? Explain your answer.

b. Would you feel the same way about having biometric information on your driver's license as on your passport? Why or why not?

c. Is it reasonable to have different biometric identification requirements for visitors from different nations? Explain your answer. What would you recommend as criteria for deciding which countries fall into what categories?

d. The checkpoints U.S. citizens pass through upon returning to the country vary greatly in the depth of the checks and the time spent. The simplest involves simply walking past the border guards who may or may not ask you your citizenship. The other end of the spectrum requires that you put up with long waits in airports where you have to line up with hundreds of other passengers while each person is questioned and must produce a passport to be scanned. Would you welcome biometric information on passports if it would speed the process, or do you think that the disadvantages of the reduction in privacy, caused by biometric information, outweigh the advantages of better security and faster border processing? Explain your answer.

PROJECT III   Setting Boundaries

Even the most ethical people sometimes face difficult choices. Acting ethically means behaving in a principled fashion and treating other people with respect and dignity. It is simple to say, but not so simple to do since some situations are complex or ambiguous. The important role of ethics in our lives has long been recognized. As far back as 44 B.C., Cicero said that ethics are indispensable to anyone who wants to have a good career. Having said that, Cicero, along with some of the greatest minds over the centuries, struggled with what the rules of ethics should be.

Our ethics are rooted in our history, culture, and religion, and our sense of ethics may shift over time. The electronic age brings with it a new dimension in the ethics debate—the amount of personal information that we can collect and store, and the speed with which we can access and process that information.

In a group, discuss how you would react to the following situations:

a. A senior marketing manager informs you that one of her employees is looking for another job and she wants you to give her access to look through her email.

b. A vice president of sales informs you that he has made a deal to provide customer information to a strategic partner, and he wants you to copy all of the customer information to a thumb drive.

c. You are asked to monitor your employee's email to discover whether he is sexually harassing another employee.

d. You are asked to install a video surveillance system in your office to find out whether employees are taking office supplies home with them.

e. You are looking on the shared network drive and discover that your boss's entire hard drive has been copied to the network for everyone to view. What do you do?

f. You have been accidentally copied on an email from the CEO, which details who will be the targets of the next round of layoffs. What do you do?

PROJECT IV   Contemplating Sharing

Bram Cohen created BitTorrent which allows users to upload and download large amounts of data. Cohen demonstrated his program at the world hacker conference, as a free, open source project aimed at computer users who need a cheap way to swap software online. Soon many TV and movie fanatics began using the program to download copyrighted materials. As a result of the hacker conference, more than 20 million people downloaded the BitTorrent program and began sharing movies and television shows across the Internet.

There is much debate surrounding the ethics of peer-to-peer networking. Do you believe BitTorrent is ethical or unethical? Justify your answer.

AYK APPLICATION PROJECTS

If you are looking for Excel projects to incorporate into your class, try any of the following after reading this chapter.

Project Number	Project Name	Project Type	Plug-In Focus Area	Project Focus	Project Skill Set	Page Number
1	Financial Destiny	Excel	T2	Personal Budget	Introductory Formulas	AYK.4
2	Cash Flow	Excel	T2	Cash Flow	Introductory Formulas	AYK.4
3	Technology Budget	Excel	T1, T2	Hardware and Software	Introductory Formulas	AYK.4
4	Tracking Donations	Excel	T2	Employee Relationships	Introductory Formulas	AYK.4
5	Convert Currency	Excel	T2	Global Commerce	Introductory Formulas	AYK.5
6	Cost Comparison	Excel	T2	Total Cost of Ownership	Introductory Formulas	AYK.5
7	Time Management	Excel or Project	T2 or T12	Project Management	Introductory Gantt Charts	AYK.6
8	Maximize Profit	Excel	T2, T4	Strategic Analysis	Intermediate Formulas or Solver	AYK.6
9	Security Analysis	Excel	T3	Filtering Data	Intermediate Conditional Formatting, Autofilter, Subtotal	AYK.7
10	Gathering Data	Excel	T3	Data Analysis	Intermediate Conditional Formatting, PivotTable	AYK.8
11	Scanner System	Excel	T2	Strategic Analysis	Intermediate	AYK.8
12	Competitive Pricing	Excel	T2	Profit Maximization	Intermediate	AYK.9
13	Adequate Acquisitions	Excel	T2	Break-Even Analysis	Intermediate	AYK.9
24	Electronic Resumes	HTML	T9, T10, T11	Electronic Personal Marketing	Introductory Structural Tags	AYK.16
25	Gathering Feedback	Dreamweaver	T9, T10, T11	Data Collection	Intermediate Organization of Information	AYK.16

Infrastructures: Sustainable Technologies

5

CHAPTER OUTLINE

What's in IT for me?

Why do you, as a business student, need to understand the underlying technology of any company? Most people think "that technical stuff" is something they will never personally encounter and for that reason do not need to know anything about MIS infrastructures. Well, those people will be challenged in the business world. When your database fails and you lose all of your sales history, you will personally feel the impact when you are unable to receive your bonus. When your computer crashes and you lose all of your confidential information, not to mention your emails, calendars, and messages, then you will understand why everyone needs to learn about MIS infrastructures. You never want to leave the critical task of backing up your data to your MIS department. You want to personally ensure that your information is not only backed up, but also safeguarded and recoverable. For these reasons, business professionals in the 21st century need to acquire a base-level appreciation of what MIS can and cannot do for their company. Understanding how MIS supports growth, operations, profitability, and most recently sustainability, is crucial whether one is new to the workforce or a seasoned *Fortune* 500 employee. One of the primary goals of this chapter is to create a more level playing field between you as a business professional and the MIS specialists with whom you will work. After reading it you should have many of the skills you need to assist in analyzing current and even some future MIS infrastructures; in recommending needed changes in processes; and in evaluating alternatives that support a company's growth, operations, and profits.

Pandora's Music Box

Napster was one of the first service providers for sharing online music. Many other companies have attempted to legally jump into the online music business, and most found little success. However, Pandora, the Internet radio site, is becoming the exception. Pandora provides users with the ability to choose specific artists or categories of music and then creates individualized playlists. Based on user feedback to Pandora's suggestions of similar tracks, the site "learns" what selections each listener prefers for his or her playlist and uses that information to generate a unique customized listening experience for each.

At the heart of Pandora's business is the Music Genome Project (MGP), a computerized jukebox of more than 700,000 works by 80,000 artists, with new ones added every day. Each selection within the MGP is categorized by hundreds of characteristics, including artist and genre and covering the qualities of melody, harmony, rhythm, form, composition, and lyrics. For example, if someone is looking for a song with a certain tempo or wants to know what the lyrics are about, Pandora can supply that information. The company has 50 employees whose sole job is to listen to and analyze music along with assigning more than 400 characteristics to each track.

Computing Merges with Connectivity

Pandora is a perfect example of cloud computing as a result of three major trends:

1. The marriage of computing and connectivity can now occur without having to be tethered to a single location. It's among the biggest disruptive forces of modern times; one that will redefine business models for decades to come.

2. The mobile Internet is now pervasive.

3. The availability of low-cost, always-on computers—smartphones—that allow sophisticated software to conduct complex tasks on the go.

Pandora is strategically planning to reach a broad, global market by embedding itself in all sorts of Internet-enabled electronic devices that can access its services directly through the cloud. Pandora's music offerings are now being embedded in everything from thin LED televisions to Blu-ray players to digital frames. Customers are listening to Pandora through their Blu-ray players, iPods, iPhones, and BlackBerrys, and soon cars will come with Pandora preinstalled.

The Pandora team envisions Pandora playing everywhere, allowing users to create as many as 100 stations, allowing for a nearly infinite list of musical opportunities. Since its founding in 2000, Pandora has registered more than 50 million listeners and adds thousands more every day.

A basic membership, which includes an occasional advertisement or two, is free. Members are allowed 40 hours a month to listen to their personal stations. If users want more than 40 hours, they can purchase unlimited playing time for 99 cents per month. Users can upgrade even further to a Pandora One account for $36 a year that includes unlimited playing time, no advertisements, and a higher-quality sound.

What drives Pandora's business? Other than its valued customer base, it is the company's solid MIS infrastructure that supports its growth, operations, and profits. So far, Pandora's investment in MIS infrastructure has delivered wonderful results as well as future opportunities. The company can now develop new applications that support its core functions more rapidly than ever. And since Pandora is located in the cloud, the company has created an MIS infrastructure that is accessible, available, flexible, scalable, reliable, and usable and that performs to meet the needs of its growing customer community.[1]

section 5.1 | MIS Infrastructures

5.1 Explain MIS infrastructure and its three primary types.

5.2 Identify the three primary areas associated with an information MIS infrastructure.

5.3 Describe the characteristics of an agile MIS infrastructure.

LO 5.1: Explain MIS infrastructure and its three primary types.

THE BUSINESS BENEFITS OF A SOLID MIS INFRASTRUCTURE

Management information systems have played a significant role in business strategies, affected business decisions and processes, and even changed the way companies operate. What is the foundation supporting all of these systems that enable business growth, operations, and profits? What supports the volume and complexity of today's user and application requirements? What protects systems from failures and crashes? It is the *MIS infrastructure*, which includes the plans for how a firm will build, deploy, use, and share its data, processes, and MIS assets. A solid MIS infrastructure can reduce costs, improve productivity, optimize business operations, generate growth, and increase profitability.

Briefly defined, *hardware* consists of the physical devices associated with a computer system, and *software* is the set of instructions the hardware executes to carry out specific tasks. In today's business environment, most hardware and software is run via a network. A *network* is a communications system created by linking two or more devices and establishing a standard methodology in which they can communicate. As more companies need to share more information, the network takes on greater importance in the infrastructure. Most companies use a specific form of network infrastructure called a client and server network. A *client* is a computer designed to request information from a server. A *server* is a computer dedicated to providing information in response to requests. A good way to understand this is when someone uses a web browser (this would be the client) to access a website (this would be a server that would respond with the web page being requested by the client). Anyone not familiar with the basics of hardware, software, or networks should review Appendix A, "Hardware and Software," and Appendix B, "Networks and Telecommunications," for more information.

In the physical world, a detailed blueprint would show how public utilities, such as water, electricity, and gas support the foundation of a building. MIS infrastructure is similar as it shows in detail how the hardware, software, and network connectivity support the firm's processes. Every company, regardless of size, relies on some form of MIS infrastructure, whether it is a few personal computers networked together sharing an Excel file or a large multinational company with thousands of employees interconnected around the world.

An MIS infrastructure is dynamic; it continually changes as the business needs change. Each time a new form of Internet-enabled device, such as an iPhone or Black-Berry, is created and made available to the public, a firm's MIS infrastructure must be revised to support the device. This moves beyond just innovations in hardware to include new types of software and network connectivity. An *enterprise architect* is a person grounded in technology, fluent in business, and able to provide the important bridge between MIS and the business. Firms employ enterprise architects to help manage change and dynamically update MIS infrastructure. Figure 5.1 displays the three primary areas where enterprise architects focus when maintaining a firm's MIS infrastructure.

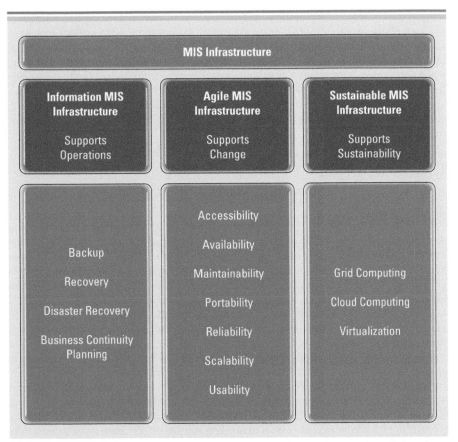

FIGURE 5.1

MIS Infrastructures

- **Supporting operations:** *Information MIS infrastructure* identifies where and how important information, such as customer records, is maintained and secured.
- **Supporting change:** *Agile MIS Infrastructure* includes the hardware, software, and telecommunications equipment that, when combined, provides the underlying foundation to support the organization's goals.
- **Supporting the environment:** *Sustainable MIS infrastructure* identifies ways that a company can grow in terms of computing resources while simultaneously becoming less dependent on hardware and energy consumption.

SUPPORTING OPERATIONS: INFORMATION MIS INFRASTRUCTURE

LO 5.2: Identify the three primary areas associated with an information MIS infrastructure.

Imagine taking a quick trip to the printer on the other side of the room, and when you turn around you find that your laptop has been stolen. How painful would you find this experience? What types of information would you lose? How much time would it take you to recover all of that information? A few things you might lose include music, movies, emails, assignments, saved passwords, not to mention that all-important 40-page paper that took you more than a month to complete. If this sounds painful then you want to pay particular attention to this section and learn how to eliminate this pain.

An information MIS infrastructure identifies where and how important information is maintained and secured. An information infrastructure supports day-to-day business operations and plans for emergencies such as power outages, floods, earthquakes, malicious attacks via the Internet, theft, and security breaches to name just a few. Managers must take every precaution to make sure their systems are operational and protected around the clock every day of the year. Losing a laptop or experiencing bad weather in one part of the country simply cannot take down systems required to operate core business processes. In the past, someone stealing company information would have to carry out boxes upon boxes of paper. Today, as data storage technologies grow in capabilities while shrinking in size, a person can simply walk out the front door of the building with the company's data files stored on a thumb drive or external hard drive. Today's managers must act responsibly to protect one of their most valued assets, information. To support continuous business operations, an information infrastructure provides three primary elements:

- Backup and recovery plan.
- Disaster recovery plan.
- Business continuity plan (see Figure 5.2).

Backup and Recovery Plan

Each year businesses lose time and money because of system crashes and failures. One way to minimize the damage of a system crash is to have a backup and recovery strategy in place. A **backup** is an exact copy of a system's information. **Recovery** is the ability to get a system up and running in the event of a system crash or failure that includes restoring the information backup. Many different types of backup and recovery media are available, including maintaining an identical replica or redundant of the storage server, external hard drives, thumb drives, and even DVDs. The primary differences between them are speed and cost.

Fault tolerance is the ability for a system to respond to unexpected failures or system crashes as the backup system immediately and automatically takes over with no loss of service. For example, fault tolerance enables a business to support continuous business operations if there is a power failure or flood. Fault tolerance is an expensive form of backup, and only mission-critical applications and operations use it. **Failover,** a specific type of fault tolerance, occurs when a redundant storage server offers an exact replica of the real-time data, and if the primary server crashes, the users are automatically directed to the secondary server or backup server. This is a high-speed and high-cost method of backup and recovery. **Failback** occurs when the primary machine recovers and resumes operations, taking over from the secondary server.

FIGURE 5.2

Areas of Support Provided by Information Infrastructure

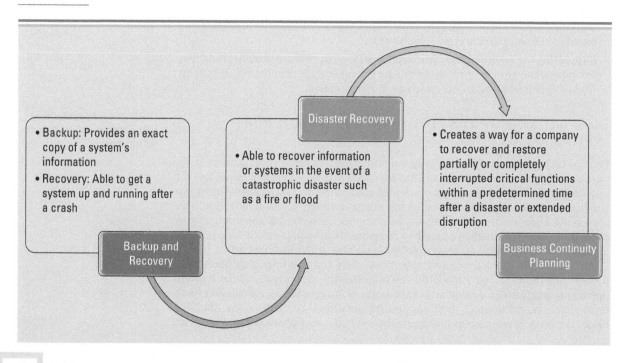

- Backup: Provides an exact copy of a system's information
- Recovery: Able to get a system up and running after a crash

Backup and Recovery

Disaster Recovery

- Able to recover information or systems in the event of a catastrophic disaster such as a fire or flood

- Creates a way for a company to recover and restore partially or completely interrupted critical functions within a predetermined time after a disaster or extended disruption

Business Continuity Planning

BUSINESS DRIVEN START-UP

Think how horrible it would be to finish your term paper at 4 a.m. and find out that your computer has a virus and you just lost your entire document. Or perhaps you submit your final paper, which is worth 50 percent of your grade, and then head off to Colorado for winter break. You return to find that you failed the course, and you frantically check email to find out what happened. A message from your professor informs you that your document was corrupt and couldn't be opened and that you had 24 hours to resend the file, which you missed because you were skiing down the slopes.

Have you ever experienced having a file corrupted? If so, what could you have done to recover from this situation? Do you think your instructor ever receives corrupted files? How did the file become corrupted? Do you think your instructor would be suspicious if you submitted a corrupted file? How could an instructor prove that your file was purchased from this site?

I Don't Have a Temperature, but I'm Positive I Have a Virus

Using DVDs or thumb drives to store your data offers a low-speed and low-cost backup method. It is a good business practice to back up data at least once a week using a low-cost method. This will alleviate the pain of having your laptop stolen or your system crash as you will still have access to your data, and it will only be a few days old.

Deciding how often to back up information and what media to use is a critical decision. Companies should choose a backup and recovery strategy in line with their goals and operational needs. If the company deals with large volumes of critical information, it will require daily, perhaps hourly, backups to storage servers. If it relies on small amounts of noncritical information, then it might require only weekly backups to external hard drives or thumb drives. A company that backs up on a weekly basis is taking the risk that, if a system crash occurs, it could lose a week's worth of work. If this risk is acceptable, a weekly backup strategy will work. If it is unacceptable, the company needs more frequent backup.

Disaster Recovery Plan

Disasters such as power outages, fires, floods, hurricanes, and even malicious activities such as hackers and viruses strike companies every day. Disasters can have the following effects on companies and their business operations.

- **Disrupting communications:** Most companies depend on voice and data communications for daily operational needs. Widespread communications outages, from either direct damage to the infrastructure or sudden spikes in usage related to an outside disaster, can be as devastating to some firms as shutting down the whole business.

- **Damaging physical infrastructures:** Fire and flood can directly damage buildings, equipment, and systems, making structures unsafe and systems unusable. Law enforcement officers and firefighters may prohibit business professionals from entering a building, thereby restricting access to retrieve documents or equipment.

- **Halting transportation:** Disasters such as floods and hurricanes can have a deep effect on transportation. Disruption to major highways, roads, bridges, railroads, and airports can prevent business professionals from reporting to work or going home, slow the delivery of supplies, and stop the shipment of products.

- **Blocking utilities:** Public utilities, such as the supply of electric power, water, and natural gas, can be interrupted for hours or days even in incidents that cause no direct damage to the physical infrastructure. Buildings are often uninhabitable and systems unable to function without public utilities.

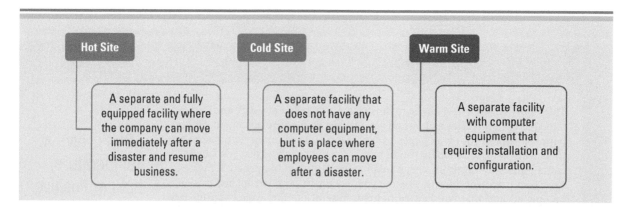

FIGURE 5.3

Sites to Support Disaster Recovery

These effects can devastate companies by causing them to cease operations for hours, days, or longer and risk losing customers whom they cannot then supply. Therefore, to combat these disasters a company can create a ***disaster recovery plan***, which is a detailed process for recovering information or a system in the event of a catastrophic disaster. This plan includes such factors as which files and systems need to have backups and their corresponding frequency and methods along with the strategic location of the storage in a separate physical site that is geographically dispersed. A company might strategically maintain operations in New York and San Francisco, ensuring that a natural disaster would not impact both locations. A disaster recovery plan also foresees the possibility that not only the computer equipment but also the building where employees work may be destroyed. A ***hot site*** is a separate and fully equipped facility where the company can move immediately after a disaster and resume business. A ***cold site*** is a separate facility that does not have any computer equipment but is a place where employees can move after a disaster. A ***warm site*** is a separate facility with computer equipment that requires installation and configuration. Figure 5.3 outlines these resources that support disaster recovery.

A disaster recovery plan usually has a disaster recovery cost curve to support it. A ***disaster recovery cost curve*** charts (1) the cost to the company of the unavailability of information and technology and (2) the cost to the company of recovering from a disaster over time. Figure 5.4 displays a disaster recovery cost curve and shows that the best recovery plan in terms of cost and time is where the two lines intersect. Creating such a curve is no small task. Managers must consider the cost of losing information and technology within each department or functional area, and across the whole company. During the first few hours of a disaster, those costs may be low, but they rise over time. With those costs in hand, a company must then determine the costs of recovery.

FIGURE 5.4

Disaster Recovery Cost Curve

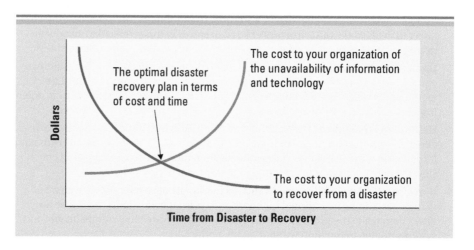

On April 18, 1906, San Francisco was rocked by an earthquake that destroyed large sections of the city and claimed the lives of more than 3,000 inhabitants. More than a century later, a rebuilt and more durable San Francisco serves as a central location for major MIS corporations as well as a major world financial center. Managers of these corporations are well aware of the potential disasters that exist along the San Andreas Fault and actively update their business continuity plans anticipating such issues as earthquakes and floods. The Union Bank of California is located in the heart of downtown San Francisco and maintains a highly detailed and well-developed business continuity plan. The company employs hundreds of business professionals scattered around the world that coordinate plans for addressing the potential loss of a facility, business professionals, or critical systems so that the company can continue to operate if a disaster happens. Its disaster recovery plan includes hot sites where staff can walk in and start working exactly as if they were in their normal location. It would be a matter of minutes, not hours, for the Union Bank of California to be up and running again in the event of a disaster.[2]

Business Continuity Plan

An *emergency* is a sudden, unexpected event requiring immediate action due to potential threat to health and safety, the environment, or property. *Emergency preparedness* ensures a company is ready to respond to an emergency in an organized, timely, and effective manner. Natural disasters and terrorist attacks are on the minds of business professionals who take safeguarding their information assets seriously. Disaster recovery plans typically focus on systems and data, ignoring cross-functional and intraorganizational business processes that can be destroyed during an emergency. For this reason many companies are turning to a more comprehensive and all-encompassing emergency preparedness plan known as *business continuity planning (BCP),* which details how a company recovers and restores critical business operations and systems after a disaster or extended disruption. BCP includes such factors as identifying critical systems, business processes, departments, and the maximum amount of time the business can continue to operate without functioning systems. BCP contains disaster recovery plans along with many additional plans, including prioritizing business impact analysis, emergency notification plans, and technology recovery strategies (see Figure 5.5).

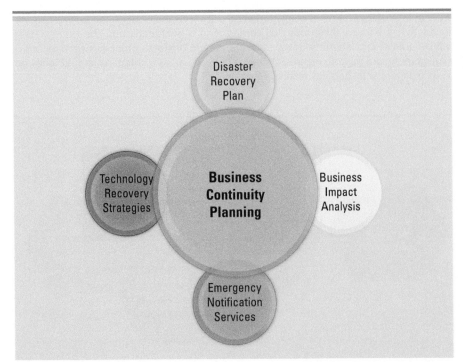

FIGURE 5.5

Business Continuity Planning Focus Areas

Business Impact Analysis   A *business impact analysis* identifies all critical business functions and the effect that a specific disaster may have upon them. A business impact analysis is primarily used to ensure a company has made the right decisions about the order of recovery priorities and strategies. For example, should the accounting department have its systems up and running before the sales and marketing departments? Will email be the first system for recovery to ensure employees can communicate with each other and outside stakeholders such as customers, suppliers, and partners? The business impact analysis is a key part of BCP as it details the order in which functional areas should be restored, ensuring the most critical are focused on first.

Emergency Notification Services   A business continuity plan typically includes an *emergency notification service*, that is, an infrastructure built for notifying people in the event of an emergency. Radio stations' occasional tests of the national Emergency Alert System are an example of a very large-scale emergency notification system. A firm will implement an emergency notification service to warn employees of unexpected events and provide them with instructions about how to handle the situation. Emergency notification services can be deployed through the firm's own infrastructure, supplied by an outside service provider on company premises, or hosted remotely by an outside service provider. All three methods provide notification using a variety of methods such as email, voice notification to a cell phone, and text messaging. The notifications can be sent to all the devices selected, providing multiple means in which to get critical information to those who need it.

Technology Recovery Strategies   Companies create massive amounts of data vital to their survival and continued operations. A *technology failure* occurs when the ability of a company to operate is impaired because of a hardware, software, or data outage. Technology failures can destroy large amounts of vital data, often causing *incidents*, unplanned interruption of a service. An *incident record* contains all of the details of an incident. *Incident management* is the process responsible for managing how incidents are identified and corrected. *Technology recovery strategies* focus specifically on prioritizing the order for restoring hardware, software, and data across the organization that best meets business recovery requirements. A technology recovery strategy details the order of importance for recovering hardware, software, data centers, and networking (or connectivity). If one of these four vital components is not functioning, the entire system will be unavailable, shutting down cross-functional business processes such as order management and payroll. Figure 5.6 displays the key areas a company should focus on when developing technology recovery strategies.

FIGURE 5.6

Key Areas of Technology Recovery Strategies

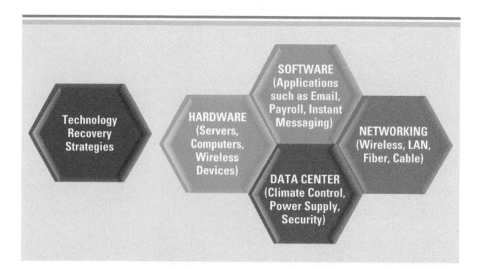

BUSINESS DRIVEN MIS

Backup and recovery are essential for any computer system. How painful would it be if someone stole your laptop right now? How much critical information would you lose? How many hours would it take you to re-create your data? Perhaps that will motivate you to implement a backup procedure. How many of you have a disaster recovery plan? Disaster recovery is needed when your best friend dumps a grande latte on your computer or you accidently wash your thumb drive.

Disaster recovery plans are crucial for any business, and you should ensure that your company has everything it needs to continue operations if there is ever a disaster, such as 9/11. You need to decide which disasters are worth worrying about and which ones are probably never going to occur. For example, if you live in Colorado, chances are good you don't have to worry about hurricanes, but avalanches are another story.

How often does a company need to back up its data? Where should the backup be stored? What types of disasters should companies in your state prepare for in case of an emergency? Why is it important to test the backup? What could happen to a company if it failed to create a disaster recovery plan?

Disaster Recovery

SUPPORTING CHANGE: AGILE MIS INFRASTRUCTURE

LO 5.3: Describe the characteristics of an agile MIS infrastructure.

Agile MIS infrastructure includes the hardware, software, and telecommunications equipment that, when combined, provides the underlying foundation to support the organization's goals. If a company grows by 50 percent in a single year, its infrastructure and systems must be able to handle a 50 percent growth rate. If they cannot, they can severely hinder the company's ability not only to grow but also to function.

The future of a company depends on its ability to meet its partners, suppliers, and customers any time of the day in any geographic location. Imagine owning an ebusiness and everyone on the Internet is tweeting and collaborating about how great your business idea is and how successful your company is going to be. Suddenly, you have 5 million global customers interested in your website. Unfortunately, you did not anticipate this many customers so quickly, and the system crashes. Users typing in your URL find a blank message stating the website is unavailable and to try back soon. Or even worse, they can get to your website but it takes three minutes to reload each time they click on a button. The buzz soon dies about your business idea as some innovative web-savvy fast follower quickly copies your idea and creates a website that can handle the massive number of customers. The characteristics of agile MIS infrastructures can help ensure your systems can meet and perform under any unexpected or unplanned changes. Figure 5.7 lists the seven abilities of an agile infrastructure.

Accessibility

Accessibility refers to the varying levels that define what a user can access, view, or perform when operating a system. Imagine the people at your college accessing the main student information system. Each person that accesses the system will have different needs and requirements; for example, a payroll employee will need to access vacation information and salary information, or a student will need to access course information and billing information. Each system user is provided with an access level that details which parts of the system the user can and cannot access and what the user can do when in the system. For example, you would not want your students to be able to view payroll information or professor's personal information; also, some users can only view

FIGURE 5.7

Agile MIS Infrastructure
Characteristics

Accessibility	• Varying levels allow system users to access, view, or perform operational functions.
Availability	• The system is operational during different time frames.
Maintainability	• The system quickly transforms to support environmental changes.
Portability	• The system is available to operate on different devices or software platforms.
Reliability	• The system functions correctly and provides accurate information.
Scalability	• The system can "scale up" or adapt to the increased demands of growth.
Usability	• The system is easy to learn and efficient and satisfying to use.

information and are not allowed to create or delete information. Top-level MIS employees require ***administrator access,*** or unrestricted access to the entire system. Administrator access can perform functions such as resetting passwords, deleting accounts, and shutting down entire systems.

Tim Berners-Lee, W3C director and inventor of the World Wide Web, stated, "the power of the web is in its universality. Access by everyone regardless of disability is an essential aspect." ***Web accessibility*** means that people with disabilities, including visual, auditory, physical, speech, cognitive, and neurological disabilities, can use the web. The ***web accessibility initiative (WAI)*** brings together people from industry, disability organizations, government, and research labs from around the world to develop guidelines and resources to help make the web accessible to people with disabilities, including auditory, cognitive, neurological, physical, speech, and visual disabilities. The goal of WAI is to allow people to access the full potential of the web, enabling people with disabilities to participate equally. For example, Apple includes screen magnification and VoiceOver on its iPhone, iPad, and iPod, which allows the blind and visually impaired to use the devices.

Availability

In a 24/7/365 ebusiness environment, business professionals need to use their systems whenever they want from wherever they want. ***Availability*** refers to the time frames when the system is operational. A system is called ***unavailable*** when it is not operating and cannot be used. ***High availability*** occurs when a system is continuously operational at all times. Availability is typically measured relative to "100 percent operational" or "never failing." A widely held but difficult-to-achieve standard of availability for a system is known as "five 9s" (99.999 percent) availability. Some companies have systems available around the clock to support ebusiness operations, global customers, and online suppliers.

Sometimes systems must be taken down for maintenance, upgrades, and fixes, which are completed during downtime. One challenge with availability is determining when to schedule system downtime if the system is expected to operate continuously. Performing maintenance during the evening might seem like a great idea, but evening in one city is morning somewhere else in the world, and business professionals scattered around the globe may not be able to perform specific job functions if the systems they need are unavailable. This is where companies deploy failover systems so they can take the primary system down for maintenance and activate the secondary system to ensure continuous operations.

Maintainability

Companies must watch today's needs, as well as tomorrow's, when designing and building systems that support agile infrastructures. Systems must be flexible enough to meet all types of company changes, environmental changes, and business changes. *Maintainability (or flexibility)* refers to how quickly a system can transform to support environmental changes. Maintainability helps to measure how quickly and effectively a system can be changed or repaired after a failure. For example, when starting a small business you might not consider that you will have global customers, a common mistake. When building your systems, you might not design them to handle multiple currencies and different languages, which might make sense if the company is not currently performing international business. Unfortunately, when the first international order arrives, which happens easily with ebusiness, the system will be unable to handle the request because it does not have the flexibility to be easily reconfigured for a new language or currency. When the company does start growing and operating overseas, the system will need to be redeveloped, which is not an easy or cheap task, to handle multiple currencies and different languages.

Building and deploying flexible systems allow easy updates, changes, and reconfigurations for unexpected business or environmental changes. Just think what might have happened if Facebook had to overhaul its entire system to handle multiple languages. Another social networking business could easily have stepped in and become the provider of choice. That certainly would not be efficient or effective for business operations.

Portability

Portability refers to the ability of an application to operate on different devices or software platforms, such as different operating systems. Apple's iTunes is readily available to users of Mac computers and also users of PC computers, smartphones, iPods, iPhones, iPads, and so on. It is also a portable application. Because Apple insists on compatibility across its products, both software and hardware, Apple can easily add to its product, device, and service offerings without sacrificing portability. Many software developers are creating programs that are portable to all three devices—the iPhone, iPod, and iPad—which increases their target market and they hope their revenue.

Reliability

Reliability (or accuracy) ensures a system is functioning correctly and providing accurate information. Inaccuracy can occur for many reasons, from the incorrect entry of information to the corruption of information during transmissions. Many argue that the information contained in Wikipedia is unreliable. Because the Wikipedia entries can be edited by any user, there are examples of rogue users inaccurately updating information. Many users skip over Google search findings that correlate to Wikipedia for this reason. Housing unreliable information on a website can put a company at risk of losing customers, placing inaccurate supplier orders, or even making unreliable business decisions. A *vulnerability* is a system weakness, such as a password that is never changed or a system left on while an employee goes to lunch, that can be exploited by a threat. Reliable systems ensure that vulnerabilities are kept at a minimum to reduce risk.

Scalability

Estimating company growth is a challenging task, in part because growth can occur in a number of different forms—the firm can acquire new customers, new product lines,

BUSINESS DRIVEN MIS

Ranking the Ab-"ilities"

Do you know how Google makes so much money? Unlike traditional businesses, Google does not make money from the users of its service. Google makes money by charging the companies that want to appear in the sponsored section of a search result. After performing a Google search, you will notice three sections on the resulting page. Along the top and side are the sponsored search results, and the middle lists the organic search results. Google's innovative marketing program, called AdWords, allows companies to bid on common search terms, and the highest bidder is posted first in the sponsored search results. Every time a user clicks on a sponsored link, the company that owns the link has to pay Google. This is also called pay-per-click and can cost anywhere from a few cents to a few dollars for each click. A general search term such as "tropical vacation" costs less than a more specific search term like "Hawaiian vacation." Whichever company bids the most for the search term appears at the top of the sponsored section. Clicking on the links in the organic search results does not incur any charges for the company that owns the link.

Rank the agile infrastructure ab-"ilities" for Google from most important to least important in terms of supporting Google's MIS infrastructure and business operations. Be sure to provide the justification behind your ranking.

or new markets. **Scalability** describes how well a system can scale up, or adapt to the increased demands of growth. If a company grows faster than anticipated, it might experience a variety of problems, from running out of storage space to taking more time to complete transactions. Anticipating expected, and unexpected, growth is key to building scalable systems that can support that development.

Performance measures how quickly a system performs a process or transaction. Performance is a key component of scalability as systems that can't scale suffer from performance issues. Just imagine your college's content management system suddenly taking five minutes to return a page after a button is pushed. Now imagine if this occurs during your midterm exam and you miss the two-hour deadline because the system is so slow. Performance issues experienced by firms can have disastrous business impacts causing loss of customers, loss of suppliers, and even loss of help-desk employees. Most users will wait only a few seconds for a website to return a request before growing frustrated and either calling the support desk or giving up and moving on to another website.

Capacity represents the maximum throughput a system can deliver; for example, the capacity of a hard drive represents its size or volume. **Capacity planning** determines future environmental infrastructure requirements to ensure high-quality system performance. If a company purchases connectivity software that is outdated or too slow to meet demand, its employees will waste a great deal of time waiting for systems to respond to user requests. It is cheaper for a company to design and implement agile infrastructure that envisions growth requirements than to update all the equipment after the system is already operational. If a company with 100 workers merges with another company and suddenly there are 400 people using the system, performance time could suffer. Planning for increases in capacity can ensure systems perform as expected. Waiting for a system to respond to requests is not productive.

Web 2.0 is a big driver for capacity planning to ensure agile infrastructures can meet the business's operational needs. Delivering videos over the Internet requires enough bandwidth to satisfy millions of users during peak periods such as Friday and Saturday evenings. Video transmissions over the Internet cannot tolerate packet loss (blocks of data loss), and allowing one additional user to access the system could degrade the video quality for every user.

BUSINESS DRIVEN DEBATE

Thanks to Moore's Law, computing devices are getting smaller, cheaper, and faster every year, allowing innovative companies to create new devices that are smaller and more powerful than current devices. Just look at desktop, laptop, notebook, and tablet computers. These are all different devices allowing users to connect and compute around the globe. Moore's Law has been accurate about computing power roughly doubling every 18 months. Do you agree or disagree that Moore's Law will continue to apply for the next 20 years? Why or why not?

Laptop?
Notebook?
Netbook?
Tablet?

Usability

Usability is the degree to which a system is easy to learn and efficient and satisfying to use. Providing hints, tips, shortcuts, and instructions for any system, regardless of its ease of use, is recommended. Apple understood the importance of usability when it designed the first iPod. One of the iPod's initial attractions was the usability of the click wheel. One simple and efficient button operates the iPod, making it usable for all ages. And to ensure ease of use, Apple also made the corresponding iTunes software intuitive and easy to use. **Serviceability** is how quickly a third party can change a system to ensure it meets user needs and the terms of any contracts, including agreed levels of reliability, maintainability, or availability. When using a system from a third party, it is important to ensure the right level of serviceability for all users, including remote employees.

section 5.2   Building Sustainable MIS Infrastructures

LEARNING OUTCOMES

5.4 Identify the environmental impacts associated with MIS.

5.5 Explain the three components of a sustainable MIS infrastructure along with their business benefits.

MIS AND THE ENVIRONMENT

LO 5.4: **Identify the environmental impacts associated with MIS.**

The general trend in MIS is toward smaller, faster, and cheaper devices. Gordon Moore, co-founder of Intel, the world's largest producer of computer chips or microprocessors, observed in 1965 that continued advances in technological innovation made it possible to reduce the size of a computer chip (the brains of a computer, or even a cell phone now) while doubling its capacity every two years. His prediction that this trend would continue has come to be known as **Moore's Law,** which refers to the computer chip performance per dollar doubles every 18 months. Although Moore originally assumed a two-year period, many sources today refer to the 18-month figure.

Moore's Law is great for many companies as they can acquire large amounts of MIS equipment for cheaper and cheaper costs. As ebusinesses continue to grow, companies equip their employees with multiple forms of electronic devices ranging from laptops to cell phones to iPads. This is great for supporting a connected corporation, significant unintended side effects include our dependence upon fossil fuels and increased need for safe disposal of outdated computing equipment. Concern about these side effects has led many companies to turn to an ecological practice known as sustainable MIS. **Sustainable, or green, MIS** describes the production, management, use, and disposal of technology in a way that minimizes damage to the environment. Sustainable MIS

BUSINESS DRIVEN ETHICS AND SECURITY

Ewaste and the Environment

By some estimates, there may be as many as 1 billion surplus or obsolete computers and monitors in the world. Consider California, where 6,000 computers become surplus every day. If not disposed of properly, this enormous ewaste stream, which can contain more than 1,000 different toxic substances, is harmful to human beings and the environment. Beryllium is found in computer motherboards, chromium in floppy disks, lead in batteries and computer monitors, and mercury in alkaline batteries. One of the most toxic chemicals known is cadmium, found in many old laptops and computer chips.

In poorer countries, where the United States and Europe export some of their ewaste, the full impact of the environmental damage is quickly being realized. These areas have little use for obsolete electronic equipment so local recyclers resell some parts and burn the rest in illegal dumps, often near residential areas, releasing toxic and carcinogenic substances into the air, land, and water.[3]

Have you ever participated in ewaste? What can you do to ensure you are safely disposing of electronic equipment including batteries? What can governments do to encourage companies to safely dispose of ewaste? What can be done to protect poorer countries from receiving ewaste? Create a list of the ways you can safely dispose of cell phones, computers, printers, ink cartridges, MP3 players, and batteries. What could you do to inform citizens of the issues associated with ewaste and educate them on safe disposal practices?

is a critical part of **corporate social responsibility**, that is, companies' acknowledged responsibility to society. Building sustainable MIS infrastructures is a core initiative and critical success factor for socially responsible corporations. Figure 5.8 displays the three primary side effects of businesses' expanded use of technology.

Increased Electronic Waste

Moore's Law has made technological devices smaller, cheaper, and faster, allowing more people from all income levels to purchase computing equipment. This increased demand is causing numerous environmental issues. **Ewaste** refers to discarded, obsolete, or broken electronic devices. Ewaste includes CDs, DVDs, thumb drives, printer cartridges, cell phones, iPods, external hard drives, TVs, VCRs, DVD players, microwaves, and so on. Some say one human year is equivalent to seven years of technological advancements. A personal computer has a life expectancy of only three to five years and a cell phone is less than two years.

Sustainable MIS disposal refers to the safe disposal of MIS assets at the end of their life cycle. It ensures that ewaste does not end up in landfills causing environmental issues. A single computer contains more than 700 chemicals; some are toxic, such as mercury, lead, and cadmium. If a computer ends up in a landfill, the toxic substances it contains can leach into our land, water, and air. Recycling costs from $15 to $50 for a monitor or computer. Many companies, including public schools and universities, simply can't afford the recycling costs.[4]

Ewaste also occurs when unused equipment stored in attics, basements, and storage facilities never reaches a recycling center. Retrieving the silver, gold, and other valuable metals from these devices is more efficient and less environmentally harmful than removing it from its natural environment.

Currently, less than 20 percent of ewaste in the United States is recycled; however, even recycling does not guarantee the equipment is disposed of safely. While some recyclers process the material ethically, others ship it to countries such as China and

FIGURE 5.8

Three Pressures Driving
Sustainable MIS Infrastructures

India, where environmental enforcement is weak. This action poses its own global environmental problems.

Increased Energy Consumption

Energy consumption is the amount of energy consumed by business processes and systems. Huge increases in technology use have greatly amplified energy consumption. The energy consumed by a computer is estimated to produce as much as 10 percent of the amount of carbon dioxide produced by an automobile. Computer servers in the United States account for about 1 percent of the total energy needs of the country. Put in perspective, this is roughly equivalent to the energy consumption of Mississippi.

Computers consume energy even when they are not being used. For convenience and to allow for automatic updates and backup, the majority of computer equipment is never completely shut down. It draws energy 24 hours a day.

Increased Carbon Emissions

The major human-generated greenhouse gases, such as carbon emissions from energy use, are very likely responsible for the increases in climatic temperature over the past half a century. Additional temperature increases are projected over the next hundred years, with serious consequences for Earth's environment, if ***carbon emissions,*** including the carbon dioxide and carbon monoxide produced by business processes and systems, are not reduced.

In the United States, coal provides more than 50 percent of electrical power. When left on continuously, a single desktop computer and monitor can consume at least 100 watts of power per hour. To generate that much energy 24 hours a day for a year would require approximately 714 pounds of coal. When that coal is burned, it releases on average 5 pounds of sulfur dioxide, 5 pounds of nitrogen oxides, and 1,852 pounds (that is almost a ton) of carbon dioxide.[5]

SUPPORTING THE ENVIRONMENT: SUSTAINABLE MIS INFRASTRUCTURE

LO 5.5: Explain the three components of a sustainable MIS infrastructure along with their business benefits.

Combating ewaste, energy consumption, and carbon emissions requires a firm to focus on creating sustainable MIS infrastructures. A sustainable MIS infrastructure identifies ways that a company can grow in terms of computing resources while simultaneously becoming less dependent on hardware and energy consumption. The components of a sustainable MIS infrastructure are displayed in Figure 5.9.

Grid Computing

When a light is turned on, the power grid delivers exactly what is needed, instantly. Computers and networks can now work that way using grid computing. ***Grid computing*** is a collection of computers, often geographically dispersed, that are coordinated to

BUSINESS DRIVEN DISCUSSION

Facebook's Energy Use

Cheap electricity is great for keeping business costs down, but it often means relying on coal for power. Facebook recently commissioned a new computing facility in Oregon and is using power from PacifiCorp, a utility that gets the majority of its energy from coal-fired power stations, which are major contributors of greenhouse gas emissions. As more and more people subscribe to Facebook, its energy needs are increasing almost exponentially.

Do you agree that Facebook made a wise business decision in selecting a utility provider that uses coal-fired power stations? What alternative sources of energy could Facebook have used to power its computing facility? Do you think Facebook's core customers care about the environment? What types of business challenges might Facebook encounter if it continues using coal-fired power stations?

FIGURE 5.9

Sustainable MIS Infrastructure Components

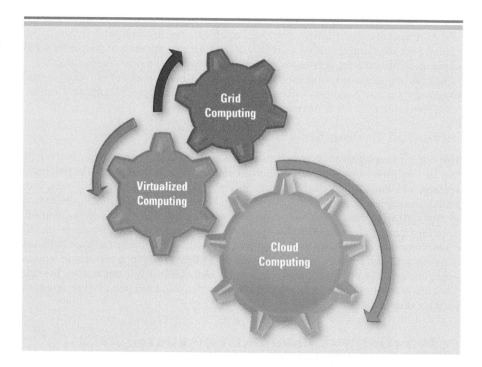

solve a common problem. With grid computing a problem is broken into pieces and distributed to many machines, allowing faster processing than could occur with a single system. Computers typically use less than 25 percent of their processing power, leaving more than 75 percent available for other tasks. Innovatively, grid computing takes advantage of this unused processing power by linking thousands of individual computers around the world to create a "virtual supercomputer" that can process intensive tasks. Grid computing makes better use of MIS resources, allowing greater scalability as systems can easily grow to handle peaks and valleys in demand, become more cost efficient, and solve problems that would be impossible to tackle with a single computer (see Figure 5.10).[6]

FIGURE 5.10

Grid Computing Example

The uses of grid computing are numerous, including the creative environment of animated movies. DreamWorks Animation used grid computing to complete many of its hit films including *Antz, Shrek, Madagascar,* and *How to Train Your Dragon.* The third *Shrek* film required more than 20 million computer hours to make (compared to 5 million for the first *Shrek* and 10 million for the second). At peak production times, DreamWorks dedicated more than 4,000 computers to its *Shrek* grid, allowing it to complete scenes in days and hours instead of months. With the increased grid computing power, the DreamWork's animators were able to add more realistic movement to water, fire, and magic scenes (see Figure 5.11). With grid computing a company can work faster or more efficiently, providing a potential competitive advantage and additional cost savings.[7]

FIGURE 5.11

Making *Shrek 2* with Grid Computing

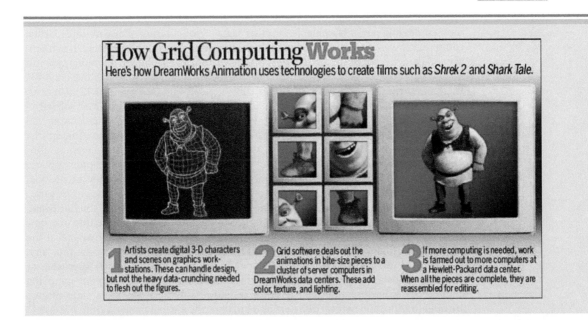

How Grid Computing **Works**
Here's how DreamWorks Animation uses technologies to create films such as *Shrek 2* and *Shark Tale.*

1 Artists create digital 3-D characters and scenes on graphics workstations. These can handle design, but not the heavy data-crunching needed to flesh out the figures.

2 Grid software deals out the animations in bite-size pieces to a cluster of server computers in DreamWorks data centers. These add color, texture, and lighting.

3 If more computing is needed, work is farmed out to more computers at a Hewlett-Packard data center. When all the pieces are complete, they are reassembled for editing.

Solving the Energy Issue with Smart Grids A *smart grid* delivers electricity using two-way digital technology. It is meant to solve the problem of the world's outdated electrical grid, making it more efficient and reliable by adding the ability to remotely monitor, analyze, and control the transmission of power. The current U.S. power grid is said to have outlived its life expectancy by as much as 30 years. Smart grids provide users with real-time usage monitoring, allowing them to choose off-peak times for noncritical or less urgent applications or processes. Residents of Boulder, Colorado, can monitor their use of electricity and control appliances remotely due to the city's large-scale smart grid system. Xcel Energy has installed 21,000 smart grid meters since the $100 million program started several years ago. Energy use by early adopters is down as much as 45 percent.[8]

Virtualized Computing

Most computers and even servers typically run only one operating system, such as Windows or Mac OS, and only one application. When a company invests in a large system such as inventory management, it dedicates a single server to house the system. This ensures the system has enough capacity to run during peak times and to scale to meet demand. Also, many systems have specific hardware requirements along with detailed software requirements, making it difficult to find two systems with the same requirements that could share the same machine. Through the use of virtualization, computers can run multiple operating systems along with multiple software applications—all at the same time. *Virtualization* creates multiple "virtual" machines on a single computing device. A good analogy is a computer printer. In the past you had to purchase a fax machine, copy machine, answering machine, and computer printer separately. This was expensive, required enough energy to run four separate machines, not to mention created additional amounts of ewaste. Today, you can buy a virtualized computer printer that functions as a fax machine, answering machine, and copy machine all on one physical machine, thereby reducing costs, power requirements, and ewaste. Virtualization is essentially a form of consolidation that can benefit sustainable MIS infrastructures in a variety of ways, for example:

- By increasing availability of applications that can give a higher level of performance depending on the hardware used.
- By increasing energy efficiency by requiring less hardware to run multiple systems or applications.
- By increasing hardware usability by running multiple operating systems on a single computer.

Originally, computers were designed to run a single application on a single operating system. This left most computers vastly underutilized (as mentioned earlier, 75 percent of most computing power is available for other tasks). Virtualization allows multiple virtual computers to exist on a single machine, which allows it to share its resources, such as memory and hard disk space, to run different applications and even different operating systems. Mac computers have the ability to run both the Apple operating system and the Windows PC operating system, with the use of virtualization software (see Figure 5.12). Unfortunately, virtualization, at least at the moment, is not available for a PC to run Mac software.

Virtualization is also one of the easiest and quickest ways to achieve a sustainable MIS infrastructure because it reduces power consumption and requires less equipment that needs to be manufactured, maintained, and later disposed of safely. Managers no longer have to assign servers, storage, or network capacity permanently to single applications. Instead, they can assign the hardware resources when and where they are needed, achieving the availability, flexibility, and scalability a company needs to thrive and grow. Also, by virtually separating the operating system and applications from the hardware, if there is a disaster or hardware failure, it is easy to port the virtual machine to a new physical machine allowing a company to recovery quickly from disasters. One of the primary uses of virtualization is for performing backup, recovery, and disaster recovery. Using virtual servers or a virtualization service provider, such as Google, Microsoft, or Amazon, to host disaster recovery is more sustainable than a single company incurring the expense of having redundant physical systems. Also, these providers' data centers are built to withstand natural disasters and are typically located far away from big cities.

BUSINESS DRIVEN INNOVATION

Virtualization is a challenging concept to understand. The formal definition is that it creates multiple "virtual" machines on a single computing device. OK, let's try that again in English. Imagine you have three cell phones, one for the company you work for, one for a company you are starting on the side, and one for personal calls. For the most part the phones are idle and they seldom ever ring at the same time. Since the phones are idle the majority of the time, you notice that it is a waste of time and resources to support idle time, especially when you are paying for cell service on each phone. You decide to use virtualization to help your situation.

Essentially, this would put three virtual cell phones on one device. The individual services and application for each phone would be independently stored on the one device. From the device's perspective, it sees three separate virtual phones. This saves time and money in expenses and maintenance. You could even use virtualization to turn your cell phone into a scanner. Visit ScanR.com and for just $5 a month you can use the camera on your phone to scan documents. Take a photo of any document, business card, or whiteboard and upload it to ScanR's website and in minutes it is returned to you in a digital file. Could be helpful if your friend has to miss class and you want to copy your lecture notes.[9]

Virtualization is a hot topic these days as more and more businesses are focusing on social responsibility and attempting to find ways to reduce their carbon footprints. Create an analogy similar to the cell phone that demonstrates virtualization. What are the potential environmental impacts associated with virtualization? What are the business advantages of virtualization? What are the business risks associated with virtualization?

Virtualization for Your Cell Phone

FIGURE 5.12

Virtualization Allows an Apple Macintosh Computer to Run OS X and Windows 7

Apple Macintosh Computer

MAC OS X
Running
Mac
software

WINDOWS 7
Running
Windows 7
software

Sharing memory and hard disk space

Virtual Data Centers   A *data center* is a facility used to house management information systems and associated components, such as telecommunications and storage systems. Data centers, sometimes referred to as server farms, consume power and require cooling and floor space while working to support business growth without

BUSINESS DRIVEN GLOBALIZATION

Data Centers on the High Seas

Google is considering constructing a floating data center three to seven miles offshore that could be both powered and cooled by the ocean. It would consist of containers stacked with servers, data storage systems, and networking equipment on barges or other platforms and could be located close to users wherever it is not feasible, cost-effective, or efficient to build on land. Bringing the data closer to the user allows the data to arrive quicker. And since the ocean is a rent-free space, data centers can be as large as 100,000 square feet without real estate fees. The ocean can provide two critical factors that support a sustainable MIS infrastructure—water for cooling and power.[10]

What are the advantages and disadvantages of housing data centers in the ocean? Do you foresee any issues for these data centers with natural disasters? What types of security issues would Google encounter with a floating data center? Do you agree that it is good business sense to house a data center on a barge in the ocean? Why or why not?

disrupting normal business operations and the quality of service. The amount of data a data center stores has grown exponentially over the years as our reliance on information increases. Backups, graphics, documents, presentations, photos, audio and video files all contribute to the ever-expanding information footprint that requires storage. One of the most effective ways to limit the power consumption and cooling requirements of a data center is to consolidate parts of the physical infrastructure, particularly by reducing the number of physical servers through virtualization. For this reason, virtualization is having a profound impact on data centers as the sheer number of servers a company requires to operate decreases, thereby boosting growth and performance while reducing environmental impact, as shown in Figure 5.13. Google, Microsoft, Amazon, and Yahoo! have all created data centers along the Columbia River in the northwestern United States. In this area, each company can benefit from affordable land, high-speed Internet access, plentiful water for cooling, and even more important, inexpensive electricity. These factors are critical to today's large-scale data centers, whose sheer size and power needs far surpass those of the previous generation. Microsoft's data center in Quincy, Washington, is larger than 10 football fields and is powered entirely by hydroelectricity, power generated from flowing water rather than from the burning of coal or other fossil fuel.[11]

If we take a holistic and integrated approach to overall company growth, the benefits of integrating information MIS infrastructures, environmental MIS infrastructures, and sustainable MIS infrastructures become obvious. For example, a company could easily create a backup of its software and important information in one or more geographically

FIGURE 5.13

Ways for Data Centers to Become Sustainable

dispersed locations using cloud computing. This would be far cheaper than building its own hot and cold sites in different areas of the country. In the case of a security breach, failover can be deployed as a virtual machine in one location of the cloud can be shut down as another virtual machine in a different location on the cloud comes online.

Cloud Computing

Imagine a cyclical business that specializes in Halloween decorations and how its sales trends and orders vary depending on the time of year. The majority of sales occur in September and October, and the remaining 10 months have relatively small sales and small system usage. The company does not want to invest in massive expensive servers that sit idle 10 months of the year just to meet its capacity spikes in September and October. The perfect solution for this company is cloud computing, which makes it easier to gain access to the computing power that was once reserved for large corporations. Small to medium-size companies no longer have to make big capital investments to access the same powerful systems that large companies run.

According to the National Institute of Standards and Technology (NIST) **_cloud computing_** is a model for enabling ubiquitous, convenient, on-demand network access to a shared pool of configurable computing resources (e.g., networks, servers, storage, applications, and services) that can be rapidly provisioned and released with minimal management effort or service provider interaction. Cloud computing offers new ways to store, access, process, and analyze information and connect people and resources from any location in the world where an Internet connection is available. As shown in Figure 5.14, users connect to the cloud from their personal computers or portable devices using a client, such as a web browser. To these individual users, the cloud appears as their personal application, device, or document. It is like storing all of your software and documents "in the cloud," and all you need is a device to access the cloud. No more hard drives, software, or processing power—that is all located in the cloud, transparent to the users. Users are not physically bound to a single computer or network; they can access their programs and documents from wherever they are, whenever they need to. Just think of having your hard drive located in the sky and you can access your information and programs using any device from wherever you are. The best part is that even if your machine crashes, is lost, or is stolen, the information hosted in the cloud is safe and always available.

FIGURE 5.14

Cloud Computing Example

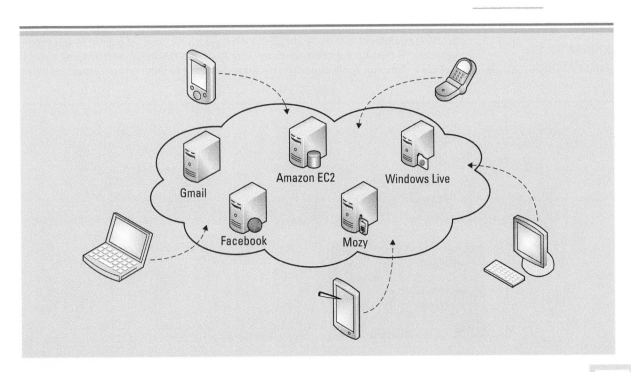

Multi-tenancy in the cloud means that a single instance of a system serves multiple customers. In the cloud, each customer is called a tenant and multiple tenants can access the same system. Multi-tenancy helps to reduce operational costs associated with implementing large systems as the costs are dispersed across many tenants as opposed to *single-tenancy,* in which each customer or tenant must purchase and maintain an individual system. With a multi-tenancy cloud approach, the service provider only has one place to update its system. With a single-tenancy cloud approach, the service provider would have to update its system in every company where the software was running. The *cloud fabric* is the software that makes possible the benefits of cloud computing, such as multi-tenancy. A *cloud fabric controller* is an individual who monitors and provisions cloud resources, similar to a server administrator at an individual company. Cloud fabric controllers provision resources, balance loads, manage servers, update systems, and ensure all environments are available and operating correctly. Cloud fabric is the primary reason cloud computing promotes all of the seven abilities, allowing a business to make its data and applications accessible, available, maintainable, portable, reliable, scalable, and usable. Figure 5.15 displays the benefits of cloud computing.

The cloud offers a company higher availability, greater reliability, and improved accessibility—all with affordable high-speed access. For flexibility, scalability, and cost efficiency, cloud computing is quickly becoming a viable option for companies of all sizes. With the cloud, you could simply purchase a single license for software such as Microsoft Office or Outlook at a far discounted rate and not worry about the hassle of installing and upgrading the software on your computer. No more worries that you don't have enough memory to run a new program because the hardware is provided in the cloud, along with the software. You simply pay to access the program. Think of this the same way you do your telephone service. You simply pay to access a vendor's service, and you do not have to pay for the equipment required to carry the call around the globe. You also don't have to worry about scalability because the system automatically handles peak loads, which can be spread out among the systems in the cloud.

Because additional cloud resources are always available, companies no longer have to purchase systems for infrequent computing tasks that need intense processing power, such as preparing tax returns during tax season or increased sales transactions during certain holiday seasons. If a company needs more processing power, it is always there in the cloud—and available on a cost-efficient basis.

With cloud computing, individuals or businesses pay only for the services they need, when they need them, and where, much as we use and pay for electricity. In the past, a company would have to pay millions of dollars for the hardware, software, and networking equipment required to implement a large system such as payroll or sales management. A cloud computing user can simply access the cloud and request a single license to a payroll application. The user does not have to incur any hardware, software,

FIGURE 5.15

Benefits of Cloud Computing

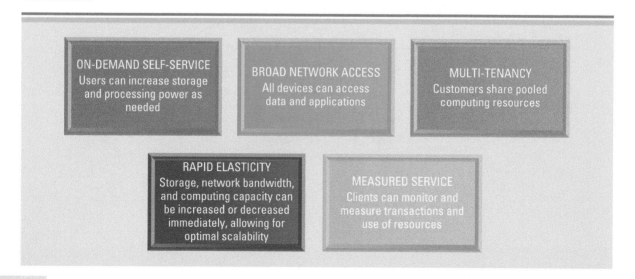

or networking expenses. As the business grows and the user requires more employees to have access to the system, the business simply purchases additional licenses. Rather than running software on a local computer or server, companies can now reach to the cloud to combine software applications, data storage, and considerable computing power. *Utility computing* offers a pay-per-use revenue model similar to a metered service such as gas or electricity. Many cloud computing service providers use utility computing cloud infrastructures, which are detailed in Figure 5.16.

Infrastructure as a Service (IaaS) *Infrastructure as a Service (IaaS)* delivers hardware networking capabilities, including the use of servers, networking, and storage, over the cloud using a pay-per-use revenue model. With IaaS the customer rents the hardware and provides its own custom applications or programs. IaaS customers save money by not having to spend a large amount of capital purchasing expensive servers, which is a great business advantage considering some servers cost more than $100,000. The service is typically paid for on a usage basis, much like a basic utility service such as electricity or gas. IaaS offers a cost-effective solution for companies that need their computing resources to grow and shrink as business demand changes. This is known as *dynamic scaling,* which means the MIS infrastructure can be automatically scaled up or down based on needed requirements.

Currently the most popular IaaS operation is Amazon's Elastic Compute Cloud, generally known as Amazon EC2, or simply EC2. EC2 provides a web interface through which customers can load and run their own applications on Amazon's computers. Customers control their own operating environment, so they can create, run, and stop services as needed, which is why Amazon describes EC2 as *elastic.* IaaS is a perfect fit for companies with research-intensive projects that need to process large amounts of information at irregular intervals, such as those in the scientific or medical fields. Cloud computing services offer these companies considerable cost savings where they can perform testing and analysis at levels that are not possible without access to additional and very costly computing infrastructure.

Software as a Service (SaaS) *Software as a Service (SaaS)* delivers applications over the cloud using a pay-per-use revenue model. Before its introduction, companies often spent huge amounts of money implementing and customizing specialized applications to satisfy their business requirements. Many of these applications were difficult to implement, expensive to maintain, and challenging to use. Usability was one of the biggest drivers for creating interest in and success for cloud computing service providers.

FIGURE 5.16

Cloud Service Delivery Models

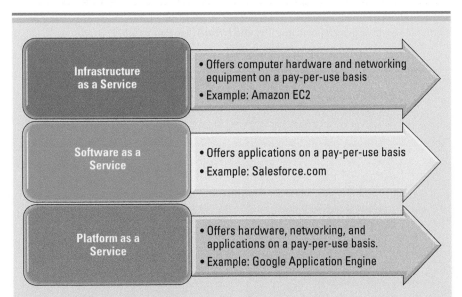

SaaS offers a number of advantages; the most obvious is tremendous cost savings. The software is priced on a per-use basis with no up-front costs, so companies get the immediate benefit of reducing capital expenditures. They also get the added benefits of scalability and flexibility to test new software on a rental basis.

Salesforce.com is one of the most popular SaaS providers. Salesforce.com built and delivered a sales automation application, suitable for the typical salesperson, that automates functions such as tracking sales leads and prospects and forecasting. Tapping the power of SaaS can provide access to a large-scale, secure infrastructure, along with any needed support, which is especially valuable for a start-up or small company with few financial resources.

Platform as a Service (PaaS)   *Platform as a Service (PaaS)* supports the deployment of entire systems including hardware, networking, and applications using a pay-per-use revenue model. PaaS is a perfect solution for a business as it passes on to the service provider the headache and challenges of buying, managing, and maintaining web development software. With PaaS the development, deployment, management, and maintenance is based entirely in the cloud and performed by the PaaS provider, allowing the company to focus resources on its core initiatives. Every aspect of development, including the software needed to create it and the hardware to run it, lives in the cloud. PaaS helps companies minimize operational costs and increase productivity by providing all the following without up-front investment:

- Increased security.
- Access to information anywhere and anytime.
- Centralized information management.
- Easy collaboration with partners, suppliers, and customers.
- Increased speed to market with significantly less cost.

One of the most popular PaaS services is Google's Application Engine, which builds and deploys web applications for a company. Google's Application Engine is easy to build, easy to maintain, and easy to scale as a company's web-based application needs grow. Google's Application Engine is free and offers a standard storage limit and enough processing power and network usage to support a web application serving about 5 million page views a month. When a customer scales beyond these initial limits, it can pay a fee to increase capacity and performance. This can turn into some huge costs savings for a small business that does not have enough initial capital to buy expensive hardware and software for its web applications. Just think, a two-person company can access the same computing resources as Google. That makes good business sense. Regardless of which cloud model a business chooses, it can select from four different cloud computing environments—public, private, community, and hybrid (see Figure 5.17).

FIGURE 5.17

Cloud Computing Environments

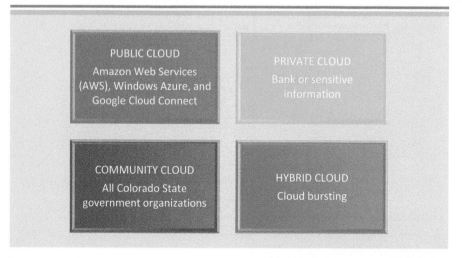

Public Cloud *Public cloud* promotes massive, global, and industrywide applications offered to the general public. In a public cloud, customers are never required to provision, manage, upgrade, or replace hardware or software. Pricing is utility-style and customers pay only for the resources they use. A few great examples of public cloud computing include Amazon Web Services (AWS), Windows Azure, and Google Cloud Connect.

Private Cloud *Private cloud* serves only one customer or organization and can be located on the customer's premises or off the customer's premises. A private cloud is the optimal solution for an organization such as the government that has high data security concerns and values information privacy. Private clouds are far more expensive than public clouds because costs are not shared across multiple customers.

Community Cloud *Community cloud* serves a specific community with common business models, security requirements, and compliance considerations. Community clouds are emerging in highly regulated industries such as financial services and pharmaceutical companies.

Hybrid Cloud *Hybrid cloud* includes two or more private, public, or community clouds, but each cloud remains separate and is only linked by technology that enables data and application portability. For example, a company might use a private cloud for critical applications that maintain sensitive data and a public cloud for nonsensitive data applications. The usage of both private and public clouds together is an example of a hybrid cloud. *Cloud bursting* is when a company uses its own computing infrastructure for normal usage and accesses the cloud when it needs to scale for peak load requirements, ensuring a sudden spike in usage does not result in poor performance or system crashes.

Deploying an MIS infrastructure in the cloud forever changes the way an organization's MIS systems are developed, deployed, maintained, and managed. Moving to the cloud is a fundamental shift from moving from a physical world to a logical world, making irrelevant the notion of which individual server applications or data reside on. As a result, organizations and MIS departments need to change the way they view systems and the new opportunities to find competitive advantages.

LEARNING OUTCOME REVIEW

Learning Outcome 5.1: Explain MIS infrastructure and its three primary types.

The three primary areas where enterprise architects focus when maintaining a firm's MIS infrastructure are:

- Supporting operations: Information MIS infrastructure identifies where and how important information, such as customer records, is maintained and secured.
- Supporting change: Agile MIS infrastructure includes the hardware, software, and telecommunications equipment that, when combined, provides the underlying foundation to support the organization's goals.
- Supporting the environment: Sustainable MIS infrastructure identifies ways that a company can grow in terms of computing resources while simultaneously becoming less dependent on hardware and energy consumption.

Learning Outcome 5.2: Identify the three primary areas associated with an information MIS infrastructure.

The three primary areas an information infrastructure provides to support continuous business operations are:

- Backup and recovery: A backup is an exact copy of a system's information. Recovery is the ability to get a system up and running in the event of a system crash or failure that includes restoring the information backup.

- Disaster recovery plan: This plan provides a detailed process for recovering information or a system in the event of a catastrophic disaster.
- Business continuity plan: This details how a company recovers and restores critical business operations and systems after a disaster or extended disruption.

Learning Outcome 5.3: Describe the characteristics of an agile MIS infrastructure.

- Accessibility refers to the varying levels that define what a user can access, view, or perform when operating a system.
- Availability refers to the time frames when the system is operational.
- Maintainability (or flexibility) refers to how quickly a system can transform to support environmental changes.
- Portability refers to the ability of an application to operate on different devices or software platforms, such as different operating systems.
- Reliability (or accuracy) ensures a system is functioning correctly and providing accurate information.
- Scalability describes how well a system can "scale up" or adapt to the increased demands of growth.
- Usability is the degree to which a system is easy to learn and efficient and satisfying to use.

Learning Outcome 5.4: Identify the environmental impacts associated with MIS.

Increased energy consumption, increased electronic waste, and increased carbon emissions are all associated with MIS. Ewaste refers to discarded, obsolete, or broken electronic devices. Sustainable MIS disposal refers to the safe disposal of MIS assets at the end of their life cycle.

Learning Outcome 5.5: Explain the three components of a sustainable MIS infrastructure along with their business benefits.

The components of a sustainable MIS infrastructure include:

- Grid computing: A collection of computers, often geographically dispersed, that are coordinated to solve a common problem.
- Cloud computing: The use of resources and applications hosted remotely on the Internet. The term comes (at least in part) from the image of a cloud to represent the Internet or some large networked environment.
- Virtualized computing: The creation of multiple "virtual" machines on a single computing device.

OPENING CASE QUESTIONS

1. **Knowledge:** List the ways that an agile MIS infrastructure supports Pandora's business.
2. **Comprehension:** Describe the reasons Pandora would create a disaster recovery plan and a business continuity plan.
3. **Application:** Apply the concepts of cloud computing to Pandora's business model.
4. **Analysis:** Analyze how Pandora is using sustainable MIS infrastructures.
5. **Synthesis:** Develop a way that Pandora could benefit from grid computing.
6. **Evaluate:** Assess the use of virtualization to support Pandora's business growth while helping the environment.

KEY TERMS

REVIEW QUESTIONS

1. How often should a business back up its data?
2. Why is it important to ensure backups are working and can be restored?
3. What is the difference between a disaster recovery plan and a business continuity plan?
4. What are the three forms of MIS infrastructures and what do they support?
5. List the characteristics of an agile MIS infrastructure and explain why they are all critical for supporting change.
6. Explain what capacity planning is and how it can help a business prepare for growth.
7. Explain the difference between fault tolerance and failover.
8. Compare the differences among a hot, cold, and warm site.
9. What is Moore's Law and how does it affect companies?
10. List the business benefits of using grid computing.
11. Identify the benefits and challenges of cloud computing
12. What is a data center and why would a business develop one.
13. List and describe the three most popular cloud computing delivery models.
14. Why would a company want to use virtualization?
15. Explain why a business today would want to follow sustainable MIS practices.
16. Explain why ebusiness is contributing to the three pressures driving sustainable MIS infrastructures.

CLOSING CASE ONE

UPS Invests $1 Billion to Go Green

United Parcel Service (UPS) will make about $1 billion in technology investments to improve the efficiency of its operations, with the goal of cutting billions more from its costs over the long term. One of its main goals is to improve the speed and efficiency of its delivery operations. To achieve that, UPS is equipping its vans with sensors that allow it to collect data about things such as fuel consumption, chosen routes, and how much time its engines spend idling. Reducing fuel consumption will help UPS not only to cut costs, but also to be more environmentally responsible. A big portion of the company's costs comes from transporting packages by air. In fact, UPS is the world's ninth-largest airline, so it is trying to conserve aircraft fuel as well by lowering flight speeds and better planning to avoid duplication of routes. But a lot of fuel is also burned by its trucks, and the sensors being implemented there could save the company millions of dollars.

UPS is installing about 200 sensors in its vehicles—in the brakes, engine box, and on the exterior—to collect data and pinpoint opportunities where drivers can adjust their driving to maximize fuel efficiency. The company wants to reduce idle time of its delivery trucks, as each hour spent idling burns about a gallon of fuel.

The company is also installing equipment to track the routes drivers take to deliver packages. Every morning the drivers are briefed on the data captured by the sensors and how they could drive differently to save fuel. UPS wants to optimize the number of times a vehicle has to start, stop, reverse, turn, or back up.

Green Data Center

The company is also investing in more efficient cooling technologies at its two data centers, which are in Mahwah, New Jersey, and Alpharetta, Georgia. During the winter, the company can shut off its chiller equipment and use outside air for cooling.

The Alpharetta data center has a 650,000-gallon water tank outside for cooling and a heat exchanger to faster dissipate the heat captured in the fluid. The water flows in a circular motion around the data center, cooling the equipment, and the heat exchanger helps lower the temperature of the hot exhaust water more quickly.

UPS is also investing in faster server processors, allowing it to consolidate existing servers through virtualization. That helps lower energy costs and also reduces the physical footprint of its servers. And the company has been consolidating smaller server rooms that were scattered around the world. These changes are saving UPS around $400,000 each year.[12]

Questions

1. Why do you think UPS is embracing sustainable technologies?
2. How is UPS developing a sustainable MIS infrastructure?
3. What business benefits will UPS gain from virtualization?
4. What role does each characteristics of an agile MIS infrastructure play in helping UPS to operate its business?
5. How could UPS benefit from cloud or grid computing?
6. What types of ethical issues might UPS encounter with the tracking technology it has placed in its trucks?
7. What types of security issues might UPS encounter with the tracking technology it has placed in its trucks?

CLOSING CASE TWO

Turning Ewaste into Gold

During the 2010 Winter Olympic Games in Vancouver, champions were not just taking home gold, silver, or bronze medals—they were also playing a role in reducing electronic waste. For the first time in Olympic history, each medal, more than 1,000 of them, was made with a tiny bit of the more than 140,000 tons of ewaste that otherwise would have been sent to landfills. The medals are the first containing metal salvaged from televisions, circuit boards, computer monitors, and electronic waste. The so-called urban ore was supplied by Teck Resources Ltd., Canada's largest base-metals producer, which provided gold, silver, and copper used to make the medals. Historically, Olympic medals have been made from mined mineral deposits; this is the first time that recycled materials have been added to them. First-place winners get gold-plated medals that are 92.5 percent silver. The second-place prizes are also 92.5 percent silver, while the third-place bronze medals are mostly copper.

All the medals have some ewaste materials from Teck's electronic recycling program located in Trail, British Columbia. Teck mixed gold, silver, and copper from the program with metals mined from the ground. The company said it couldn't provide the exact percentage of mined versus recycled material in the finished medals. Each gold medal contained a little more than 1.5 percent of ewaste materials, while each copper medal contained just over 1 percent, and the silver medals contained only small pieces. The ewaste came from old computer monitor's glass, various computer parts, and other surplus or discarded technologies.

Several different processing methods were used to extract the materials. First, the company shredded the equipment to separate out the various metals, glass, and other usable parts. To remove the metals that could not be recovered by the shredding process, the parts were fed into a furnace operating at a temperature greater than 2,000 degrees (Fahrenheit). The materials were then combined with other metals to create the medals. Each medal was hand-cropped, ensuring no two are alike, another first in Olympic history. The medals, designed by Canadian artist Corrine Hunt, were also the first nonflat medals made for the Games, with a wavy form to represent the ocean and mountain snowdrifts, both characteristic of Vancouver's environment. In addition to representing the athletes' outstanding achievements, the 2010 Olympic medals gave new life to the precious metals recoverable from ewaste.[13]

Questions

1. Why would the Olympics benefit from creating a strong environmental MIS infrastructure?
2. How can the Olympics help support ethical ewaste initiatives?
3. Why would a sporting event like the Olympics be concerned with reducing its carbon footprint?
4. What could the Olympics do to help shed light on global environmental MIS issues?
5. How could Moore's Law enable future Olympic medals to be made from more ewaste?

CRITICAL BUSINESS THINKING

1. Universities Are Switching to Gmail

Schools around the world are moving to cloud computing applications such as Google Docs & Spreadsheets and Google Calendar. Yale had planned to move from its own email system to Google Mail, but at the last minute decided to cancel the project. The reason was because school administrators and faculty members did not believe the move could support their business requirements.

Do you agree or disagree that Google Gmail would be unable to replace a university's private email system? What are the advantages and disadvantages of a private email system? What are the advantages and disadvantages of using a cloud application such as Google Gmail? What choice would you make if you were the primary decision maker for choosing your school's email system?[14]

2. Desktop Virtualization

Every day users are becoming more comfortable with accessing and storing information in the cloud. This creates increased demand on MIS personnel to help manage, control, and provide access to that information—not just on company-issued computers, but on any number of devices, including personal ones. More and more employees want to be able to utilize their own computing devices—cell phones, netbooks, laptops—instead of company-issued ones. For instance, many students graduating from college have been exposed to Macs and may even own one, yet they are finding PCs as the standard computer of choice for most companies. Do you think it is a good business practice to allow your employees to use their personal devices for work-related business? What are the challenges of allowing users to port business applications to their personal devices? What are the challenges of allowing users to connect to corporate systems with personal devices?

3. iTunes in the Cloud

Apple is considering a cloud version of its iTunes software that could possibly provide a host of new services for its users as they would no longer be required to save iTunes to their computers as it would reside in the cloud. With cloud computing, the software for iTunes would reside in centralized servers in data centers, rather than on a specific user computer. What would be the benefits to customers if they could host iTunes in the clouds and access it using a variety of devices? What would be your fears if you were to use iTunes in the cloud?

4. Sustainable Departments

Energy prices and global warming are discussed daily in the news as the environmental impact of ewaste is just beginning to be recognized. Sustainability and corporate social responsibility need to be taken seriously by all managers as everyone should take an active role in helping to preserve the environment. List the different departments in a business and the types of environmental issues they typically encounter. Which department do you think creates the most ewaste? Which department uses the greatest amount of electricity or has the largest carbon footprint? What can each department do to help combat its environmental issues? Why do all managers, and for that matter all employees, need to be aware of environmental issues and ways they can create sustainable MIS infrastructures?

5. Making the Smart Grid Smart

ISO, a regional electricity company in New England, has launched an $18 million project in part because of an $8 million three-year federal grant. The project is designed to speed up the installation of 30 smart-grid devices covering every state in New England. The smart-grid devices will provide control room operators at ISO with enhanced tools to monitor and measure performance of the region's electrical grid, allowing the company to improve its ability to detect and address problems on the system. System status information coming into ISO will increase from once every four seconds to 30 times per second. Would you invest in ISO if you had the chance? Why or why not? If you were awarded an $8 million three-year federal grant, what type of sustainable infrastructure would you create?[15]

6. Planning for Disaster Recovery

You are the new senior analyst in the MIS department at Beltz, a large snack food manufacturing company. The company is located on the beautiful shoreline in Charleston, North Carolina. The company's location is one of its best and worst features. The weather and surroundings are beautiful, but the threat of hurricanes and other natural disasters is high. What types of information should be contained in Beltz's disaster recovery plan that will minimize any risks involved with a natural disaster?

7. Comparing Backup and Recovery Systems

Research the Internet to find three different vendors of backup and recovery systems. Compare and contrast the three systems and determine which one you would recommend if you were installing a backup and recovery system for a medium-sized business, with 3,500 employees, that maintains information on the stock market. Compile your findings in a presentation that you can give to your class that details the three systems' strengths and weaknesses, along with your recommendation.

8. Cool Schools

Very large computers and data centers incur huge energy costs keeping electronic components cooled. Where is your school's data center located? How big is it? What security measures does the facility enforce? Can you get a tour of it? If it is on campus, how is the facility cooled? How is the power supplied? Heating and cooling computer systems are certainly a big issue. Think of ways you could reuse the heat from a data center, such as sending it to a college dorm. Could alternative resources, such as a nearby river or a lake, provide added cooling? What unanticipated environmental issues could this create?

9. Box.net in the Cloud

Box.net was started by two college students, Aaron Levie and Dylan Smith, who needed a secure place to collaborate on group projects. The two immediately understood the value of cloud computing, and they created Box.net to allow them to share ideas and collaborate on documents in a virtual work space located in the cloud. They knew the cloud would allow them to access their documents from anywhere and on any device and that there was no chance of their papers being stolen or accidently destroyed. Levie and Smith recognized the business opportunity of their site and jumped at turning Box.net into a real business. Explain how Box.net could help you if you were working on a project with four other students. What would be the challenges of using Box.net?[16]

ENTREPRENEURIAL CHALLENGE

BUILD YOUR OWN BUSINESS

1. On your way to work this morning, you stopped for gas. When you were inside paying, someone broke into your car and stole your computer bag. You did not notice until you arrived at your business and began looking for your bag. As you begin to realize all of the data you just lost—customer lists, profit and loss analysis, tax returns, email, sales information, payroll files, and so on—you begin to wonder when you last backed up your hard drive. Now that you have been stung by a painful data loss experience, you realize the importance of having a backup strategy. Create a detailed backup strategy and disaster recovery plan for your business. Be sure to include details such as the types of backup you will perform, frequency of backups, and location of backups. (Be sure to identify your business and the name of your company.)

2. Rank the characteristics of an agile MIS infrastructure in order of importance to your business and be sure to provide detailed information on each characteristic and your justification for its ranking.

3. Cloud computing is a business driven MIS infrastructure that supports growth, operations, and profits. It helps today's businesses innovate by using resources and applications hosted remotely as a shared service on the Internet. You have decided to research the different types of cloud computing services. Create a report listing the types of services your business should implement and the advantages and disadvantages of each.

APPLY YOUR KNOWLEDGE BUSINESS PROJECTS

PROJECT I   Ranking MIS characteristics

In a group, review the list of MIS infrastructure characteristics that support growth and rank them in order of their impact on a company's success, using 1 to indicate the biggest impact and 7 the least.

MIS Infrastructure Characteristics	Business Impact
Accessibility	
Availability	
Maintainability	
Portability	
Reliability	
Scalability	
Usability	

PROJECT II   Designing a Company Infrastructure

Components of an MIS infrastructure include everything from documentation to business concepts to software and hardware. Deciding which components to implement and how to implement them can be a challenge. New MIS components are released daily, and business needs continually change. An MIS infrastructure that meets your company's needs today may not meet those needs tomorrow. Building an MIS infrastructure that is accessible, available, flexible, reliable, scalable, usable, and performs well is key to your company's growth, operations, and profitability.

You are the manager for a large clothing company called Xedous. You are responsible for developing the initial MIS infrastructure. Create a list of questions you will need answered to develop it. Here are examples of a few of the questions you might ask:

- What are the company's growth expectations?
- Will systems be able to handle additional users?
- How long will information be stored in the systems?
- How much customer history must be stored?
- What are the company's business hours?
- What are the company's backup requirements?

PROJECT III   Recycle Your Cell Phone

For all those excited to get a new iPhone with its numerous applications and cool games, what are you going to do with your old cell phone? You can help the environment and recycle your phone, PDA, charger, and batteries. Recycling cell phones helps to save energy and keep reusable materials out of landfills. Cell phones are made of plastic, copper, and precious metals, which require energy to extract and manufacture. If you decide to recycle your cell phone be sure to terminate the service, delete any contacts or stored information, and take out the SIM card.

If your old cell phone is still working, you might also want to consider donating it to charity. Many programs will accept working cell phones that they donate to people in need, such as survivors of domestic violence, because old cell phones can still dial 911 even after the service is disconnected. To find local agencies where you can donate your cell phone, visit ncadv.org. Cell phones are only a small percentage of the total computer equipment organizations replace each year. What happens to all of those old laptops, notebooks, servers, and monitors? What is the environmental impact of throwing a computer system into a landfill? What can companies do to recycle their computer equipment? What can the government do to help motivate companies and individuals to recycle?

PROJECT IV   Back on Your Feet

You are working for GetSmart, a document creation company for legal professionals. Due to the highly sensitive nature of their work, employees must store all information on the network drive and are not allowed to back up the data to a CD, flash drive, or any other type of external storage, including home computers. The company has been following this policy for the past three years without any problems. You return to work Monday morning after a long weekend to find that the building was struck by lightning, destroying several servers. Unfortunately, the backup network also failed, so all the data from your department have been lost.

Because of this loss, the MIS manager and four colleagues who developed the company backup policy were fired.

You have been placed on a committee with several of your peers to revamp the backup and recovery policies and create a new disaster recovery plan. You must create policies and procedures that will preserve the sensitive nature of the documents, while ensuring the company is safe from disasters. Be sure to address a worst-case scenario where the entire building is lost.

PROJECT V   Growing, Growing, Gone

You are the founder of Black Pearl, a small comic book start-up. The good news is Black Pearl is tremendously successful, with 34 employees in a functional and creative office in downtown Chicago. The comics you produce are of extremely high quality. The artwork is unmatched, and fans find the story lines compelling. Black Pearl comics are quickly becoming classics with extremely loyal customers. You produce all the comics and sell them in your store and via the Internet to individuals all over the United States.

You had a vision when you started Black Pearl. You knew the potential of your business model to revamp the comic industry. You purchased high-end computers and customizable software to support your operations. Now, you are faced with a new dilemma. You have a large international following and you have decided to pursue international opportunities. You would like to open stores in Japan, France, and Brazil over the next year. To determine whether this is possible you need to evaluate if your MIS infrastructure is agile enough to support international requirements. Brainstorm all of the business nuances that will be different when working with international companies and customers. Create a list of questions your MIS department will need to answer to determine if your system is agile enough to support international business.

PROJECT VI   Excuses, Excuses, Excuses

Here are a few examples of the strangest and most unusual excuses employees use when missing work.

- I have a sunburn.
- I'm not sure why but I woke up in Canada.
- I was caught selling an alligator.
- I was locked in the trunk of an abandoned car.
- I have a note from my mom that I could not go to work yesterday.
- I'm just not into it today.
- I was riding my motorcycle and I accidentally hit a nun.
- Some person threw poison ivy at me and now I have a rash on my face.
- I need to stay home as I am convinced I can catch my spouse having an affair.

- I was chasing a seagull and fell down and had to go to the hospital.
- I have a migraine from eating too many jalapeño peppers.

This chapter focuses on MIS infrastructures, the main building blocks that function together to control the entire organization's systems. If your systems cannot operate, then your organization cannot work, similar to how your health controls your ability to work. Attempting to do business with an organization when its systems have crashed, Internet access is down, or wireless network is malfunctioning is very frustrating. When these types of issues occur, companies do not want to broadcast that they are experiencing technical difficulties because of hackers, an unpaid utility bill, or squirrels got into the data center and ate through all of the wires (yes, that has really happened).

How many times have you called a company and the customer service representative has stated that the system is down or that the system is really slow today? How many times have you missed submitting an assignment because your Internet service was down? Why is it important for an organization to have its systems available 24 hours a day, 7 days a week, and 365 days a year? Why would a company hide the real reason that its systems are malfunctioning? What could happen if customers were informed that the systems were down due to hackers? How can an organization safeguard its systems?

PROJECT VII   Ewaste Not, Want Not

On Earth Day every year many people, including corporate citizens, devote themselves to recycling and reducing, along with identifying items they can repurpose. Companies, such as Dell and Microsoft, two producers of materials that eventually become ewaste, have joined forces with an electronics recycling program run by Goodwill Industries International. Goodwill reports that the program has diverted about 96 million pounds in electronics from landfills.[17]

Assisting in a similar effort are office supply stores Office Depot and Staples that offer their own sorting and recycling services for used electronics. Apple has even jumped on this bandwagon, allowing customers to turn their old products in to retail locations when they buy something new.

There are so many opportunities to reduce ewaste. Make a list of how the popular technology manufacturers are already trying to reduce ewaste. Would starting a company that helped people locate used computers or other technologies for reuse be a worthwhile venture? Why or why not? Create a list of new alternatives any company could adopt to reuse, recycle, and reduce ewaste.

PROJECT VIII   One Laptop Per Child

The One Laptop Per Child (OLPC) project intends to create a $100 laptop for distribution to the world's poorest children. The machine, called the OLPC or XO laptop, has a rubberized keyboard and an ultra-bright screen readable in daylight; when flipped, it converts to an electronic book reader. To keep the cost as low as possible (at $175 it is currently a bit more than the target), the computer has a host of free software and other tools to support learning opportunities. A special type of networking allows machines within a hundred feet or so to communicate with each other and relays a single Internet connection for them to use (where the Internet is available). The XO is targeted at communities where power generation is unreliable or nonexistent; it gets its power via a hand crank, pull cord, or foot pedal.[18]

Do you agree that the One Laptop Per Child project will help educate children around the world? How does the XO computer provide learning opportunities for children in poor regions of the world? What issues could these children encounter if they have an XO laptop? How will cloud computing play an important role in the XO laptop, especially in terms of keeping costs low and data safe? What do you think the typical environment will be like where the XO laptop will be used? What issues will users of the XO laptop encounter that are not common in the United States? What can the creators of the XO laptop do to ensure its functionality even in the most extreme environments?

AYK APPLICATION PROJECTS

If you are looking for Excel projects to incorporate into your class, try any of the following after reading this chapter.

Project Number	Project Name	Project Type	Plug-In	Focus Area	Project Level	Skill Set	Page Number
8	Book Boxes	Excel	T2, T4	Strategic Analysis	Intermediate	Formulas or Solver	AYK.6
9	Security Analysis	Excel	T3	Filtering Data	Intermediate	Conditional Formatting, Autofilter, Subtotal	AYK.7
10	Gathering Data	Excel	T3	Data Analysis	Intermediate	Conditional Formatting	AYK.8
11	Splashem	Excel	T2	Strategic Analysis	Intermediate	Formulas	AYK.8
12	Bill's Boots	Excel	T2	Profit Maximization	Intermediate	Formulas	AYK.9
13	Adequate Acquisitions	Excel	T2	Break Even Analysis	Intermediate	Formulas	AYK.9
15	Assessing the Value of Information	Excel	T3	Data Analysis	Intermediate	PivotTable	AYK.10
16	Growth, Trends, and Forecasts	Excel	T2, T3	Data Forecasting	Advanced	Average, Trend, Growth	AYK.11
18	Formatting Grades	Excel	T3	Data Analysis	Advanced	If, LookUp	AYK.12
22	Gizmo Turnover	Excel	T3	Data Mining	Advanced	PivotTable	AYK.15
24	Mountain Cycle	Excel	T4	Business Analysis	Advanced	Goal Seek	AYK.16
25	Lutz Motors	Excel	T4	Sales Analysis	Advanced	Scenario Manager	AYK.16

6

CHAPTER

Data: Business Intelligence

CHAPTER OUTLINE

What's in IT for me?

This chapter introduces the concepts of information and data and their relative importance to business professionals and firms. It distinguishes between data stored in transactional databases and powerful business intelligence gleaned from data warehouses. Students who understand how to access, manipulate, summarize, sort, and analyze data to support decision making find success. Information has power, and understanding that power will help you compete in the global marketplace. This chapter will provide you with an overview of database fundamentals and the characteristics associated with high-quality information. It will also explain how the various bits of data stored across multiple, operational databases can be transformed in a centralized repository of summarized information in a data warehouse, which can be used for discovering business intelligence.

You, as a business student, need to understand the differences between transactional data and summarized information and the different types of questions you could use a transactional database to answer versus a data warehouse. You need to be aware of the complexity of storing data in databases and the level of effort required to transform operational data into meaningful, summarized information. You need to realize the power of information and the competitive advantage a data warehouse brings an organization in terms of facilitating business intelligence. Armed with the power of information, business students will make smart, informed, and data-supported managerial decisions.

Informing Information

Since the beginning of time, man has been using pictures and images to communicate, moving from caveman drawings to hieroglyphics to the Internet. Today, it is easier than ever to paint a picture worth 100,000 words, thanks to technological advances. The primary advantages are databases and data warehouses that capture enormous amounts of data. Informing means accessing large amounts of data from different management information systems. According to a recent analysis of press releases by *PR Newswire*, an article or advertisement that uses visual images can significantly improve the number of views a message generates. This can be a true competitive advantage in the digital age.

An infographic (or information graphic) displays information graphically so it can be more easily understood. Infographics cut straight to the point by taking complex information and presenting it in a simple visual format. Infographics can present the results of large data analysis, looking for patterns and relationships that monitor changes in variables over time. Because infographics can easily become overwhelming, users need to be careful to not display too much data or the resulting infographics can result in information overload. Effective infographics can achieve outstanding results for marketing, advertising, and public relations. According to *PR Newswire*, infographics gain the greatest competitive advantage when they have the following:

- Survey results that are too hard to understand in text format.
- Statistical data that are not interesting for readers.
- Comparison research where the impact can be far more dramatic when presented visually.
- Messages for multilingual audiences.
- Any information that can use a visual element to make it more interesting (see Figures 6.1, 6.2, and 6.3 for examples).[1]

FIGURE 6.1

Hotels.com Travel Infographic

FIGURE 6.2

Emerson's Food Waste
Infographic

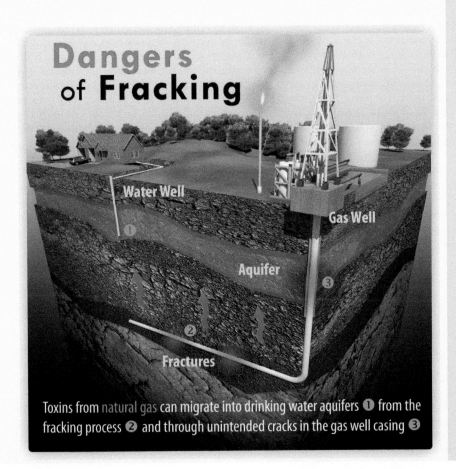

FIGURE 6.3

SC Johnson Consumer
Environmental Behaviors
Infographic

section 6.1 | Data, Information, and Databases

LO 6.1: Explain the four primary traits that determine the value of information.

THE BUSINESS BENEFITS OF HIGH-QUALITY INFORMATION

Information is powerful. Information can tell an organization how its current operations are performing and help it estimate and strategize about how future operations might perform. The ability to understand, digest, analyze, and filter information is key to growth and success for any professional in any industry. Remember that new perspectives and opportunities can open up when you have the right data that you can turn into information and ultimately business intelligence.

Information is everywhere in an organization. Managers in sales, marketing, human resources, and management need information to run their departments and make daily decisions. When addressing a significant business issue, employees must be able to obtain and analyze all the relevant information so they can make the best decision possible. Information comes at different levels, formats, and granularities. *Information granularity* refers to the extent of detail within the information (fine and detailed or coarse and abstract). Employees must be able to correlate the different levels, formats, and granularities of information when making decisions. For example, a company might be collecting information from various suppliers to make needed decisions, only to find that the information is in different levels, formats, and granularities. One supplier might send detailed information in a spreadsheet, while another supplier might send summary information in a Word document, and still another might send a collection of information from emails. Employees will need to compare these different types of information for what they commonly reveal to make strategic decisions. Figure 6.4 displays the various levels, formats, and granularities of organizational information.

Successfully collecting, compiling, sorting, and finally analyzing information from multiple levels, in varied formats, and exhibiting different granularities can provide tremendous insight into how an organization is performing. Exciting and unexpected results can include potential new markets, new ways of reaching customers, and even new methods of doing business. After understanding the different levels, formats, and granularities of information, managers next want to look at the four primary traits that help determine the value of information (see Figure 6.5).

Information Type: Transactional and Analytical

As discussed previously in the text, the two primary types of information are transactional and analytical. Transactional information encompasses all of the information contained within a single business process or unit of work, and its primary purpose is to support daily operational tasks. Organizations need to capture and store transactional information to perform operational tasks and repetitive decisions such as analyzing daily sales reports and production schedules to determine how much inventory to carry. Consider Walmart, which handles more than 1 million customer transactions every hour, and Facebook, which keeps track of 400 million active users (along with their photos, friends, and web links). In addition, every time a cash register rings up a sale, a deposit or withdrawal is made from an ATM, or a receipt is given at the gas pump, capturing and storing of the transactional information are required.

Information Levels
Individual, Department, Enterprise

- Individual knowledge, goals, and strategies
- Departmental goals, revenues, expenses, processes, and strategies
- Enterprise revenues, expenses, processes, and strategies

Information Formats
Document, Presentation, Spreadsheet, Database

- Letters, memos, faxes, emails, reports, marketing materials, and training materials
- Product, strategy, process, financial, customer, and competitor
- Sales, marketing, industry, financial, competitor, customer, and order spreadsheets
- Customer, employee, sales, order, supplier, and manufacturer databases

Information Granularities
Detail (Fine), Summary, Aggregate (Coarse)

- Reports for each salesperson, product, and part
- Reports for all sales personnel, all products, and all parts
- Reports across departments, organizations, and companies

FIGURE 6.4

Levels, Formats, and Granularities of Organizational Information

Analytical information encompasses all organizational information, and its primary purpose is to support the performing of managerial analysis tasks. Analytical information is useful when making important decisions such as whether the organization should build a new manufacturing plant or hire additional sales personnel. Analytical information makes it possible to do many things that previously were difficult to accomplish, such as spot business trends, prevent diseases, and fight crime. For example, credit card companies crunch through billions of transactional purchase records to identify fraudulent activity. Indicators such as charges in a foreign country or consecutive purchases of gasoline send a red flag highlighting potential fraudulent activity.

Walmart was able to use its massive amount of analytical information to identify many unusual trends, such as a correlation between storms and Pop-Tarts. Yes, Walmart

FIGURE 6.5

The Four Primary Traits of the Value of Information

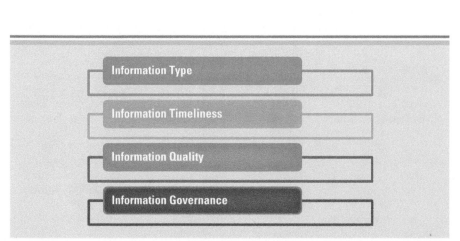

Information Type

Information Timeliness

Information Quality

Information Governance

discovered an increase in the demand for Pop-Tarts during the storm season. Armed with the valuable information the retail chain was able to stock up on Pop-Tarts that were ready for purchase when customers arrived. Figure 6.6 displays different types of transactional and analytical information.

Information Timeliness

Timeliness is an aspect of information that depends on the situation. In some firms or industries, information that is a few days or weeks old can be relevant, while in others information that is a few minutes old can be almost worthless. Some organizations, such as 911 response centers, stock traders, and banks, require up-to-the-second information. Other organizations, such as insurance and construction companies, require only daily or even weekly information.

Real-time information means immediate, up-to-date information. *Real-time systems* provide real-time information in response to requests. Many organizations use real-time systems to uncover key corporate transactional information. The growing demand for real-time information stems from organizations' need to make faster and more effective decisions, keep smaller inventories, operate more efficiently, and track performance more carefully. Information also needs to be timely in the sense that it meets employees' needs, but no more. If employees can absorb information only on an hourly or daily basis, there is no need to gather real-time information in smaller increments.

Most people request real-time information without understanding one of the biggest pitfalls associated with real-time information—continual change. Imagine the following scenario: Three managers meet at the end of the day to discuss a business problem. Each manager has gathered information at different times during the day to create a picture of the situation. Each manager's picture may be different because of the time differences. Their views on the business problem may not match because the information they are basing their analysis on is continually changing. This approach may not speed up decision making, and it may actually slow it down. Business decision makers must evaluate the timeliness for the information for every decision. Organizations do not want to find themselves using real-time information to make a bad decision faster.

Information Quality

Business decisions are only as good as the quality of the information used to make them. *Information inconsistency* occurs when the same data element has different values. Take for example the amount of work that needs to occur to update a customer who had changed her last name due to marriage. Changing this information in only a few organizational systems will lead to data inconsistencies causing customer 123456 to be associated with two last names. *Information integrity issues* occur when a system produces

FIGURE 6.6

Transactional versus Analytical Information

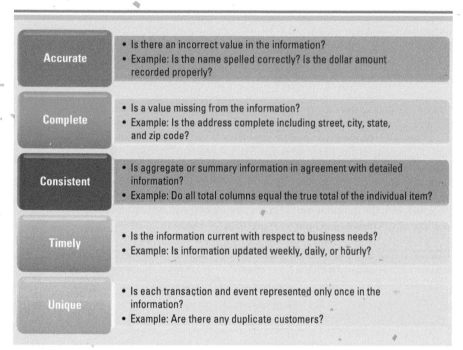

FIGURE 6.7

Five Common Characteristics of High-Quality Information

incorrect, inconsistent, or duplicate data. Data integrity issues can cause managers to consider the system reports invalid and will make decisions based on other sources.

To ensure your systems do not suffer from data integrity issues, review Figure 6.7 for the five characteristics common to high-quality information: accuracy, completeness, consistency, timeliness, and uniqueness. Figure 6.8 provides an example of several problems associated with using low-quality information including:

1. *Completeness.* The customer's first name is missing.
2. Another issue with *completeness.* The street address contains only a number and not a street name.
3. *Consistency.* There may be a duplication of information since there is a slight difference between the two customers in the spelling of the last name. Similar street addresses and phone numbers make this likely.

FIGURE 6.8

Example of Low-Quality Information

1. Missing information (no first name)   2. Incomplete information (no street)   5. Inaccurate information (invalid email)

ID	Last Name	First Name	Street	City	State	Zip	Phone	Fax	Email
113	Smith		123 S. Main	Denver	CO	80210	(303) 777-1258	(303) 777-5544	ssmith@aol.com
114	Jones	Jeff	12A	Denver	CO	80224	(303) 666-6868	(303) 666-6868	(303) 666-6868
115	Roberts	Jenny	1244 Colfax	Denver	CO	85231	759-5654	853-6584	jr@msn.com
116	Robert	Jenny	1244 Colfax	Denver	CO	85231	759-5654	853-6584	jr@msn.com

3. Probable duplicate information (similar names, same address, phone number)   4. Potential wrong information (are the phone and fax numbers the same or is this an error?)   6. Incomplete information (missing area codes)

BUSINESS DRIVEN MIS

Determining Information Quality Issues

Real People magazine is geared toward working individuals and provides articles and advice on everything from car maintenance to family planning. The magazine is currently experiencing problems with its distribution list. More than 30 percent of the magazines mailed are returned because of incorrect address information, and each month it receives numerous calls from angry customers complaining that they have not yet received their magazines. Below is a sample of *Real People*'s customer information. Create a report detailing all the issues with the information, potential causes of the information issues, and solutions the company can follow to correct the situation.

ID	First Name	Middle Initial	Last Name	Street	City	State	Zip Code
433	M	J	Jones	13 Denver	Denver	CO	87654
434	Margaret	J	Jones	13 First Ave.	Denver	CO	87654
434	Brian	F	Hoover	Lake Ave.	Columbus	OH	87654
435	Nick	H	Schweitzer	65 Apple Lane	San Francisco	OH	65664
436	Richard	A		567 55th St.	New York	CA	98763
437	Alana	B	Smith	121 Tenny Dr.	Buffalo	NY	142234
438	Trevor	D	Darrian	90 Fresrdestil	Dallas	TX	74532

4. *Accuracy.* This may be inaccurate information because the customer's phone and fax numbers are the same. Some customers might have the same number for phone and fax, but the fact that the customer also has this number in the email address field is suspicious.

5. Another issue with *accuracy*. There is inaccurate information because a phone number is located in the email address field.

6. Another issue with *completeness*. The information is incomplete because there is not a valid area code for the phone and fax numbers.

Nestlé uses 550,000 suppliers to sell more than 100,000 products in 200 countries. However, due to poor information, the company was unable to evaluate its business effectively. After some analysis, it found that it had 9 million records of vendors, customers, and materials, half of which were duplicated, obsolete, inaccurate, or incomplete. The analysis discovered that some records abbreviated vendor names while other records spelled out the vendor names. This created multiple accounts for the same customer, making it impossible to determine the true value of Nestlé's customers. Without being able to identify customer profitability, a company runs the risk of alienating its best customers.[2]

Knowing how low-quality information issues typically occur can help a company correct them. Addressing these errors will significantly improve the quality of company information and the value to be extracted from it. The four primary reasons for low-quality information are:

1. Online customers intentionally enter inaccurate information to protect their privacy.

2. Different systems have different information entry standards and formats.

3. Data-entry personnel enter abbreviated information to save time or erroneous information by accident.

4. Third-party and external information contains inconsistencies, inaccuracies, and errors.

Understanding the Costs of Using Low-Quality Information Using the wrong information can lead managers to make erroneous decisions. Erroneous decisions in turn can cost time, money, reputations, and even jobs. Some of the serious business consequences that occur due to using low-quality information to make decisions are:

- Inability to accurately track customers.
- Difficulty identifying the organization's most valuable customers.
- Inability to identify selling opportunities.
- Lost revenue opportunities from marketing to nonexistent customers.
- The cost of sending nondeliverable mail.
- Difficulty tracking revenue because of inaccurate invoices.
- Inability to build strong relationships with customers.

Understanding the Benefits of Using High-Quality Information High-quality information can significantly improve the chances of making a good decision and directly increase an organization's bottom line. One company discovered that even with its large number of golf courses, Phoenix, Arizona, is not a good place to sell golf clubs. An analysis revealed that typical golfers in Phoenix are tourists and convention-eers who usually bring their clubs with them. The analysis further revealed that two of the best places to sell golf clubs in the United States are Rochester, New York, and Detroit, Michigan. Equipped with this valuable information, the company was able to strategically place its stores and launch its marketing campaigns.

High-quality information does not automatically guarantee that every decision made is going to be a good one, because people ultimately make decisions and no one is per-fect. However, such information ensures that the basis of the decisions is accurate. The success of the organization depends on appreciating and leveraging the true value of timely and high-quality information.

Information Governance

Information is a vital resource and users need to be educated on what they can and can-not do with it. To ensure a firm manages its information correctly, it will need special pol-icies and procedures establishing rules on how the information is organized, updated, maintained, and accessed. Every firm, large and small, should create an information policy concerning data governance. *Data governance* refers to the overall management of the availability, usability, integrity, and security of company data. A company that sup-ports a data governance program has a defined a policy that specifies who is accountable for various portions or aspects of the data, including its accuracy, accessibility, consis-tency, timeliness, and completeness. The policy should clearly define the processes con-cerning how to store, archive, back up, and secure the data. In addition, the company should create a set of procedures identifying accessibility levels for employees. Then, the firm should deploy controls and procedures that enforce government regulations and compliance with mandates such as Sarbanes-Oxley.

STORING INFORMATION USING A RELATIONAL DATABASE MANAGEMENT SYSTEM

LO 6.2: Describe a database, a database management system, and the relational database model.

The core component of any system, regardless of size, is a database and a database management system. Broadly defined, a *database* maintains information about vari-ous types of objects (inventory), events (transactions), people (employees), and places (warehouses). A *database management system (DBMS)* creates, reads, updates, and deletes data in a database while controlling access and security. Managers send requests to the DBMS, and the DBMS performs the actual manipulation of the data in the data-base. Companies store their information in databases, and managers access these sys-tems to answer operational questions such as how many customers purchased Product A in December or what were the average sales by region. There are two primary tools available for retrieving information from a DBMS. First is a *query-by-example (QBE)*

BUSINESS DRIVEN DEBATE

Securing Credit Card Data

Without a data governance policy, a company might be leaving its data vulnerable to hackers and theft. Consider TJX Co., the parent company of T.J. Maxx, which had 45 million credit and debit card numbers stolen from its data systems. The credit card industry provides security rules that mandate vendors encrypt credit card data and limit storage of credit card numbers from point-of-sale terminals. T.J. Maxx did not have a data governance policy adhering to these stipulations and was actively storing the customer information and credit card numbers for years.[3]

Who do you think is to blame for the T.J. Maxx credit card data theft—the company for not implementing the proper data governance policies or the hackers?

tool that helps users graphically design the answer to a question against a database. Second is a *structured query language (SQL)* that asks users to write lines of code to answer questions against a database. Managers typically interact with QBE tools, and MIS professionals have the skills required to code SQL. Figure 6.9 displays the relationship between a database, a DBMS, and a user. Some of the more popular examples of DBMS include MySQL, Microsoft Access, SQL Server, FileMaker, Oracle, and FoxPro.

A *data element (or data field)* is the smallest or basic unit of information. Data elements can include a customer's name, address, email, discount rate, preferred shipping method, product name, quantity ordered, and so on. *Data models* are logical data structures that detail the relationships among data elements using graphics or pictures.

Metadata provides details about data. For example, metadata for an image could include its size, resolution, and date created. Metadata about a text document could contain document length, data created, author's name, and summary. Each data element is given a description, such as Customer Name; metadata is provided for the type of data (text, numeric, alphanumeric, date, image, binary value) and descriptions of potential predefined values such as a certain area code; and finally the relationship is defined. A *data dictionary* compiles all of the metadata about the data elements in the data model. Looking at a data model along with reviewing the data dictionary provides tremendous insight into the database's functions, purpose, and business rules.

DBMS use three primary data models for organizing information—hierarchical, network, and the relational database, the most prevalent. A *relational database model* stores information in the form of logically related two-dimensional tables. A *relational*

FIGURE 6.9

Relationship of Database, DBMS, and User

database management system allows users to create, read, update, and delete data in a relational database. Although the hierarchical and network models are important, this text focuses only on the relational database model.

Storing Data Elements in Entities and Attributes

For flexibility in supporting business operations, managers need to query or search for the answers to business questions such as which artist sold the most albums during a certain month. The relationships in the relational database model help managers extract this information. Figure 6.10 illustrates the primary concepts of the relational database model—entities, attributes, keys, and relationships. An ***entity*** (also referred to as a table) stores information about a person, place, thing, transaction, or event. The entities, or tables, of interest in Figure 6.10 are *TRACKS, RECORDINGS, MUSICIANS,* and *CATEGORIES.* Notice that each entity is stored in a different two-dimensional table (with rows and columns).

Attributes (also called columns or fields) are the data elements associated with an entity. In Figure 6.10 the attributes for the entity *TRACKS* are *TrackNumber, TrackTitle, TrackLength,* and *RecordingID.* Attributes for the entity *MUSICIANS* are *MusicianID, MusicianName, MusicianPhoto,* and *MusicianNotes.* A ***record*** is a collection of related data elements (in the *MUSICIANS* table these include "3, Lady Gaga, gag.tiff, Do not bring young kids to live shows"). Each record in an entity occupies one row in its respective table.

Creating Relationships Through Keys

To manage and organize various entities within the relational database model, you use primary keys and foreign keys to create logical relationships. A ***primary key*** is a field (or group of fields) that uniquely identifies a given record in a table. In the table *RECORDINGS,* the primary key is the field *RecordingID* that uniquely identifies each record in the table. Primary keys are a critical piece of a relational database because they provide a way of distinguishing each record in a table; for instance, imagine you need to find information

FIGURE 6.10

Primary Concepts of the Relational Database Model

Entities   **Foreign keys**

TRACKS

TrackNumber	TrackTitle	TrackLength	RecordingID
1	I Won't	3:45	1
2	Begin Again	4:14	1
3	You Got Me	4:00	1
4	Fallin For you	3:35	1
1	I Gotta Feelin	4:49	2
2	Imma Be	4:17	2
3	Boom Boom Pow	4:11	2
4	Meet Me Halfway	4:44	2

Primary keys

RECORDINGS

RecordingID	RecordingTitle	MuscianID	CategoryID
1	Breakthrough	1	1
2	The E.N.D.	2	1
3	Monkey Business	2	1
4	Elephunk	2	1
5	The Fame Monster	3	1
6	Raymond v. Raymond	4	2

Attributes

CATEGORIES

CategoryID	CategoryName
1	Pop
2	R&B
3	Rock
4	Country
5	Blues
6	Classical

MUSICIANS

MusicianID	MusicianName	MusicianPhoto	MusicianNotes
1	Colby Caillat	Colby.jpg	Next concert in Boston 7/1/2011
2	Black Eyed Peas	BYP.bmp	New album due 12/25/2011
3	Lady Gaga	Gaga.tiff	Do not bring young kids to live shows
4	Usher	Usher.bmp	Current album #1 on Billboard

Records

BUSINESS DRIVEN START-UP

The Rylaxer

Living in a cramped dorm room is a common college occurrence. This was the experience of Ryan Dickerson, a Syracuse University student, who found himself wedged into a tiny dorm room with only enough room to fit a bed, desk, and chair. Spotting an entrepreneurial opportunity, Dickerson innovatively created a hybrid bed and couch, calling his new product the Rylaxer. During the day the Rylaxer functioned as a couch and during the night it transformed into a bed, solving his limited space issue. The Rylaxer is made of environmentally friendly foam and is available in two sizes and a variety of colors. Of course, you can pay extra for a custom cover with your school's name, Greek letters, or favorite sports team's logo.[4]

Why would a spreadsheet be ineffective for running Dickerson's business? Why would he want to create a database to support his business needs? If you were building the Rylaxer database, what are a few of the entities and associated attributes you might create? Why would you want to create primary and foreign keys? How will you use these keys to turn data into information?

on a customer named Steve Smith. Simply searching the customer name would not be an ideal way to find the information because there might be 20 customers with the name Steve Smith. This is the reason the relational database model uses primary keys to uniquely identify each record. Using Steve Smith's unique ID allows a manager to search the database to identify all information associated with this customer.

A *foreign key* is a primary key of one table that appears as an attribute in another table and acts to provide a logical relationship between the two tables. For instance, Black Eyed Peas in Figure 6.10 is one of the musicians appearing in the *MUSICIANS* table. Its primary key, *MusicianID,* is "2." Notice that *MusicianID* also appears as an attribute in the *RECORDINGS* table. By matching these attributes, you create a relationship between the *MUSICIANS* and *RECORDINGS* tables that states the Black Eyed Peas *(MusicianID 2)* have several recordings including The E.N.D., Monkey Business, and Elepunk. In essence, *MusicianID* in the *RECORDINGS* table creates a logical relationship (who was the musician that made the recording) to the *MUSICIANS* table. Creating the logical relationship between the tables allows managers to search the data and turn it into useful information.

LO 6.3: Identify the business advantages of a relational database.

USING A RELATIONAL DATABASE FOR BUSINESS ADVANTAGES

Many business managers are familiar with Excel and other spreadsheet programs they can use to store business data. Although spreadsheets are excellent for supporting some data analysis, they offer limited functionality in terms of security, accessibility, and flexibility and can rarely scale to support business growth. From a business perspective, relational databases offer many advantages over using a text document or a spreadsheet, as displayed in Figure 6.11.

Increased Flexibility

Databases tend to mirror business structures, and a database needs to handle changes quickly and easily, just as any business needs to be able to do. Equally important, databases need to provide flexibility in allowing each user to access the information in whatever way best suits his or her needs. The distinction between logical and physical views is important in understanding flexible database user views. The *physical view of information* deals with the physical storage of information on a storage device.

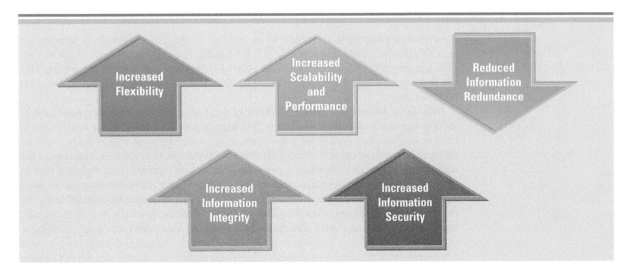

FIGURE 6.11

Business Advantages of a
Relational Database

The *logical view of information* focuses on how individual users logically access information to meet their own particular business needs.

In the database illustration from Figure 6.10, for example, one user could perform a query to determine which recordings had a track length of four minutes or more. At the same time, another user could perform an analysis to determine the distribution of recordings as they relate to the different categories. For example, are there more R&B recordings than rock, or are they evenly distributed? This example demonstrates that while a database has only one physical view, it can easily support multiple logical views that provides for flexibility.

Consider another example—a mail-order business. One user might want a report presented in alphabetical format, in which case last name should appear before first name. Another user, working with a catalog mailing system, would want customer names appearing as first name and then last name. Both are easily achievable, but different logical views of the same physical information.

Increased Scalability and Performance

In its first year of operation, the official website of the American Family Immigration History Center, www.ellisisland.org, generated more than 2.5 billion hits. The site offers immigration information about people who entered America through the Port of New York and Ellis Island between 1892 and 1924. The database contains more than 25 million passenger names that are correlated to 3.5 million images of ships' manifests.[5]

The database had to be scalable to handle the massive volumes of information and the large numbers of users expected for the launch of the website. In addition, the database needed to perform quickly under heavy use. Some organizations must be able to support hundreds or thousands of users including employees, partners, customers, and suppliers, who all want to access and share the same information. Databases today scale to exceptional levels, allowing all types of users and programs to perform information-processing and information-searching tasks.

Reduced Information Redundancy

Information redundancy is the duplication of data, or the storage of the same data in multiple places. Redundant data can cause storage issues along with data integrity issues, making it difficult to determine which values are the most current or most accurate. Employees become confused and frustrated when faced with incorrect information causing disruptions to business processes and procedures. One primary goal of a database is to eliminate information redundancy by recording each piece of information in only one place in the database. This saves disk space, makes performing information updates easier, and improves information quality.

Increased Information Integrity (Quality)

Information integrity is a measure of the quality of information. ***Integrity constraints*** are rules that help ensure the quality of information. The database design needs to consider integrity constraints. The database and the DBMS ensures that users can never violate these constraints. There are two types of integrity constraints: (1) relational and (2) business critical.

Relational integrity constraints are rules that enforce basic and fundamental information-based constraints. For example, a relational integrity constraint would not allow someone to create an order for a nonexistent customer, provide a markup percentage that was negative, or order zero pounds of raw materials from a supplier. A ***business rule*** defines how a company performs certain aspects of its business and typically results in either a yes/no or true/false answer. Stating that merchandise returns are allowed within 10 days of purchase is an example of a business rule. ***Business-critical integrity constraints*** enforce business rules vital to an organization's success and often require more insight and knowledge than relational integrity constraints. Consider a supplier of fresh produce to large grocery chains such as Kroger. The supplier might implement a business-critical integrity constraint stating that no product returns are accepted after 15 days past delivery. That would make sense because of the chance of spoilage of the produce. Business-critical integrity constraints tend to mirror the very rules by which an organization achieves success.

The specification and enforcement of integrity constraints produce higher-quality information that will provide better support for business decisions. Organizations that establish specific procedures for developing integrity constraints typically see an increase in accuracy that then increases the use of organizational information by business professionals.

Increased Information Security

Managers must protect information, like any asset, from unauthorized users or misuse. As systems become increasingly complex and highly available over the Internet on many different devices, security becomes an even bigger issue. Databases offer many security features including passwords to provide authentication, access levels to determine who can access the data, and access controls to determine what type of access they have to the information.

For example, customer service representatives might need read-only access to customer order information so they can answer customer order inquiries; they might not have or need the authority to change or delete order information. Managers might require access to employee files, but they should have access only to their own employees' files, not the employee files for the entire company. Various security features of databases can ensure that individuals have only certain types of access to certain types of information.

Security risks are increasing as more and more databases and DBMS systems are moving to data centers run in the cloud. The biggest risks when using cloud computing are ensuring the security and privacy of the information in the database. Implementing data governance policies and procedures that outline the data management requirements can ensure safe and secure cloud computing.

LO 6.4: Explain the business benefits of a data-driven website.

DRIVING WEBSITES WITH DATA

A ***content creator*** is the person responsible for creating the original website content. A ***content editor*** is the person responsible for updating and maintaining website content. ***Static information*** includes fixed data incapable of change in the event of a user action. ***Dynamic information*** includes data that change based on user actions. For example, static websites supply only information that will not change until the content editor changes the information. Dynamic information changes when a user requests information. A dynamic website changes information based on user requests such as movie ticket availability, airline prices, or restaurant reservations. Dynamic website information is stored in a ***dynamic catalog***, or an area of a website that stores information about products in a database.

BUSINESS DRIVEN ETHICS AND SECURITY

Peter Warden is not your typical Facebook user. He is a young entrepreneur from Boulder, Colorado, who used the online social networking site's data to illustrate people's interests and common names across the United States. Warden collected data from more than 200 million Facebook profiles, and then he created a visualization map showing connections between locations that share friends.

Warden gathered the data from public profiles using "crawling" software similar to what search engines use to find content. Analyzing these data could provide useful information, such as displaying links between people with similar income, employment, and social connections. When Facebook learned what Warden was doing, the company threatened to sue him unless he deleted the data immediately. Warden did not have the funds required to fight the lawsuit and was forced to comply with Facebook's request and deleted the data.[6]

Do you agree or disagree that Warden's use of the information was unethical? Do you agree with Facebook's decision to have Warden delete all the data he collected? What other social networking sites could Warden use to collect public information? How much of your personal information do you think is available to the public for data collection efforts such as Warden's?

Facebook Fiasco

Websites change for site visitors depending on the type of information they request. Consider, for example, an automobile dealer. The dealer would create a database containing data elements for each car it has available for sale including make, model, color, year, miles per gallon, a photograph, and so on. Website visitors might click on Porsche and then enter their specific requests such as price range or year made. Once the user hits "go" the website automatically provides a custom view of the requested information. The dealer must create, update, and delete automobile information as the inventory changes.

A ***data-driven website*** is an interactive website kept constantly updated and relevant to the needs of its customers using a database. Data-driven capabilities are especially useful when a firm needs to offer large amounts of information, products, or services. Visitors can become quickly annoyed if they find themselves buried under an avalanche of information when searching a website. A data-driven website can help limit the amount of information displayed to customers based on unique search requirements. Companies even use data-driven websites to make information in their internal databases available to customers and business partners.

There are a number of advantages to using the web to access company databases. First, web browsers are much easier to use than directly accessing the database using a custom-query tool. Second, the web interface requires few or no changes to the database model. Finally, it costs less to add a web interface in front of a DBMS than to redesign and rebuild the system to support changes. Additional data-driven website advantages include:

- **Easy to manage content:** Website owners can make changes without relying on MIS professionals; users can update a data-driven website with little or no training.

- **Easy to store large amounts of data:** Data-driven websites can keep large volumes of information organized. Website owners can use templates to implement changes for layouts, navigation, or website structure. This improves website reliability, scalability, and performance.

- **Easy to eliminate human errors:** Data-driven websites trap data-entry errors, eliminating inconsistencies while ensuring all information is entered correctly.

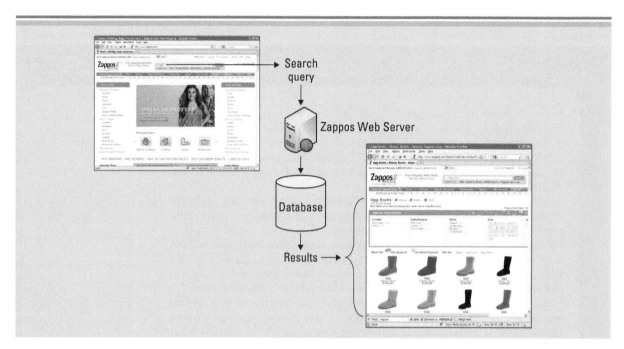

FIGURE 6.12

Zappos.com—A Data-Driven
Website

FIGURE 6.13

BI in a Data-Driven Website

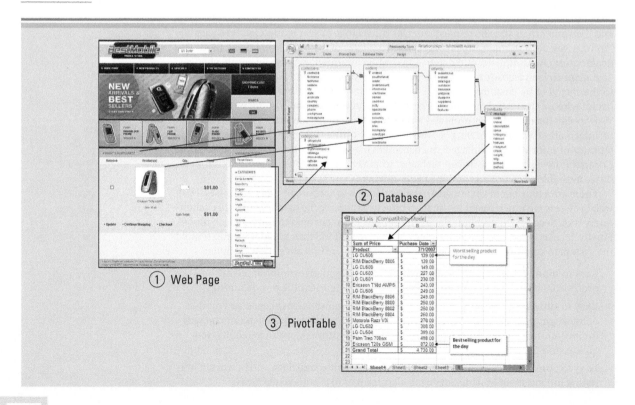

Zappos credits its success as an online shoe retailer to its vast inventory of nearly 3 million products available through its dynamic data-driven website. The company built its data-driven website catering to a specific niche market: consumers who were tired of finding that their most-desired items were always out of stock at traditional retailers. Zappos' highly flexible, scalable, and secure database helped it rank as the most-available Internet retailer. Figure 6.12 displays Zappos data-driven website illustrating a user querying the database and receiving information that satisfies the user's request.[7]

Companies can gain valuable business knowledge by viewing the data accessed and analyzed from their website. Figure 6.13 displays how running queries or using analytical tools, such as a PivotTable, on the database that is attached to the website can offer insight into the business, such as items browsed, frequent requests, items bought together, and so on.

section 6.2 | Business Intelligence

LEARNING OUTCOMES

6.5 Define a data warehouse, and provide a few reasons it can make a manager more effective.

6.6 Explain ETL and the role of a data mart in business.

6.7 Define data mining, and explain the three common forms for mining structured and unstructured data.

6.8 Identify the advantages of using business intelligence to support managerial decision making.

THE BUSINESS BENEFITS OF DATA WAREHOUSING

LO 6.5: Define a data warehouse, and provide a few reasons it can make a manager more effective.

In the 1990s as organizations began to need more timely information about their business, they found that traditional management information systems were too cumbersome to provide relevant information efficiently and efficiently. Most of the systems were in the form of operational databases that were designed for specific business functions, such as accounting, order entry, customer service, and sales, and were not appropriate for business analysis for the reasons shown in Figure 6.14.

During the latter half of the 20th century, the numbers and types of operational databases increased. Many large businesses found themselves with information scattered across multiple systems with different file types (such as spreadsheets, databases, and even word processing files), making it almost impossible for anyone to use the information from multiple sources. Completing reporting requests across operational systems could take days or weeks using antiquated reporting tools that were ineffective for running a business. From this idea, the data warehouse was born as a place where relevant information could be stored and accessed for making strategic queries and reports.

A ***data warehouse*** is a logical collection of information, gathered from many different operational databases, that supports business analysis activities and decision-making tasks. The primary purpose of a data warehouse is to combine information, more specifically, strategic information, throughout an organization into a single repository in such a way that the people who need that information can make decisions and undertake business analysis. A key idea within data warehousing is to collect information from multiple systems in a common location that uses a universal querying tool. This allows operational databases to run where they are most efficient for the business, while providing a common location using a familiar format for the strategic or enterprisewide reporting information.

Data warehouses go even a step further by standardizing information. Gender, for instance can be referred to in many ways (Male, Female, M/F, 1/0), but it should be standardized on a data warehouse with one common way of referring to each data element that stores gender (M/F). Standardizing of data elements allows for greater accuracy, completeness, and consistency as well as increases the quality of the information

FIGURE 6.14

Reasons Business Analysis
Is Difficult from Operational
Databases

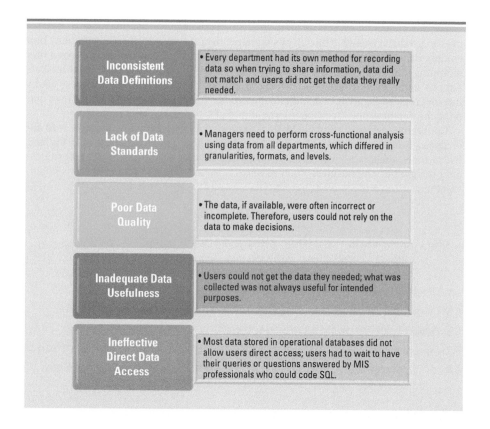

Inconsistent Data Definitions	• Every department had its own method for recording data so when trying to share information, data did not match and users did not get the data they really needed.
Lack of Data Standards	• Managers need to perform cross-functional analysis using data from all departments, which differed in granularities, formats, and levels.
Poor Data Quality	• The data, if available, were often incorrect or incomplete. Therefore, users could not rely on the data to make decisions.
Inadequate Data Usefulness	• Users could not get the data they needed; what was collected was not always useful for intended purposes.
Ineffective Direct Data Access	• Most data stored in operational databases did not allow users direct access; users had to wait to have their queries or questions answered by MIS professionals who could code SQL.

in making strategic business decisions. The data warehouse then is simply a tool that enables business users, typically managers, to be more effective in many ways, including:

- Developing customer profiles.
- Identifying new-product opportunities.
- Improving business operations.
- Identifying financial issues.
- Analyzing trends.
- Understanding competitors.
- Understanding product performance.

LO 6.6: **Explain ETL and the role of a data mart in business.**

PERFORMING BUSINESS ANALYSIS WITH DATA MARTS

Businesses collect a tremendous amount of transactional information as part of their routine operations. Marketing, sales, and other departments would like to analyze these data to understand their operations better. While databases store the details of all transactions (for instance, the sale of a product) and events (hiring a new employee), data warehouses store that same information but in an aggregated form more suited to supporting decision-making tasks. Aggregation, in this instance, can include totals, counts, averages, and the like.

The data warehouse modeled in Figure 6.15 compiles information from internal databases (or transactional and operational databases) and external databases through extraction, transformation, and loading. *Extraction, transformation, and loading (ETL)* is a process that extracts information from internal and external databases, transforms it using a common set of enterprise definitions, and loads it into a data warehouse. The data warehouse then sends portions (or subsets) of the information to data marts. A *data mart* contains a subset of data warehouse information. To distinguish between

FIGURE 6.15

Data Warehouse Model

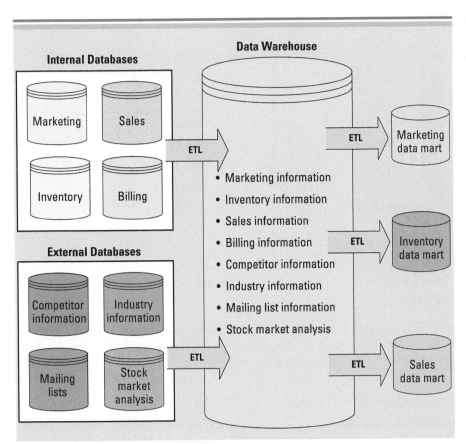

data warehouses and data marts, think of data warehouses as having a more organizational focus and data marts as having a functional focus. Figure 6.15 provides an illustration of a data warehouse and its relationship to internal and external databases, ETL, and data marts.

Multidimensional Analysis

A relational database contains information in a series of two-dimensional tables. In a data warehouse and data mart, information contains layers of columns and rows. For this reason, most data warehouses and data marts are multidimensional databases. A dimension is a particular attribute of information. Each layer in a data warehouse or data mart represents information according to an additional dimension. An *information cube* is the common term for the representation of multidimensional information. Figure 6.16 displays a cube (cube a) that represents store information (the layers), product information (the rows), and promotion information (the columns).

After creating a cube of information, users can begin to slice-and-dice the cube to drill down into the information. The second cube (cube b) in Figure 6.16 displays a slice representing promotion II information for all products at all stores. The third cube (cube c) in Figure 6.16 displays only information for promotion III, product B, at store 2. By using multidimensional analysis, users can analyze information in a number of ways and with any number of dimensions. Users might want to add dimensions of information to a current analysis including product category, region, and even forecasted versus actual weather. The true value of a data warehouse is its ability to provide multidimensional analysis that allows users to gain insights into their information.

Data warehouses and data marts are ideal for off-loading some of the querying against a database. For example, querying a database to obtain an average of sales for Product B at Store 2 while Promotion III is under way might create a considerable processing

FIGURE 6.16

A Cube of Information for Performing a Multidimensional Analysis on Three Stores for Five Products and Four Promotions

burden for a database, increasing the time it takes another person to enter a new sale into the same database. If an organization performs numerous queries against a database (or multiple databases), aggregating that information into a data warehouse will be beneficial.

Information Cleansing or Scrubbing

Maintaining quality information in a data warehouse or data mart is extremely important. To increase the quality of organizational information and thus the effectiveness of decision making, businesses must formulate a strategy to keep information clean. ***Information cleansing or scrubbing*** is a process that weeds out and fixes or discards inconsistent, incorrect, or incomplete information.

Specialized software tools exist that use sophisticated procedures to analyze, standardize, correct, match, and consolidate data warehouse information. This step is vitally important because data warehouses often contain information from several different databases, some of which can be external to the organization. In a data warehouse, information cleansing occurs first during the ETL process and again once the information is in the data warehouse. Companies can choose information cleansing software from several different vendors including Oracle, SAS, Ascential Software, and Group 1 Software. Ideally, scrubbed information is accurate and consistent.

Looking at customer information highlights why information cleansing is necessary. Customer information exists in several operational systems. In each system, all the details could change—from the customer ID to contact information—depending on the business process the user is performing (see Figure 6.17).

Figure 6.18 displays a customer name entered differently in multiple operational systems. Information cleansing allows an organization to fix these types of inconsistencies in the data warehouse. Figure 6.19 displays the typical events that occur during information cleansing.

Achieving perfect information is almost impossible. The more complete and accurate a company wants its information to be, the more it costs (see Figure 6.20). Companies may also trade accuracy for completeness. Accurate information is correct, while complete information has no blanks. A birth date of 2/31/10 is an example of complete but inaccurate information (February 31 does not exist). An address containing Denver, Colorado, without a zip code is an example of accurate information that is incomplete. Many firms complete ***data quality audits*** to determine the accuracy and completeness of its data. Most organizations determine a percentage of accuracy and completeness high enough to make good decisions at a reasonable cost, such as 85 percent accurate and 65 percent complete.

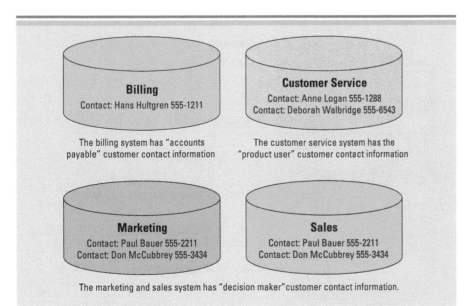

FIGURE 6.17

Contact Information in
Operational Systems

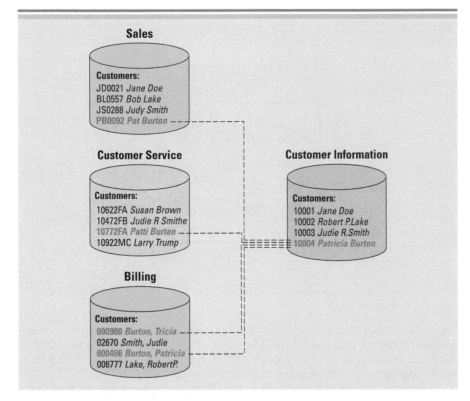

FIGURE 6.18

Standardizing a Customer Name
in Operational Systems

UNCOVERING TRENDS AND PATTERNS WITH DATA MINING

LO 6.7: Define data mining, and
explain the three common forms for
mining structured and unstructured
data.

Companies are collecting more data than ever. Historically, data were housed functionally in systems that were unable to talk to each other, such as customer service, finance, and human resources. ***Data mining*** is the process of analyzing data to extract information not offered by the raw data alone. Data mining can also begin at a summary information level (coarse granularity) and progress through increasing levels of detail (drilling down), or the reverse (drilling up). Companies use data-mining techniques to compile

FIGURE 6.19

Information Cleansing Activities

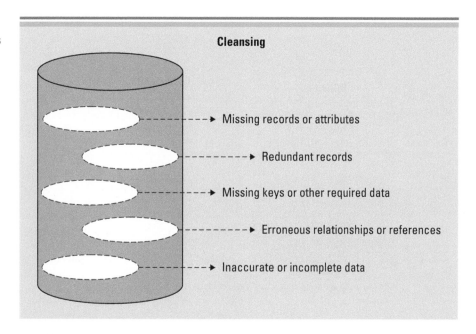

Cleansing

Missing records or attributes

Redundant records

Missing keys or other required data

Erroneous relationships or references

Inaccurate or incomplete data

FIGURE 6.20

The Cost of Accurate and
Complete Information

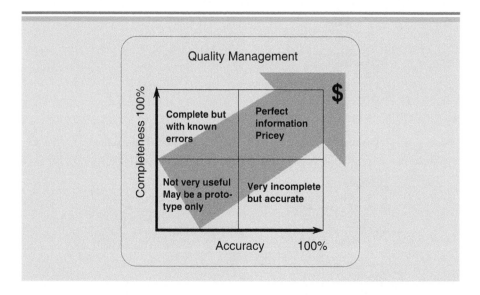

Quality Management

Completeness 100%

$

Complete but with known errors

Perfect information Pricey

Not very useful May be a proto-type only

Very incomplete but accurate

Accuracy   100%

a complete picture of their operations, all within a single view, allowing them to identify trends and improve forecasts. Consider Best Buy, which used data-mining tools to identify that 7 percent of its customers accounted for 43 percent of its sales, so the company reorganized its stores to accommodate those customers.[8]

To perform data mining, users need data-mining tools. **Data-mining tools** use a variety of techniques to find patterns and relationships in large volumes of information that predict future behavior and guide decision making. Data mining uncovers trends and patterns, which analysts use to build models that, when exposed to new information sets, perform a variety of information analysis functions. Data-mining tools for data warehouses help users uncover business intelligence in their data. Some of the key areas where businesses are using data mining include:

■ Analyzing customer buying patterns to predict future marketing and promotion campaigns.

■ Building budgets and other financial information.

BUSINESS DRIVEN GLOBALIZATION

Congratulations! You have just been hired as a consultant for Integrity Information Inc., a start-up business intelligence consulting company. Your first job is to help work with the sales department in securing a new client, The Warehouse. The Warehouse has been operating in the United States for more than a decade, and its primary business is to sell wholesale low-cost products. The Warehouse is interested in hiring Integrity Information Inc. to clean up the data that are stored in its U.S. database. To determine how good your work is, the client would like your analysis of the following spreadsheet. The Warehouse is also interested in expanding globally and wants to purchase several independent wholesale stores located in Australia, Thailand, China, Japan, and the United Kingdom. Before the company moves forward with the venture, it wants to understand what types of data issues it might encounter as it begins to transfer data from each global entity to the data warehouse. Please create a list detailing the potential issues The Warehouse can anticipate encountering as it consolidates the global databases into a single data warehouse.[9]

Integrity Information Inc.

CUST ID	First Name	Last Name	Address	City	State	Zip	Phone	Last Order Date
233620	Christopher	Lee	12421 W Olympic Blvd	Los Angeles	CA	75080-1100	(972)680-7848	4/18/2014
233621	Bruce	Brandwen	268 W 44th St	New York	PA	10036-3906	(212)471-6077	5/3/2014
233622	Glr	Johnson	4100 E Dry Creek Rd	Littleton	CO	80122-3729	(303)712-5461	5/6/2014
233623	Dave	Owens	466 Commerce Rd	Staunton	VA	24401-4432	(540)851-0362	3/19/2014
233624	John	Coulbourn	124 Action St	Maynard	MA	1754	(978)987-0100	4/24/2014
233629	Dan	Gagliardo	2875 Union Rd	Cheektowaga	NY	14227-1461	(716)558-8191	5/4/2014
23362	Damanceee	Allen	1633 Broadway	New York	NY	10019-6708	(212)708-1576	
233630	Michael	Peretz	235 E 45th St	New York	NY	10017-3305	(212)210-1340	4/30/2014
233631	Jody	Veeder	440 Science Dr	Madison	WI	53711-1064	(608)238-9690 X227	3/27/2014
233632	Michael	Kehrer	3015 SSE Loop 323	Tyler	TX	75701	(903)579-3229	4/28/2014
233633	Erin	Yoon	3500 Carillon Pt	Kirkland	WA	98033-7354	(425)897-7221	3/25/2014
233634	Madeline	Shefferly	4100 E Dry Creek Rd	Littleton	CO	80122-3729	(303)486-3949	3/33/2014
233635	Steven	Conduit	1332 Enterprise Dr	West Chester	PA	19380-5970	(610)692-5900	4/27/2014
233636	Joseph	Kovach	1332 Enterprise Dr	West Chester	PA	19380-5970	(610)692-5900	4/28/2014
233637	Richard	Jordan	1700 N	Philadelphia	PA	19131-4728	(215)581-6770	3/19/2014
233638	Scott	Mikolajczyk	1655 Crofton Blvd	Crofton	MD	21114-1387	(410)729-8155	4/28/2014
233639	Susan	Shragg	1875 Century Park E	Los Angeles	CA	90067-2501	(310)785-0511	4/29/2014
233640	Rob	Ponto	29777 Telegraph Rd	Southfield	MI	48034-1303	(810)204-4724	5/5/2014
233642	Lauren	Butler	1211 Avenue Of The Americas	New York	NY	10036-8701	(212)852-7494	4/22/2014
233643	Christopher	Lee	12421 W Olympic Blvd	Los Angeles	CA	90064-1022	(310)689-2577	3/25/2014
233644	Michelle	Decker	6922 Hollywood Blvd	Hollywood	CA	90028-6117	(323)817-4655	5/8/2014
233647	Natalia	Galeano	1211 Avenue Of The Americas	New York	NY	10036-8701	(646)728-6911	4/23/2014
233648	Bobbie	Orchard	4201 Congress St	Charlotte	NC	28209-4617	(704)557-2444	5/11/2014
233650	Ben	Konfino	1111 Stewart Ave	Bethpage	NY	11714-3533	(516)803-1406	3/19/2014
233651	Lenee	Santana	1050 Techwood Dr NW	Atlanta	GA	30318-KKRR	(404)885-2000	3/22/2014
233652	Lauren	Monks	7700 Wisconsin Ave	Bethesda	MD	20814-3578	(301)771-4772	3/19/2005
233653	Mark	Woolley	10950 Washington Blvd	Culver City	CA	90232-4026	(310)202-2900	4/20/2014

- Detecting fraud by identifying deceptive spending patterns.
- Finding the best customers who spend the most money.
- Keeping customers from leaving or migrating to competitors.
- Promoting and hiring employees to ensure success for both the company and the individual.

Data mining enables these companies to determine relationships among such internal factors as price, product positioning, or staff skills, and external factors such as economic indicators, competition, and customer demographics. In addition, it enables companies to determine the impact on sales, customer satisfaction, and corporate profits and to drill down into summary information to view detailed transactional data. With data mining, a retailer could use point-of-sale records of customer purchases to send targeted promotions based on an individual's purchase history. By mining demographic data from comment or warranty cards, the retailer could develop products and promotions to appeal to specific customer segments.

Netflix uses data mining to analyze each customer's film-viewing habits to provide recommendations for other customers with Cinematch, its movie recommendation system. Using Cinematch, Netflix can present customers with a number of additional movies they might want to watch based on the customer's current preferences. Netflix's innovative use of data mining provides its competitive advantage in the movie rental industry.[10]

Data mining uses specialized technologies and functionalities such as query tools, reporting tools, multidimensional analysis tools, statistical tools, and intelligent agents. Data mining approaches decision making with a few different activities in mind including:

- Classification—assigns records to one of a predefined set of classes.
- Estimation—determines values for an unknown continuous variable behavior or estimated future value.
- Affinity grouping—determines which things go together.
- Clustering—segments a heterogeneous population of records into a number of more homogeneous subgroups.

Data mining occurs on *structured data* that are already in a database or a spreadsheet. *Unstructured data* do not exist in a fixed location and can include text documents, PDFs, voice messages, emails, and so on. *Text mining* analyzes unstructured data to find trends and patterns in words and sentences. Text mining a firm's customer support email might identify which customer service representative is best able to handle the question, allowing the system to forward it to the right person. *Web mining* analyzes unstructured data associated with websites to identify consumer behavior and website navigation. Three common forms for mining structured and unstructured data are:

- Cluster analysis
- Association detection
- Statistical analysis.

Cluster Analysis

Cluster analysis is a technique used to divide information sets into mutually exclusive groups such that the members of each group are as close together as possible to one another and the different groups are as far apart as possible. Cluster analysis segments customer information to help organizations identify customers with similar behavioral traits, such as clusters of best customers or onetime customers. Cluster analysis also has the ability to uncover naturally occurring patterns in information (see Figure 6.21).

A great example of using cluster analysis in business is to create target-marketing strategies based on zip codes. Evaluating customer segments by zip code allows a business to assign a level of importance to each segment. Zip codes offer valuable insight into such things as income levels, demographics, lifestyles, and spending habits. With target marketing, a business can decrease its costs while increasing the success rate of the marketing campaign.

BUSINESS DRIVEN DISCUSSION

Often criticized for accruing large amounts of data about people, Google is now giving users an easy way to find out what information it stores about them. The company provides a service called Google Dashboard that summarizes the data that it collects in users' accounts on their products such as Gmail, Picasa Reader, and YouTube. Using the Dashboard, users can then adjust their privacy settings for the various Google applications, even allowing users to review and delete recent Google searches.[11]

Google Dashboard is giving users what they want—control over their own data. How is Google using data mining to collect information on users? What privacy issues does Google create by the massive amounts of personal data it stores? Will the Dashboard prevent Google from tracking users across the web if it wants to?

Google Dashboard

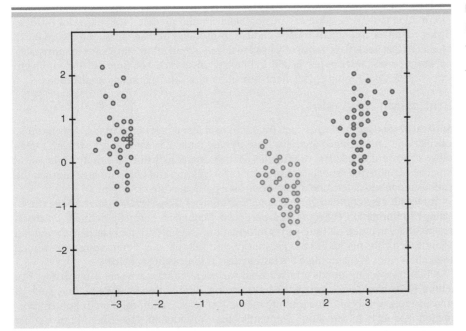

FIGURE 6.21

Example of Cluster Analysis

Association Detection

Association detection reveals the relationship between variables along with the nature and frequency of the relationships. Many people refer to association detection algorithms as association rule generators because they create rules to determine the likelihood of events occurring together at a particular time or following each other in a logical progression. Percentages usually reflect the patterns of these events; for example, "55 percent of the time, events A and B occurred together," or "80 percent of the time that items A and B occurred together, they were followed by item C within three days."

FIGURE 6.22

Market Basket Analysis

One of the most common forms of association detection analysis is market basket analysis. *Market basket analysis* analyzes such items as websites and checkout scanner information to detect customers' buying behavior and predict future behavior by identifying affinities among customers' choices of products and services (see Figure 6.22). Market basket analysis is frequently used to develop marketing campaigns for cross-selling products and services (especially in banking, insurance, and finance) and for inventory control, shelf-product placement, and other retail and marketing applications.

Statistical Analysis

Statistical analysis performs such functions as information correlations, distributions, calculations, and variance analysis. Data-mining tools offer knowledge workers a wide range of powerful statistical capabilities so they can quickly build a variety of statistical models, examine the models' assumptions and validity, and compare and contrast the various models to determine the best one for a particular business issue.

Forecasting is a common form of statistical analysis. *Time-series information* is time-stamped information collected at a particular frequency. Formally defined, *forecasts* are predictions based on time-series information. Examples of time-series information include web visits per hour, sales per month, and calls per day. Forecasting data-mining tools allow users to manipulate the time series for forecasting activities.

When discovering trends and seasonal variations in transactional information, use a time-series forecast to change the transactional information by units of time, such as transforming weekly information into monthly or seasonal information or hourly information into daily information. Companies base production, investment, and staffing decisions on a host of economic and market indicators in this manner. Forecasting models allow organizations to consider all sorts of variables when making decisions.

LO 6.8: Identify the advantages of using business intelligence to support managerial decision making.

SUPPORTING DECISIONS WITH BUSINESS INTELLIGENCE

Many organizations today find it next to impossible to understand their own strengths and weaknesses, let alone their biggest competitors, because the enormous volume of organizational data is inaccessible to all but the MIS department. Organization data include far more than simple structured data elements in a database; the set of data also includes unstructured data such as voice mail, customer phone calls, text messages, video clips, along with numerous new forms of data, such as tweets from Twitter.

BUSINESS DRIVEN INNOVATION

News Dots

Gone are the days of staring at boring spreadsheets and trying to understand how the data correlate. With innovative data visualization tools, managers can arrange different ways to view the data, providing new forms of pattern recognition not offered by simply looking at numbers. *Slate,* a news publication, developed a new data visualization tool called News Dots that offers readers a different way of viewing the daily news through trends and patterns. The News Dots tool scans about 500 stories a day from major publications and then tags the content with important keywords such as people, places, companies, and topics. Surprisingly, the majority of daily news overlaps as the people, places, and stories are frequently connected. Using News Dots you can visualize how the news fits together, almost similar to a giant social network. News Dots uses circles (or dots) to represent the tagged content and arranges them according to size. The more frequently a certain topic is tagged, the larger the dot and its relationship to other dots. The tool is interactive and users simply click on a dot to view which stories mention that topic and which other topics it connects to in the network such as a correlation among the U.S. government, Federal Reserve, Senate, bank, and Barack Obama.[12]

How can data visualization help identify trends? What types of business intelligence could you identify if your college used a data visualization tool to analyze student information? What types of business intelligence could you identify if you used a data visualization tool to analyze the industry where you plan to compete?

The Problem: Data Rich, Information Poor

An ideal business scenario would be as follows: As a business manager on his way to meet with a client reviews historical customer data, he realizes that the client's ordering volume has substantially decreased. As he drills down into the data, he notices the client had a support issue with a particular product. He quickly calls the support team to find out all of the information and learns that a replacement for the defective part can be shipped in 24 hours. In addition, he learns that the client has visited the website and requested information on a new product line. Armed with all this information, the business manager is prepared for a productive meeting with his client. He now understands the client's needs and issues, and he can address new sales opportunities with confidence.

For many companies the above example is simply a pipe dream. Attempting to gather all of the client information would actually take hours or even days to compile. With so much data available, it is surprisingly hard for managers to get information, such as inventory levels, past order history, or shipping details. Managers send their information requests to the MIS department where a dedicated person compiles the various reports. In some situations, responses can take days, by which time the information may be outdated and opportunities lost. Many organizations find themselves in the position of being data rich and information poor. Even in today's electronic world, managers struggle with the challenge of turning their business data into business intelligence.

The Solution: Business Intelligence

Employee decisions are numerous and they include providing service information, offering new products, and supporting frustrated customers. Employees can base their decisions on data, experience, or knowledge and preferably a combination of all three.

Business intelligence can provide managers with the ability to make better decisions. A few examples of how different industries use business intelligence include:

- **Airlines:** Analyze popular vacation locations with current flight listings.
- **Banking:** Understand customer credit card usage and nonpayment rates.
- **Health care:** Compare the demographics of patients with critical illnesses.
- **Insurance:** Predict claim amounts and medical coverage costs.
- **Law enforcement:** Track crime patterns, locations, and criminal behavior.
- **Marketing:** Analyze customer demographics.
- **Retail:** Predict sales, inventory levels, and distribution.
- **Technology:** Predict hardware failures.

Figure 6.23 displays how organizations using BI can find the cause to many issues and problems simply by asking "Why?" The process starts by analyzing a report such as sales amounts by quarter. Managers will drill down into the report looking for why sales are up or why sales are down. Once they understand why a certain location or product is experiencing an increase in sales, they can share the information in an effort to raise enterprisewide sales. Once they understand the cause for a decrease in sales, they can take effective action to resolve the issue. Here are a few examples of how managers can use BI to answer tough business questions:

- **Where has the business been?** Historical perspective offers important variables for determining trends and patterns.
- **Where is the business now?** Looking at the current business situation allows managers to take effective action to solve issues before they grow out of control.
- **Where is the business going?** Setting strategic direction is critical for planning and creating solid business strategies.

Ask a simple question—such as who is my best customer or what is my worst-selling product—and you might get as many answers as you have employees. Databases, data warehouses, and data marts can provide a single source of "trusted" data that can answer questions about customers, products, suppliers, production, finances, fraud, and even employees. They can also alert managers to inconsistencies or help determine the cause and effects of enterprisewide business decisions. All business aspects can benefit from the added insights provided by business intelligence, and you, as a business student, will benefit from understanding how MIS can help you make intelligent decisions.

Visual Business Intelligence

Informing is accessing large amounts of data from different management information systems. *Infographics (information graphics)* displays information graphically so

FIGURE 6.23

How BI Can Answer Tough Customer Questions

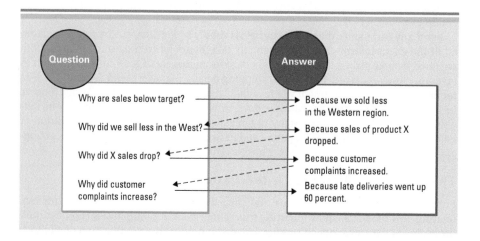

it can be easily understood. Infographics can present the results of large data analysis looking for patterns and relationships that monitor changes in variables over time. **Data visualization** describes technologies that allow users to "see" or visualize data to transform information into a business perspective. **Data visualization tools** move beyond Excel graphs and charts into sophisticated analysis techniques such as pie charts, controls, instruments, maps, time-series graphs, and more. Data visualization tools can help uncover correlations and trends in data that would otherwise go unrecognized. **Business intelligence dashboards** track corporate metrics such as critical success factors and key performance indicators and include advanced capabilities such as interactive controls allowing users to manipulate data for analysis. The majority of business intelligence software vendors offer a number of different data visualization tools and business intelligence dashboards.

LEARNING OUTCOME REVIEW

Learning Outcome 6.1: Explain the four primary traits that determine the value of information.

Information is data converted into a meaningful and useful context. Information can tell an organization how its current operations are performing and help it estimate and strategize about how future operations might perform. It is important to understand the different levels, formats, and granularities of information along with the four primary traits that help determine the value of information, which include (1) information type: transactional and analytical; (2) information timeliness; (3) information quality; (4) information governance.

Learning Outcome 6.2: Describe a database, a database management system, and the relational database model.

A database maintains information about various types of objects (inventory), events (transactions), people (employees), and places (warehouses). A database management system (DBMS) creates, reads, updates, and deletes data in a database while controlling access and security. A DBMS provides methodologies for creating, updating, storing, and retrieving data in a database. In addition, a DBMS provides facilities for controlling data access and security, allowing data sharing, and enforcing data integrity. The relational database model allows users to create, read, update, and delete data in a relational database.

Learning Outcome 6.3: Identify the business advantages of a relational database.

Many business managers are familiar with Excel and other spreadsheet programs they can use to store business data. Although spreadsheets are excellent for supporting some data analysis, they offer limited functionality in terms of security, accessibility, and flexibility and can rarely scale to support business growth. From a business perspective, relational databases offer many advantages over using a text document or a spreadsheet, including increased flexibility, increased scalability and performance, reduced information redundancy, increased information integrity (quality), and increased information security.

Learning Outcome 6.4: Explain the business benefits of a data-driven website.

A data-driven website is an interactive website kept constantly updated and relevant to the needs of its customers using a database. Data-driven capabilities are especially useful when the website offers a great deal of information, products, or services because visitors are frequently annoyed if they are buried under an avalanche of information when searching a website. Many companies use the web to make some of the information in their internal databases available to customers and business partners.

Learning Outcome 6.5: Define a data warehouse, and provide a few reasons it can make a manager more effective.

A data warehouse is a logical collection of information, gathered from many different operational databases, that supports business analysis and decision making. The primary value of a data warehouse is to combine information, more specifically, strategic information, throughout an organization into a single repository in such a way that the people who need that information can make decisions and undertake business analysis.

Learning Outcome 6.6: Explain ETL and the role of a data mart in business.

Extraction, transformation, and loading (ETL) is a process that extracts information from internal and external databases, transforms it using a common set of enterprise definitions, and loads it into a data warehouse. The data warehouse then sends portions (or subsets) of the information to data marts. A data mart contains a subset of data warehouse information. To distinguish between data warehouses and data marts, think of data warehouses as having a more organizational focus and data marts as having a functional focus.

Learning Outcome 6.7: Define data mining, and explain the three common forms for mining structured and unstructured data.

Data mining is the process of analyzing data to extract information not offered by the raw data alone. Data mining can also begin at a summary information level (coarse granularity) and progress through increasing levels of detail (drilling down), or the reverse (drilling up). Data mining occurs on structured data that are already in a database or a spreadsheet. Unstructured data do not exist in a fixed location and can include text documents, PDFs, voice messages, emails, and so on. Three common forms for mining structured and unstructured data are cluster analysis, association detection, and statistical analysis.

Learning Outcome 6.8: Identify the advantages of using business intelligence to support managerial decision making.

Many organizations today find it next to impossible to understand their own strengths and weaknesses, let alone their biggest competitors, due to enormous volumes of organizational data being inaccessible to all but the MIS department. Organization data include far more than simple structured data elements in a database; the set of data also includes unstructured data such as voice mail, customer phone calls, text messages, video clips, along with numerous new forms of data, such as tweets from Twitter. Managers today find themselves in the position of being data rich and information poor, and they need to implement business intelligence systems to solve this challenge.

OPENING CASE QUESTIONS

1. **Knowledge:** List the reasons a business would want to display information in a graphic or visual format.

2. **Comprehension:** Describe how a business could use a business intelligence digital dashboard to gain an understanding of how the business is operating.

3. **Application:** Explain how a marketing department could use data visualization tools to help with the release of a new product.

4. **Analysis:** Categorize the five common characteristics of high-quality information and rank them in order of importance for Hotels.com.

5. **Synthesis:** Develop a list of some possible entities and attributes located in the Hotels.com database.

6. **Evaluate:** Assess how Hotels.com is using BI to identify trends and change associated business processes.

KEY TERMS

REVIEW QUESTIONS

1. How does a database turn data elements into information?
2. Why does a business need to be concerned with the quality of its data?
3. How can data governance help protect a business from hackers?
4. Why would a company care about the timeliness of its data?
5. What are the five characteristics common to high-quality information?
6. What is data governance and its importance to a company?
7. What are the four primary traits that help determine the value of information?
8. What is the difference between an entity and an attribute?
9. What are the advantages of a relational database?
10. What are the advantages of a data-driven website?
11. What is a data warehouse and why would a business want to implement one?
12. Why would you need to use multidimensional analysis?
13. What is the purpose of information cleansing (or scrubbing)?
14. Why would a department want a data mart instead of just accessing the entire data warehouse?
15. Why would a business be data rich, but information poor?

CLOSING CASE ONE

Data Visualization: Stories for the Information Age

At the intersection of art and algorithm, data visualization schematically abstracts information to bring about a deeper understanding of the data, wrapping it in an element of awe. While the practice of visually representing information is arguably the foundation of all design, a newfound fascination with data visualization has been emerging. After *The New York Times* and *The Guardian* recently opened their online archives to the public, artists rushed to dissect nearly two centuries worth of information, elevating this art form to new prominence.

For artists and designers, data visualization is a new frontier of self-expression, powered by the proliferation of information and the evolution of available tools. For enterprise, it is a platform for displaying products and services in the context of the cultural interaction that surrounds them, reflecting consumers' increasing demand for corporate transparency.

"Looking at something ordinary in a new way makes it extraordinary," says Aaron Koblin, one of the more recent pioneers of the discipline. As technology lead of Google's Creative Labs in San Francisco, he spearheaded the search giant's Chrome Experiments series designed to show off the speed and reliability of the Chrome browser.

Forget Pie Charts and Bar Graphs

Data visualization has nothing to do with pie charts and bar graphs. And it's only marginally related to "infographics," information design that tends to be about objectivity and clarification. Such representations simply offer another iteration of the data—restating it visually and making it easier to digest. Data visualization, on the other hand, is an interpretation, a different way to look at and think about data that often exposes complex patterns or correlations.

Data visualization is a way to make sense of the ever-increasing stream of information with which we're bombarded and provides a creative antidote to the analysis paralysis that can result from the burden of processing such a large volume of information. "It's not about clarifying data," says Koblin. "It's about contextualizing it."

Today algorithmically inspired artists are reimagining the art-science continuum through work that frames the left-brain analysis of data in a right-brain creative story. Some use data visualization as a bridge between alienating information and its emotional impact—see Chris Jordan's portraits of global mass culture. Others take a more technological angle and focus on cultural utility—the Zoetrope project offers a temporal and historical visualization of the ephemeral web. Still others are pure artistic indulgence—like Koblin's own Flight Patterns project, a visualization of air traffic over North America.

How Business Can Benefit

There are real implications for business here. Most cell phone providers, for instance, offer a statement of a user's monthly activity. Most often it's an overwhelming table of various numerical measures of how much you talked, when, with whom, and how much it cost. A visual representation of this data might help certain patterns emerge, revealing calling habits and perhaps helping users save money.

Companies can also use data visualization to gain new insight into consumer behavior. By observing and understanding what people do with the data—what they find useful and what they dismiss as worthless—executives can make the valuable distinction between what consumers say versus what they do. Even now, this can be a tricky call to make from behind the two-way mirror of a traditional qualitative research setting.

It's essential to understand the importance of creative vision along with the technical mastery of software. Data visualization isn't about using all the data available, but about deciding which patterns and elements to focus on, building a narrative, and telling the story of the raw data in a different, compelling way.

Ultimately, data visualization is more than complex software or the prettying up of spreadsheets. It's not innovation for the sake of innovation. It's about the most ancient of social rituals: storytelling. It's about telling the story locked in the data differently, more engagingly, in a way that draws us in, makes our eyes open a little wider and our jaw drop ever so slightly. And as we process it, it can sometimes change our perspective altogether.[13]

Questions

1. Identify the effects poor information might have on a data visualization project.
2. How does data visualization use database technologies?
3. How could a business use data visualization to identify new trends?
4. What is the correlation between data mining and data visualization?
5. Is data visualization a form of business intelligence? Why or why not?
6. What security issues are associated with data visualization?
7. What might happen to a data visualization project if it failed to cleanse or scrub its data?

CLOSING CASE TWO

Zillow

Zillow.com is an online web-based real estate site helping homeowners, buyers, sellers, renters, real estate agents, mortgage professionals, property owners, and property managers find and share information about real estate and mortgages. Zillow allows users to access, anonymously and free of charge, the kinds of tools and information previously reserved for real estate professionals. Zillow's databases cover more than 90 million homes, which represents 95 percent of the homes in the United States. Adding to the sheer size of its databases, Zillow recalculates home valuations for each property every day, so it can provide historical graphs on home valuations over time. In some areas, Zillow is able to display 10 years of valuation history, a value-added benefit for many of its customers. This collection of data represents an operational data warehouse for anyone visiting the website.

As soon as Zillow launched its website, it immediately generated a massive amount of traffic. As the company expanded its services, the founders knew the key to its success would be the site's ability to quickly process and manage massive amounts of data, in real time. The company identified a need for accessible, scalable, reliable, secure databases that would enable it to continue to increase the capacity of its infrastructure indefinitely without sacrificing performance. Zillow's traffic continues to grow despite the weakened real estate market; the company is experiencing annual traffic growth of 30 percent and about a third of all U.S. mortgage professionals visit the site in a given month.

Data Mining and Business Intelligence

Zestimate values on Zillow use data-mining features for spotting trends across property valuations. Data mining also allows the company to see how accurate Zestimate values are over time. Zillow has also built the industry's first search by monthly payment, allowing users to find homes that are for sale and rent based on a monthly payment they can afford. Along with the monthly payment search, users can also enter search criteria such as the number of bedrooms or bathrooms.

Zillow also launched a new service aimed at changing the way Americans shop for mortgages. Borrowers can use Zillow's new Mortgage Marketplace to get custom loan quotes from lenders without having to give their names, addresses, phone numbers, or Social Security numbers, or field unwanted telephone calls from brokers competing for their business. Borrowers reveal their identities only after contacting the lender of their choice. The company is entering a field of established mortgage sites such as LendingTree.com and Experian Group's Lowermybills.com, which charge mortgage companies for borrower information. Zillow, which has an advertising model, says it does not plan to charge for leads.

For mortgage companies, the anonymous leads come free; they can make a bid based on information provided by the borrower, such as salary, assets, credit score, and the type of loan. Lenders can browse borrower requests and see competing quotes from other brokers before making a bid.[14]

Questions

1. List the reasons Zillow would need to use a database to run its business.
2. Describe how Zillow uses business intelligence to create a unique product for its customers.
3. How could the marketing department at Zillow use a data mart to help with the release of a new product launch?
4. Categorize the five common characteristics of high-quality information and rank them in order of importance to Zillow.
5. Develop a list of some possible entities and attributes of Zillow's mortgage database.
6. Assess how Zillow uses a data-driven website to run its business.

CRITICAL BUSINESS THINKING

1. Information—Business Intelligence or a Diversion from the Truth?

President Obama used part of his commencement address at Virginia's Hampton University to criticize the flood of incomplete information or downright incorrect information that flows in the 24-hour news cycle. The president said, "You're coming of age in a 24/7 media environment that bombards us with all kinds of content and exposes us to all kinds of arguments, some of which don't always rank all that high on the truth meter. With iPods and iPads and Xboxes and PlayStations—none of which I know how to work—information becomes a distraction, a diversion, a form of entertainment, rather than a tool of empowerment, rather than the means of emancipation."[15]

Do you agree or disagree with President Obama's statement? Who is responsible for verifying the accuracy of online information? What should happen to companies that post inaccurate information? What should happen to individuals who post inaccurate information? What should you remember when reading or citing sources for online information?

2. Illegal Database Access

Goldman Sachs has been hit with a $3 million lawsuit by a company that alleges the brokerage firm stole intellectual property from its database that had market intelligence facts. The U.S. District Court for the Southern District of New York filed the lawsuit in 2010 claiming Goldman Sachs employees used other people's access credentials to log into Ipreo's proprietary database, dubbed Bigdough. Offered on a subscription basis, Bigdough provides detailed information on more than 80,000 contacts within the financial industry. Ipreo complained to the court that Goldman Sachs employees illegally accessed Bigdough at least 264 times in 2008 and 2009.[16]

Do you agree or disagree with the lawsuit? Should Goldman Sachs be held responsible for rogue employees' behavior? What types of policies should Goldman Sachs implement to ensure this does not occur again?

3. Data Storage

Information is one of the most important assets of any business. Businesses must ensure information accuracy, completeness, consistency, timeliness, and uniqueness. In addition, business must have a reliable backup service. In part thanks to cloud computing, there are many data hosting services on the Internet. These sites offer storage of information that can be accessed from anywhere in the world.

These data hosting services include Hosting (www.hosting.com), Mozy (www.mozy.com), My Docs Online (www.mydocsonline.com), and Box (www.box.net). Visit a few of these sites along with a several others you find through research. Which sites are free? Are there limits to how much you can store? If so, what is the limit? What type of information can you store (video, text, photos, etc.)? Can you allow multiple users with different passwords to access your storage area? Are you contractually bound for a certain duration (annual, etc.)? Are different levels of services provided such as personal, enterprise, work group? Does it make good business sense to store business data on the Internet? What about personal data?

4. Gathering Business Intelligence

When considering new business opportunities, you need knowledge about the competition. One of the things many new business owners fail to do is to gather business intelligence on their competitors, such as how many there are and what differentiates each of them. You may find there are too many and that they would be tough competition for you. Or, you may find that there are few competitors and the ones who are out there offer very little value.

Generate a new business idea you could launch on the Internet. Research the Internet to find similar business in the area you have chosen. How many sites did you find that are offering the same products or services you are planning to offer? Did you come across any sites from another country that have a unique approach that you did not see on any of the sites in your own country? How would you use this information in pursuing your business idea?

5. Free Data!

The U.S. Bureau of Labor Statistics states that its role is as the "principal fact-finding agency for the federal government in the broad field of labor economics and statistics." And the data that the bureau provides via its website are available to anyone, free. This can represent a treasure trove of business intelligence and data mining for those who take advantage of this resource. Visit the website www.bls.gov. What type of information does the site provide? What information do you find most useful? What sort of information concerning employment and wages is available? How is this information categorized? How would this type of information be helpful to a business manager? What type of demographic information is available? How could this benefit a new start-up business?[17]

6. Explaining Relational Databases

You have been hired by Vision, a start-up clothing company. Your manager, Holly Henningson, is unfamiliar with databases and their associated business value. Henningson has asked you to create a report detailing the basics of databases. She would also like you to provide a detailed explanation of relational databases along with their associated business advantages.

7. Entities and Attributes

Martex Inc. is a manufacturer of athletic equipment, and its primary lines of business include running, tennis, golf, swimming, basketball, and aerobics equipment. Martex currently supplies four primary vendors including Sam's Sports, Total Effort, The Underline, and Maximum Workout. Martex wants to build a database to help it organize its products. In a group, identify the different types of entities, attributes, keys, and relationships Martex will want to consider when designing its relational database.

8. Compiling Information

You are currently working for the Public Transportation Department of Chatfield. The department controls all forms of public transportation, including buses, subways, and trains. Each department has about 300 employees and maintains its own accounting, inventory, purchasing, and human resource systems. Generating reports across departments is a difficult task and usually involves gathering and correlating the information from the many different databases. It typically takes about two weeks to generate the quarterly balance sheets and profit and loss statements. Your team has been asked to compile a report recommending what the Public Transportation Department of Chatfield can do to alleviate its information and system issues. Be sure that your report addresses the various reasons departmental reports are presently difficult to obtain as well as how you plan to solve this problem.[18]

9. Information Timeliness

Information timeliness is a major consideration for all organizations. Organizations need to decide the frequency of backups and the frequency of updates to a data warehouse. In a team, describe the timeliness requirements for backups and updates to a data warehouse for each of the following:

- Weather tracking systems.
- Car dealership inventories.
- Vehicle tire sales forecasts.
- Interest rates.
- Restaurant inventories.
- Grocery store inventories.

10. Improving Information Quality

HangUps Corporation designs and distributes closet organization structures. The company operates five systems—order entry, sales, inventory management, shipping, and billing. The company has severe information quality issues including missing, inaccurate, redundant, and incomplete information. The company wants to implement a data warehouse containing information from the five different systems to help maintain a single customer view, drive business decisions, and perform multidimensional analysis. Identify how the organization can improve its information quality when it begins designing and building its data warehouse.

ENTREPRENEURIAL CHALLENGE

BUILD YOUR OWN BUSINESS

1. Provide an example of your business data that fits each of the five common characteristics of high-quality information. Explain why each characteristic is important to your business data and what might happen if your business data were of low quality. (Be sure to identify your business and the name of your company.)

2. Identify the different entities and their associated attributes that would be found in your potential relational database model for your sales database.

3. Identify the benefits of having a data warehouse for your business. What types of data marts would you want to extract from your data warehouse to help you run your business and make strategic decisions.

APPLY YOUR KNOWLEDGE BUSINESS PROJECTS

PROJECT I   Mining the Data Warehouse

Alana Smith is a senior buyer for a large wholesaler that sells different types of arts and crafts to greeting card stores such as Hallmark. Smith's latest marketing strategy is to send all of her customers a new line of handmade picture frames from Russia. All of her information supports her decision for the new line. Her analysis predicts that the frames should sell an average of 10 to 15 per store, per day. Smith is excited about the new line and is positive it will be a success.

One month later Smith learns the frames are selling 50 percent below expectations and averaging between five and eight frames sold daily in each store. She decides to access the company's data warehouse information to determine why sales are below expectations. Identify several different dimensions of information that Smith will want to analyze to help her decide what is causing the problems with the picture frame sales.

PROJECT II   Different Dimensions

The focus of data warehousing is to extend the transformation of data into information. Data warehouses offer strategic level, external, integrated, and historical information so businesses can make projections, identify trends, and make key business decisions. The data warehouse collects and stores integrated sets of historical information from multiple operational systems and feeds them to one or more data marts. It may also provide end user access to support enterprisewide views of information.

You are currently working on a marketing team for a large corporation that sells jewelry around the world. Your boss has asked you to look at the following dimensions of data to determine which ones you want in your data mart for performing sales and market analysis (see Figure AYK.1). As a team, categorize the different dimensions ranking them from 1 to 5, with 1 indicating that the dimension offers the highest value and must be in your data mart and 5 indicating that the dimension offers the lowest value and does not need to be in your data mart.

PROJECT III   Understanding Search

Pretend that you are a search engine. Choose a topic to query. It can be anything such as your favorite book, movie, band, or sports team. Search your topic on Google, pick three or four pages from the results, and print them out. On each printout, find the individual words from your query (such as

FIGURE AYK.1

Data Warehouse Data

Dimension	Value (1–5)	Dimension	Value (1–5)
Product number		Season	
Store location		Promotion	
Customer net worth		Payment method	
Number of sales personnel		Commission policy	
Customer eating habits		Manufacturer	
Store hours		Traffic report	
Salesperson ID		Customer language	
Product style		Weather	
Order date		Customer gender	
Product quantity		Local tax information	
Ship date		Local cultural demographics	
Current interest rate		Stock market closing	
Product cost		Customer religious affiliation	
Customer's political affiliation		Reason for purchase	
Local market analysis		Employee dress code policy	
Order time		Customer age	
Customer spending habits		Employee vacation policy	
Product price		Employee benefits	
Exchange rates		Current tariff information	
Product gross margin			

"Boston Red Sox" or "The Godfather") and use a highlighter to mark each word with color. Do that for each of the documents that you print out. Now tape those documents on a wall, step back a few feet, and review your documents.

If you did not know what the rest of a page said and could judge only by the colored words, which document do you think would be most relevant? Is there anything that would make a document look more relevant? Is it better to have the words be in a large heading or to occur several times in a smaller font? Do you prefer it if the words are at the top or the bottom of the page? How often do the words need to appear? Come up with two or three things you would look for to see if a document matched a query well. This exercise mimics search engine processes and should help you understand why a search engine returns certain results over others.

PROJECT IV   Predicting Netflix

Netflix Inc., the largest online movie rental service, provides more than 12 million subscribers access to more than 100,000 unique DVD titles along with a growing on-demand library in excess of 10,000 choices. Data and information are so important to Netflix that it created The Netflix Prize, an open competition for anyone who could improve the data used in prediction ratings for films (an increase of 10 percent), based on previous ratings. The winner would receive a $1 million prize.

The ability to search, analyze, and comprehend information is vital for any organization's success. It certainly was for Netflix, as it was happy to pay anyone $1 million to improve the quality of its information. In a group, explain how Netflix might use databases, data warehouses, and data marts to predict customer movie recommendations. Here are a few characteristics you might want to analyze to get you started:

- Customer demographics.
- Movie genre, rating, year, producer, type.
- Actor information.
- Internet access.
- Location for mail pickup.

PROJECT V   The Crunch Factory

The Crunch Factory is one of the fourth-largest gyms operating in Australia, and each gym operates its own system with its own database. Unfortunately, the company failed to develop any data-capturing standards and now faces the challenges associated with low-quality enterprisewide information. For example, one system has a field to capture email addresses while another system does not. Duplicate customer information among the different systems is another major issue, and the company continually finds itself sending conflicting or competing messages to customers from different gyms. A customer could also have multiple accounts within the company, one representing a membership, another representing additional classes, and yet another for a personal trainer. The Crunch Factory has no way to identify that the different customer accounts are actually for the same customer.

To remain competitive and be able to generate business intelligence The Crunch Factory has to resolve these challenges. The Crunch Factory has just hired you as its data quality expert. Your first task is to determine how the company can turn its low-quality information into high-quality business intelligence. Create a plan that The Crunch Factory can implement that details the following:

- Challenges associated with low-quality information.
- Benefits associated with high-quality information.
- Recommendations on how the company can clean up its data.

PROJECT VI   Too Much of a Good Thing

The Castle, a premium retailer of clothes and accessories, created an enterprisewide data warehouse so all its employees could access information for decision making. The Castle soon discovered that it is possible to have too much of a good thing. The Castle employees found themselves inundated with data and unable to make any decisions, a common occurrence called analysis paralysis. When sales representatives queried the data warehouse to determine if a certain product in the size, color, and category was available, they would get hundreds of results showing everything from production orders to supplier contracts. It became easier for the sales representatives to look in the warehouse themselves than to check the system. Employees found the data warehouse was simply too big, too complicated, and contained too much irrelevant information.

The Castle is committed to making its data warehouse system a success and has come to you for help. Create a plan that details the value of the data warehouse to the business, how it can be easier for all employees to use, along with the potential business benefits the company can derive from its data warehouse.

PROJECT VII   Twitter Buzz

Technology tools that can predict sales for the coming week, decide when to increase inventory, and determine when additional staff is required are extremely valuable. Twitter is not just for tweeting your whereabouts anymore. Twitter and other social-media sites have become great tools for gathering business intelligence on customers, including what they like, dislike, need, and want. Twitter is easy to use, and businesses can track every single time a customer makes a statement about a particular product or service. Good businesses turn this valuable information into intelligence spotting trends and patterns in customer opinion.

Do you agree that a business can use Twitter to gain business intelligence? How many companies do you think are aware of Twitter and exactly how they can use it to gain BI? How do you think Twitter uses a data warehouse? How do you think companies store Twitter information? How would a company use Twitter in a data mart? How would a company use cubes to analyze Twitter data?

AYK APPLICATION PROJECTS

If you are looking for Access projects to incorporate into your class, try any of the following after reading this chapter.

Project Number	Project Name	Project Type	Plug-In	Focus Area	Project Level	Skill Set	Page Number
28	Daily Invoice	Access	T5, T6, T7, T8	Business Analysis	Introductory	Entities, Relationships, and Databases	AYK.17
29	Billing Data	Access	T5, T6, T7, T8	Business Intelligence	Introductory	Entities, Relationships, and Databases	AYK.19
30	Inventory Data	Access	T5, T6, T7, T8	SCM	Intermediate	Entities, Relationships, and Databases	AYK.20
31	Call Center	Access	T5, T6, T7, T8	CRM	Intermediate	Entities, Relationships, and Databases	AYK.21
32	Sales Pipeline	Access	T5, T6, T7, T8	Business Intelligence	Advanced	Entities, Relationships, and Databases	AYK.23
33	Online Classified Ads	Access	T5, T6, T7, T8	Ecommerce	Advanced	Entities, Relationships, and Databases	AYK.23

Enterprise Applications: Business Communications

CHAPTER OUTLINE

What's in IT for me?

This chapter introduces high-profile strategic initiatives an organization can undertake to help it gain competitive advantages and business efficiencies—supply chain management, customer relationship management, and enterprise resource planning. At the simplest level, organizations implement enterprise systems to gain efficiency in business processes, effectiveness in supply chains, and an overall understanding of customer needs and behaviors. Successful organizations recognize the competitive advantage of maintaining healthy relationships with employees, customers, suppliers, and partners. Doing so has a direct and positive effect on revenue and greatly adds to a company's profitability.

You, as a business student, must understand the critical relationship your business will have with its employees, customers, suppliers, and partners. You must also understand how to analyze your organizational data to ensure you are not just meeting but exceeding expectations. Enterprises are technologically empowered as never before to reach their goals of integrating, analyzing, and making intelligent business decisions.

opening case study

Zappos Is Passionate for Customers

Tony Hsieh's first entrepreneurial effort began at the age of 12 when he started his own custom button business. Realizing the importance of advertising, Hsieh began marketing his business to other kids through directories, and soon his profits soared to a few hundred dollars a month. Throughout his adolescence, Hsieh started several businesses, and by the time he was in college he was making money selling pizzas out of his Harvard dorm room. Another entrepreneurial student, Alfred Lin, bought pizzas from Hsieh and resold them by the slice, making a nice profit. Hsieh and Lin quickly became friends.

After Harvard, Hsieh founded LinkExchange in 1996, a company that helped small businesses exchange banner ads. A mere two years later, Hsieh sold LinkExchange to Microsoft for $265 million. Using the profits from the sale, Hsieh and Lin formed a venture capital company that invested in start-up businesses. One investment that caught their attention was Zappos, an online etailer of shoes. Both entrepreneurs viewed the $40 billion shoe market as an opportunity they could not miss, and in 2000 Hsieh took over as Zappos' CEO with Lin as his chief financial officer.

Today, Zappos is leading its market and offering an enormous selection of more than 90,000 styles of handbags, clothing, and accessories for more than 500 brands. One reason for Zappos' incredible success was Hsieh's decision to use the advertising and marketing budget for customer service, a tactic that would not have worked before the Internet. Zappos' passionate customer service strategy encourages customers to order as many sizes and styles of products as they want, ships them for free, and offers free return shipping. Zappos encourages customer communication, and its call center receives more than 5,000 calls a day with the longest call to date lasting more than four hours.

Zappos' extensive inventory is stored in a warehouse in Kentucky right next to a UPS shipping center. Only available stock is listed on the website, and orders as late as 11 P.M. are still guaranteed next-day delivery. To facilitate supplier and partner relationships, Zappos built an extranet that provides its vendors with all kinds of product information, such as items sold, times sold, price, customer, and so on. Armed with these kinds of details, suppliers can quickly change manufacturing schedules to meet demand.

Zappos Culture

Along with valuing its partners and suppliers, Zappos also places a great deal of value on its employee relationships. Zappos employees have fun, and walking through the offices you will see all kinds of things not normally seen in business environments—bottle-cap pyramids, cotton-candy machines, and bouncing balls. Building loyal employee relationships is a critical success factor at Zappos, and to facilitate this relationship the corporate headquarters are located in the same building as the call center (where most employees work) in Las Vegas. All employees receive 100 percent company-paid health insurance along with a daily free lunch.

Of course, the Zappos culture does not work for everyone, and the company pays to find the right employees through "The Offer," which extends to new employees the option of quitting and receiving payment for time worked plus an additional $1,000 bonus. Why the $1,000 bonus for quitting? Zappos management believes that is a small price to pay to find those employees who do not have the sense of commitment Zappos requires. Less than 10 percent of new hires take The Offer.

Zappos' unique culture stresses the following:

1. Delivering WOW through service.
2. Embracing and driving change.
3. Creating fun and a little weirdness.
4. Being adventurous, creative, and open-minded.
5. Pursuing growth and learning.
6. Building open and honest relationships with communication.
7. Building a positive team and family spirit.
8. Doing more with less.
9. Being passionate and determined.
10. Being humble.

Zappos' Sale to Amazon

Amazon.com purchased Zappos for $880 million. Zappos employees shared $40 million in cash and stock, and the Zappos management team remained in place. Having access to Amazon's world-class warehouses and supply chain is sure to catapult Zappos' revenues, though many wonder whether the Zappos culture will remain. It'll be interesting to watch![1]

section 8.1 | Supply Chain Management

8.1 Explain integrations and the role they play in connecting a corporation.

8.2 Describe supply chain management along with its associated benefits and challenges.

LO 8.1: Explain integrations and the role they play in connecting a corporation.

BUILDING A CONNECTED CORPORATION THROUGH INTEGRATIONS

Until the 1990s, each department in the United Kingdom's Ministry of Defense and Army headquarters had its own information system, and each system had its own database. Sharing information was difficult, requiring employees to manually input the same information into different systems multiple times. Often, management could not even compile the information it needed to answer questions, solve problems, and make decisions.

To combat this challenge the ministry integrated its systems, or built connections among its many databases. These connections or ***integrations*** allow separate systems to communicate directly with each other, eliminating the need for manual entry into multiple systems. Building integrations allows the sharing of information across databases along with dramatically increasing its quality. The army can now generate reports detailing its state of readiness and other essential intelligence, tasks that were nearly impossible before the integrations. ***Eintegration*** is the use of the Internet to provide customers with the ability to gain personalized information by querying corporate databases and their information sources. ***Application integration*** is the integration of a company's existing management information systems. ***Data integration*** is the integration of data from multiple sources, which provides a unified view of all data.

Two common methods are used for integrating databases. The first is to create forward and backward integrations that link processes (and their underlying databases) in the value chain. A ***forward integration*** takes information entered into a given system and sends it automatically to all downstream systems and processes. A ***backward integration*** takes information entered into a given system and sends it automatically to all upstream systems and processes. Figure 8.1 demonstrates how this method works across the systems or processes of sales, order entry, order fulfillment, and billing. In the order entry system, for example, an employee can update the customer's information. Via the integrations, that information is sent upstream to the sales system and downstream to the order fulfillment and billing systems. Ideally, an organization wants to build both forward

FIGURE 8.1

A Forward and Backward Customer Information Integration Example

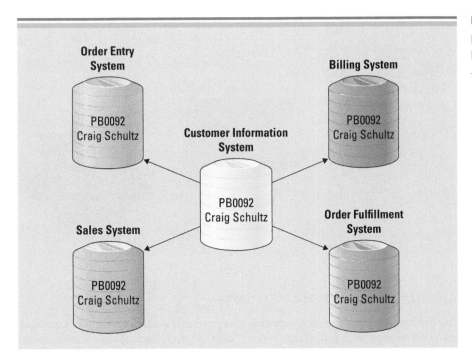

FIGURE 8.2

Integrating Customer
Information among Databases

and backward integrations, which provide the flexibility to create, update, and delete information in any of the systems. However, integrations are expensive and difficult to build and maintain, causing most organizations to invest in forward integrations only.

The second integration method builds a central repository for a particular type of information. Figure 8.2 provides an example of customer information integrated using this method across four different systems in an organization. Users can create, update, and delete customer information only in the central customer database. As users perform these tasks, integrations automatically send the new and/or updated customer information to the other systems. The other systems limit users to read-only access of the customer information stored in them. Both integration methods do not entirely eliminate information redundancy, but they do ensure information consistency among multiple systems.

Integration Tools

Enterprise systems provide enterprisewide support and data access for a firm's operations and business processes. These systems can manage customer information across the enterprise, letting you view everything your customer has experienced from sales to support. Enterprise systems are often available as a generic, but highly customizable, group of programs for business functions such as accounting, manufacturing, and marketing. Generally, the development tools for customization are complex programming tools that require specialist capabilities.

Enterprise application integration (EAI) connects the plans, methods, and tools aimed at integrating separate enterprise systems. A legacy system is a current or existing system that will become the base for upgrading or integrating with a new system. EAI reviews how legacy systems fit into the new shape of the firm's business processes and devises ways to efficiently reuse what already exists while adding new systems and data.

Integrations are achieved using **middleware**—several different types of software that sit between and provide connectivity for two or more software applications. Middleware translates information between disparate systems. **Enterprise application integration (EAI) middleware** takes a new approach to middleware by packaging commonly used applications together, reducing the time needed to integrate applications from multiple vendors. The remainder of this chapter covers the three enterprise systems most organizations use to integrate their disparate departments and separate operational systems: supply chain management (SCM), customer relationship management, and enterprise resource planning (see Figure 8.3).

FIGURE 8.3

The Three Primary Enterprise
Systems

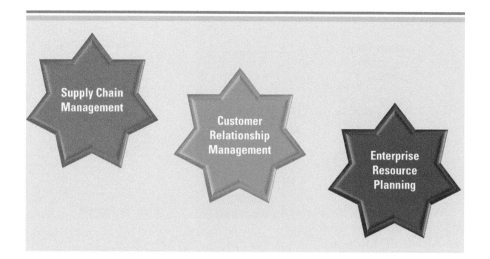

LO 8.2: **Describe supply chain man-agement along with its associated benefits and challenges.**

SUPPLY CHAIN MANAGEMENT

The average company spends nearly half of every dollar it earns on suppliers and raw materials to manufacture products. It is not uncommon to hear of critical success factors focusing on getting the right products, to the right place, at the right time, at the right cost. For this reason, tools that can help a company source raw materials, manufacture products, and deliver finished goods to retailers and customers are in high demand. A *supply chain* consists of all parties involved, directly or indirectly, in obtaining raw materials or a product. Figure 8.4 highlights the five basic supply chain activities a company undertakes to manufacture and distribute products. To automate and enable sophisticated decision making in these critical areas, companies are turning to systems that provide demand forecasting, inventory control, and information flows between suppliers and customers.

Supply chain management (SCM) is the management of information flows between and among activities in a supply chain to maximize total supply chain effectiveness and corporate profitability. In the past, manufacturing efforts focused primarily on quality improvement efforts within the company; today these efforts reach across the entire supply chain, including customers, customers' customers, suppliers, and suppliers' suppliers. Today's supply chain is an intricate network of business partners linked through communication channels and relationships. Supply chain management systems manage and enhance these relationships with the primary goal of creating a fast, efficient, and low-cost network of business relationships that take products from concept to market. SCM systems create the integrations or tight process and information linkages between all participants in the supply chain. Supply chain management performs three main business processes (see Figure 8.5):

1. Materials flow from suppliers and their upstream suppliers at all levels.
2. Materials are transformed into semifinished and finished products—the organization's own production processes.
3. Products are distributed to customers and their downstream customers at all levels.

Consider a customer purchasing a mountain bike from a dealer. Dozens of steps are required to complete this transaction from beginning to end. The customer places an order with the dealer. The dealer purchases the bike from the manufacturer. The manufacturer purchases the raw materials required to make the bike such as aluminum, rubber tires, brakes, accessories, and packaging from different suppliers. The raw materials are stored in the manufacturer's warehouse until a production order requires the bike to be built, at which time the finished product is sent to the dealer or, in some cases, directly to the customer. The supply chain for a bike manufacturer includes all processes and people required to fulfill the customer's order (see Figure 8.6).

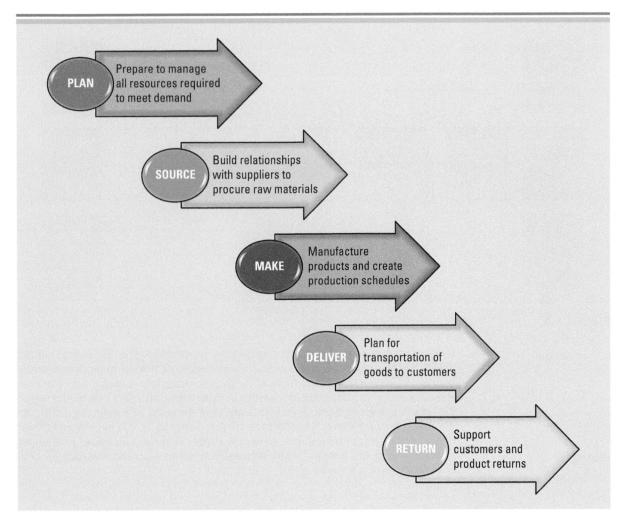

FIGURE 8.4

The Five Basic Supply Chain
Activities

Walmart and Procter & Gamble (P&G) have implemented a successful SCM system that links Walmart's distribution centers directly to P&G's manufacturing centers (see Figure 8.7). The customer generates order information by purchasing a product from Walmart. Walmart supplies the order information to its warehouse or distributor. The warehouse or distributor transfers the order information to P&G, which provides pricing and availability information to the store and replenishes the product to the distributor. Payment is transferred electronically. Effective and efficient supply chain management systems can enable an organization to have these impacts on Porter's Five Forces Model[2]:

- Decrease the power of its buyers.

- Increase its supplier power.

- Increase buyers' switching costs to reduce the threat of substitute products or services.

- Create entry barriers to reduce the threat of new entrants.

- Increase efficiencies while seeking a competitive advantage through cost leadership (see Figure 8.8).

THE BENEFITS OF SCM

Better forecasts for tomorrow result in better preparedness today. Technology advances have significantly improved the ability to perform the five basic supply chain activities such as access to advanced modeling and simulation tools that can combine

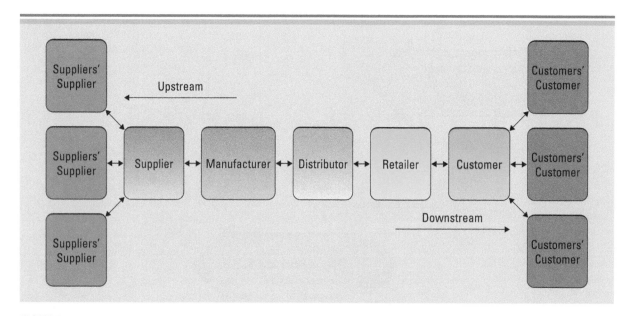

FIGURE 8.5

A Typical Supply Chain

information from multiple sources to build forecasts that look days, weeks, and months ahead. It is now common, for instance, for suppliers to participate in product development and for retailers to contribute to marketing campaigns. Considerable evidence shows that supply chain integration results in superior supply chain capabilities, which drives a firm's profitability. Although firms have dreamed of integrating their supply chains for a long time, it is only recently that advances in MIS have brought these dreams to life. Improved visibility across the supply chain and increased profitability for the firm are the primary business benefits received when implementing supply chain management systems.

FIGURE 8.6

Supply Chain for a Bike Manufacturer

FIGURE 8.7

Supply Chain for a Product Purchased from Walmart

Improved Visibility

Supply chain visibility is the ability to view all areas up and down the supply chain in real time. To react to demand, an organization needs to know all customer events triggered upstream and downstream and so must their suppliers and their suppliers' suppliers. Without this information, supply chain participants are blind to the supply and demand needs occurring in the marketplace, a factor required to implement successful business strategies. To improve visibility across the supply chain, firms can use supply chain planning systems and supply chain execution systems. *Supply chain planning systems* use advanced mathematical algorithms to improve the flow and efficiency of the supply chain while reducing inventory. To yield accurate results, however, supply chain planning systems require information inputs that are correct and up-to-date regarding customers, orders, sales, manufacturing, and distribution capabilities.

Ideally, the supply chain consists of multiple firms that function as efficiently and effectively as a single firm, with full information visibility. *Supply chain execution systems* ensure supply chain cohesion by automating the different activities of the supply chain. For example, a supply chain execution system might electronically route orders from a manufacturer to a supplier using *electronic data interchange (EDI)*, a standard format for the electronic exchange of information between supply chain participants. Figure 8.9 details how supply chain planning and supply chain execution systems interact with the supply chain.

A good example of inventory issues that occur when a company does not have a clear vision of its entire supply chain is the bullwhip effect. The *bullwhip effect* occurs when

FIGURE 8.8

Effective and Efficient Supply Chain Management's Effect on Porter's Five Forces

FIGURE 8.9

Supply Chain Planning's and
Supply Chain Execution's Roles
in the Supply Chain

distorted product-demand information ripples from one partner to the next throughout the supply chain. The misinformation regarding a slight rise in demand for a product could cause different members in the supply chain to stockpile inventory. These changes ripple throughout the supply chain, magnifying the issue and creating excess inventory and costs for all. For example, if a car dealership is having a hard time moving a particular brand of car, it might offer significant discounts to try to move the inventory. Without this critical information, the car manufacturer might see a rise in demand for this particular brand of car and increase production orders, not realizing that the dealerships are actually challenged with selling the inventory. Today, integrated supply chains provide managers with the visibility to see their suppliers' and customers' supply chains, ensuring that supply always meets demand.

Increased Profitability

Supply chain management systems can increase profitability across an organization. For example, a manufacturing plant manager might focus on keeping the inventory of Product A as low as possible, which will directly reduce the manufacturing costs and make the plant manager look great. However, the plant manager and the business might not realize that these savings are causing increased costs in other areas, such as having to pay more to procure raw materials for immediate production needs or increasing costs due to expedited shipping services. Only an end-to-end view or an integrated supply chain would uncover these issues, allowing a firm to adjust business strategies to increase profitability across the enterprise.

Customers are also more demanding than ever before. Because information is so readily available, they know exactly what they want, when they want it, and how they want it delivered. If your company can't meet their demand, the competition is simply a mouse-click away. Couple supply chain complexity with today's demanding customers and a firm's costs can easily escalate out of control. ***Demand planning systems*** generate demand forecasts using statistical tools and forecasting techniques, so companies can respond faster and more effectively to consumer demands through supply chain enhancements. Firms are implementing demand planning systems to understand customer demand and production capabilities so they can estimate supply chain costs that ultimately impact the firm's performance and business strategies. Innovative wireless technologies, such as radio-frequency identification (RFID), are also enabling companies to operate with improved speed and accuracy, ensuring that they can satisfy continuously changing customer demands.

BUSINESS DRIVEN ETHICS AND SECURITY

Zappos, Staples, and Amazon are just a few of the companies taking advantage of the latest innovation in warehouse management by replacing traditional order fulfillment technologies such as conveyor belts with little orange robots. The Kiva Mobile Fulfillment System (Kiva MFS) takes advantage of a unique order fulfillment system that improves productivity, speed, accuracy, and flexibility. Watching an order fulfillment center equipped with Kiva MFS robots is amazing; the operators stand still while the products come to them. Inventory pods store the products that are carried and transferred by a small army of little orange robots, eliminating the need for traditional systems such as conveyors and sorters.[3]

What impact could Kiva MFS have on visibility and profitability of the supply chain? How would your warehouse employees react if you told them you were looking at implementing Kiva robots? What ethical issues arise in the replacement of human labor with robots? What security concerns could a company face when implementing Kiva MFS robots?

Kiva's Robots

A supply chain is only as strong as its weakest link. Companies use supply chain management metrics to measure the performance of supply chains to quickly identify weak links. A few of the common supply chain management metrics include:

- **Back order:** An unfilled customer order for a product that is out of stock.
- **Inventory cycle time:** The time it takes to manufacture a product and deliver it to the retailer.
- **Customer order cycle time:** The agreed upon time between the purchase of a product and the delivery of the product.
- **Inventory turnover:** The frequency of inventory replacement.

THE CHALLENGES OF SCM

The primary challenges associated with supply chain management include costs and complexity. Supply chain management systems can cost millions of dollars for the software and millions of dollars more for help with the implementation. Just walk into any manufacturing plant, distribution center, or factory floor and you will witness the complexity and costs associated with supply chain management. Supply chains cross entire organizations touching multiple departments and spanning organizationwide business processes. Revamping just a single business process can be difficult for a company. Revamping all business processes that touch the supply chain is an incredibly difficult and complex task but is typically required for the SCM system to become effective. And, to top it all off, the supply chain reaches beyond the borders of the organization into partner, supplier, and customer domains, adding another layer of complexity for SCM. A lack of adequate collaboration among marketing, sales, and manufacturing within a company and suppliers, partners, and distributors outside of a company can easily sabotage SCM efforts sending the multimillion-dollar investment down the drain.

The move toward globalization is also increasing supply chain complexity. As supply chains span geographical locations, issues such as time zone differences, transportation fees, cultural and language barriers, and exchange rates all add additional layers to the already complex supply chain. Government relationships, taxes, and local laws also tend to differ across global regions, creating more confusion and issues in supplier relationships. The bottom line is that SCM systems are complex and costly and implementing them correctly can be challenging even for the most sophisticated organization.

BUSINESS DRIVEN DEBATE

Fixing the Post Office

Lines at the post office are frustrating, and they are also becoming unprofitable as the U.S. Postal Service faces billion-dollar losses for the first time in its history. What is causing this failure? It could be any number of things, but ebusiness competition is one of the primary challengers stealing the Postal Service's market share. Stamps.com allows you to customize and print your own stamps 24 hours a day. If you are getting married, you can place your engagement picture on the stamp for the invitations. If you are starting your own business, you can purchase stamps showing your business logo. And, Stamps.com goes beyond simply delivering a product by tracking customer spending and recommending optimal delivery methods along with postage discounts. Now that is something you can't get at the post office. Talk about a competitive advantage![4]

Why do you think the U.S. Postal Service is losing its market share and becoming unprofitable? What does the Postal Service's supply chain look like? Who are its partners, suppliers, distributors, and customers? What can the Postal Service do to revamp its supply chain so it can become profitable? Many people believe the Postal Service should not be supported by the government, and that if it can't operate efficiently it should fail. Do you agree? Why or why not?

THE FUTURE OF SCM

There is a great commercial that depicts the future of supply chain management. A man wearing a uniform is walking through a home and quietly replaces an empty cereal box with a full one just as the child opens the kitchen cabinet. He then produces a new bag of dog food as soon as the hungry dog's bowl is empty and finally reaches into the shower to hand a new bottle of shampoo to the man in the shower who had just run out. The next wave in supply chain management will be home-based supply chain fulfillment. No more running to the store to replace your products as your store will come to you as soon as you need a new product.

Walgreens is differentiating itself from other national chains as the family's just-in-time supplier, developing custom websites for each household that allow families to order electronically and then pick up their goods at a self-service counter or drive-through window at their convenience. Walgreens even calls its customers to let them know their prescription medications are soon going to run out and offers to fulfill the new prescription.

As the supply chain management market matures, it is becoming even more sophisticated and incorporating additional functionality such as marketing, customer service, and even product development to its extended supply chain. Advanced communications tools, easy-to-use decision support systems, and building trust among participants when sharing information are all making the home-based supply chain possible. A few of the fastest-growing SCM components include:

- **Collaborative demand planning**—reduces inventory investments, while improving customer satisfaction.
- **Collaborative engineering**—reduces product development costs.
- **Selling chain management**—automates order processes from initial customer inquiry to final product delivery.
- **Supply chain event management (SCEM)**—increases real-time information sharing among supply chain partners focusing on reducing response time to unexpected events.

section 8.2 | Customer Relationship Management and Enterprise Resource Planning

8.3 Describe customer relationship management along with its associated benefits and challenges.

8.4 Describe enterprise resource planning along with its associated benefits and challenges.

CUSTOMER RELATIONSHIP MANAGEMENT

LO 8.3: Describe customer relationship management along with its associated benefits and challenges.

Today, most competitors are simply a mouse-click away, and this intense competition is forcing firms to switch from sales-focused business strategies to customer-focused business strategies. Customers are one of a firm's most valuable assets, and building strong loyal customer relationships is a key competitive advantage. Harley-Davidson offers an excellent example of a company that knows the value of customer loyalty, and it finds itself in the coveted position of demand outweighing its supply. No other motorcycle in the world has the look, feel, and sound of a Harley-Davidson. Demand for Harley-Davidson motorcycles outweighs supply and some models have up to a two-year waiting list. Knowing the value of its customers, Harley-Davidson started the Harley's Owners Group (HOG), which is the largest motorcycle club in the world with more than 600,000 members. HOG offers a wide array of events, rides, and benefits to its members and is a key competitive advantage as it helps to build a strong sense of community among Harley-Davidson owners. Harley-Davidson has built a customer following that is extremely loyal, a difficult task to accomplish in any industry.[5]

Customer relationship management (CRM) is a means of managing all aspects of a customer's relationship with an organization to increase customer loyalty and retention and an organization's profitability. CRM allows an organization to gain insights into customers' shopping and buying behaviors. Every time a customer communicates with a company, the firm has the chance to build a trusting relationship with that particular customer. Harley-Davidson realizes that it takes more than just building and selling motorcycles to fulfill the dreams of its loyal customers. For this reason, the company strives to deliver unforgettable experiences along with its top-quality products. When the company began selling products online it found itself facing a dilemma—its online strategy for selling accessories directly to consumers would bypass Harley-Davidson's dealers, who depend on the higha-margin accessories for store revenues. The solution was to deploy Harley-Davidson.com, which prompts customers to select a participating Harley-Davidson dealership before placing any online orders. The selected dealership is then responsible for fulfilling the order. This strategy ensured that the dealers remained the focus point of each customer's buying experiences. To guarantee that every customer has a highly satisfying online buying experience, the company asks the dealers to agree to a number of standards including:

- Checking online orders twice daily.
- Shipping online orders within 24 hours.
- Responding to customer inquiries within 24 hours.[6]

Harley-Davidson still monitors online customer metrics such as time taken to process orders, number of returned orders, and number of incorrect orders, guaranteeing that the company delivers on its critical success factor of providing prompt, excellent customer service consistently to all its loyal customers.

A primary component of managing a customer relationship is knowing when and why the customer is communicating with the company. Imagine an irate customer that has just spent an hour on the phone with your call center complaining about a defective product. While the customer is on the phone, your sales representative decides to drop by the customer's office in an attempt to sell additional products. Obviously, this is not the ideal time to try to up-sell or cross-sell products to this particular customer. A customer relationship management system would inform the sales representative that the customer was on the phone with customer service and even provide details of the call. Then your sales representative could stop by and offer assistance in resolving the product issue, which might help restore the relationship with the customer and provide opportunities for future sales.

The complicated piece of this puzzle is that customers have many communication channels they can use to contact a company including call centers, websites, email, faxes, and telephones. To make matters even more complex, a single customer can communicate with a firm using all of the different communication channels multiple times. Keeping track of customer communications is important if the firm wants to continue to build and manage that relationship. A CRM system can track every form of customer communication providing this information to all employees (see Figure 8.10). The firm can then implement strategies for the best ways to communicate effectively with each and every customer. With a CRM system a firm can obtain an overview of the customer's products, preferences, account information, communications, and purchasing history, allowing it to send customized product offers, expedite shipping, ensure satisfaction, and other marketing and sales techniques that can greatly add to sales and profits.

FIGURE 8.10

Customer Relationship Management Overview

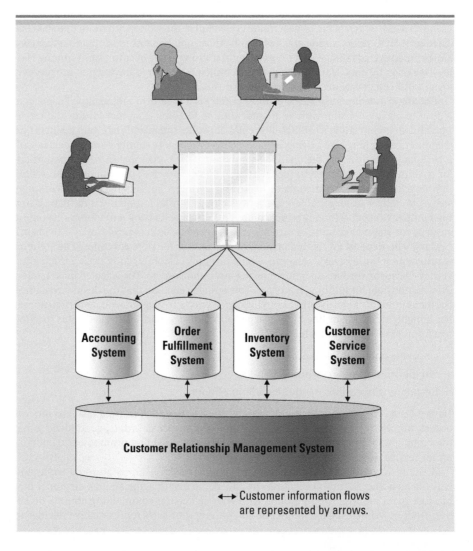

← → Customer information flows are represented by arrows.

THE BENEFITS OF CRM

Companies that understand individual customer needs are best positioned to achieve success. Of course, building successful customer relationships is not a new business practice; however, implementing CRM systems allows a company to operate more efficiently and effectively in the area of supporting customer needs. CRM moves far beyond technology by identifying customer needs and designing specific marketing campaigns tailored to each. This enables a firm to treat customers as individuals, gaining important insights into their buying preferences and shopping behaviors. Firms that treat their customers well reap the rewards and generally see higher profits and highly loyal customers. Identifying the most valuable customers allows a firm to ensure that these customers receive the highest levels of customer service and are offered the first opportunity to purchase new products. Firms can find their most valuable customers by using the RFM formula—recency, frequency, and monetary value. In other words, an organization must track:

- How r*ecently* a customer purchased items.
- How *frequently* a customer purchases items.
- The *monetary value* of each customer purchase.

After gathering this initial CRM information, the firm can analyze it to identify patterns and create marketing campaigns and sales promotions for different customer segments. For example, if a customer buys only at the height of the season, the firm should send a special offer during the off-season. If a certain customer segment purchases shoes but never accessories, the firm can offer discounted accessories with the purchase of a new pair of shoes. If the firm determines that its top 20 percent of customers are responsible for 80 percent of the revenue, it can focus on ensuring these customers are always satisfied and receive the highest levels of customer service.

Evolution of CRM

There are three phases in the evolution of CRM: (1) reporting, (2) analyzing, and (3) predicting. **CRM reporting technologies** help organizations identify their customers across other applications. **CRM analysis technologies** help organizations segment their customers into categories such as best and worst customers. **CRM predicting technologies** help organizations predict customer behavior, such as which customers are at risk of leaving. Figure 8.11 highlights a few of the important questions an organization can answer in these areas by using CRM technologies.

FIGURE 8.11

Evolution of CRM

REPORTING Customer Identification: Asking What Happened	ANALYZING Customer Segmentation: Asking Why It Happened	PREDICTING Customer Prediction: Asking What Will Happen
• What is the total revenue by customer? • How many units did we make? • What were total sales by product? • How many customers do we have? • What are the current inventory levels?	• Why did sales not meet forecasts? • Why was production so low? • Why did we not sell as many units as previous years? • Who are our customers? • Why was revenue so high? • Why are inventory levels low?	• What customers are at risk of leaving? • Which products will our customers buy? • Who are the best customers for a marketing campaign? • How do we reach our customers? • What will sales be this year? • How much inventory do we need to preorder?

BUSINESS DRIVEN GLOBALIZATION

Banking on Customer Relationships

Barclays Bank, a leader in the global financial markets, maintains business operations in more than 70 countries. Barclays chose to invest in CRM technologies to help it gain valuable insights into its personal and business customers, many of which carry credit cards. The purpose of the CRM system was to predict the financial behavior of individual customers and assess whether a customer is likely to pay back a loan in full within the agreed-upon time period and interest rate. Surprisingly, Barclays' CRM system quickly identified that about 50 percent of its customers were nonprofitable, and that 90 percent of its profits were generated by fewer than 30 percent of its customers.

This valuable information allowed Barclays to revamp its offerings and charge customers an interest rate based on risk assessment. Barclays also identifies groups of profitable customers, both on a corporate and personal level, which it can then target for new financial products.[7]

How can a business like Barclays use RFM (recency, frequency, and monetary value) to improve customer relations? Provide three examples of questions a bank would ask in each of the following categories: CRM reporting technologies, CRM analysis technologies, and CRM predicting technologies.

Operational and Analytical CRM

The two primary components of a CRM strategy are operational CRM and analytical CRM. **Operational CRM** supports traditional transactional processing for day-to-day front-office operations or systems that deal directly with the customers. **Analytical CRM** supports back-office operations and strategic analysis and includes all systems that do not deal directly with the customers. Figure 8.12 provides an overview of the two.

FIGURE 8.12

Operational CRM and Analytical CRM

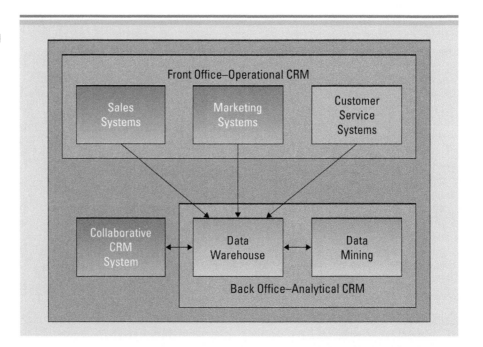

Figure 8.13 shows the different technologies marketing, sales, and customer service departments can use to perform operational CRM.

Marketing and Operational CRM

Companies are no longer trying to sell one product to as many customers as possible; instead, they are trying to sell one customer as many products as possible. Marketing departments switch to this new way of doing business by using CRM technologies that allow them to gather and analyze customer information to tailor successful marketing campaigns. In fact, a marketing campaign's success is directly proportional to the organization's ability to gather and analyze the right customer information. The three primary operational CRM technologies a marketing department can implement to increase customer satisfaction are:

1. List generator.
2. Campaign management.
3. Cross-selling and up-selling.

List Generator   *List generators* compile customer information from a variety of sources and segment it for different marketing campaigns. These sources include website visits, questionnaires, surveys, marketing mailers, and so on. After compiling the customer list, it can be filtered based on criteria such as household income, gender, education level, political facilitation, age, or other factors. List generators provide the marketing department with valuable information on the type of customer it must target to find success for a marketing campaign.

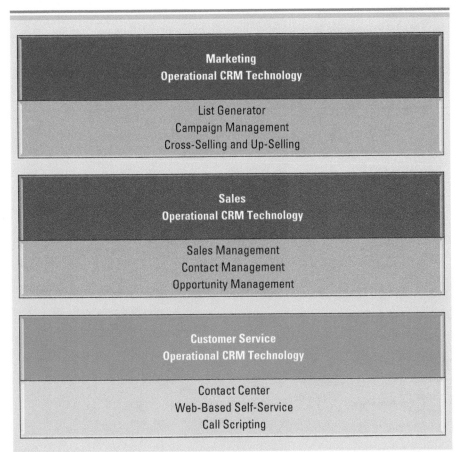

FIGURE 8.13

Operational CRM Technologies

Campaign Management   *Campaign management systems* guide users through marketing campaigns by performing such tasks as campaign definition, planning, scheduling, segmentation, and success analysis. These advanced systems can even calculate the profitability and track the results for each marketing campaign.

Cross-Selling and Up-Selling   Two key sales strategies a marketing campaign can deploy are cross-selling and up-selling. *Cross-selling* is selling additional products or services to an existing customer. For example, if you were to purchase Tim Burton's movie *Alice in Wonderland* on Amazon, you would also be asked if you want to purchase the movie's soundtrack or the original book. Amazon is taking advantage of cross-selling by offering customers goods across its book, movie, and music product lines. *Up-selling* is increasing the value of the sale. McDonald's performs up-selling by asking customers whether they would like to super-size their meals for an extra cost. CRM systems offer marketing departments all kinds of information about customers and products, which can help identify up-selling and cross-selling opportunities to increase revenues.

Sales and Operational CRM

Sales departments were the first to begin developing CRM systems. They had two primary motivations to track customer sales information electronically. First, sales representatives were struggling with the overwhelming amount of customer account information they were required to maintain and track. Second, managers found themselves hindered because much of their vital customer and sales information remained in the heads of their sales representatives, even if the sales representative left the company. Finding a way to track customer information became a critical success factor for many sales departments. *Customer service and support (CSS)* is a part of operational CRM that automates service requests, complaints, product returns, and information requests.

Figure 8.14 depicts the typical sales process, which begins with an opportunity and ends with billing the customer for the sale. Leads and potential customers are the lifeblood of all sales organizations, whether they sell computers, clothing, consulting, or cars. How leads are handled can make the difference between revenue growth and decline.

Sales force automation (SFA) automatically tracks all the steps in the sales process. SFA products focus on increasing customer satisfaction, building customer relationships,

FIGURE 8.14

A Typical Sales Process

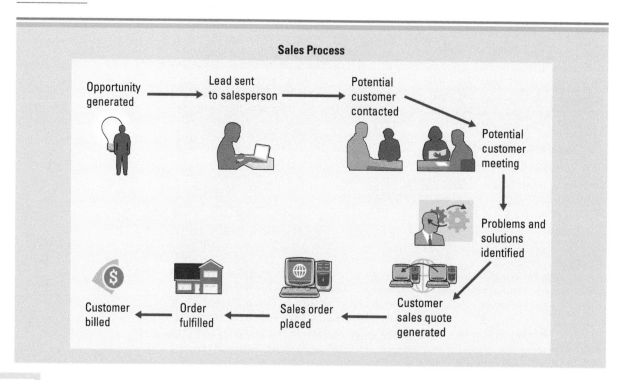

Sales Process

Opportunity generated → Lead sent to salesperson → Potential customer contacted → Potential customer meeting → Problems and solutions identified → Customer sales quote generated → Sales order placed → Order fulfilled → Customer billed and improving product sales. The three primary operational CRM technologies a sales department can adopt are:

1. Sales management CRM systems.
2. Contact management CRM systems.
3. Opportunity management CRM systems.

Sales Management CRM Systems   *Sales management CRM systems* automate each phase of the sales process, helping individual sales representatives coordinate and organize all their accounts. Features include calendars, reminders for important tasks, multimedia presentations, and document generation. These systems can even provide an analysis of the sales cycle and calculate how each individual sales representative is performing during the sales process.

Contact Management CRM Systems   A *contact management CRM system* maintains customer contact information and identifies prospective customers for future sales, using tools such as organizational charts, detailed customer notes, and supplemental sales information. For example, a contact management system can take an incoming telephone number and automatically display the person's name along with a comprehensive history including all communications with the company. This allows the sales representative to personalize the phone conversation and ask such things as, "How is your new laptop working, Sue?" or "How was your family vacation to Colorado?" The customer feels valued since the sales associate knows her name and even remembers details of their last conversation.

Opportunity Management CRM Systems   *Opportunity management CRM systems* target sales opportunities by finding new customers or companies for future sales. They determine potential customers and competitors and define selling efforts including budgets and schedules. Advanced systems can even calculate the probability of a sale, which can save sales representatives significant time and money when qualifying new customers. The primary difference between contact management and opportunity management is that contact management deals with existing customers and opportunity management with new or potential customers.

Customer Service and Operational CRM

Most companies recognize the importance of building strong customer relationships during the marketing and sales efforts, but they must continue this effort by building strong post-sale relationships also. A primary reason firms lose customers is due to negative customer service experiences. Providing outstanding customer service is challenging, and many CRM technologies can assist organizations with this important activity. The three primary ones are:

1. Contact center.
2. Web-based self-service.
3. Call scripting.

Contact Center   A *contact center* or *call center* is where customer service representatives answer customer inquiries and solve problems, usually by email, chat, or phone. It is one of the best assets a customer-driven organization can have because maintaining a high level of customer support is critical to obtaining and retaining customers. Figure 8.15 highlights a few of the services contact center systems offer.

Contact centers also track customer communication histories along with problem resolutions—information critical for providing a comprehensive customer view to the service representative. Representatives who can quickly comprehend the customer's concerns provide tremendous value to the customer and to the company. Nothing makes frustrated customers happier than not having to explain their problems all over again to yet another customer service representative.

BUSINESS DRIVEN INNOVATION

Nice Emotions

New emotion-detection software called Perform, created by Nice Systems, helps firms improve customer service by identifying callers who are displeased or upset. Perform determines a baseline of emotion and can detect emotional issues during the first few seconds of a call; any variation from the baseline activates an alert. When an elderly person who was highly distressed over medical costs hung up during a phone call to the insurance company, Perform identified the customer's frustration and automatically emailed a supervisor. The supervisor was able to review a recording of the conversation and immediately called the customer back suggesting ways to lower the costs.[8]

How do you think emotion-detection software will affect customer relationships? What other departments or business processes could benefit from its use? Create a new product that uses emotion-detection software. What business problem would your product solve and who would be your primary customers?

FIGURE 8.15

Common Services Provided by Contact Centers

Automatic call distribution: Routes inbound calls to available agents.
Interactive voice response (IVR): Directs customers to use touch-tone phones or keywords to navigate or provide information.
Predictive dialing: Automatically dials outbound calls and forwards answered calls to an available agent.

Web-Based Self-Service   *Web-based self-service systems* allow customers to use the web to find answers to their questions or solutions to their problems. FedEx uses web-based self-service systems to let customers electronically track packages without having to talk to a customer service representative. Another feature of web-based self-service is *click-to-talk* functions, which allow customers to click on a button and talk with a representative via the Internet. Powerful customer-driven features such as these add value to any organization by providing customers with real-time information that helps resolve their concerns.

Call Scripting   Companies that market and sell highly technical products have a difficult time finding competent customer service representatives. *Call scripting systems* gather product details and issue resolution information that can be automatically generated into a script for the representative to read to the customer. These systems even provide questions the representative can ask the customer to troubleshoot the problem and find a resolution. This feature not only helps reps answer difficult questions quickly but also presents a uniform response so customers don't receive different answers.

Analytical CRM

Analytical CRM provides information about customers and products that was once impossible to locate, such as which type of marketing and sales campaign to launch and which customers to target and when. Unlike operational CRM, which automates call centers and sales forces with the aim of enhancing customer service, analytical CRM works by using business intelligence to identify patterns in product sales and customer behaviors. Analytical CRM tools can slice-and-dice vast amounts of information to create custom views of customers, products, and market segments highlighting opportunities for cross-selling and up-selling. *Website personalization* occurs when a website has stored enough data about a person's likes and dislikes to fashion offers more likely to appeal to that person. Many marketers use CRM to personalize customer communications and decide which customers are worth pursuing. Here are a few examples of the information insights analytical CRM can help an organization gain.

- **Find new profitable customers:** Analytical CRM could highlight that the most profitable market segment consists of women between 35 and 45 years old who drive SUVs and live within 30 miles of the city limits. The firm could then find a way to locate these customers for mailings and other opportunities.

- **Exceed customer expectations:** Analytical CRM helps a firm move past the typical "Dear Mr. Smith" greeting by personalizing communications. For example, if the firm knows the customer's favorite brand and size of shoe it can notify the customer that a pair of size 12 Nike cross trainers are available for him to try on the next time he visits the store.

- **Discover the activities the firm performs the best:** Analytical CRM can determine what an organization does better than its competitors. If a restaurant caters more lunches to midsized companies than its competition does, it can purchase a specialized mailing targeting these customers for future mailings.

- **Eliminate competition:** Analytical CRM can determine sales trends allowing the company to provide customers with special deals outsmarting its competition. A sports store might identify its best customers for outdoor apparel and invite them to a private sale right before the competition runs its sale.

- **Care about customers:** Analytical CRM can determine what customers want and need, so a firm can contact them with an invitation to a private sale, reminder that a product needs a tune-up, or send them a personalized letter along with a discount coupon to help spark a renewed relationship.

Measuring CRM Success

Using CRM metrics to track and monitor performance is a best practice for many companies. Figure 8.16 displays a few common CRM metrics a manager can use to track the success of the system. Just remember that you only want to track between five and seven of the hundreds of CRM metrics available.

THE CHALLENGES OF CRM

A standard rule of business states that the customer is always right. Although most businesses use this as their motto, they do not actually mean it. Ebusiness firms must adhere to this rule as the power of the customer grows exponentially in the information age. Various websites and videos on YouTube reveal the power of the individual consumer (see Figure 8.17). A decade ago if you had a complaint against a company you could make a phone call or write a letter. Now you can contact hundreds or thousands of people around the globe and voice your complaint or anger with a company or product. You—the customer—can now take your power directly to millions of people and companies have to listen.

FIGURE 8.16

CRM Metrics

Sales Metrics	Customer Service Metrics	Marketing Metrics
Number of prospective customers	Cases closed same day	Number of marketing campaigns
Number of new customers	Number of cases handled by agent	New customer retention rates
Number of retained customers	Number of service calls	Number of responses by marketing campaign
Number of open leads	Average number of service requests by type	Number of purchases by marketing campaign
Number of sales calls	Average time to resolution	Revenue generated by marketing campaign
Number of sales calls per lead	Average number of service calls per day	Cost per interaction by marketing campaign
Amount of new revenue	Percentage compliance with service-level agreement	Number of new customers acquired by marketing campaign
Amount of recurring revenue	Percentage of service renewals	Customer retention rate
Number of proposals given	Customer satisfaction level	Number of new leads by product

FIGURE 8.17

The Power of the Customer

BUSINESS DRIVEN START-UP

You might not want to put the fact that you won the Straightjacket Award on your résumé unless you worked for Rackspace, a Texas company that specializes in hosting websites. At Rackspace, the coveted Straightjacket Award is won by the employee who best delivers "fanatical customer support," one of the firm's critical success factors. The company motivates its customer service representatives by dividing them into teams, each responsible for its own profitability. The company then measures such things as customer turnover, upselling, cross-selling, and referrals. The team with the highest scores wins the Straightjacket Award and each member receives a 20 percent bonus.[9]

Assume your professor has hired you as the employee relationship manager for your class. What type of award would you create to help increase class participation? What type of award would you create to help increase the overall average on exams? What type of award would you create to help increase student collaboration? Be sure to name your awards and describe their details. Also, what type of metrics would you create to measure your awards? How could a CRM system help you implement your awards?

Straightjacket Customer Service

THE FUTURE OF CRM

Organizations are discovering a wave of other key business areas where it is beneficial to build strong relationships beyond customers. These include supplier relationship management (SRM), partner relationship management (PRM), and employee relationship management (ERM).

Supplier relationship management (SRM) focuses on keeping suppliers satisfied by evaluating and categorizing suppliers for different projects. SRM applications help companies analyze suppliers based on a number of key variables including prices, inventory availability, and business focus or strategies. It can then determine the best supplier to collaborate with and develop strong relationships with to streamline processes, outsource services, and provide products the firm could not offer alone.

Partner relationship management (PRM) discovers optimal sales channels by selecting the right partners and identifying mutual customers. A PRM system offers real-time sales channel information about such things as inventory availability, pricing strategies, and shipping information, allowing a company to expand its market by offering specialized products and services.

Employee relationship management (ERM) provides web-based self-service tools that streamline and automate the human resource department. Employees are the backbone of an enterprise and the communication channel to customers, partners, and suppliers. Their relationship with the company is far more complex and long-lasting than the relationship with customers, thus many enterprises are turning to ERM systems to help retain key employees.

ENTERPRISE RESOURCE PLANNING

LO 8.4: Describe enterprise resource planning along with its associated benefits and challenges.

Today's managers require real-time views into their businesses so they can make decisions when they need to. *Enterprise resource planning (ERP)* integrates all departments and functions throughout an organization into a single IT system (or integrated set of IT systems) so employees can make decisions by viewing enterprisewide information about all business operations.

Many organizations fail to maintain consistency across business operations. If a single department, such as sales, decides to implement a new system without considering other departments, like marketing and accounting, inconsistencies can occur throughout the company, and operations can become discontinuous, like silos. Enterprise resource planning systems provide organizations with consistency. They allow for the effective planning and controlling of all the resources required to plan, source, make, and deliver goods and services. Figure 8.18 shows how an ERP system takes data from across the enterprise, consolidates and correlates it, and generates enterprisewide organizational reports.

The key word in enterprise resource planning is *enterprise*. At the core of an ERP system is a central database that gathers transactional data from operational systems across the company. Each time information is altered, it is automatically updated throughout the entire system. For example, sales representatives can access the ERP system to view all necessary information to process orders such as credit rating, order history, inventory levels, and delivery schedules. Once the order is complete, the ERP system automatically routes it to the next department in the order process, as illustrated in Figure 8.19. ERP systems facilitate the order process, ensuring customers receive their purchases faster and with fewer errors. ERP systems can support numerous business processes far beyond order processing, such as employee benefits and financial reporting. An ERP system can also support supplier and customer business processes infiltrating the entire value chain and helping the organization achieve greater operational efficiency (see Figure 8.20).

THE BENEFITS OF ERP

The first generation of ERP systems focused on improving the manufacturing process through automation, primarily addressing back-office business processes such as inventory ordering and product distribution. The second generation of ERP systems extended its reach into the front office and primarily addressed customer issues including marketing and sales. The third generation of ERP systems, known as ERP-II, allows a company to compete on a functional level by adopting an enterprisewide approach using the Internet to connect all participants in the value chain. Figure 8.21 shows how ERP has grown to accommodate the needs of the entire organization.

The current generation of ERP, ERP-II is composed of two primary components—core and extended. **Core ERP components** are the traditional components included in most ERP systems and primarily focus on internal operations. **Extended ERP components** are

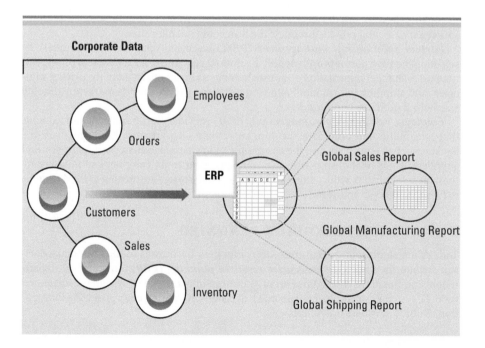

FIGURE 8.18

Enterprise Resource Planning System Overview

BUSINESS DRIVEN MIS

Classic Cars Inc. operates high-end automotive dealerships that offer luxury cars along with luxury service. The company is proud of its extensive inventory, top-of-the-line mechanics, and especially its exceptional service, which includes operating a cappuccino bar at each dealership.

The company currently has 40 sales representatives at four locations. Each location maintains its own computer systems, and all sales representatives have their own contact management systems. This splintered approach to operations causes numerous problems in customer communication, pricing strategy, and inventory control, such as:

- A customer can get different quotes at different dealerships for the same car.
- Sales representatives frequently steal each other's customers and commissions.
- Sales representatives send their customers to other dealerships to see specific cars that turn out not to be on the lot.
- Marketing campaigns are typically generic and not designed to target specific customers.
- If a sales representative quits, all his or her customer information is lost.

You work for Customer One, a small consulting company that specializes in enterprisewide strategies. The owner of Classic Cars Inc. has hired you to help him formulate a strategy to put his company back on track. Develop a proposal detailing how an ERP system can alleviate the company's problems and create new sales opportunities.

Classic Cars

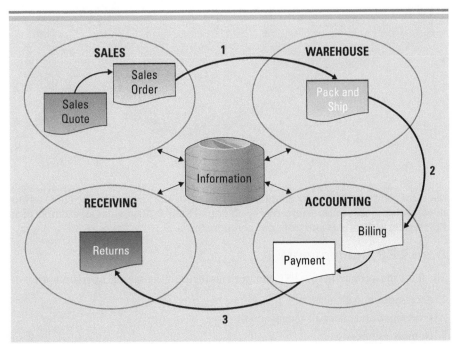

FIGURE 8.19

ERP Process Flow

FIGURE 8.20

The Organization Before
and After ERP

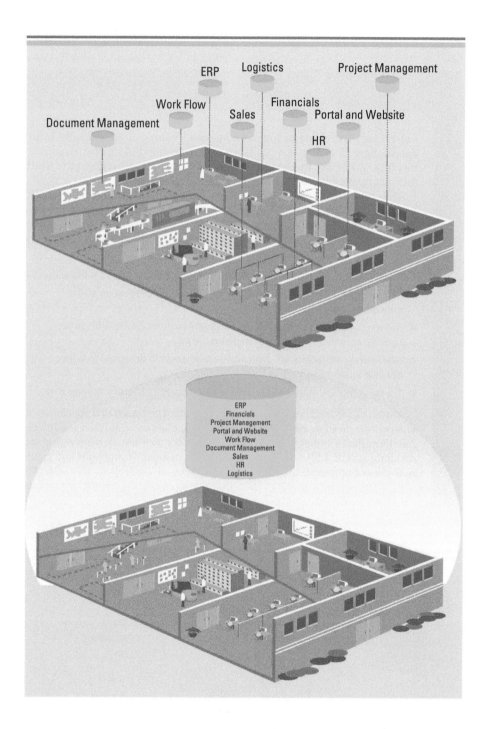

the extra components that meet organizational needs not covered by the core components and primarily focus on external operations. Figure 8.22 provides an example of an ERP system with its core and extended components.

Core ERP Components

The three most common core ERP components focusing on internal operations are:

1. Accounting and finance.
2. Production and materials management.
3. Human resources.

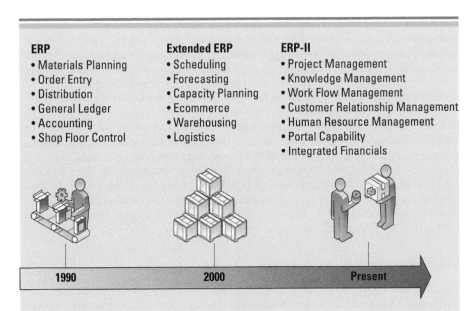

FIGURE 8.21

The Evolution of ERP

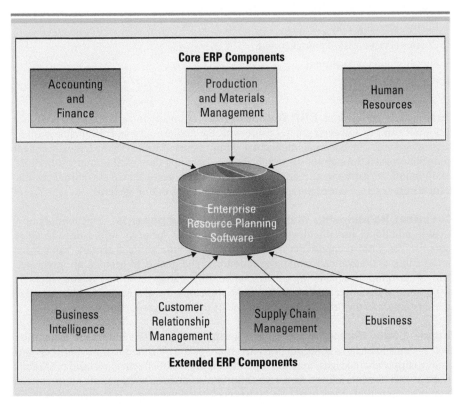

FIGURE 8.22

Core ERP Components and
Extended ERP Components

Accounting and Finance ERP Components   *Accounting and finance ERP components* manage accounting data and financial processes within the enterprise with functions such as general ledger, accounts payable, accounts receivable, budgeting, and asset management. One of the most useful features of an ERP accounting/finance component is credit management. Most organizations manage their relationships with customers by setting credit limits, or limits on how much a customer can owe at any one time. ERP financial systems correlate customers' orders with their account balances to determine credit availability. They also perform all types of advanced profitability modeling techniques.

Production and Materials Management ERP Components *Production and materials management ERP components* handle production planning and execution tasks such as demand forecasting, production scheduling, job cost accounting, and quality control. Demand forecasting helps determine production schedules and materials purchasing. A company that makes its own product prepares a detailed production schedule, and a company that buys products for resale develops a materials requirement plan.

Human Resources ERP Components *Human resources ERP components* track employee information including payroll, benefits, compensation, and performance assessment and ensure compliance with all laws. They even allow the organization to perform detailed employee analysis, such as identifying who is likely to leave the company unless additional compensation or benefits are provided, and whether the most talented people are working in areas where they can have the greatest impact. Human resource components can also identify which employees are using which resources, such as online training and long-distance telephone services.

Extended ERP Components

Extended ERP components meet the organizational needs not covered by the core components and primarily focus on external operations. Many are Internet-enabled and require interaction with customers, suppliers, and business partners outside the organization. The four most common extended ERP components are:

1. Business intelligence.
2. Customer relationship management.
3. Supply chain management.
4. Ebusiness.

Business Intelligence ERP Components Many organizations have found that ERP tools can provide even greater value with the addition of powerful business intelligence systems. The business intelligence components of ERP systems typically collect information used throughout the organization (including data used in many other ERP components), organize it, and apply analytical tools to assist managers with decisions. Data warehouses are one of the most popular extensions to ERP systems.

Customer Relationship Management ERP Components ERP vendors now include additional functionality that provides services formerly found only in CRM systems. The CRM components in ERP systems include contact centers, sales force automation, and advanced marketing functions. The goal is to provide an integrated view of customer data, enabling a firm to effectively manage customer relationships by responding to customer needs and demands while identifying the most (and least) valuable customers so the firm can better allocate its marketing resources.

Supply Chain Management ERP Components ERP vendors are expanding their systems to include SCM functions that manage the information flows between and among supply chain stages, maximizing total supply chain effectiveness and profitability. SCM components allow a firm to monitor and control all stages in the supply chain from the acquisition of raw materials to the receipt of finished goods by customers.

Ebusiness ERP Components The newest extended ERP components are the ebusiness components that allow companies to establish an Internet presence and fulfill online orders. Two of the primary features of ebusiness components are elogistics and eprocurement. *Elogistics* manages the transportation and storage of goods. *Eprocurement* is the business-to-business (B2B) online purchase and sale of supplies and services. A common mistake many businesses make is jumping into online business without properly integrating the entire organization on the ERP system. One large toy manufacturer announced less than a week before Christmas that it would be unable to fulfill any of its online orders. The company had all the toys in the warehouse, but it could not organize the basic order processing function to get the toys delivered to consumers on time.

Measuring ERP Success

One of the best methods of measuring ERP success is the balanced scorecard, created by Dr. Robert Kaplan and Dr. David Norton, both from the Harvard Business School. The ***balanced scorecard*** is a management system, as well as a measurement system, that a firm uses to translate business strategies into executable tasks. It provides feedback for both internal and external business processes, allowing continuous improvement. Kaplan and Norton describe the balanced scorecard as follows: "The balanced scorecard retains traditional financial measures. But financial measures tell the story of past events, an adequate story for industrial age companies for which investments in long-term capabilities and customer relationships were not critical for success. These financial measures are inadequate, however, for guiding and evaluating the journey that information age companies must make to create future value through investment in customers, suppliers, employees, processes, technology, and innovation."[10] The balanced scorecard uses four perspectives to monitor an organization:

1. The learning and growth perspective.
2. The internal business process perspective.
3. The customer perspective.
4. The financial perspective (see Figure 8.23).

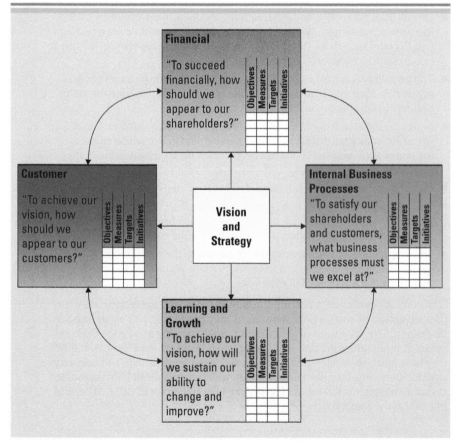

FIGURE 8.23

The Four Primary Perspectives of the Balanced Scorecard

BUSINESS DRIVEN DISCUSSION

Bean Integration

At Flavors, a premium coffee shop, customers receive more than just a great cup of coffee—they also get exposure to music, art, literature, and town events. Flavors offers the following:

- Music center—information about all live music events occurring in the area and an open microphone two nights a week for local musicians.
- Art gallery—a space in the store filled with great pieces from local artists.
- Book clubs—a way for customers to meet to discuss current and classic literature.
- Coffee sampler—free tastings in which experts showcase coffees from around the world.
- Community calendar—weekly meetings to help customers find ways to become more involved in their community.
- Brewing courses—lessons in the finer details of the brewing, grinding, and blending equipment for sale in Flavor stores, from the traditional press to a digital espresso machine. Also includes a trouble-shooting guide developed by brewing specialists.

Flavors' sales are great and profits are soaring; however, operations need an overhaul. The following is a quick look at Flavors' current nonfood offerings.

- Flavors does not receive any information about how many customers attend live events in the music center. Musicians typically maintain a fan email list and CD sales records for the event; however, they don't always provide this information to the store.
- The art gallery is run by several local artists who pay Flavors a small commission on each sale. Flavors has no input on the art displayed in the store or information about who purchases it.
- Book club events are booked and run through the local bookstore, Pages Up, which runs a tab during the meetings and pays Flavor with a check at the end of each month. Flavors has no access to book club customer information or sales information.
- Coffee sampler events are run through Flavors' primary operations.
- Community event information is open to all members of the community. Each event is run by a separate organization, which provides monthly event feedback to Flavors in a variety of formats from Word to Access files.
- Brewing and machine resource courses are run by the equipment manufacturers, and all customer and sales information is provided to Flavors in a Word document at the end of each year.

Flavors' owners want to revamp the way the company operates so they can take advantage of enterprise systems, and they have hired you as an integration expert. They also want to gain a better understanding of how the different events they host affect the different areas of their business. For example, should they have more open-microphone nights and fewer book clubs? The other way around? Currently, they have no way to tell which events result in higher sales. Create an integration strategy so Flavors can take advantage of CRM, SCM, and ERP across the company.

THE CHALLENGES OF ERP

One of the biggest challenges of an ERP system is cost. ERP systems contain multiple complex components that are not only expensive to purchase, but also expensive to implement. Costs can include the software itself, plus consulting charges, hardware expenses, and training fees. A large firm can easily spend millions of dollars and many years completing an ERP implementation. The biggest issue facing an ERP implementation is that it fundamentally changes the way the entire organization operates, causing employees to learn and adjust to new business processes. Many ERP failures occur because the business managers and MIS professionals underestimate the complexity of the planning, development, and training required with an ERP implementation. As a manager, you must carefully assess your company's needs and choose the right ERP system and ensure proper support for all new processes, while avoiding too much change too fast.

THE FUTURE OF ENTERPRISE SYSTEMS: INTEGRATING SCM, CRM, AND ERP

Applications such as SCM, CRM, and ERP are the backbone of ebusiness, yet most organizations today have to piece together these systems. A firm might choose its CRM components from Siebel, SCM components from i2, and financial components and HR management components from Oracle. Figure 8.24 identifies the general audience and purpose for each of these applications, and Figure 8.25 shows where they are integrated and the underlying premise of an integrated organization. Integrating all of these enterprise systems allows an organization to function as a single unit meeting customer, partner, and supplier needs.

If one application performs poorly, the entire customer value delivery system is affected. For example, no matter how great a company is at CRM, if its SCM system does not work and the customer never receives the finished product, the company will lose that customer. The world-class enterprises of tomorrow must be built on world-class applications implemented today.

FIGURE 8.24

Primary Uses and Business Benefits of Strategic Initiatives

FIGURE 8.25

Integrations between SCM, CRM, and ERP

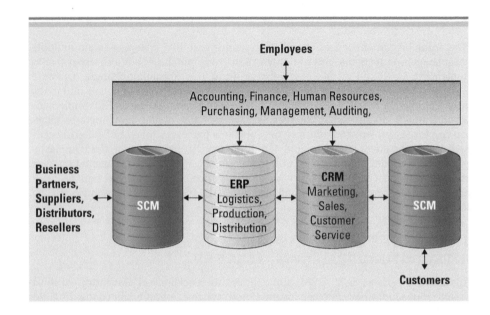

Learning Outcome 8.1: Explain integrations and the role they play in connecting a corporation.

Integrations allow separate systems to communicate directly with each other, eliminating the need for manual entry into multiple systems. Building integrations allows the sharing of information across databases along with dramatically increasing its quality.

Learning Outcome 8.2: Describe supply chain management along with its associated benefits and challenges.

A supply chain consists of all parties involved, directly or indirectly, in obtaining raw materials or a product. To automate and enable sophisticated decision making in these critical areas, companies are turning to systems that provide demand forecasting, inventory control, and information flows between suppliers and customers. Supply chain management (SCM) is the management of information flows between and among activities in a supply chain to maximize total supply chain effectiveness and corporate profitability. In the past, manufacturing efforts focused primarily on quality improvement efforts within the company; today these efforts reach across the entire supply chain, including customers, customers' customers, suppliers, and suppliers' suppliers. Today's supply chain is an intricate network of business partners linked through communication channels and relationships.

Improved visibility across the supply chain and increased profitability for the firm are the primary business benefits received when implementing supply chain management systems. Supply chain visibility is the ability to view all areas up and down the supply chain in real time. The primary challenges associated with supply chain management include costs and complexity. The next wave in supply chain management will be home-based supply chain fulfillment. No more running to the store to replace your products as your store will come to you as soon as you need a new product.

Learning Outcome 8.3: Describe customer relationship management along with its associated benefits and challenges.

Customer relationship management (CRM) is a means of managing all aspects of a customer's relationship with an organization to increase customer loyalty and retention and an organization's profitability. CRM allows an organization to gain insights into customers' shopping and buying behaviors.

Every time a customer communicates with a company, the firm has the chance to build a trusting relationship with that particular customer.

Companies that understand individual customer needs are best positioned to achieve success. Building successful customer relationships is not a new business practice; however, implementing CRM systems allows a company to operate more efficiently and effectively in the area of supporting customer needs. CRM moves far beyond technology by identifying customer needs and designing specific marketing campaigns tailored to each.

A decade ago if you had a complaint against a company you could make a phone call or write a letter. Now you can contact people around the globe and voice your complaint or anger with a company or product. Companies have to listen, making CRM the primary challenge facing organizations.

Organizations are discovering a wave of other key business areas where it is beneficial to build strong relationships beyond customers. These include supplier relationship management (SRM), partner relationship management (PRM), and employee relationship management (ERM).

Learning Outcome 8.4: Describe enterprise resource planning along with its associated benefits and challenges.

Enterprise resource planning (ERP) integrates all departments and functions throughout an organization into a single IT system (or integrated set of IT systems) so employees can make decisions by viewing enterprisewide information about all business operations. Enterprise resource planning systems provide organizations with consistency. They allow for the effective planning and controlling of all the resources required to plan, source, make, and deliver goods and services.

The first generation of ERP systems focused on improving the manufacturing process through automation, primarily addressing back-office business processes such as inventory ordering and product distribution. The second generation of ERP systems extended its reach into the front office and primarily addressed customer issues including marketing and sales. The third generation of ERP systems, known as ERP-II, allows a company to compete on a functional level, adopting an enterprisewide approach using the Internet to connect all participants in the value chain

One of the biggest challenges of an ERP system is cost. ERP systems contain multiple complex components that are not only expensive to purchase, but also expensive to implement. Costs can include the software itself, plus consulting charges, hardware expenses, and training fees.

Applications such as SCM, CRM, and ERP are the backbone of ebusiness, yet most organizations today have to piece together these systems. A firm might choose its CRM components from Siebel, SCM components from i2, and financial components and HR management components from Oracle. Integrating all of these enterprise systems allows an organization to function as a single unit meeting customer, partner, and supplier needs.

OPENING CASE QUESTIONS

1. **Knowledge:** Define SCM and how it can benefit Zappos.
2. **Comprehension:** Explain CRM and why Zappos would benefit from the implementation of a CRM system.
3. **Application:** Demonstrate why Zappos would need to implement SCM, CRM, and ERP for a connected corporation.
4. **Analysis:** Analyze the merger between Zappos and Amazon and assess potential issues for Zappos customers.
5. **Synthesis:** Propose a plan for how Zappos can use Amazon's supply chain to increase sales and customer satisfaction.
6. **Evaluate:** Argue for or against the following statement: "In the electronic age customer relationships are more important than ever and Zappos provides the new benchmark that all corporations should follow."

KEY TERMS

Accounting and finance ERP
  component, 323
Analytical CRM, 312
Application integration, 300
Backward integration, 300
Balanced scorecard, 325
Bullwhip effect, 305
Call scripting system, 316
Campaign management
  system, 314
Click-to-talk, 316
Contact center or call center, 315
Contact management CRM
  system, 315
Core ERP component, 320
CRM analysis technologies, 311
CRM predicting technologies, 311
CRM reporting technologies, 311
Cross-selling, 314
Customer relationship manage-
  ment (CRM), 309
Customer service and support
  (CSS), 314
Data integration, 300

Demand planning system, 306
Eintegration, 300
Electronic data interchange
  (EDI), 305
Elogistics, 324
Employee relationship manage-
  ment (ERM), 319
Enterprise application
  integration (EAI), 301
Enterprise application
  integration (EAI)
  middleware, 301
Enterprise resource planning
  (ERP), 319
Enterprise system, 301
Eprocurement, 324
Extended ERP component, 320
Forward integration, 300
Human resources ERP
  component, 324
Integration, 300
List generator, 313
Middleware, 301
Operational CRM, 312

Opportunity management CRM
  system, 315
Partner relationship management
  (PRM), 319
Production and materials
  management ERP
  component, 324
Sales force automation (SFA), 314
Sales management CRM
  system, 315
Supplier relationship management
  (SRM), 319
Supply chain, 302
Supply chain execution
  system, 305
Supply chain management
  (SCM), 302
Supply chain planning
  system, 305
Supply chain visibility, 305
Up-selling, 314
Web-based self-service
  system, 316
Website personalization, 316

REVIEW QUESTIONS

1. How do integrations connect a corporation?

2. What is the difference between forward and backward integrations?

3. What are the five primary activities in a supply chain?

4. What is the bullwhip effect and how can it impact a supply chain and a firm's profitability?

5. What are supply chain planning systems, supply chain execution systems, and demand planning systems?

6. What are the challenges associated with SCM systems?

7. Why are customer relationships important to an organization? Do you agree that every business needs to focus on customers to survive in the information age?

8. What is the difference between operational and analytical CRM?

9. How can a sales department use CRM to improve operations?

10. How can a marketing department use CRM to improve operations?

11. What is the difference between customer relationship management, supplier relationship management, and employee relationship management?

12. What is an enterprise resource planning system?

13. What are the components in a core ERP system?

14. What are the components in an extended ERP system?

15. What does a company need to integrate to become connected?

CLOSING CASE ONE

Can Customer Loyalty Be a Bad Thing?

What happens when you find out that your business's most faithful customers aren't necessarily the most profitable ones? The economic crisis has jolted companies into the need to redouble efforts to foster customer loyalty. Numerous articles now tout the increased importance of giving customers premium service in troubled times to ensure customer retention. The underlying reasoning is simple—through their continued patronage, loyal customers help a company to weather the storm.

Without question, there is some truth to this logic. No firm can survive for long without loyal customers. The problem, however, is that success through loyalty isn't nearly so simple. Like most big ideas, there are conditions where it is unarguably correct, and less popular but equally true conditions where it is wrong.

Loyalty is a big idea. At its most basic level, it is a feeling of attachment that causes someone to be willing to continue a relationship. And while exclusive loyalty has been replaced in customers' hearts and minds with multiple loyalties for many if not most product categories, often greater than 50 percent of a company's customers would classify themselves as holding some level of loyalty to a particular company. Even if we narrow our classification of loyalty to customers who feel loyal and give the majority of their purchases in a category to the firm, typically we find this to represent one-third of a firm's customers.

The fly in the ointment is that typically only 20 percent of a firm's customers are actually profitable. And many—often most—of a company's profitable customers are not loyal. This presents managers with a loyalty problem, although not one that they expect. If typically most loyal customers in a firm aren't profitable, how does a customer loyalty strategy ever generate a positive return on investment? Instead of asking whether you have enough loyal customers in your customer base, you need to ask yourself three more complex questions: (1) which loyal customers are good for the business, (2) how do we hang onto them, and (3) how do we get more customers like them.

In this slow economy, customers in both B2B and B2C settings are naturally much more sensitive to economic issues. Furthermore, companies in B2B relationships are often more reliant on their vendor partners to help them shoulder this burden. There is nothing inherently wrong with this, and managers need to recognize that their job is to meet customers' needs to deserve their loyalty.

But the simple solution to improving customer loyalty in a down market is to offer price deals. Firms that track their customer loyalty can be guaranteed that loyalty scores will increase with each substantial decrease in price.

But that's a bad loyalty strategy. This doesn't mean businesses shouldn't find ways to be more efficient so they can pass cost savings on to customers. But price-driven loyalty is always the lowest form of loyalty. It means the firm isn't offering differentiated value to its customers.

The place to begin any loyalty strategy is to determine which loyal customers are profitable and which are not. A closer examination of these two types of customers always reveals very different reasons for their loyalty. Unprofitable loyal customers tend to be loyal for one of two reasons: (1) they are driven by unprofitable pricing or exchange policies, or (2) they demand an excessive amount of service that they are not willing to pay fairly to receive.

Profitable loyal customers, on the other hand, are almost always driven by differentiating aspects of the product or service offering. The key to a successful loyalty strategy is to become clear as to what these differentiating aspects are, and to focus on tangibly improving these elements. It is also imperative to actively tell customers and prospective customers that these are the things the company stands for and that the firm is committed to being best at. By doing this, the best customers will have the necessary information to clearly articulate why an organization deserves their loyalty in good times and in bad.[11]

Questions

1. Why are customer relationships important to an organization? Do you agree that every business needs to focus on customers to survive in the information age?

2. How can a company find its most loyal customers?

3. Choose a business (maybe Starbucks, Disney, or Nissan). Answer each of the following questions based on your business choice.

   a. Which loyal customers are good for the business?

   b. How do we hang onto them?

   c. How do we get more customers like them?

4. Do you agree or disagree with the following statement: "The fly in the ointment is that typically only 20 percent of a firm's customers are actually profitable. And many—often most—of a company's profitable customers are not loyal."

CLOSING CASE TWO

Got Milk? It's Good for You—Unless It's Contaminated!

Dong Lizhong bet that being a dairy farmer was his golden ticket out of a factory job in China. Unfortunately, a contamination crisis in 2008 shattered his dairy business when babies mysteriously started developing kidney stones from contaminated baby formula. A chemical called melamine, an additive used to make plastic, was discovered in the milk supply of one of China's third-largest dairy producers. Four infants died from the contamination and at least 53,000 fell ill. According to the official Xinhua news agency, officials knew about problems with the milk for months before informing the public.

China's four largest dairy organizations, accounting for nearly half the country's milk market, pulled their goods off shelves. More than 20 countries, including France, India, and South Korea, banned not only dairy products from China, but also candies, cookies, and chocolates. "This is a disastrous setback. I estimate that it will take one or two years to rebuild confidence in dairy products," says Luo Yunbo, dean of the College of Food Science & Nutritional Engineering at China Agricultural University.

The local milk-collection station in Dong Lizhong's village discontinued purchasing milk. Farmers continued to milk their cows, but they drank the milk themselves or poured the milk into their cabbage fields.

Cutting Corners

Chinese do not traditionally drink milk. However, as the country has grown more affluent over the past few decades, the domestic dairy industry has skyrocketed. China's two largest dairy companies have greatly benefited from this new trend: China Mengniu Dairy and Inner Mongolia Yili Industrial Group. Simultaneously, numerous entrepreneurs—from dairy farmers to milk-collection station owners to milk distributors—have jumped into the supply chain of dairy products to make their fortunes. Due to the fierce competition within China's dairy industry, a few companies decided to cut corners to reduce costs, regardless of the consequences.

As Mengniu and Yili expanded at breathtaking speed, they found themselves in the unique position where supply could not keep up with demand. According to KPMG, China consumes 25 million tons of milk yearly, putting its dairy market ahead of France and Germany. In their quest for more raw milk, Mengniu and Yili have expanded outside their base in the northern province of Inner Mongolia and set up production facilities in other parts of China. Most of the quality problems in milk were found in dairy farms in Hebei and Inner Mongolia provinces, where the competition for raw milk supplies has been the fiercest.

Most dairy farmers in Hebei province traditionally sold their milk to milk-collection stations established by local heavyweight Sanlu. In recent years, new privately owned milk-collection stations to buy raw milk for Mengniu and Yili started popping up next to existing stations. These new entrants captured raw milk supplies by offering dairy farmers slightly higher prices. "This competition broke the rules. As milk buyers fought over milk supplies, their standards for quality fell," says Roger Liu, vice chairman of American Dairy Inc., a Heilongjiang province-based powdered milk company.

Additives to Boost Protein

Many of the milking stations do not have the equipment to test milk for additives. At the Nanxincheng station, 16 households bring their dairy cows in the area to be milked in the red brick farmhouse. The farmers hook up the cows to a milking machine, which pumps the milk directly into a big vat. "They didn't test the milk here. They sent it to Sanlu for testing," says Du Yanjun, a government inspector who was posted to monitor the Nanxincheng station after the contamination crisis broke.

The milk is collected from the stations and shipped by middlemen to big dairy companies such as Sanlu, which would do their own testing and grading. It now appears that unscrupulous middlemen added melamine to the raw milk to increase protein levels in their milk samples, so their milk would be graded higher. However, ingesting melamine can also cause kidney stones or kidney failure, especially in infants.

Matthew Estes, president and CEO of BabyCare, had looked into switching from Australian and New Zealand sources of milk for the company's infant-formula business in China. BabyCare tested possible Chinese suppliers and realized it could not locate a suitable supplier in China. "We couldn't the find quality that met our standards. We chose to not sell in China rather than take the risk," he says.

Stiff Sentences

A Chinese court sentenced two of the middlemen to death and a dairy boss to life in prison for their roles in the milk contamination scandal. The swift trial and harsh sentences show Beijing's resolve in tackling the country's stubborn food safety problems and an eagerness by the communist leadership to move past the embarrassing scandal.[12]

Questions

1. List 10 products that could possibly be affected by a problem in the U.S. milk supply chain. What would be the damages to an ice cream business that used contaminated milk in its manufacturing process? Who do you think should be held liable for such an issue?

2. Do you think a CRM system could have helped communicate issues in the milk production supply chain? How could a company use a CRM system to perform damage control after finding out about contaminated milk in the supply chain?

3. Do you agree with the Chinese court in sentencing of the middlemen to death and a dairy boss to life in prison for their roles in the milk contamination scandal? Do you think the United States should implement similar laws for unethical corporate behavior?

4. Many companies in the United States use Chinese suppliers in the sourcing of raw materials and manufacturing of products. Research the Internet and find three examples of recent issues for U.S. companies because of Chinese products. What will happen in the long run as companies use Chinese suppliers?

CRITICAL BUSINESS THINKING

1. Political Supply Chains

The U.S. government brokered a deal with the United Arab Emirates (UAE) allowing the UAE government-owned firm Dubai Ports World (DPW) to operate six major U.S. ports (New York, New Jersey, Baltimore, New Orleans, Miami, Philadelphia) after DPW purchased the current United Kingdom-based port operator, P&O, the fourth largest port company in the world.

Some citizens are worried that the federal government may be outsourcing U.S. port operations to a company prone to terrorist infiltration by allowing a firm from the United Arab Emirates to run port operations within the United States. The United Arab Emirates has had people involved in terrorism. Some of its financial institutions laundered the money for the 9/11 terrorists. You have been called in on an investigation to determine the potential effects on U.S. businesses' supply chains if these ports were shut down due to terrorist activities. Create an argument for or against outsourcing these ports to the UAE. Be sure to detail the effect on U.S. businesses' supply chains if these ports are subjected to terrorist acts.[13]

2. Analyzing Dell's Supply Chain Management System

Dell's supply chain strategy is legendary. If you want to build a successful SCM system, your best bet is to model your SCM system after Dell's. In a team, research Dell's supply chain management strategy on the web and create a report discussing any new SCM updates and strategies the company is currently using that were not discussed in this text. Be sure to include a graphical presentation of Dell's current supply chain model.

3. Total Recall

The Firestone Tire Company issued a recall for all tires issued on a certain brand of Ford's sport-utility vehicles. The tire treads on some SUVs separated during use, which could cause a fatal accident as the defect caused vehicles to roll over. In the beginning Firestone denied it had a tire problem, stating that Ford had incorrectly matched its SUVs with the wrong brand of tires. It also suggested that the shock absorbers might have been rubbing against the tires, causing the defect. Firestone soon recalled the tires as the company received more and more pressure from government and consumer advocacy groups. Interestingly, all of the defective tires were manufactured at the same tire factory and the company soon shut down that facility. Information was soon found that Firestone had recalled the identical type of tire in South America and had already settled a lawsuit for an accident caused by the tread defect. Discuss each of the following factors in relation to this case: quality, inventory, ethics, supply chain visibility, profitability, customer loyalty.[14]

4. Finding Shelf Space at Walmart

Walmart's business strategy of being a low-cost provider by managing its supply chain down to the minutia has paid off greatly. Each week, approximately 100 million customers, or one-third of the U.S. population, visit Walmart's U.S. stores. Walmart is currently the world's largest retailer and the second-largest corporation behind ExxonMobil. It was founded by Sam Walton in 1962 and is the largest private employer in the United States and Mexico. Walmart is also the largest grocery retailer in the United States, with an estimated 20 percent of the retail grocery and consumables business, and the largest toy seller in the United States, with an estimated 45 percent of the retail toy business, having surpassed Toys "R" Us in the late 1990s.

Walmart's business model is based on selling a wide variety of general merchandise at "always low prices." The reason Walmart can offer such low prices is due to its innovative use of information technology tools to create its highly sophisticated supply chain. Walmart has famously invited its major suppliers to jointly develop powerful supply chain partnerships. These are designed to increase product flow efficiency and, consequently, Walmart's profitability.[15]

You are the owner of a high-end collectible toy company. You create everything from authentic sports figure replicas to famous musicians and movie characters including Babe Ruth, Hulk Hogan, Mick Jagger, Ozzy Osbourne, Alien, and the Terminator. It would be a huge win for your company if you could get your collectibles into Walmart. Compile a strategic plan highlighting the steps required to approach Walmart as your supply chain partner. Be sure to address the pros and cons of partnering with the chain, including the cost to revamp your current supply chain to meet Walmart's tough supply chain requirements.

5. Customer Relationship Management Strategies

On average, it costs an organization six times more to sell to a new customer than to sell to an existing customer. As the co-owner of a medium-sized sports equipment distributor, you have recently been notified that sales for the past three months have decreased by an average of 20 percent. The reasons for the decline in sales are numerous, including a poor economy and some negative publicity your company received regarding a defective product line. In a group, explain how implementing a CRM system can help you understand and combat the decline in sales. Be sure to justify why a CRM system is important to your business and its future growth.

Also, search the Internet for at least one recent and authoritative article that compares or ranks customer relationship management systems. Select two packages from the list and compare their functions and features as described in the article(s) you found as well as on each company's website. Find references in the literature where companies that are using each package have reported their experiences, both good and bad. Draw on any other comparisons you can find. Prepare a presentation for delivery in class on the strengths and weaknesses of each package, which one you favor, and why.

6. Searching for Employee Loyalty

You are the CEO of Razz, a start-up web-based search company, which is planning to compete directly with Google. The company had an exceptional first year and is currently receiving over 500,000 hits a day from customers all over the world. You have hired 250 people in the past four months, doubling the size of your organization. With so many new employees starting so quickly you are concerned about how your company's culture will evolve and whether your employees are receiving enough attention. You are already familiar with customer relationship management and how CRM systems can help an organization create strong customer relationships. However, you are unfamiliar with employee relationship management and you are wondering what ERM systems might be able to offer your employees and your company. Research the web, create a report detailing features and functions of ERM systems, and determine what value will be added to your organization if you decide to implement an ERM solution.

7. Driving Up Profits with Loyalty (or Driving Down?)

The Butterfly Café is located in downtown San Francisco and offers specialty coffee, teas, and organic fruits and vegetables. The café holds a number of events to attract customers such as live music, poetry readings, book clubs, charity events, and local artist's night. A listing of all participants attending each event is tracked in the café's database. The café uses the information for marketing campaigns and offers customers who attend multiple events additional discounts. A marketing database company, InTheKnow.com, has offered to pay the Butterfly Café a substantial amount of money for access to its customer database, which it will then sell to other local businesses. The owner of the Butterfly Café, Penny Dirks, has come to you for advice. She is not sure if her customers would appreciate her selling their personal information and how it might affect her business. However, the amount of money InTheKnow.com is offering is enough to finance her much-needed new patio for the back of the café. InTheKnow.com has promised that the sale will be completely confidential. What should Dirks do?

8. Supporting Customers

Creative.com is an ebusiness that sells craft materials and supplies over the Internet. You have just started as the vice president of customer service, and you have a team of 45 customer service representatives. Currently, the only form of customer service is the toll-free number and the company is receiving a tremendous number of calls regarding products, orders, and shipping information. The average wait time for a customer to speak to a customer service representative is 35 minutes. Orders are being cancelled and Creative.com is losing business due to its lack of customer service. Create a strategy to revamp the customer service center and get the company back on track.

9. Implementing an ERP System

Blue Dog Inc. is a leading manufacturer in the high-end sunglasses industry, reaching record revenue levels of more than $250 million last year. Blue Dog is currently deciding on the possibility of implementing an ERP system to help decrease production costs and increase inventory control. Many of the executives are nervous about making such a large investment in an ERP system due to its low success rates. As a senior manager at Blue Dog Inc., you have been asked to compile a list of the potential benefits and risks associated with implementing an ERP system along with your recommendations for the steps the company can take to ensure a successful implementation. Be sure to also explain why ERP systems include CRM and SCM components, and the advantages the company can gain by implementing all of the components for a connected corporation.

ENTREPRENEURIAL CHALLENGE

BUILD YOUR OWN BUSINESS

1. Netflix reinvented the video rental business using supply chain technology. Netflix is the largest online DVD rental service, offering flat-rate rental by mail and over the Internet to customers. Customers can create their own personal list of movie favorites and the DVDs are delivered by the U.S. Postal Service from one of Netflix's warehouses. Customers can keep the DVD for as long as they want and simply return it by mail to receive their next selection. Netflix's business is video rental, but it used technology to revamp its supply chain to completely disrupt the entire video rental industry. Define a way that you can revamp or reinvent your business using supply chain technologies.

2. Business is booming, and you have achieved your goal of driving operating costs down, which helps to drive revenues up. One of your best new products is from China, and it is accounting for a 20 percent increase in your profits. Yesterday, a dockworkers union strike began and shut down all of the West Coast shipping docks from San Francisco to Canada. Work will resume when the union agrees to new labor contracts, which could take months. You need to quickly assess the impact of the shutdown on your business. How will you keep business running if you cannot receive your shipments? What strategies do you recommend to help the business continue working while the supply chain is disrupted by the strike?

3. The web contains numerous examples of customer power. Examples include www.ihatedell .net and www.donotbuydodge.ca. Customers are using YouTube, MySpace, blogs, and a number of other web tools to slam or praise companies. Do you believe that the most influential person in your business is the customer? How could customers hurt or help your business? Will your employees agree that customers are the most important part of the business?

APPLY YOUR KNOWLEDGE BUSINESS PROJECTS

PROJECT I Shipping Problems

Entrepreneurship is in Alyssa Stuart's blood. Stuart has been starting businesses since she was 10 years old, and she finally has the perfect business of custom-made furniture. Customers who visit her shop can choose from a number of different fabrics and 50 different styles of couch and chair designs to create their custom-made furniture. Once the customer decides on a fabric pattern and furniture design, the information is sent to China where the furniture is built and shipped to the customer via the West Coast. Stuart is excited about her business; all of her hard work has finally paid off as she has more than 17,000 customers and 875 orders currently in the pipe.

Stuart's business is booming. Her high-quality products and outstanding customer service have created an excellent reputation for her business. But the business is at risk of losing everything and she has come to you for help solving her supply chain issues. The parcel delivery companies such as FedEx and UPS are on strike and Alyssa is not sure how she is going to get her raw materials or finished products delivered. What strategies do you recommend for Alyssa's business to continue working to overcome the strike?

PROJECT II   Great Stories

When customers have an unpleasant customer experience, the company no longer has to worry about them telling a few friends and family; the company now has to worry about them telling everyone. Internet service providers are giving frustrated consumers another means of fighting back. Free or low-cost computer space for Internet websites is empowering consumers to tell not only their friends, but also the world about the way they have been treated. A few examples of disgruntled customer stories from the Internet include:

- A bike-riding tourist requires stitches after being bitten on the leg by a dog. The tourism company is banned from renting bikes and in turn bars the tourist from taking any future tours.

- A customer leaving Best Buy refuses to voluntarily show the receipt to the guard at the door. The Best Buy employees try to seize the customer's cart and then decide to park a car behind the customer's vehicle.

- Enterprise Rent-A-Car operates a high-stress business, and frequently its customers find that the company did not honor reservations, did not have cars ready for reservations, rented cars with empty tanks of gas, and charged higher rates to corporate account holders.

The pervasive nature of the Internet is increasing customer power and changing business from product-focused to a customer-focused. Explain the difference between product-focused business and customer-focused business and why CRM is more important than ever before?

PROJECT III   JetBlue on YouTube

JetBlue took an unusual and interesting CRM approach by using YouTube to apologize to its customers. JetBlue's founder and former CEO, David Neeleman, apologized to customers via YouTube after a very bad week for the airline: 1,100 flights were canceled due to snowstorms, causing thousands of passengers to be stranded at airports around the country. Neeleman's unrehearsed, unrefined, and sincere YouTube apology made customers understand the issues and accept the company's apology.

You are the founder and CEO of GoodDog, a large pet food manufacturing company. Recently, at least 16 pet deaths have been tied to tainted pet food, fortunately not manufactured by your company. A recall of potentially deadly pet food has dog and cat owners studying their animals for even the slightest hint of illness and swamping veterinarians nationwide with calls about symptoms. Create a strategy for using YouTube as a vehicle to communicate with your customers as they fear for their pets' lives. Be sure to highlight the pros and cons of using YouTube as a customer communication vehicle. Are there any other new technologies you could use as a customer communication vehicle that would be more effective than YouTube? With all the new advances in technology and the many ways to reach customers, do you think using YouTube is a smart approach? What else could you do to help gain back customers' trust?

PROJECT IV   Gaining Business Intelligence from Strategic Initiatives

You are a new employee in the customer service department at Premier One, a large office supply distributor. The company has been in business for three years and focuses on providing top of the line office supplies at a low cost. The company currently has 90 employees and operates in seven states.

Sales over the past three years have tripled, and the manual systems currently in place are no longer sufficient to run the business. Your first task is to meet with your new team and create a presentation for the president and chief executive officer describing supply chain management, customer relationship management, and enterprise resource planning. The presentation should highlight the main benefits Premier One can receive from these enterprise systems along with any additional added business value that can be gained from the systems.

PROJECT V   Second Life CRM

New virtual worlds such as Second Life are becoming the first point of contact between many firms and customers. To say the least, virtual relationships are far different from traditional relationships. Firms such as Adidas, Dell, Reuters, and Toyota are all embracing Second Life; however, beyond opening a virtual office in a virtual world, they are struggling with how to build virtual customer relationships.

PA Consulting quickly learned that building a virtual office to answer customer queries is not nearly good enough to find and attract loyal customers. The company realized that real people behind the avatars need to be housed in a real office similar to having a call center to answer questions for online shopping. When a potential customer wants to speak to a human, one must appear or else the customer will leave the website.

You are the executive director of CRM at StormPeak, an advanced technological company that develops robots. You are in charge of overseeing the first virtual site being built in Second Life. Create a CRM strategy for doing business in a virtual world. Here are a few questions to get you started:

- How will customer relationships be different in a virtual world?
- What is your strategy for managing customer relationships in this new virtual environment?
- How will supporting Second Life customers differ from supporting traditional customers?
- How will supporting Second Life customers differ from supporting website customers?
- What customer security issues might you encounter in Second Life?
- What customer ethical issues might you encounter in Second Life?

PROJECT VI   Searching Telephone Calls

Imagine being able to search a database of customer phone calls to find specific requests or to be able to sort through digital customer complaints to detect the exact moment when the interaction between the customer service representative and the customer went wrong. A new tool called Find It allows the sorting of digital voice records as easily as using Google to sift through documents. Find It is opening limitless business opportunities as organizations begin to understand how they can use this technology to help employees search voice mails or recorded calls for keywords and phrases.

You have recently started your own marketing firm and you want to use the power of Find It to help your customers query all of their unique data records, including digital voice recordings. Now all you need is to prepare your marketing materials to send to potential customers. Create a marketing pitch that you will deliver to customers detailing the business opportunities they could uncover if they purchase Find It. Your marketing pitch can be a one-page document, a catchy tune, a video, or a PowerPoint presentation.

PROJECT VII   Sharptooth Incorporated

Stephen Kern is the founder and CEO of Sharptooth, a small business that buys and sells comic strips to magazines and newspapers around the country. Some of Sharptooth's artists have made it big and are syndicated in hundreds of magazines and newspapers, while others are new to the industry. Kern started in the business as an artist and began contracting other artists when he realized he had a knack for promoting and marketing comic materials. His artistic background is great for spotting talented young artists, but not so great for running the business.

Kern recently began selling comics to new forms of media such as blogs, websites, and other online tools. He has hired you to build him a new system to track all online comic sales. You quickly notice that Kern has a separate system for each of his different lines of business including newspaper sources, magazine sources, billboard sources, and now online sources. You notice that each system works independently to perform its job of creating, updating, and maintaining sales information, but you are wondering how he operates his business as a whole. Create a list of issues Kern will encounter if he continues to run his business with four separate systems performing the same operations. What could happen to the business if he cannot correlate the details of each? Be sure to highlight at least 10 issues where separate systems could cause problems.

PROJECT VIII   Eating In

Having been employed by the same company for more than 20 years, Mary Lou Smith was shocked when she was suddenly terminated along with about 900 of her co-workers. It took Smith a few weeks to recover from the shock, then she finally began focusing her efforts on searching for a new job. Smith was sure her loyal employment history and strong skill set would land her a new job in no time; however, after several months of searching she wasn't having any luck. With her emergency funds quickly being depleted, Smith knew she had to find a new job soon or else she'd need to start selling her assets or cashing in her retirement.

The one positive aspect of having so much free time was that she could focus on her true passion, cooking. She began making a little money by catering lunches and dinners for local businesses and neighbors. Smith overheard a neighbor remark that she was hosting a large party and didn't have enough time to prepare the meal. Almost jokingly, Smith asked her how much she'd be willing to pay for a catered event. Soon Smith was catering for numerous neighbors and small businesses and she knew she had to make a decision if she would go into business for herself or continue searching for other employment.

After a year in the catering business, Smith was earning a good living and building a stellar reputation. She began catering for all types of events, including weddings, and business was so good that she hired several employees to help grow her business. As Smith begins to plan her expansion, she has asked for you help in answering the following questions:

1. How important is customer loyalty for Smith's business? What can she do to ensure her customers remain loyal? How could one disgruntled customer hurt business? What can she do to combat this challenge?

2. Research the business Yelp.com. What service does Yelp.com perform? Would a small business see Yelp.com as an opportunity or a threat? What are the pros and cons a customer should be aware of when using yelp.com?

3. Smith's responsibilities include forecasting, inventory control, scheduling, and ensuring high-quality products. What types of forecasts would she require to run her business? What types of inventory would she want to track? What might happen if her inventory tracking tool was off by 50 percent? What types of schedules does Smith need to generate? What things might occur to disrupt schedules and cause her to reschedule? How can a supply chain management system help run the business?

4. Smith wants to create a business based on loyal customers and loyal employees. She offers her employees bonuses for new ideas, recipes, or business referrals. What risks is Smith encountering by offering these bonuses? One employee idea that she has implemented is turning out to be a competitive advantage for her business; however, the employee has quit and is now working for a competitor. Should Smith still pay the employee the bonus? What should she do to ensure she is building strong employee relationships?

5. Smith overheard one of her customers talking about enterprise systems such as CRM, SCM, and ERP. However, she is sure they are available only to big companies that have lots of capital. Research the Internet and find examples of enterprise systems for small business. Do you think she should invest in these types of systems to run her business? Why or why not?

AYK APPLICATION PROJECTS

If you are looking for Excel projects to incorporate into your class, try any of the following after reading this chapter.

Project Number	Project Name	Project Type	Plug-In	Focus Area	Project Level	Skill Set	Page Number
9	Security Analysis	Excel	T3	Filtering Data	Intermediate	Conditional Formatting, Autofilter, Subtotal	AYK.7
10	Gathering Data	Excel	T3	Data Analysis	Intermediate	Conditional Formatting	AYK.8
11	Scanner System	Excel	T2	Strategic Analysis	Intermediate	Formulas	AYK.8
12	Competitive Pricing	Excel	T2	Profit Maximization	Intermediate	Formulas	AYK.9
13	Adequate Acquisitions	Excel	T2	Break Even Analysis	Intermediate	Formulas	AYK.9
15	Assessing the Value of Information	Excel	T3	Data Analysis	Intermediate	PivotTable	AYK.10
16	Growth, Trends, and Forecasts	Excel	T2, T3	Data Forecasting	Advanced	Average, Trend, Growth	AYK.11
18	Formatting Grades	Excel	T3	Data Analysis	Advanced	If, LookUp	AYK.12
22	Turnover Rates	Excel	T3	Data Mining	Advanced	PivotTable	AYK.15
23	Vital Information	Excel	T3	Data Mining	Advanced	PivotTable	AYK.15
24	Breaking Even	Excel	T4	Business Analysis	Advanced	Goal Seek	AYK.16
25	Profit Scenario	Excel	T4	Sales Analysis	Advanced	Scenario Manager	AYK.16

APPLY YOUR KNOWLEDGE

Apply Your Knowledge Project Overview

Project Number	Project Name	Project Type	Plug-In	Focus Area	Project Level	Skill Set	Page Number
1	Financial Destiny	Excel	T2	Personal Budget	Introductory	Formulas	AYK.4
2	Cash Flow	Excel	T2	Cash Flow	Introductory	Formulas	AYK.4
3	Technology Budget	Excel	T1, T2	Hardware and Software	Introductory	Formulas	AYK.4
4	Tracking Donations	Excel	T2	Employee Relationships	Introductory	Formulas	AYK.4
5	Convert Currency	Excel	T2	Global Commerce	Introductory	Formulas	AYK.5
6	Cost Comparison	Excel	T2	Total Cost of Ownership	Introductory	Formulas	AYK.5
7	Time Management	Excel or Project	T12	Project Management	Introductory	Gantt Charts	AYK.6
8	Maximize Profit	Excel	T2, T4	Strategic Analysis	Intermediate	Formulas or Solver	AYK.6
9	Security Analysis	Excel	T3	Filtering Data	Intermediate	Conditional Formatting, Autofilter, Subtotal	AYK.7
10	Gathering Data	Excel	T3	Data Analysis	Intermediate	Conditional Formatting	AYK.8
11	Scanner System	Excel	T2	Strategic Analysis	Intermediate	Formulas	AYK.8
12	Competitive Pricing	Excel	T2	Profit Maximization	Intermediate	Formulas	AYK.9
13	Adequate Acquisitions	Excel	T2	Break-Even Analysis	Intermediate	Formulas	AYK.9
14	Customer Relations	Excel	T3	CRM	Intermediate	PivotTable	AYK.9
15	Assessing the Value of Information	Excel	T3	Data Analysis	Intermediate	PivotTable	AYK.10
16	Growth, Trends, and Forecasts	Excel	T2, T3	Data Forecasting	Advanced	Average, Trend, Growth	AYK.11
17	Shipping Costs	Excel	T4	SCM	Advanced	Solver	AYK.12
18	Formatting Grades	Excel	T3	Data Analysis	Advanced	If, LookUp	AYK.12

(Continued)

Project Number	Project Name	Project Type	Plug-In	Focus Area	Project Level	Skill Set	Page Number
19	Moving Dilemma	Excel	T2, T3	SCM	Advanced	Absolute vs. Relative Values	AYK.13
20	Operational Efficiencies	Excel	T3	SCM	Advanced	PivotTable	AYK.14
21	Too Much Information	Excel	T3	CRM	Advanced	PivotTable	AYK.14
22	Turnover Rates	Excel	T3	Data Mining	Advanced	PivotTable	AYK.15
23	Vital Information	Excel	T3	Data Mining	Advanced	PivotTable	AYK.15
24	Breaking Even	Excel	T4	Business Analysis	Advanced	Goal Seek	AYK.16
25	Profit Scenario	Excel	T4	Sales Analysis	Advanced	Scenario Manager	AYK.16
26	Electronic Résumés	HTML	T9, T10, T11	Electronic Personal Marketing	Introductory	Structural Tags	AYK.17
27	Gathering Feedback	Dreamweaver	T9, T10, T11	Data Collection	Intermediate	Organization of Information	AYK.17
28	Daily Invoice	Access	T5, T6, T7, T8	Business Analysis	Introductory	Entities, Relationships, and Databases	AYK.17
29	Billing Data	Access	T5, T6, T7, T8	Business Intelligence	Introductory	Entities, Relationships, and Databases	AYK.19
30	Inventory Data	Access	T5, T6, T7, T8	SCM	Intermediate	Entities, Relationships, and Databases	AYK.20
31	Call Center	Access	T5, T6, T7, T8	CRM	Intermediate	Entities, Relationships, and Databases	AYK.21
32	Sales Pipeline	Access	T5, T6, T7, T8	Business Intelligence	Advanced	Entities, Relationships, and Databases	AYK.23
33	Online Classified Ads	Access	T5, T6, T7, T8	Ecommerce	Advanced	Entities, Relationships, and Databases	AYK.23

NOTE: Many of the Excel projects support multiple data files. Therefore the naming convention that you see in the text may not be the same as what you see in a data folder. As an example, in the text we reference data files as AYK1_Data.xlsx; however, you may see a file named AYK1_Data_Version_1.xlsx, or AYK1_Data_Version_2.xlsx.

Project 1:

Financial Destiny

You have been introduced to Microsoft Excel and are ready to begin using it to help track your monthly expenses and take charge of your financial destiny. The first step is to create a personal budget so you can see where you are spending money and if you need to decrease your monthly expenses or increase your monthly income.

Create a template for a monthly budget of your income and expenditures, with some money set aside for savings (or you can use the data file, AYK1_Data.xlsx, we created). Create variations of this budget to show how much you could save if you cut back on certain expenses, found a roommate, or got a part-time job. Compare the costs of a meal plan to costs of groceries. Consider how much interest would be earned if you saved $100 a month, or how much debt paid on student loans or credit card bills. To expand your data set, make a fantasy budget for 10 years from now, when you might own a home, have student loan payments, and have a good salary.

> **Data File: AYK1_Data.xlsx**

Project 2:

Cash Flow

Gears is a five-year-old company that specializes in bike components. The company is having trouble paying for its monthly supplies and would like to perform a cash flow analysis so it can understand its financial position. Cash flow represents the money an investment produces after subtracting cash expenses from income. The statement of cash flows summarizes sources and uses of cash, indicates whether enough cash is available to carry on routine operations, and offers an analysis of all business transactions, reporting where the firm obtained its cash and how it chose to allocate the cash. The cash flow statement shows where money comes from, how the company is going to spend it, and when the company will require additional cash. Gears would like to project a cash flow statement for the next month.

Using the data file AYK2_Data.xlsx complete the cash flow statement for Gears using Excel. Be sure to create formulas so the company can simply input numbers in the future to determine cash flow.

> **Data File: AYK2_Data.xlsx**

Project 3:

Technology Budget

Tally is a start-up website development company located in Seattle, Washington. The company currently has seven employees and is looking to hire six new employees in the next month.

You are in charge of purchasing for Tally. Your first task is to purchase computers for the new employees. Your budget is $250,000 to buy the best computer systems with a scanner, three color printers, and business software. Use the web to research various products and calculate the costs of different systems using Excel. Use a variety of Excel formulas as you analyze costs and compare prices. Use the data file AYK3_Data.xlsx as a template.

> **Data File: AYK3_Data.xlsx**

Project 4:

Tracking Donations

Lazarus Consulting is a large computer consulting company in New York. Pete Lazarus, the CEO and founder, is well known for his philanthropic efforts. Pete knows that most of his employees contribute to nonprofit organizations and wants to reward them for their efforts while encouraging others to contribute to charities. Pete began a program that matches 50 percent of each employee donation. The only stipulations are that the charity must be a nonprofit organization and the company will match only up to $2,000 per year per employee.

Open the data file AYK4_Data.xlsx and determine the following:

- What was the total donation amount per organization?
- What were the average donations per organization?

Data File: AYK4_Data.xlsx

Project 5:

Convert Currency

You have decided to spend the summer traveling abroad with your friends. Your trip is going to take you to France, England, Italy, Switzerland, Germany, Norway, and Ireland. You want to use Excel to convert currencies as you travel around the world.

Locate one of the exchange rate calculators on the Internet (www.xe.com or www .x-rates.com). Find the exchange rates for each of the countries listed above and create formulas in Excel to convert $100, $500, and $1,000. Use the data file AYK5_Data.xlsx as a template.

Data File: AYK5_Data.xls

Project 6:

Cost Comparison

You are thinking about purchasing a new computer since the machine you are using now is four years old, slow, not always reliable, and does not support the latest operating system. Your needs for the new computer are simple: anti-virus software, email, web browsing, word processing, spreadsheet, database, iTunes, and some lightweight graphical tools. Your concern is what the total cost of ownership will be for the next three years. You have to factor in a few added costs beyond just the initial purchase price for the computer itself, such as: added hardware (this could include a new printer, docking station, or scanner), software (purchase of a new operating system), training (you're thinking about pursuing web training to get an internship next term), subsequent software upgrades, and maintenance.

- It is useful to think about costs over time—both direct as well as indirect costs. Part of the reason this distinction is important is that a decision should rest not on the nominal sum of the purchase, but rather on the present value of the purchase.
- A dollar today is worth more than a dollar one year from now.

FIGURE AYK.1

Sample Layout of New Computer Spreadsheet

	A	B	C	D	E	F
1		COST OF NEW COMPUTER				
2	Discount Rate	1	0.9325	0.9109	0.7051	
3		Time 0	Year 1	Year 2	Year 3	Present Value Costs
4	Computer					
5	Software					
6	Additional Hardware					
7	Training					
8	Software upgrades					
9	Maintenance					
10						
11	Total Costs					
12						

- The relevant discount rate (interest rate) is your marginal cost of capital corresponding to a level of risk equal with the purchase.
- Use the data file AYK6_Data.xlsx as a template.

Data File: AYK6_Data.xlsx

Project 7:

Time Management

You have just been hired as a business analyst by a new start-up company called Multi-Media. Multi-Media is an interactive agency that constructs phased and affordable website marketing, providing its clients with real and measurable solutions that are supported by easy-to-use tools. Since the company is very new to the business arena, it needs help in creating a project management plan for developing its own website. The major tasks for the development team have been identified but you need to create the timeline.

1. The task names, durations, and any prerequisites are:

   - Analyze and plan—two weeks. Cannot start anything else until done.
   - Create and organize content—four weeks. Can start to develop "look and feel" before this is done.
   - Develop the "look and feel"—four weeks. Start working on graphics and HTML at the same time.
   - Produce graphics and HTML documents—two weeks. Create working prototype after the first week.
   - Create a working prototype—two weeks. Give to test team when complete.
   - Test, test, test—four weeks.
   - Upload to a web server and test again—one week.
   - Maintain.

2. Using Microsoft Excel or Microsoft Project, create a Gantt chart using the information provided above.

Project 8:

Maximize Profit

Books, Books, Books is a wholesale distributor of popular books. The business buys overstocked books and sells them for a discount of more than 50 percent to local area bookstores. The owner of the company, BK Kane, would like to determine the best approach to boxing books so he can make the most profit possible. The local bookstores accept all shipments from Books, Books, Books because of BK's incredibly low prices. BK can order as many overstocked books as he requires, and this week's options include:

Title	Weight	Cost	Sale Price
Harry Potter and the Deathly Hallows, J. K. Rowling	5 lb	$9	$17
The Children of Húrin, J. R. R. Tolkien	4 lb	$8	$13
The Time Traveler's Wife, Audrey Niffenegger	3.5 lb	$7	$11
The Dark River, John Twelve Hawks	3 lb	$6	$ 9
The Road, Cormac McCarthy	2.5 lb	$5	$ 7
Slaughterhouse-Five, Kurt Vonnegut	1 lb	$4	$ 5

When packing a single box, BK must adhere to the following:

- 20 books or less.
- Books by three different authors.
- Between four and eight books from each author.
- Weight equal to or less than 50 pounds.

BK has come to you to help him determine which books he should order to maximize his profit based on the above information. Using the data file AYK8_Data.xlsx, determine the optimal book order for a single box of books.

Data File: AYK8_Data.xlsx

Project 9:

Security Analysis

SecureWorks, Inc., is a small computer security contractor that provides computer security analysis, design, and software implementation for the U.S. government and commercial clients. SecureWorks competes for both private and U.S. government computer security contract work by submitting detailed bids outlining the work the company will perform if awarded the contracts. Because all of the work involves computer security, a highly sensitive area, almost all of SecureWorks tasks require access to classified material or company confidential documents. Consequently, all of the security engineers (simply known as "engineers" within the company) have U.S. government clearances of either Secret or Top Secret. Some have even higher clearances for the 2 percent of SecureWorks work that involves so-called "black box" security work. Most of the employees also hold clearances because they must handle classified documents.

Leslie Mamalis is SecureWorks' human resources (HR) manager. She maintains all employee records and is responsible for semiannual review reports, payroll processing, personnel records, recruiting data, employee training, and pension option information. At the heart of an HR system are personnel records. Personnel record maintenance includes activities such as maintaining employee records, tracking cost center data, recording and maintaining pension information, and absence and sick leave record keeping. While most of this information resides in sophisticated database systems, Leslie maintains a basic employee worksheet for quick calculations and ad hoc report generation. Because SecureWorks is a small company, Leslie can take advantage of Excel's excellent list management capabilities to satisfy many of her personnel information management needs.

Leslie has asked you to assist with a number of functions (she has provided you with a copy of her "trusted" personnel data file, AYK9_Data.xlsx):

1. Copy the worksheet Data to a new worksheet called Sort. Sort the employee list in ascending order by department, then by last name, then by first name.

2. Copy the worksheet Data to a new worksheet called Autofilter. Using the Autofilter feature, create a custom filter that will display employees whose birth date is greater than or equal to 1/1/1965 and less than or equal to 12/31/1975.

3. Copy the worksheet Data to a new worksheet called Subtotal. Using the subtotal feature create a sum of the salary for each department.

4. Copy the worksheet Data to a new worksheet called Formatting. Using the salary column, change the font color to red if the cell value is greater than or equal to 55000. You must use the conditional formatting feature to complete this step.

Data File: AYK9_Data.xlsx

Project 10:

Gathering Data

You have just accepted a new job offer from a firm that has offices in San Diego, Los Angeles, and San Francisco. You need to decide which location to move to. Because you have not visited any of these three cities and want to get in a lot of golf time, you determine that the main factor that will affect your decision is weather.

Go to www.weather.com and locate the box in which you can enter the city or zip code for which you want information. Enter San Diego, CA, and when the data appear, click the Averages and Records tab. Print this page and repeat this for Los Angeles and San Francisco. You will want to focus on the Monthly Average and Records section on the top of the page.

1. Create a spreadsheet to summarize the information you find.

2. Record the temperature and rainfall in columns, and group the cities into four groups of rows labeled Average High, Average Low, Mean, and Average Precipitation.

3. Fill in the appropriate data for each city and month.

4. Because rain is your greatest concern, use conditional formatting to display the months with an average precipitation below 2.5 inches in blue and apply boldface.

5. You also want to be in the warmest weather possible while in California. Use conditional formatting to display the months with average high temperatures above 65 degrees in green and apply an italic font face.

6. Looking at the average high temperatures above 65 degrees and average precipitation below two inches, to which city do you think you should relocate? Explain your answer.

Project 11:

Scanner System

FunTown is a popular amusement park filled with roller coasters, games, and water features. Boasting 24 roller coasters, 10 of which exceed 200 feet and 70 miles per hour, and five water parks, the park's attendance remains steady throughout the season. Due to the park's popularity, it is not uncommon for entrance lines to exceed one hour on busy days. FunTown would like your help to find a solution to decrease park entrance lines.

FunTown would like to implement a handheld scanner system that can allow employees to walk around the front gates and accept credit card purchases and print tickets on the spot. The park anticipates an overall increase in sales of 4 percent per year with online ticketing, with an expense of 6 percent of total sales for the scanning equipment. FunTown has created a data file for you to use, AYK11_Data.xlsx, that compares scanning sales and traditional sales. You will need to create the necessary formulas to calculate all the assumptions including:

- Tickets sold at the booth.
- Tickets sold by the scanner.
- Revenues generated by booth sales.
- Revenues generated by scanner sales.
- Scanner ticket expense.
- Revenue with and without scanner sales.
- Three year row totals.

Data File: AYK11_Data.xlsx

Project 12:

Competitive Pricing

Bill Schultz is thinking of starting a store that specializes in handmade cowboy boots. Bill is a longtime rancher in the town of Taos, New Mexico. Bill's reputation for honesty and integrity is well-known around town, and he is positive that his new store will be highly successful.

Before opening his store, Bill is curious about how his profit, revenue, and variable costs will change depending on the amount he charges for his boots. Bill would like you to perform the work required for this analysis and has given you the data file AYK12_Data. xlsx. Here are a few things to consider while you perform your analysis:

- Current competitive prices for custom cowboy boots are between $225 and $275 a pair.
- Variable costs will be either $100 or $150 a pair depending on the types of material Bill chooses to use.
- Fixed costs are $10,000 a month.

  Data File: AYK12_Data.xlsx

Project 13:

Adequate Acquisitions

XMark.com is a major Internet company specializing in organic food. XMark.com is thinking of purchasing GoodGrow, another organic food Internet company. GoodGrow has current revenues of $100 million, with expenses of $150 million. Current projections indicate that GoodGrow's revenues are increasing at 35 percent per year and its expenses are increasing by 10 percent per year. XMark.com understands that projections can be erroneous, however; the company must determine the number of years before GoodGrow will return a profit.

You need to help XMark.com determine the number of years required to break even, using annual growth rates in revenue between 20 percent and 60 percent and annual expense growth rates between 10 percent and 30 percent. You have been provided with a template, AYK13_Data.xlsx, to assist with your analysis.

  Data File: AYK13_Data.xlsx

Project 14:

Customer Relations

Schweizer Distribution specializes in distributing fresh produce to local restaurants in the Chicago area. The company currently sells 12 different products through the efforts of three sales representatives to 10 restaurants. The company, like all small businesses, is always interested in finding ways to increase revenues and decrease expenses.

The company's founder, Bob Schweizer, has recently hired you as a new business analyst. You have just graduated from college with a degree in marketing and a specialization in customer relationship management. Bob is eager to hear your thoughts and ideas on how to improve the business and help the company build strong lasting relationships with its customers.

Bob has provided you with last year's sales information in the data file AYK14_Data. xlsx. Help Bob analyze his distribution company by using a PivotTable to determine the following:

1. Who is Bob's best customer by total sales?
2. Who is Bob's worst customer by total sales?
3. Who is Bob's best customer by total profit?
4. Who is Bob's worst customer by total profit?

5. What is Bob's best-selling product by total sales?

6. What is Bob's worst-selling product by total sales?

7. What is Bob's best-selling product by total profit?

8. What is Bob's worst-selling product by total profit?

9. Who is Bob's best sales representative by total profit?

10. Who is Bob's worst sales representative by total profit?

11. What is the best sales representative's best-selling product (by total profit)?

12. Who is the best sales representative's best customer (by total profit)?

13. What is the best sales representative's worst-selling product (by total profit)?

14. Who is the best sales representative's worst customer (by total profit)?

Data File: AYK14_Data.xlsx

Project 15:

Assessing the Value of Information

Recently Santa Fe, New Mexico, was named one of the safest places to live in the United States. Since then housing development projects have been springing up all around Santa Fe. Six housing development projects are currently dominating the local market—Pinon Pine, Rancho Hondo, Creek Side, Vista Del Monte, Forest View, and Santa Fe South. These six projects each started with 100 homes, have sold all of them, and are currently developing phase two.

As one of the three partners and real estate agents of Affordable Homes Real Estate, it is your responsibility to analyze the information concerning the past 600 home sales and choose which development project to focus on for selling homes in phase two. Because your real estate firm is so small, you and your partners have decided that the firm should focus on selling homes in only one of the development projects.

From the New Mexico Real Estate Association you have obtained a spreadsheet file that contains information concerning each of the sales for the first 600 homes. It contains the following fields:

Column	Name	Description
A	LOT #	The number assigned to a specific home within each project.
B	PROJECT #	A unique number assigned to each of the six housing development projects (see table on the next page).
C	ASK PRICE	The initial posted asking price for the home.
D	SELL PRICE	The actual price for which the home was sold.
E	LIST DATE	The date the home was listed for sale.
F	SALE DATE	The date on which the final contract closed and the home was sold.
G	SQ. FT.	The total square footage for the home.
H	# BATH.	The number of bathrooms in the home.
I	# BDRMS	The numb er of bedrooms in the home.

The following numbers have been assigned to each of the housing development projects:

Project Number	Project Name
23	Pinon Pine
47	Rancho Hondo
61	Creek Side
78	Vista Del Monte
92	Forest View
97	Santa Fe South

It is your responsibility to analyze the sales list and prepare a report that details which housing development project your real estate firm should focus on. Your analysis should be from as many angles as possible.

1. You do not know how many other real estate firms will also be competing for sales in each of the housing development projects.

2. Phase two for each housing development project will develop homes similar in style, price, and square footage to their respective first phases.

3. As you consider the information provided to you, think in terms of what information is important and what information is not important. Be prepared to justify how you went about your analysis.

4. Upon completing your analysis, please provide concise, yet detailed and thorough, documentation (in narrative, numeric, and graphic forms) that justifies your decision.

Data file: AYK15_Data.xlsx

Project 16:

Growth, Trends, and Forecasts

Founded in 2002, Analytics Software provides innovative search software, website accessibility testing software, and usability testing software. All serve as part of its desktop and enterprise content management solutions for government, corporate, educational, and consumer markets. The company's solutions are used by website publishers, digital media publishers, content managers, document managers, business users, consumers, software companies, and consulting services companies. Analytics Software solutions help organizations develop long-term strategies to achieve web content accessibility, enhance usability, and comply with U.S. and international accessibility and search standards.

You manage the customer service group for the company and have just received an email from CIO Sue Downs that the number of phone calls from customers having problems with one of your newer applications is on the increase. This company has a 10-year history of approximately 1 percent in turnover a year, and its focus had always been on customer service. With the informal motto of "Grow big, but stay small," it takes pride in 100 percent callbacks in customer care, knowing that its personal service was one thing that made it outstanding.

The rapid growth to six times its original customer-base size has forced the company to deal with difficult questions for the first time, such as, "How do we serve this many customers?"

One option might be for the company to outsource its customer service department. Before deciding to do that, Analytics Software needs to create a growth, trend, forecast analysis for future predictions.

1. Create a weekly analysis from the data provided in AYK16_Data.xlsx.

2. The price of the products, the actual product type, and any warrantee information is irrelevant.

3. Develop a growth, trend, and forecast analysis. You should use a three-day moving average; a shorter moving average might not display the trend well, and a much longer moving average would shorten the trend too much.

4. Upon completing your analysis, please provide concise yet detailed and thorough documentation (in narrative, numeric, and graphic forms) that justifies your recommendations.

Data File: AYK16_Data.xlsx

Project 17:

Shipping Costs

One of the main products of the Fairway Woods Company is custom-made golf clubs. The clubs are manufactured at three plants (Denver, Colorado; Phoenix, Arizona; and Dallas, Texas) and are then shipped by truck to five distribution warehouses in Sacramento, California; Salt Lake City, Utah; Chicago, Illinois; Albuquerque, New Mexico; and New York City, New York. Since shipping costs are a major expense, management has begun an analysis to determine ways to reduce them. For the upcoming golf season, the output from each manufacturing plant and how much each warehouse will require to satisfy its customers have been estimated.

The CIO from Fairway Woods Company has created a data file for you, AYK17_Data.xlsx, of the shipping costs from each manufacturing plant to each warehouse as a baseline analysis. Some business rules and requirements you should be aware of include:

■ The problem presented involves the shipment of goods from three plants to five regional warehouses.

■ Goods can be shipped from any plant to any warehouse, but it costs more to ship goods over long distances than over short distances.

1. Your goal is to minimize the costs of shipping goods from production plants to warehouses, thereby meeting the demand from each metropolitan area while not exceeding the supply available from each plant. To complete this project it is recommended that you use the Solver function in Excel to assist with the analysis.

2. Specifically you want to focus on:

■ Minimizing the total shipping costs.

■ Total shipped must be less than or equal to supply at a plant.

■ Total shipped to warehouses must be greater than or equal to the warehouse demand.

■ Number to ship must be greater than or equal to 0.

Data File: AYK17_Data.xlsx

Project 18:

Formatting Grades

Professor Streterstein is a bit absentminded. His instructor's grade book is a mess, and he would like your help cleaning it up and making it easier to use. In Professor Streterstein's course, the maximum possible points a student can earn is 750. The following table displays the grade equivalent to total points for the course.

Total Points	Calculated Grade
675	A
635	A–
600	B
560	B–
535	C
490	C–
450	D
0	F

Help Professor Streterstein rework his grade book. Open the data file AYK18_Data.xlsx and perform the following:

1. Reformat the workbook so it is readable, understandable, and consistent. Replace column labels, format and align the headings, add borders and shading as appropriate.

2. Add a column in the grade book for final grade next to the total points earned column.

3. Use the VLookup Function to automatically assess final grades based on the total points column.

4. Using the If Function, format the workbook so each student's grade shows a pass or fail—P for pass, F for fail—based on the total points.

   Data File: AYK18_Data.xlsx

Project 19:

Moving Dilemma

Pony Espresso is a small business that sells specialty coffee drinks at office buildings. Each morning and afternoon, trucks arrive at offices' front entrances, and the office employees purchase various beverages such as Java du Jour and Café de Colombia. The business is profitable. Pony Espresso offices, however, are located north of town, where lease rates are less expensive, and the principal sales area is south of town. This means the trucks must drive across town four times each day.

The cost of transportation to and from the sales area plus the power demands of the trucks' coffee brewing equipment are a significant portion of variable costs. Pony Espresso could reduce the amount of driving and, therefore, the variable costs, if it moved the offices closer to the sales area.

Pony Espresso presently has fixed costs of $10,000 per month. The lease of a new office, closer to the sales area, would cost an additional $2,200 per month. This would increase the fixed costs to $12,200 per month.

Although the lease of new offices would increase the fixed costs, a careful estimate of the potential savings in gasoline and vehicle maintenance indicates that Pony Espresso could reduce the variable costs from $0.60 per unit to $0.35 per unit. Total sales are unlikely to increase as a result of the move, but the savings in variable costs should increase the annual profit.

Consider the information provided to you from the owner in the data file AYK19_Data. xlsx. Especially look at the change in the variability of the profit from month to month. From

November through January, when it is much more difficult to lure office workers out into the cold to purchase coffee, Pony Espresso barely breaks even. In fact, in December, the business lost money.

1. Develop the cost analysis on the existing lease information using the monthly sales figures provided to you in the data file.
2. Develop the cost analysis from the new lease information provided above.
3. Calculate the variability that is reflected in the month-to-month standard deviation of earnings for the current cost structure and the projected cost structure.
4. Do not consider any association with downsizing such as overhead—simply focus on the information provided to you.
5. You will need to calculate the EBIT (earnings before interest and taxes).

Data File: AYK19_Data.xlsx

Project 20:

Operational Efficiencies

Hoover Transportation, Inc., is a large distribution company located in Denver, Colorado. The company is currently seeking to gain operational efficiencies in its supply chain by reducing the number of transportation carriers that it is using to outsource. Operational efficiencies for Hoover Transportation, Inc., suggest that reducing the number of carriers from the Denver distribution center to warehouses in the selected states will lead to reduced costs. Brian Hoover, the CEO of Hoover Transportation, requests that the number of carriers transporting products from its Denver distribution center to wholesalers in Arizona, Arkansas, Iowa, Missouri, Montana, Oklahoma, Oregon, and Washington be reduced from the current five carriers to two carriers.

Carrier selection should be based on the assumptions that all environmental factors are equal and historical cost trends will continue. Review the historical data from the past several years to determine your recommendation for the top two carriers that Hoover Transportation should continue to use.

1. Analyze the last 24 months of Hoover's Transportation carrier transactions found in the data file AYK20_Data.xlsx.
2. Create a report detailing your recommendation for the top two carriers with which Hoover Transportation should continue to do business. Be sure to use PivotTables and PivotCharts in your report. A few questions to get you started include:

   ▪ Calculate the average cost per carrier.
   ▪ Calculate the total shipping costs per state.
   ▪ Calculate the total shipping weights per state.
   ▪ Calculate the average shipping costs per pound.
   ▪ Calculate the average cost per carrier.

Data File: AYK20_Data.xlsx

Project 21:

Too Much Information

You have just landed the job of vice president of operations for The Pitt Stop Restaurants, a national chain of full-service, casual-themed restaurants. During your first week on the job, Suzanne Graham, your boss and CEO of the company, has asked you to provide an analysis of how well the company's restaurants are performing. Specifically, she would like to know which units and regions are performing extremely well, which are performing moderately well, and which are underperforming. Her goal is to identify where to spend time and focus efforts to improve the overall health of the company.

Review the data file AYK21_Data.xlsx and determine how best to analyze and interpret the data. Create a formal presentation of your findings. A few things to consider include:

- Should underperforming restaurants be closed or sold?
- Should high-performing restaurants be expanded to accommodate more seats?
- Should the company spend more or less on advertising?
- In which markets should the advertising budget be adjusted?
- How are The Pitt Stop Restaurants performing compared to the competition?
- How are units of like size performing relative to each other?

Data File: AYK21_Data.xlsx

Project 22:

Turnover Rates

Employee turnover rates are at an all-time high at Gizmo's Manufacturing plants. The company is experiencing severe worker retention issues, which are leading to productivity and quality control problems. The majority of the company's workers perform a variety of tasks and are paid by the hour. The company currently tests potential applicants to ensure they have the skills necessary for the intense mental concentration and dexterity required to fill the positions. Since significant costs are associated with employee turnover, Gizmo Manufacturing wants to find a way to predict which applicants have the characteristics of being a short-term versus a long-term employee.

1. Review the information that Gizmo Manufacturing has collected from two of its different data sources. The first data file, AYK22_Data_A.xlsx, contains information regarding employee wages. The second data file, AYK22_Data_B.xlsx, contains information regarding employee retention.

2. Using Excel analysis functions, determine the employee characteristics that you would recommend Gizmo Manufacturing look for when hiring new personnel. It is highly recommended that you use PivotTables as part of your analysis.

3. Prepare a report based on your findings (which should include several forms of graphical representation) for your recommendations.

Data Files: AYK22_Data_A.xlsx and AYK22_Data_B.xlsx

Project 23:

Vital Information

Martin Resorts, Inc., owns and operates four Spa and Golf resorts in Colorado. The company has five traditional lines of business: (1) golf sales; (2) golf lessons; (3) restaurants; (4) retail and rentals; and (5) hotels. David Logan, director of marketing technology at Martin Resorts, Inc., and Donald Mayer, the lead strategic analyst for Martin Resorts, are soliciting your input for their CRM strategic initiative.

Martin Resorts' IT infrastructure is pieced together with various systems and applications. Currently, the company has a difficult time with CRM because its systems are not integrated. The company cannot determine vital information such as which customers are golfing and staying at the hotel or which customers are staying at the hotel and not golfing.

For example, the three details that the customer Diego Titus (1) stayed four nights at a Martin Resorts' managed hotel, (2) golfed three days, and (3) took an all-day spa treatment the first day are discrete facts housed in separate systems. Martin Resorts hopes that by using data warehousing technology to integrate its data, the next time Diego reserves lodging for another trip, sales associates may ask him if he would like to book a spa treatment as well, and even if he would like the same masseuse that he had on his prior trip.

Martin Resorts is excited about the possibility of taking advantage of customer segmentation and CRM strategies to help increase its business.

The company wants to use CRM and data warehouse technologies to improve service and personalization at each customer touch point. Using a data warehousing tool, important customer information can be accessed from all of its systems either daily, weekly, monthly, or once or twice per year. Analyze the sample data in AYK23_Data.xlsx for the following:

1. Currently, the quality of the data within the above disparate systems is low. Develop a report for David and Donald discussing the importance of high-quality information and how low-quality information can affect Martin Resorts' business.

2. Review the data that David and Donald are working with from the data warehouse in the data file AYK23_Data.xlsx.

   a. Give examples from the data showing the kind of information Martin Resorts might be able to use to gain a better understanding of its customers. Include the types of data quality issues the company can anticipate and the strategies it can use to help avoid such issues.

   b. Determine who are Martin Resorts' best customers, and provide examples of the types of marketing campaigns the company should offer these valuable customers.

   c. Prepare a report that summarizes the benefits Martin Resorts can receive from using business intelligence to mine the data warehouse. Include a financial analysis of the costs and benefits.

   Data File: AYK23_Data.xlsx

Project 24:
Breaking Even

Mountain Cycle specializes in making custom mountain bikes. The company founder, PJ Steffan, is having a hard time making the business profitable. Knowing that you have great business knowledge and solid financial sense, PJ has come to you for advice.

PJ would like you to determine how many bikes Mountain Cycle needs to sell per year to break even. Using Goal Seek in Excel solve using the following:

- Fixed cost equals $65,000
- Variable cost equals $1,575
- Bike price equals $2,500

Project 25:
Profit Scenario

Murry Lutz owns a small shop, Lutz Motors, that sells and services vintage motorcycles. Murry is curious how his profit will be affected by his sales over the next year.

Murry would like your help creating best, worst, and most-likely scenarios for his motorcycle sales over the next year. Using Scenario Manager, help Murry analyze the information in the data file AYK25_Data.xlsx.

   Data File: AYK25_Data.xlsx

Project 26:
Electronic Résumés

Résumés are the currency of the recruitment industry. They are the cornerstone of communication between candidates, recruiters, and employers. Technology is automating elements of the recruitment process, but a complete solution requires proper handling of the actual development of all the pieces and parts that comprise not just a résumé, but also an erésumé. Electronic résumés, or erésumés, have moved into the mainstream of today's job market at lightning speed. Erésumés have stepped up the efficiency of job placement to such a point that you could get a call from a recruiter just hours after submitting your erésumé. With this kind of opportunity, you cannot afford to be left in the dark ages of using only a paper résumé.

In the text or HTML editor of your choice, write your erésumé as though you were really putting it online and inviting prospective employers to see it. We recommend typing in all the text and then later adding the HTML tags (rather than trying to type in the tags as you go).

Use the following checklist to make sure you're covering the basics. You do not need to match it exactly; it just shows what can be done.

- Add structural tags.
- Add paragraphs and headings.
- Find an opportunity to include a list.
- Add inline styles.
- Play with the alignment of elements.
- Add appropriate font selection, font size, and color.

Project 27:
Gathering Feedback

Gathering feedback from website's visitors can be a valuable way of assessing a site's success, and it can help build a customer or subscriber database. For example, a business could collect the addresses of people who are interested in receiving product samples, email newsletters, or notifications of special offers.

Adding form elements to a web page is simple: They are created using a set of HTML form tags that define menus, text fields, buttons, and so on. Form elements are generally used to collect information from a web page.

In the text or HTML editor of your choice, create a web page form that would collect information for a customer ordering a customized bicycle. Use proper web page design and HTML tools to understand the process and function of form elements. Be sure to pay attention to:

- Form layout and design.
- Visual elements, including labels, alignment, font selection, font size, color.
- Required versus nonrequired fields.
- Drop-down boxes, text fields, and radio buttons.

Project 28:
Daily Invoice

Foothills Animal Hospital is a full-service small animal veterinary hospital located in Morrison, Colorado, specializing in routine medical care, vaccinations, laboratory testing, and surgery. The hospital has experienced tremendous growth over the past six months due to customer referrals. While Foothills Animal Hospital has typically kept its daily service records in a workbook format, it feels the need to expand its reporting capabilities to develop a relational database as a more functional structure.

Foothills Animal Hospital needs help developing a database, specifically:

- Create a customer table—name, address, phone, and date of entrance.
- Create a pet table—pet name, type of animal, breed, gender, color, neutered/spayed, weight, and comments.
- Create a medications table—medication code, name of medication, and cost of medication.
- Create a visit table—details of treatments performed, medications dispensed, and date of the visit.
- Produce a daily invoice report.

Figure AYK.2 displays a sample daily invoice report that the Foothills Animal Hospital accountants have requested. Foothills Animal Hospital organizes its treatments using the codes displayed in Figure AYK.3. The entities and primary keys for the database have been identified in Figure AYK.4.

The following business rules have been identified:

1. A customer can have many pets but must have at least one.
2. A pet must be assigned to one and only one customer.
3. A pet can have one or more treatments per visit but must have at least one.
4. A pet can have one or more medications but need not have any.

Your job is to complete the following tasks:

1. Develop and describe the entity-relationship diagram.
2. Use normalization to assure the correctness of the tables (relations).

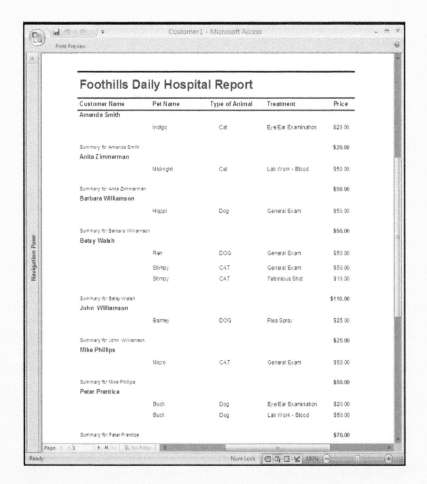

FIGURE AYK.2

Foothills Animal Hospital Daily Invoice Report

Treatment Code	Treatment	Price
0100	Tetrinious Shot	$10.00
0201	Rabonius Shot	$20.00
0300	General Exam	$50.00
0303	Eye/Ear Examination	$20.00
0400	Spay/Neuter	$225.00
0405	Reset Dislocation	$165.00
0406	Amputation of Limb	$450.00
0407	Wrap Affected Area	$15.00
0408	Cast Affected Area	$120.00
1000	Lab Work—Blood	$50.00
1003	Lab Work—Misc	$35.00
2003	Flea Spray	$25.00
9999	Other Not Listed	$10.00

FIGURE AYK.3

Treatment Codes, Treatments, and Price Descriptions

FIGURE AYK.4

Entity Names and Primary Keys Foothills Animal Hospital

Entity	Primary Key
CUSTOMER	Customer Number
PET	Pet Number
VISIT	Visit Number
VISIT DETAIL	Visit Number and Line Number (a composite key)
TREATMENT	Treatment Code
MEDICATION	Medication Code

3. Create the database using a personal DBMS package (preferably Microsoft Access).

4. Use the data in Figure AYK.3 to populate your tables. Feel free to enter your own personal information.

5. Use the DBMS package to create the basic report in Figure AYK.2.

Project 29:
Billing Data

On-The-Level Construction Company is a Denver-based construction company that specializes in subcontracting the development of single-family homes. In business since 1998, On-The-Level Construction has maintained a talented pool of certified staff and independent consultants providing the flexibility and combined experience required to meet the needs of its nearly 300 completed projects in the Denver metropolitan area. The field of operation methods that On-The-Level Construction is responsible for includes structural development, heating and cooling, plumbing, and electricity.

The company charges its clients by billing the hours spent on each contract. The hourly billing rate is dependent on the employee's position according to the field of operations (as noted above). Figure AYK.5 shows a basic report that On-The-Level Construction foremen would like to see every week concerning what projects are being assigned, the overall assignment hours, and the charges for the assignment. On-The-Level Construction organizes its internal structure in four different operations—Structure (500), Plumbing (501), Electrical (502), and Heating and Ventilation (503). Each of these operational departments can and should have many subcontractors who specialize in that area. On-The-Level Construction has decided to implement a relational database model to track project details according to project name, hours assigned, and charges per hour for each job description. Originally, On-The-Level Construction decided to let one of its employees handle the construction of the database. However, that employee has not had the time to completely implement the project. On-The-Level Construction has asked you to take over and complete the development of the database.

The entities and primary keys for the database have been identified in Figure AYK.6.

The following business rules have been identified:

1. A job can have many employees assigned but must have at least one.

2. An employee must be assigned to one and only one job number.

FIGURE AYK.5

On-The-Level-Construction Detail Report

3. An employee can be assigned to work on one or more projects.
4. A project can be assigned to only one employee but need not be assigned to any employee.

Your job is to complete the following tasks:

1. Develop and describe the entity relationship diagram.
2. Use normalization to assure the correctness of the tables (relations).
3. Create the database using a personal DBMS package (preferably Microsoft Access).
4. Use the DBMS package to create the basic report in Figure AYK.5.
5. You may not be able to develop a report that looks exactly like the one in Figure AYK.5. However, your report should include the same information.
6. Complete personnel information is tracked by another database. For this application, include only the minimum: employee number, last name, and first name.
7. Information concerning all projects, employees, and jobs is not readily available. You should create information for several fictitious projects, employees, and jobs to include in your database.

FIGURE AYK.6

Entity Classes and Primary Keys for On-The-Level Construction

Entity	Primary Key
PROJECT	Project Number
EMPLOYEE	Employee Number
JOB	Job Number
ASSIGNMENT	Assignment Number

Project 30:

Inventory Data

An independent retailer of mobile entertainment and wireless phones, iToys.com has built its business on offering the widest selection, expert advice, and outstanding customer service. However, iToys.com does not use a formal, consistent inventory tracking system. Periodically, an iToys.com employee visually checks to see what items are in stock. Although iToys.com does try to keep a certain level of each "top seller" in stock, the lack of a formal inventory tracking system has led to the overstocking of some items and understocking of other items. On occasion, a customer will request a hot item, and it is only then that iToys.com realizes that the item is out of stock. If an item is not available, iToys.com risks losing a customer to a competitor.

Lately, iToys.com has become concerned with its inventory management methods. The owner of iToys.com, Dan Connolly, wants to better manage his inventory. The company receives orders by mail, by telephone, or through its website. Regardless of how the orders are received, Dan needs a database to automate the inventory checking and ordering process.

Dan has provided you with a simplified version of the company's current system (an Excel workbook) for recording inventory and orders in an Excel spreadsheet data file AYK30_Data.xlsx.

1. Develop an ERD diagram before you begin to create the database. You will need to use the information provided here as well as the data given in the Excel workbook.

2. Create the database using a personal DBMS package (preferably Microsoft Access) that will track items (i.e., products), orders, order details, categories, suppliers, and shipping methods.

3. In addition to what is mentioned above, the database needs to track the inventory levels for each product, according to a reorder level and lead time.

4. At this time, Dan does not need information stored about the customer; he simply needs you to focus on the inventory structure.

5. Develop a query that will display the products that need to be ordered from their supplier. To complete this, you will want to compare a reorder level with how many units are in stock.

6. Develop several reports that display:

   a. Each product ordered by its supplier. The report should include the product name, quantity on hand, and reorder level.

   b. Each supplier ordered by shipping method.

   c. Each product that requires more than five days lead time. (Hint: You will want to create a query for this first).

   d. Each product ordered by category.

7. Here are some additional business rules to assist you in completing this task:

   a. An order must have at least one product, but can contain more than one product.

   b. A product can have one or more orders, but need not have any orders.

   c. A product must belong to one and only one category, but a category may contain many different products.

   d. A product can only be stocked by one supplier, but a supplier can provide more than one product.

   e. A supplier will use one type of shipping method, but shipping methods can be used by more than one supplier.

   Data File: AYK30_Data.xlsx

Project 31:
Call Center

A manufacturing company, Teleworks, has been a market leader in the wireless telephone business for the past 10 years. Other firms have imitated its product with some degree of success, but Teleworks occupies a dominant position in the marketplace because it has a first-mover advantage with a quality product.

Recently Teleworks began selling a new, enhanced wireless phone. This new phone does not replace its current product, but offers additional features, greater durability, and better performance for a somewhat higher price. Offering this enhanced phone has established a new revenue stream for the company.

Many sales executives at Teleworks seem to subscribe to the-more-you-have, the-more-you-want theory of managing customer data. That is, they believe they can never accumulate too much information about their customers, and that they can do their jobs more effectively by collecting infinite amounts of customer details. Having a firm grasp on a wide range of customer-focused details—specifically reports summarizing call center information—can be critical in enabling your company to successfully manage a customer relationship management (CRM) solution that creates a positive impact.

To continue to provide excellent customer support, and in anticipation of increased calls due to the release of its new product, Teleworks needs a database that it can use to record, track, and query call center information. Teleworks CIO KED Davisson has hired you to develop this database.

1. Teleworks has provided you with a data file AYK31_Data.xlsx; its current approach for recording cell center information is a spreadsheet file.

2. Develop an ERD diagram before you begin to create the database.

3. Create the database using a personal DBMS package (preferably Microsoft Access) that will allow data analysts to enter call center data according to the type of issue and the customer, assign each call to a consultant, and prioritize the call.

4. Develop a query that will display all issues that are "open."

5. Develop a screen form to browse all issues.

6. Develop several reports that display:

   a. All closed issues.

   b. Each issue in detail ordered by issue ID.

   c. Each issue in detail ordered by consultant.

   d. Each issue in detail ordered by category.

   e. Each issue in detail ordered by status.

7. Here are some additional business rules to assist you in completing this task:

   a. An issue must have at least one customer.

   b. A customer can have more than one issue.

   c. Each issue must be assigned to one consultant.

   d. Each consultant can be assigned to more than one issue.

   e. An issue can only belong to one category.

   f. An issue must be assigned only one status code.

   g. An issue must be assigned a priority code.

8. Priorities are assigned accordingly:

Priority Level
Critical
High
Moderate
Standard
Low

9. Status is recorded as either open or closed.

10. The categories of each issue need to be recorded as:

Category
Hardware/Phone
Software/Voice mail
Internet/Web

Data File: AYK31_Data.xlsx

Project 32:

Sales Pipeline

Sales drive any organization. This is true for every for-profit business irrespective of size or industry type. If customers are not buying your goods or services, you run the risk of not having a business. This is when tough decisions have to be made like whether to slash budgets, lay off staff, or seek additional financing.

Unfortunately, you do not wield ultimate power over your customers' buying habits. While you can attempt to influence buying behavior through strategic marketing, smart businesses remain one step ahead by collecting and analyzing historical and current customer information from a range of internal and external sources to forecast future sales. In other words, managing the sales pipeline is an essential ingredient to business success.

You have recently been hired by RealTime Solutions, a new company that collects information to understand, manage, and predict specific sales cycle (including the supply chain and lead times) in the automobile business. Having an accurate forecast of future sales will allow the company to increase or decrease the production cycle as required and manage personnel levels, inventory, and cash flow.

Using a personal DBMS package (preferably Microsoft Access) create a sales pipeline database that will:

1. Track opportunities from employees to customers.
   - Opportunities should have a ranking, category, source of opportunity, open date, closed date, description.
2. Create a form for inputting customer, employee, and opportunity data.
3. Create a few reports that display:
   - All open opportunities, including relevant customer and employee information.
   - Closed opportunities, including relevant customer and employee information.
   - All customers.
4. Create your own data to test the integrity of the relationships. Use approximately 10 records per table.

Project 33:

Online Classified Ads

With the emergence of the Internet as a worldwide standard for communicating information, *The Morrison Post,* a medium-size community newspaper in central Colorado, is creating an electronic version of its paper-based classified ads.

Advertisers can place a small ad that lists items that they wish to sell and provide a means (e.g., telephone number and email) by which prospective buyers can contact them. The nature of a sale via the newspaper's classified system goes as follows:

- During the course of the sale, the information flows in different directions at different stages.
- First, there is a downstream flow of information (from seller to buyer): the listing in print in the newspaper. (Thus, the classified ad listing is just a way of bringing a buyer and seller together.)
- When a potential purchaser's interest has been raised, then that interest must be relayed upstream, usually by telephone or by email.
- Finally, a meeting should result that uses face-to-face negotiation to finalize the sale, if the sale can be agreed.

By placing the entire system on the Internet, the upstream and downstream communications are accomplished using a web browser. The sale becomes more of an auction, because many potential buyers, all with equal status, can bid for the same item. So it is fairer for all purchasers and gets a better deal for the seller.

Any user who is trying to buy an item can:

- View items for sale.
- Bid on an item they wish to purchase.

Any user who is trying to sell an item can:

- Place a new item for sale.
- Browse a list of the items that he or she is trying to sell, and examine the bids that have been made on each of those items.
- Accept a bid on an item that he or she is selling.

Your job is to complete the following:

1. Develop and describe the entity-relationship diagram for the database that will support the listed activities.
2. Use normalization to ensure the correctness of the tables.
3. Create the database using a personal DBMS package.
4. Use Figure AYK.7 as a baseline for your database design.

   Data File: AYK33_Data.xlsx

FIGURE AYK.7

The Morrison Post Classified Section
New User Registration

In order to bid on existing "for-sale" items, or sell your own items, you need to register first. Once you have done that, you will have full access to the system.

EMail Address:
First Name:
Last Name:
Address:

City:
State:
Postal Code:
Country:
Password:
Verify Password:

Submit   Reset

GLOSSARY

3G A service that brings wireless broadband to mobile phones.

A

acceptable use policy (AUP) A policy that a user must agree to follow to be provided access to corporate email, information systems, and the Internet.

access point (AP) The computer or network device that serves as an interface between devices and the network.

accessibility Refers to the varying levels that define what a user can access, view, or perform when operating a system.

accounting and finance ERP component Manages accounting data and financial processes within the enterprise with functions such as general ledger, accounts payable, accounts receivable, budgeting, and asset management.

active RFID tags Have their own transmitter and a power source (typically a battery).

adaptive computer devices Input devices designed for special applications for use by people with different types of special needs.

administrator access Unrestricted access to the entire system.

advanced encryption standard (AES) Introduced by the National Institute of Standards and Technology (NIST), AES is an encryption standard designed to keep government information secure.

adware Software, while purporting to serve some useful function and often fulfilling that function, also allows Internet advertisers to display advertisements without the consent of the computer user.

agile methodology Aims for customer satisfaction through early and continuous delivery of useful software components developed by an iterative process using the bare minimum requirements.

agile MIS infrastructure Includes the hardware, software, and telecommunications equipment that, when combined, provides the underlying foundation to support the organization's goals.

alpha testing Assess if the entire system meets the design requirements of the users.

analysis phase The firm analyzes its end-user business requirements and refines project goals into defined functions and operations of the intended system.

analytical CRM Supports back-office operations and strategic analysis and includes all systems that do not deal directly with the customers.

analytical information Encompasses all organizational information, and its primary purpose is to support the performing of managerial analysis or semistructured decisions.

analytics The science of fact-based decision making.

anti-spam policy Simply states that email users will not send unsolicited emails (or spam).

antivirus software Scans and searches hard drives to prevent, detect, and remove known viruses, adware, and spyware.

applet A program that runs within another application such as a website.

appliance A computer dedicated to a single function, such as a calculator or computer game.

application integration The integration of a company's existing management information systems to each other.

application programming interface (API) A set of routines, protocols, and tools for building software applications.

application service provider license Specialty software paid for on a license basis or per-use basis or usage-based licensing.

application software Used for specific information processing needs, including payroll, customer relationship management, project management, training, and many others.

arithmetic-logic unit (ALU) Performs all arithmetic operations (for example, addition and subtraction) and all logic operations (such as sorting and comparing numbers).

artificial intelligence (AI) Simulates human thinking and behavior such as the ability to reason and learn.

As-Is process model Represents the current state of the operation that has been mapped, without any specific improvements or changes to existing processes.

asset tracking Occurs when a company places active or semi-passive RFID tags on expensive products or assets to gather data on the items' location with little or no manual intervention.

association detection Reveals the relationship between variables along with the nature and frequency of the relationships.

asynchronous communication Communication such as email in which the message and the response do not occur at the same time.

attenuation Represents the loss of a network signal strength measured in decibels (dB) and occurs because the transmissions gradually dissipate in strength over longer distances or because of radio interference or physical obstructions such as walls.

attribute The data elements associated with an entity.

augmented reality The viewing of the physical world with computer-generated layers of information added to it.

authentication A method for confirming users' identities.

authorization The process of providing a user with permission including access levels and abilities such as file access, hours of access, and amount of allocated storage space.

automatic vehicle location (AVL) Uses GPS tracking to track vehicles.

automation Involves computerizing manual tasks making them more efficient and effective and dramatically lowering operational costs.

availability Refers to the time frames when the system is operational.

B

backup An exact copy of a system's information.

backward integration Takes information entered into a given system and sends it automatically to all upstream systems and processes.

balanced scorecard A management system, as well as a measurement system, that a firm uses to translate business strategies into executable tasks.

bandwidth The maximum amount of data that can pass from one point to another in a unit of time.

benchmark Baseline values the system seeks to attain.

benchmarking A process of continuously measuring system results, comparing those results to optimal system performance (benchmark values), and identifying steps and procedures to improve system performance.

best practice The most successful solutions or problem-solving methods that have been developed by a specific organization or industry.

biometrics   The identification of a user based on a physical characteristic, such as a fingerprint, iris, face, voice, or handwriting.

bit   The smallest element of data and has a value of either 0 or 1.

bit rate   The number of bits transferred or received per unit of time.

black-hat hacker   Breaks into other people's computer systems and may just look around or may steal and destroy information.

blog, or web log   An online journal that allows users to post their own comments, graphics, and video.

bluetooth   Wireless PAN technology that transmits signals over short distances between cell phones, computers, and other devices.

bottleneck   Occurs when resources reach full capacity and cannot handle any additional demands; they limit throughput and impede operations.

brainstorming   A technique for generating ideas by encouraging participants to offer as many ideas as possible in a short period of time without any analysis until all the ideas have been exhausted

broadband   A high-speed Internet connection that is always connected.

broadband over power line (BPL)   Technology makes possible high-speed Internet access over ordinary residential electrical lines and offers an alternative to DSL or high-speed cable modems.

bugs   Defects in the code of an information system.

bullwhip effect   Occurs when distorted product-demand information ripples from one partner to the next throughout the supply chain.

business continuity planning (BCP)   Details how a company recovers and restores critical business operations and systems after a disaster or extended disruption.

business facing process   Invisible to the external customer but essential to the effective management of the business; they include goal setting, day-to-day planning, giving performance feedback and rewards, and allocating resources.

business impact analysis   A process that identifies all critical business functions and the effect that a specific disaster may have upon them.

business intelligence (BI)   Information collected from multiple sources such as suppliers, customers, competitors, partners, and industries that analyze patterns, trends, and relationships for strategic decision making.

business intelligence dashboards   Track corporate metrics such as critical success factors and key performance indicators and include advanced capabilities such as interactive controls, allowing users to manipulate data for analysis.

business model   A plan that details how a company creates, delivers, and generates revenues.

business process   Standardized set of activities that accomplish a specific task.

business process improvement   Attempts to understand and measure the current process and make performance improvements accordingly.

business process management (BPM) system   Focus on evaluating and improving processes that include both person-to-person workflow and system-to-system communications.

business process model   A graphic description of a process, showing the sequence of process tasks, which is developed for a specific purpose and from a selected viewpoint.

business process modeling (or mapping)   The activity of creating a detailed flowchart or process map of a work process that shows its inputs, tasks, and activities in a structured sequence.

business process patent   A patent that protects a specific set of procedures for conducting a particular business activity.

business process reengineering (BPR)   The analysis and redesign of workflow within and between enterprises.

business requirement   The specific business requests the system must meet to be successful.

business rule   Defines how a company performs a certain aspect of its business and typically results in either a yes/no or true/false answer.

business strategy   A leadership plan that achieves a specific set of goals or objectives.

business-critical integrity constraint   Enforces business rules vital to an organization's success and often requires more insight and knowledge than relational integrity constraints.

business-to-business (B2B)   Applies to businesses buying from and selling to each other over the Internet.

business-to-consumer (B2C)   Applies to any business that sells its products or services directly to consumers online.

buyer power   One of Porter's five forces; measures the ability of buyers to directly affect the price they are willing to pay for an item.

C

cable modem (or broadband modem)   A type of digital modem used with high-speed cable Internet service.

cache memory   A small unit of ultra-fast memory that is used to store recently accessed or frequently accessed data so that the CPU does not have to retrieve this data from slower memory circuits such as RAM.

call scripting system   Gathers product details and issue resolution information that can be automatically generated into a script for the representative to read to the customer.

campaign management system   Guides users through marketing campaigns by performing such tasks as campaign definition, planning, scheduling, segmentation, and success analysis

capacity   Represents the maximum throughput a system can deliver; for example, the capacity of a hard drive represents the size or volume.

capacity planning   Determines future environmental infrastructure requirements to ensure high-quality system performance.

carbon emissions   Includes the carbon dioxide and carbon monoxide in the atmosphere, produced by business processes and systems.

cardinality   Expresses the specific number of instances in an entity.

cartography   The science and art of making an illustrated map or chart.

central processing unit (CPU) (or microprocessor)   The actual hardware that interprets and executes the program (software) instructions and coordinates how all the other hardware devices work together.

certificate authority   A trusted third party, such as VeriSign, that validates user identities by means of digital certificates.

change agent   A person or event that is the catalyst for implementing major changes for a system to meet business changes.

chief information officer (CIO)   Responsible for (1) overseeing all uses of MIS and (2) ensuring that MIS strategically aligns with business goals and objectives.

chief knowledge officer (CKO)   Responsible for collecting, maintaining, and distributing company knowledge.

chief privacy officer (CPO)   Responsible for ensuring the ethical and legal use of information within a company.

chief security officer (CSO)   Responsible for ensuring the security of business systems and developing strategies and safeguards against attacks from hackers and viruses.

chief technology officer (CTO)   Responsible for ensuring the speed, accuracy, availability, and reliability for MIS.

Child Online Protection Act (COPA)   A law that protects minors from accessing inappropriate material on the Internet.

chipless RFID tags   Use plastic or conductive polymers instead of silicon-based microchips, allowing them to be washed or exposed to water without damaging the chip.

clickstream data   Exact pattern of a consumer's navigation through a site.

click-fraud   The abuse of pay-per-click, pay-per-call, and pay-per-conversion revenue models by repeatedly clicking on a link to increase charges or costs for the advertiser.

click-to-talk   Allows customers to click on a button and talk with a representative via the Internet.

client   A computer designed to request information from a server.

client/server network   A model for applications in which the bulk of the back-end processing, such as performing a physical search of a database, takes place on a server, while the front-end processing, which involves communicating with the users, is handled by the clients.

cloud bursting   When a company uses its own computing infrastructure for normal usage and accesses the cloud when it needs to scale for high/peak load requirements, ensuring a sudden spike in usage does not result in poor performance or system crashes.

cloud computing   A model for enabling ubiquitous, convenient, on-demand network access to a shared pool of configurable computing resources (e.g., networks, servers, storage, applications, and services) that can be rapidly provisioned and released with minimal management effort or service provider interaction.

cloud fabric   The software that makes the benefits of cloud computing possible, such as multi-tenancy.

cloud fabric controller   An individual who monitors and provisions cloud resources similar to a server administrator at an individual company.

cluster analysis   A technique used to divide information sets into mutually exclusive groups such that the members of each group are as close together as possible to one another and the different groups are as far apart as possible.

coaxial cable   Cable that can carry a wide range of frequencies with low signal loss.

cold site   A separate facility that does not have any computer equipment but is a place where employees can move after a disaster.

collaboration system   A set of tools that supports the work of teams or groups by facilitating the sharing and flow of information.

collective intelligence   Collaborating and tapping into the core knowledge of all employees, partners, and customers.

communication device   Equipment used to send information and receive it from one location to another.

communication plan   Defines the how, what, when, and who regarding the flow of project information to stakeholders and is key for managing expectations.

community cloud   Serves a specific community with common business models, security requirements, and compliance considerations.

competitive advantage   A feature of a product or service on which customers place a greater value than on similar offerings from competitors.

competitive click-fraud   A computer crime where a competitor or disgruntled employee increases a company's search advertising costs by repeatedly clicking on the advertiser's link.

competitive intelligence   The process of gathering information about the competitive environment, including competitors' plans, activities, and products, to improve a company's ability to succeed.

complex instruction set computer (CISC) chips   Type of CPU that can recognize as many as 100 or more instructions, enough to carry out most computations directly.

composite entities   Entities that exist to represent the relationship between two other entities.

computer   An electronic device operating under the control of instructions stored in its own memory that can accept, manipulate, and store data.

computer-aided software engineering (CASE)   Software tools provide automated support for the development of the system.

confidentiality   The assurance that messages and information remain available only to those authorized to view them.

consolidation   The aggregation of data from simple roll-ups to complex groupings of interrelated information.

consumer-to-business (C2B)   Applies to any consumer who sells a product or service to a business on the Internet.

consumer-to-consumer (C2C)   Applies to customers offering goods and services to each other on the Internet.

contact center or call center   Where customer service representatives answer customer inquiries and solve problems, usually by email, chat, or phone.

contact management CRM system   Maintains customer contact information and identifies prospective customers for future sales, using tools such as organizational charts, detailed customer notes, and supplemental sales information.

content creator   The person responsible for creating the original website content.

content editor   The person responsible for updating and maintaining website content.

content filtering   Occurs when organizations use software that filters content, such as emails, to prevent the accidental or malicious transmission of unauthorized information.

content management system (CMS)   Helps companies manage the creation, storage, editing, and publication of their website content.

control objectives for information and related technologies (COBIT)   A set of best practices that helps an organization to maximize the benefits of an information system, while at the same time establishing appropriate controls to ensure minimum errors.

control panel   A Windows feature that provides a group of options that sets default values for the Windows operating system.

control unit   Interprets software instructions and literally tells the other hardware devices what to do, based on the software instructions.

conversion   The process of transferring information from a legacy system to a new system.

copyright   The legal protection afforded an expression of an idea, such as a song, book, or video game.

core ERP component   The traditional components included in most ERP systems and primarily focus on internal operations.

core process   Business processes, such as manufacturing goods, selling products, and providing service that make up the primary activities in a value chain.

corporate social responsibility   Companies' acknowledged responsibility to society.

corrective maintenance   Makes system changes to repair design flaws, coding errors, or implementation issues.

counterfeit software   Software that is manufactured to look like the real thing and sold as such.

course management software   Contains course information such as a syllabus and assignments and offers drop boxes for quizzes and homework along with a grade book.

cracker   A hacker with criminal intent.

critical path   Estimates the shortest path through the project ensuring all critical tasks are completed from start to finish.

critical success factors (CSFs)   Crucial steps companies perform to achieve their goals and objectives and implement their strategies.

CRM analysis technologies   Help organizations segment their customers into categories such as best and worst customers.

CRM predicting technologies   Help organizations predict customer behavior, such as which customers are at risk of leaving.

CRM reporting technologies   Help organizations identify their customers across other applications.

cross-selling   Selling additional products or services to an existing customer.

crowdsourcing   Refers to the wisdom of the crowd.

cryptography   The science that studies encryption, which is the hiding of messages so that only the sender and receiver can read them.

customer-facing process   Results in a product or service that is received by an organization's external customer.

customer relationship management (CRM)   A means of managing all aspects of a customer's relationship with an organization to increase customer loyalty and retention and an organization's profitability.

customer service and support (CSS)   A part of operational CRM that automates service requests, complaints, product returns, and information requests.

cyberbulling   Threats, negative remarks, or defamatory comments transmitted via the Internet or posted on a website.

cybermediation   Refers to the creation of new kinds of intermediaries that simply could not have existed before the advent of ebusiness.

cyberterrorism   The use of computer and networking technologies against persons or property to intimidate or coerce governments, individuals, or any segment of society to attain political, religious, or ideological goals.

cyberterrorists   Seek to cause harm to people or to destroy critical systems or information and use the Internet as a weapon of mass destruction.

cybervandalism   The electronic defacing of an existing website.

cyberwar   An organized attempt by a country's military to disrupt or destroy information and communication systems for another country.

cycle time   The time required to process an order.

D

data   Raw facts that describe the characteristics of an event or object.

data center   A facility used to house management information systems and associated components, such as telecommunications and storage systems.

data dictionary   Compiles all of the metadata about the data elements in the data model.

data element (or data field)   The smallest or basic unit of information.

data integration   The integration of data from multiple sources, which provides a unified view of all data.

data mart   Contains a subset of data warehouse information.

data mining   The process of analyzing data to extract information not offered by the raw data alone.

data-mining tool   Uses a variety of techniques to find patterns and relationships in large volumes of information that predict future behavior and guide decision making.

data model   Logical data structures that detail the relationships among data elements using graphics or pictures.

data quality audit   Determines the accuracy and completeness of its data.

data visualization   Describes technologies that allow users to "see" or visualize data to transform information into a business perspective.

data visualization tools   Moves beyond Excel graphs and charts into sophisticated analysis techniques such as pie charts, controls, instruments, maps, time-series graphs, etc.

data warehouse   A logical collection of information, gathered from many different operational databases, that supports business analysis activities and decision-making tasks.

database   Maintains information about various types of objects (inventory), events (transactions), people (employees), and places (warehouses).

database management system (DBMS)   Creates, reads, updates, and deletes data in a database while controlling access and security.

data-driven website   An interactive website kept constantly updated and relevant to the needs of its customers using a database.

decision support system (DSS)   Model information using OLAP, which provides assistance in evaluating and choosing among different courses of action.

decrypt   Decodes information and is the opposite of encrypted.

demand planning system   Generates demand forecasts using statistical tools and forecasting techniques, so companies can respond faster and more effectively to consumer demands through supply chain enhancements.

dependency   A logical relationship that exists between the project tasks, or between a project task and a milestone.

design phase   Establishes descriptions of the desired features and operations of the system including screen layouts, business rules, process diagrams, pseudo code, and other documentation.

destructive agents   Malicious agents designed by spammers and other Internet attackers to farm email addresses off websites or deposit spyware on machines.

development phase   Takes all the detailed design documents from the design phase and transforms them into the actual system.

development testing   Programmers test the system to ensure it is bug-free.

digital certificate   A data file that identifies individuals or organizations online and is comparable to a digital signature.

digital Darwinism   Implies that organizations that cannot adapt to the new demands placed on them for surviving in the information age are doomed to extinction.

digital dashboard   Tracks KPIs and CSFs by compiling information from multiple sources and tailoring it to meet user needs.

digital divide   A worldwide gap giving advantage to those with access to technology.

digital rights management   A technological solution that allows publishers to control their digital media to discourage, limit, or prevent illegal copying and distribution.

digital subscriber line (DSL)   Provides high-speed digital data transmission over standard telephone lines using broadband modem technology allowing both Internet and telephone services to work over the same phone lines.

disaster recovery cost curve   Charts (1) the cost to the company of the unavailability of information and technology and (2) the cost to the company of recovering from a disaster over time.

disaster recovery plan   A detailed process for recovering information or a system in the event of a catastrophic disaster.

discovery prototyping   Builds a small-scale representation or working model of the system to ensure it meets the user and business requirements.

disintermediation   Occurs when a business sells direct to the customer online and cuts out the intermediary.

disruptive technology   A new way of doing things that initially does not meet the needs of existing customers.

domain name hosting (web hosting)   A service that allows the owner of a domain name to maintain a simple website and provide email capacity.

domain name system (DNS)   Converts IP address into domains, or identifying labels that use a variety of recognizable naming conventions.

dot-com   The original term for a company operating on the Internet.

downtime   Refers to a period of time when a system is unavailable.

drill-down   Enables users to view details, and details of details, of information.

drive-by hacking   A computer attack where an attacker accesses a wireless computer network, intercepts data, uses network services, and/or sends attack instructions without entering the office or organization that owns the network.

dual boot   Provides the user with the option of choosing the operating system when the computer is turned on.

dumpster diving   Looking through people's trash, another way hackers obtain information.

dynamic catalog   An area of a website that stores information about products in a database.

dynamic host configuration protocol (DHCP)   Allows dynamic IP address allocation so users do not have to have a preconfigured IP address to use the network.

dynamic information   Includes data that change based on user actions. For example, static websites supply only information that will not change until the content editor changes the information.

dynamic scaling   Means that the MIS infrastructure can be automatically scaled up or down based on needed requirements.

E

ebook   An electronic book that can be read on a computer or special reading device.

ebusiness   Includes ecommerce along with all activities related to internal and external business operations such as servicing customer accounts, collaborating with partners, and exchanging real-time information.

ebusiness model   A plan that details how a company creates, delivers, and generates revenues on the Internet.

ecommerce   The buying and selling of goods and services over the Internet.

edge matching (warping, rubber sheeting)   Occurs when paper maps are laid edge to edge, and items that run across maps but do not match are reconfigured to match.

ediscovery (or electronic discovery)   Refers to the ability of a company to identify, search, gather, seize, or export digital information in responding to a litigation, audit, investigation, or information inquiry.

effectiveness MIS metrics   Measure the impact MIS has on business processes and activities including customer satisfaction and customer conversion rates.

efficiency MIS metrics   Measure the performance of MIS itself such as throughput, transaction speed, and system availability.

egovernment   Involves the use of strategies and technologies to transform government(s) by improving the delivery of services and enhancing the quality of interaction between the citizen-consumer within all branches of government.

eintegration   The use of the Internet to provide customers with the ability to gain personalized information by querying corporate databases and their information sources.

electronic data interchange (EDI)   A standard format for the electronic exchange of information between supply chain participants.

elogistics   Manages the transportation and storage of goods.

email privacy policy   Details the extent to which email messages may be read by others.

embedded operating system   Used for a single purpose in computer appliances and special-purpose applications, such as an automobile, ATM, or media player.

emergency   A sudden, unexpected event requiring immediate action due to potential threat to health and safety, the environment, or property.

emergency notification service   An infrastructure built for notifying people in the event of an emergency.

emergency preparedness   Ensures a company is ready to respond to an emergency in an organized, timely, and effective manner.

employee monitoring policy   States explicitly how, when, and where the company monitors its employees.

employee relationship management (ERM)   Provides web-based self-service tools that streamline and automate the human resource department.

encryption   Scrambles information into an alternative form that requires a key or password to decrypt.

energy consumption   The amount of energy consumed by business processes and systems.

enterprise application integration (EAI)   Connects the plans, methods, and tools aimed at integrating separate enterprise systems.

enterprise application integration (EAI) middleware   Takes a new approach to middleware by packaging commonly used applications together, reducing the time needed to integrate applications from multiple vendors.

enterprise architect   A person grounded in technology, fluent in business, and able to provide the important bridge between MIS and the business.

enterprise resource planning (ERP)   Integrates all departments and functions throughout an organization into a single IT system (or integrated set of IT systems) so employees can make decisions by viewing enterprisewide information about all business operations.

enterprise system   Provides enterprisewide support and data access for a firm's operations and business processes.

entity   Stores information about a person, place, thing, transaction, or event.

entity-relationship diagram (ERD)   A technique for documenting the entities and relationships in a database environment.

entry barrier   A feature of a product or service that customers have come to expect and entering competitors must offer the same for survival.

epolicies   Policies and procedures that address information management along with the ethical use of computers and the Internet in the business environment.

eprocurement   The business-to-business (B2B) online purchase and sale of supplies and services.

eshop (estore or etailer)   An online version of a retail store where customers can shop at any hour.

estimated-time-enroute (ETE)   The time remaining before reaching a destination using the present speed; typically used for navigation applications.

estimated-time-of-arrival (ETA)   The time of day of an expected arrival at a certain destination; typically used for navigation applications.

ethernet   A physical and data layer technology for LAN networking.

ethical computer use policy   Contains general principles to guide computer user behavior.

ethics   The principles and standards that guide our behavior toward other people.

ewaste   Refers to discarded, obsolete, or broken electronic devices.

executive information system (EIS)   A specialized DSS that supports senior-level executives and unstructured, long-term, nonroutine decisions requiring judgment, evaluation, and insight.

executive sponsor   The person or group who provides the financial resources for the project.

expert system   Computerized advisory programs that imitate the reasoning processes of experts in solving difficult problems.

explicit knowledge   Consists of anything that can be documented, archived, and codified, often with the help of IT.

extended ERP component   The extra components that meet organizational needs not covered by the core components and primarily focus on external operations.

extraction, transformation, and loading (ETL)   A process that extracts information from internal and external databases, transforms it using a common set of enterprise definitions, and loads it into a data warehouse.

extranet   An extension of an intranet that is only available to authorized outsiders, such as customers, partners, and suppliers.

extreme programming (XP) methodology   Breaks a project into four phases, and developers cannot continue to the next phase until the previous phase is complete.

F

fact   The confirmation or validation of an event or object.

failback   Occurs when the primary machine recovers and resumes operations, taking over from the secondary server.

failover   A specific type of fault tolerance, occurs when a redundant storage server offers an exact replica of the real-time data, and if the primary server crashes the users are automatically directed to the secondary server or backup server.

fault tolerance   A general concept that a system has the ability to respond to unexpected failures or system crashes as the backup system immediately and automatically takes over with no loss of service.

feasibility   The measure of the tangible and intangible benefits of an information system.

feedback   Information that returns to its original transmitter (input, transform, or output) and modifies the transmitter's actions.

fiber optic (or optical fiber)   Refers to the technology associated with the transmission of information as light impulses along a glass wire or fiber.

field   A characteristic of a table.

file transfer protocol (FTP)   A simple network protocol that allows the transfer of files between two computers on the Internet.

firewall   Hardware and/or software that guard a private network by analyzing incoming and outgoing information for the correct markings.

first-mover advantage   An advantage that occurs when a company can significantly increase its market share by being first to market with a competitive advantage.

flash memory   A special type of rewritable read-only memory (ROM) that is compact and portable.

folksonomy   Similar to taxonomy except that crowdsourcing determines the tags or keyword-based classification system.

forecasts   Predictions based on time-series information.

foreign key   A primary key of one table that appears as an attribute in another table and acts to provide a logical relationship between the two tables.

forward integration   Takes information entered into a given system and sends it automatically to all downstream systems and processes.

fourth-generation languages (4GL)   Programming languages that look similar to human languages.

fuzzy logic   A mathematical method of handling imprecise or subjective information.

G

Gantt chart   A simple bar chart that lists project tasks vertically against the project's time frame, listed horizontally.

genetic algorithm   An artificial intelligence system that mimics the evolutionary, survival-of-the-fittest process to generate increasingly better solutions to a problem.

geocache   A GPS technology adventure game that posts on the Internet the longitude and latitude location of an item for users to find.

geocoding   Spatial databases is a coding process that takes a digital map feature and assigns it an attribute that serves as a unique ID (tract number, node number) or classification (soil type, zoning category).

geocoin   A round coin-sized object that is uniquely numbered and hidden in geocache.

geographic information system (GIS)   Stores, views, and analyzes geographic data, creating multidimensional charts or maps.

gigabyte (GB)   Roughly 1 billion bytes.

gigahertz (GHz)   The number of billions of CPU cycles per second.

GIS map automation   Links business assets to a centralized system where they can be tracked and monitored over time.

global positioning system (GPS)   A satellite-based navigation system providing extremely accurate position, time, and speed information.

goal-seeking analysis   Finds the inputs necessary to achieve a goal such as a desired level of output.

goods   Material items or products that customers will buy to satisfy a want or need. Clothing, groceries, cell phones, and cars are all examples of goods that people buy to fulfill their needs.

granularity   Refers to the level of detail in the model or the decision-making process.

grid computing   A collection of computers, often geographically dispersed, that are coordinated to solve a common problem.

H

hackers   Experts in technology who use their knowledge to break into computers and computer networks, either for profit or motivated by the challenge.

hactivists   Have philosophical and political reasons for breaking into systems and will often deface the website as a protest.

hard drive   A secondary storage medium that uses several rigid disks coated with a magnetically sensitive material and housed together with the recording heads in a hermetically sealed mechanism.

hardware   Consists of the physical devices associated with a computer system

help desk   A group of people who respond to users' questions.

high availability   Occurs when a system is continuously operational at all times.

high-speed Internet cable connection   Provides Internet access using a cable television company's infrastructure and a special cable modem.

hot site   A separate and fully equipped facility where the company can move immediately after a disaster and resume business.

human resources ERP component   Tracks employee information including payroll, benefits, compensation, and performance assessment and ensures compliance with all laws.

hybrid cloud   Includes two or more private, public, or community clouds, but each cloud remains separate and is only linked by technology that enables data and application portability.

hypertext markup language (HTML) Links documents allowing users to move from one to another simply by clicking on a hot spot or link.

hypertext transport protocol (HTTP) The Internet protocol web browsers use to request and display web pages using universal resource locators.

I

identity theft The forging of someone's identity for the purpose of fraud.

IEEE 802.11n (or Wireless-N) The newest standard for wireless networking.

implementation phase The organization places the system into production so users can begin to perform actual business operations with it.

incident Unplanned interruption of a service.

incident management The process responsible for managing how incidents are identified and corrected.

incident record Contains all of the details of an incident.

infographics (information graphics) Displays information graphically so it can be easily understood.

information Data converted into a meaningful and useful context.

information age The present time, during which infinite quantities of facts are widely available to anyone who can use a computer.

information architecture The set of ideas about how all information in a given context should be organized.

information cleansing or scrubbing A process that weeds out and fixes or discards inconsistent, incorrect, or incomplete information.

information compliance The act of conforming, acquiescing, or yielding information.

information cube The common term for the representation of multidimensional information.

information ethics Govern the ethical and moral issues arising from the development and use of information technologies, as well as the creation, collection, duplication, distribution, and processing of information itself (with or without the aid of computer technologies).

information governance Refers to the overall management of the availability, usability, integrity, and security of company data.

information granularity The extent of detail within the information (fine and detailed or coarse and abstract).

information inconsistency Occurs when the same data element has different values.

information integrity A measure of the quality of information.

information integrity issue Occurs when a system produces incorrect, inconsistent, or duplicate data.

information management Examines the organizational resource of information and regulates its definitions, uses, value, and distribution ensuring it has the types of data/information required to function and grow effectively.

information MIS infrastructure Identifies where and how important information, such as customer records, is maintained and secured.

information privacy policy Contains general principles regarding information privacy.

information property An ethical issue that focuses on who owns information about individuals and how information can be sold and exchanged.

information reach Measures the number of people a firm can communicate with all over the world.

information redundancy The duplication of data, or the storage of the same data in multiple places.

information richness Refers to the depth and breadth of details contained in a piece of textual, graphic, audio, or video information.

information secrecy The category of computer security that addresses the protection of data from unauthorized disclosure and confirmation of data source authenticity.

information security plan Details how an organization will implement the information security policies.

information security policies Identify the rules required to maintain information security, such as requiring users to log off before leaving for lunch or meetings, never sharing passwords with anyone, and changing passwords every 30 days.

informing Accessing large amounts of data from different management information systems.

Infrastructure as a Service (IaaS) The delivery of computer hardware capability, including the use of servers, networking, and storage, as a service.

input device Equipment used to capture information and commands.

insiders Legitimate users who purposely or accidentally misuse their access to the environment and cause some kind of business-affecting incident.

in-sourcing (in-house development) Uses the professional expertise within an organization to develop and maintain its information technology systems.

instant messaging (sometimes called IM or IMing) A service that enables "instant" or real-time communication between people.

Institute of Electrical and Electronics Engineers (IEEE) An organization that researches and institutes electrical standards for communication and other technologies.

intangible benefits Difficult to quantify or measure.

integration Allows separate systems to communicate directly with each other, eliminating the need for manual entry into multiple systems.

integration testing Verifies that separate systems can work together passing data back and forth correctly.

integrity constraint Rules that help ensure the quality of information.

intellectual property Intangible creative work that is embodied in physical form and includes copyrights, trademarks, and patents.

intelligent agent A special-purpose knowledge-based information system that accomplishes specific tasks on behalf of its users.

intelligent system Various commercial applications of artificial intelligence.

interactivity Measures advertising effectiveness by counting visitor interactions with the target ad, including time spent viewing the ad, number of pages viewed, and number of repeat visits to the advertisement.

intermediaries Agents, software, or businesses that provide a trading infrastructure to bring buyers and sellers together.

Internet A massive network that connects computers all over the world and allows them to communicate with one another.

Internet censorship Government attempts to control Internet traffic, thus preventing some material from being viewed by a country's citizens.

Internet protocol TV (IPTV) Distributes digital video content using IP across the Internet and private IP networks.

Internet protocol version 6 (IPv6) The "next generation" protocol designed to replace the current version Internet protocol, IP version 4 (IPv4)

Internet service provider (ISP) A company that provides access to the Internet for a monthly fee.

Internet use policy Contains general principles to guide the proper use of the Internet.

interoperability   The capability of two or more computer systems to share data and resources, even though they are made by different manufacturers.

intranet   A restricted network that relies on Internet technologies to provide an Internet-like environment within the company for information sharing, communications, collaboration, web publishing, and the support of business process.

intrusion detection software (IDS)   Features full-time monitoring tools that search for patterns in network traffic to identify intruders.

IP address   A unique number that identifies where computers are located on the network.

iterative development   Consists of a series of tiny projects.

K

key performance indicators (KPIs)   Quantifiable metrics a company uses to evaluate progress towards critical success factors.

kill switch   A trigger that enables a project manager to close the project before completion.

knowledge   Skills, experience, and expertise coupled with information and intelligence that creates a person's intellectual resources.

knowledge management (KM)   Involves capturing, classifying, evaluating, retrieving, and sharing information assets in a way that provides context for effective decisions and actions.

knowledge management system (KMS)   Supports the capturing, organization, and dissemination of knowledge (i.e., know-how) throughout an organization.

knowledge worker   Individuals valued for their ability to interpret and analyze information.

L

latitude   Represents a north/south measurement of position.

legacy system   An old system that is fast approaching or beyond the end of its useful life within an organization.

list generator   Compiles customer information from a variety of sources and segments it for different marketing campaigns.

local area network (LAN)   Connects a group of computers in proximity, such as in an office building, school, or home.

location-based services (LBS)   Applications that use location information to provide a service.

logical view of information   Shows how individual users logically access information to meet their own particular business needs.

longitude   Represents an east/west measurement of position.

long tail   Referring to the tail of a typical sales curve.

loyalty program   A program to reward customers based on spending.

M

magnetic medium   A secondary storage medium that uses magnetic techniques to store and retrieve data on disks or tapes coated with magnetically sensitive materials.

magnetic tape   An older secondary storage medium that uses a strip of thin plastic coated with a magnetically sensitive recording medium.

mail bomb   Sends a massive amount of email to a specific person or system that can cause that user's server to stop functioning.

maintainability (or flexibility)   Refers to how quickly a system can transform to support environmental changes.

maintenance phase   The organization performs changes, corrections, additions, and upgrades to ensure the system continues to meet its business goals.

management information systems   A business function, like accounting and human resources, which moves information about people, products, and processes across the company to facilitate decision making and problem solving.

managerial level   Employees are continuously evaluating company operations to hone the firm's abilities to identify, adapt to, and leverage change.

many-to-many relationship (M:N)   Between two entities in which an instance of one entity is related to many instances of another and one instance of the other can be related to many instances of the first entity.

market basket analysis   Analyzes such items as websites and checkout scanner information to detect customers' buying behavior and predict future behavior by identifying affinities among customers' choices of products and services.

market share   The proportion of the market that a firm captures.

mashup   A website or web application that uses content from more than one source to create a completely new product or service.

mashup editor   WYSIWYGs or What You See Is What You Get tools.

mass customization   The ability of an organization to tailor its products or services to the customers' specifications.

megabyte (MB or M or Meg)   Roughly 1 million bytes.

megahertz (MHz)   The number of millions of CPU cycles per second.

memory cards   Contain high-capacity storage that holds data such as captured images, music, or text files.

memory sticks   Provide nonvolatile memory for a range of portable devices including computers, digital cameras, MP3 players, and PDAs.

metadata   Details about data.

Metcalfe's Law   The value of a network increases as its number of users grows.

methodology   A set of policies, procedures, standards, processes, practices, tools, techniques, and tasks that people apply to technical and management challenges.

metrics   Measurements that evaluate results to determine whether a project is meeting its goals.

metropolitan area network (MAN)   A large computer network usually spanning a city.

microblogging   The practice of sending brief posts (140 to 200 characters) to a personal blog, either publicly or to a private group of subscribers who can read the posts as IMs or as text messages.

middleware   Several different types of software that sit between and provide connectivity for two or more software applications.

MIS infrastructure   Includes the plans for how a firm will build, deploy, use, and share its data, processes, and MIS assets.

mobile business (or mbusiness, mcommerce)   The ability to purchase goods and services through a wireless Internet-enabled device.

model   A simplified representation or abstraction of reality.

modem   A device that enables a computer to transmit and receive data.

Moore's Law   Refers to the computer chip performance per dollar doubling every 18 months.

multiple-in/multiple-out (MIMO) technology   Multiple transmitters and receivers allow sending and receiving greater amounts of data than traditional networking devices.

multitasking   Allows more than one piece of software to be used at a time.

multi-tenancy   A single instance of a system serves multiple customers.

multi-valued attribute   Having the potential to contain more than one value for an attribute.

mutation   The process within a genetic algorithm of randomly trying combinations and evaluating the success (or failure) of the outcome.

N

national service providers (NSPs)   Private companies that own and maintain the worldwide backbone that supports the Internet.

nearshore outsourcing   Contracting an outsourcing arrangement with a company in a nearby country.

network   A communications system created by linking two or more devices and establishing a standard methodology in which they can communicate.

network access points (NAPs)   Traffic exchange points in the routing hierarchy of the Internet that connects NSPs.

network convergence   The efficient coexistence of telephone, video, and data communication within a single network, offering convenience and flexibility not possible with separate infrastructures.

network effect   Describes how products in a network increase in value to users as the number of users increases.

network operating system (NOS)   Operating system that runs a network, steering information between computers and managing security and users.

network topology   Refers to the geometric arrangement of the actual physical organization of the computers (and other network devices) in a network.

network transmission media   Refers to the various types of media used to carry the signal between computers.

network user license   Enables anyone on the network to install and use the software.

neural network   A category of AI that attempts to emulate the way the human brain works.

nonrepudiation   A contractual stipulation to ensure that ebusiness participants do not deny (repudiate) their online actions.

nonvolatile   Does not require constant power to function.

null-valued attribute   Assigned to an attribute when no other value applies or when a value is unknown.

O

object-oriented language   Languages group data and corresponding processes into objects.

offshore outsourcing   Using organizations from developing countries to write code and develop systems.

off-the-shelf application software   Supports general business processes and does not require any specific software customization to meet the organization's needs.

one-to-many relationship (1:M)   A relationship between two entities in which an instance of one entity can be related to many instances of a related entity.

one-to-one relationship (1:1)   A relationship between two entities in which an instance of one entity can be related to only one instance of a related entity.

online analytical processing (OLAP)   The manipulation of information to create business intelligence in support of strategic decision making.

online training   Runs over the Internet or on a CD or DVD, and employees complete the training on their own time at their own pace.

online transaction processing (OLTP)   The capturing of transaction and event information using technology to (1) process the information according to defined business rules, (2) store the information, and (3) update existing information to reflect the new information.

onshore outsourcing   Engaging another company within the same country for services.

open source   Refers to any software whose source code is made available free for any third party to review and modify.

open system   Consists of non-proprietary hardware and software based on publicly known standards that allows third parties to create add-on products to plug into or interoperate with the system.

operating system software   Controls the application software and manages how the hardware devices work together.

operational CRM   Supports traditional transactional processing for day-to-day front-office operations or systems that deal directly with the customers.

operational level   Employees develop, control, and maintain core business activities required to run the day-to-day operations.

opportunity management CRM system   Targets sales opportunities by finding new customers or companies for future sales.

optimization analysis   An extension of goal-seeking analysis, finds the optimum value for a target variable by repeatedly changing other variables, subject to specified constraints.

opt out   Customer specifically chooses to deny permission of receiving emails.

output device   Equipment used to see, hear, or otherwise accept the results of information processing requests

outsourcing   An arrangement by which one organization provides a service or services for another organization that chooses not to perform them in-house.

P

packet   A single unit of binary data routed through a network.

packet footer   Represents the end of the packet or transmission end.

packet header   Lists the destination (for example, in IP packets the destination is the IP address) along with the length of the message data.

packet-switching   Occurs when the sending computer divides a message into a number of efficiently sized units of data called packets, each of which contains the address of the destination computer.

paradigm shift   Occurs when a new radical form of business enters the market that reshapes the way companies and organizations behave.

parallel implementation   Uses both the legacy system and new system until all users verify that the new system functions correctly.

partner relationship management (PRM)   Discovers optimal sales channels by selecting the right partners and identifying mutual customers.

passive RFID tags   Do not have a power source.

patent   An exclusive right to make, use, and sell an invention granted by a government to the inventor.

pay-per-call   Generates revenue each time users click on a link that takes them directly to an online agent waiting for a call.

pay-per-click   Generates revenue each time a user clicks on a link to a retailer's website.

pay-per-conversion   Generates revenue each time a website visitor is converted to a customer.

peer-to-peer (P2P) network   A computer network that relies on the computing power and bandwidth of the participants in the network rather than a centralized server.

performance   Measures how quickly a system performs a process or transaction.

personal area networks (PAN) Provide communication over a short distance that is intended for use with devices that are owned and operated by a single user.

personal information management (PIM) Software handles contact information, appointments, task lists, and email.

personalization Occurs when a company knows enough about a customer's likes and dislikes that it can fashion offers more likely to appeal to that person, say by tailoring its website to individuals or groups based on profile information, demographics, or prior transactions.

PERT (Program Evaluation and Review Technique) chart A graphical network model that depicts a project's tasks and the relationships between them.

pharming Reroutes requests for legitimate websites to false websites.

pharming attack Uses a zombie farm, often by an organized crime association, to launch a massive phishing attack.

phased implementation Installs the new system in phases (for example, by department) until it is verified that it works correctly.

phishing A technique to gain personal information for the purpose of identity theft, usually by means of fraudulent emails that look as though they came from legitimate sources.

phishing expedition A masquerading attack that combines spam with spoofing.

physical security Tangible protection such as alarms, guards, fireproof doors, fences, and vaults.

physical view of information The physical storage of information on a storage device.

pilot implementation A small group uses the new system until it is verified that it works correctly, then the remaining users migrate to the new system.

pirated software The unauthorized use, duplication, distribution, or sale of copyrighted software.

planning phase Establishes a high-level plan of the intended project and determines project goals.

Platform as a Service (PaaS) Supports the deployment of entire systems including hardware, networking, and applications using a pay-per-use revenue model.

plunge implementation Discards the legacy system and immediately migrates all users to the new system.

podcasting Converts an audio broadcast to a digital music player.

portability Refers to the ability of an application to operate on different devices or software platforms, such as different operating systems.

Porter's Five Forces Model A model for analyzing the competitive forces within the environment in which a company operates, to assess the potential for profitability in an industry.

preventive maintenance Makes system changes to reduce the chance of future system failure.

primary key A field (or group of fields) that uniquely identifies a given record in a table.

primary storage Computer's main memory, which consists of the random access memory (RAM), cache memory, and read-only memory (ROM) that is directly accessible to the CPU.

primary value activities Found at the bottom of the value chain, these include business processes that acquire raw materials and manufacture, deliver, market, sell, and provide after-sales services.

privacy The right to be left alone when you want to be, to have control over your personal possessions, and not to be observed without your consent.

private cloud Serves only one customer or organization and can be located on the customers' premises or off the customer's premises.

product differentiation An advantage that occurs when a company develops unique differences in its products with the intent to influence demand.

production The process where a business takes raw materials and processes them or converts them into a finished product for its goods or services.

production and materials management ERP component Handles production planning and execution tasks such as demand forecasting, production scheduling, job cost accounting, and quality control.

productivity The rate at which goods and services are produced based upon total output given total inputs.

project Temporary activity a company undertakes to create a unique product, service, or result.

project assumption Factors considered to be true, real, or certain without proof or demonstration.

project constraint Specific factors that can limit options including budget, delivery dates, available skilled resources, and organizational policies.

project deliverable Any measurable, tangible, verifiable outcome, result, or item that is produced to complete a project or part of a project.

project management The application of knowledge, skills, tools, and techniques to project activities to meet project requirements.

project management office (PMO) An internal department that oversees all organizational projects.

project manager An individual who is an expert in project planning and management, defines and develops the project plan, and tracks the plan to ensure the project is completed on time and on budget.

project milestones Represent key dates when a certain group of activities must be performed.

project objective Quantifiable criteria that must be met for the project to be considered a success.

project plan A formal, approved document that manages and controls project execution.

project requirements document Defines the specifications for product/output of the project and is key for managing expectations, controlling scope, and completing other planning efforts.

project scope Describes the business needs and the justification, requirements, and current boundaries for the project.

project scope statement Links the project to the organization's overall business goals.

project stakeholder Individuals and organizations actively involved in the project or whose interests might be affected as a result of project execution or project completion.

protocol A standard that specifies the format of data as well as the rules to be followed during transmission.

prototyping A modern design approach where the designers and system users use an iterative approach to building the system.

proxy Software that prevents direct communication between a sending and receiving computer and is used to monitor packets for security reasons.

public cloud Promotes massive, global, industrywide applications offered to the general public.

public key encryption (PKE) Uses two keys: a public key that everyone can have and a private key for only the recipient.

Q

query-by-example (QBE) tool   Helps users graphically design the answer to a question against a database.

R

radio-frequency identification (RFID)   Uses electronic tags and labels to identify objects wirelessly over short distances.

random access memory (RAM)   The computer's primary working memory, in which program instructions and data are stored so that they can be accessed directly by the CPU via the processor's high-speed external data bus.

rapid application development (RAD) methodology (also called rapid prototyping)   Emphasizes extensive user involvement in the rapid and evolutionary construction of working prototypes of a system, to accelerate the systems development process.

rational unified process (RUP) methodology   Provides a framework for breaking down the development of software into four "gates."

read-only memory (ROM)   The portion of a computer's primary storage that does not lose its contents when one switches off the power.

real simple syndication (RSS)   A web format used to publish frequently updated works, such as blogs, news headlines, audio, and video in a standardized format.

real-time communication   Occurs when a system updates information at the same rate it receives it.

real-time information   Immediate, up-to-date information.

real-time system   Provides real-time information in response to requests.

record   A collection of related data elements.

recovery   The ability to get a system up and running in the event of a system crash or failure that includes restoring the information backup.

reduced instruction set computer (RISC) chips   Limits the number of instructions the CPU can execute to increase processing speed.

redundancy   Occurs when a task or activity is unnecessarily repeated.

regional service providers (RSPs)   Offer Internet service by connecting to NSPs, but they also can connect directly to each other.

reintermediation   Steps are added to the value chain as new players find ways to add value to the business process.

relational database management system   Allows users to create, read, update, and delete data in a relational database.

relational database model   Stores information in the form of logically related two-dimensional tables.

relational integrity constraint   Rules that enforce basic and fundamental information-based constraints.

reliability (or accuracy)   Ensures a system is functioning correctly and providing accurate information.

reputation system   Where buyers post feedback on sellers.

requirements definition document   Prioritizes all of the business requirements by order of importance to the company.

requirements management   The process of managing changes to the business requirements throughout the project.

responsibility matrix   Defines all project roles and indicates what responsibilities are associated with each role.

return on investment (ROI)   Indicates the earning power of a project.

RFID accelerometer   A device that measures the acceleration (the rate of change of velocity) of an item and is used to track truck speeds or taxi cab speeds.

RFID reader (RFID interrogator)   A transmitter/receiver that reads the contents of RFID tags in the area.

RFID tag   An electronic identification device that is made up of a chip and antenna.

rivalry among existing competitors   One of Porter's five forces; high when competition is fierce in a market and low when competitors are more complacent.

router   An intelligent connecting device that examines each packet of data it receives and then decides which way to send it toward its destination.

S

safe mode   Occurs if the system is failing and will load only the most essential parts of the operating system and will not run many of the background operating utilities.

sales force automation (SFA)   Automatically tracks all the steps in the sales process.

sales management CRM system   Automates each phase of the sales process, helping individual sales representatives coordinate and organize all their accounts.

satellite   A space station that orbits the Earth receiving and transmitting signals from Earth-based stations over a wide area.

scalability   Describes how well a system can scale up or adapt to the increased demands of growth.

script kiddies or script bunnies   Find hacking code on the Internet and click-and-point their way into systems to cause damage or spread viruses.

scripting language   A programming method that provides for interactive modules to a website.

scrum methodology   Uses small teams to produce small pieces of software using a series of "sprints," or 30-day intervals, to achieve an appointed goal.

search engine   Website software that finds other pages based on keyword matching.

search engine optimization (SEO)   Combines art along with science to determine how to make URLs more attractive to search engines, resulting in higher search engine ranking.

search engine ranking   Evaluates variables that search engines use to determine where a URL appears on the list of search results.

secondary storage   Consists of equipment designed to store large volumes of data for long-term storage.

secure hypertext transfer protocol (SHTTP or HTTPS)   A combination of HTTP and SSL to provide encryption and secure identification of an Internet server.

secure sockets layer (SSL)   A standard security technology for establishing an encrypted link between a web server and a browser, ensuring that all data passed between them remains private.

semantic web   A component of Web 3.0 that describes things in a way that computers can understand.

semi-passive RFID tags   Include a battery to run the microchip's circuitry, but communicate by drawing power from the RFID reader.

semistructured decision   Occurs in situations in which a few established processes help to evaluate potential solutions, but not enough to lead to a definite recommended decision.

sensitivity analysis   A special case of what-if analysis, is the study of the impact on other variables when one variable is changed repeatedly.

server   A computer dedicated to providing information in response to requests.

serviceability   How quickly a third party or vendor can change a system to ensure it meets user needs and the terms of any contracts, including agreed levels of reliability, maintainability or availability.

services   Tasks that customers will buy to satisfy a want or need.

shopping bot Software that will search several retailer websites and provide a comparison of each retailer's offerings including price and availability.

sign-off Users' actual signatures, indicating they approve all of the business requirements.

single-tenancy Each customer or tenant must purchase and maintain an individual system.

single-user license Restricts the use of the software to one user at a time.

single-valued attribute Having only a single value of each attribute of an entity.

site license Enables any qualified users within the organization to install the software, regardless of whether the computer is on a network. Some employees might install the software on a home computer for working remotely.

slice-and-dice The ability to look at information from different perspectives.

smart card A device about the size of a credit card, containing embedded technologies that can store information and small amounts of software to perform some limited processing.

smart grid Delivers electricity using two-way digital technology.

smartphones Offer more advanced computing ability and connectivity than basic cell phones.

social bookmarking Allows users to share, organize, search, and manage bookmarks.

social engineering Hackers use their social skills to trick people into revealing access credentials or other valuable information.

social media Refers to websites that rely on user participation and user-contributed content.

social media policy Outlines the corporate guidelines or principles governing employee online communications.

social network An application that connects people by matching profile information

social networking The practice of expanding your business and/or social contacts by constructing a personal network.

social networking analysis (SNA) Maps group contacts identifying who knows each other and who works together.

social tagging Describes the collaborative activity of marking shared online content with keywords or tags as a way to organize it for future navigation, filtering, or search.

software The set of instructions the hardware executes to carry out specific tasks.

Software as a Service (SaaS) Delivers applications over the cloud using a pay-per-use revenue model.

software customization Modifies software to meet specific user or business requirements.

software engineering A disciplined approach for constructing information systems through the use of common methods, techniques, or tools.

software updates (software patch) Occurs when the software vendor releases updates to software to fix problems or enhance features.

software upgrade Occurs when the software vendor releases a new version of the software, making significant changes to the program.

source code Contains instructions written by a programmer specifying the actions to be performed by computer software.

source document The original transaction record.

spam Unsolicited email.

spatial data (geospatial data or geographic information) Identifies the geographic location of features and boundaries on Earth, such as natural or constructed features, oceans, and more.

spear phishing A phishing expedition in which the emails are carefully designed to target a particular person or organization.

spyware A special class of adware that collects data about the user and transmits it over the Internet without the user's knowledge or permission.

SSL Certificate An electronic document that confirms the identity of a website or server and verifies that a public key belongs to a trustworthy individual or company.

standard packet format Includes a packet header, packet body containing the original message, and packet footer.

static information Includes fixed data that are not capable of change in the event of a user action.

statistical analysis Performs such functions as information correlations, distributions, calculations, and variance analysis.

status report Periodic reviews of actual performance versus expected performance.

strategic level Managers develop overall business strategies, goals, and objectives as part of the company's strategic plan.

streaming A method of sending audio and video files over the Internet in such a way that the user can view the file while it is being transferred.

streamlining Improves business process efficiencies simplifying or eliminating unnecessary steps.

structured data Data already in a database or a spreadsheet.

structured decision Involves situations where established processes offer potential solutions.

structured query language (SQL) Users write lines of code to answer questions against a database.

stylus A pen-like device used to tap the screen to enter commands.

supplier power One of Porter's five forces; measures the suppliers' ability to influence the prices they charge for supplies (including materials, labor, and services).

supplier relationship management (SRM) Focuses on keeping suppliers satisfied by evaluating and categorizing suppliers for different projects.

supply chain All parties involved, directly or indirectly, in obtaining raw materials or a product.

supply chain execution system Ensures supply chain cohesion by automating the different activities of the supply chain.

supply chain management (SCM) The management of information flows between and among activities in a supply chain to maximize total supply chain effectiveness and corporate profitability.

supply chain planning system Uses advanced mathematical algorithms to improve the flow and efficiency of the supply chain while reducing inventory.

supply chain visibility The ability to view all areas up and down the supply chain in real time.

support value activities Found along the top of the value chain and includes business processes, such as firm infrastructure, human resource management, technology development, and procurement, that support the primary value activities.

sustainable MIS disposal Refers to the safe disposal of MIS assets at the end of their life cycle.

sustainable MIS infrastructure Identifies ways that a company can grow in terms of computing resources while simultaneously becoming less dependent on hardware and energy consumption.

sustainable, or "green," MIS Describes the production, management, use, and disposal of technology in a way that minimizes damage to the environment.

sustaining technology   Produces an improved product customers are eager to buy, such as a faster car or larger hard drive.

swim lane   Layout arranges the steps of a business process into a set of rows depicting the various elements.

switching costs   Costs that make customers reluctant to switch to another product or service.

synchronous communication   Communications that occur at the same time such as IM or chat.

system   A collection of parts that link to achieve a common purpose.

system clock   Works like a wristwatch and uses a battery mounted on the motherboard to provide power when the computer is turned off.

system restore   Enables a user to return to the previous operating system.

system software   Controls how the various technology tools work together along with the application software.

system testing   Verifies that the units or pieces of code function correctly when integrated.

systems development life cycle (SDLC)   The overall process for developing information systems, from planning and analysis through implementation and maintenance.

systems thinking   A way of monitoring the entire system by viewing multiple inputs being processed or transformed to produce outputs while continuously gathering feedback on each part.

T

table   Composed of rows and columns that represent an entity.

tacit knowledge   The knowledge contained in people's heads.

tag   Specific keywords or phrases incorporated into website content for means of classification or taxonomy.

tangible benefits   Easy to quantify and typically measured to determine the success or failure of a project.

taxonomy   The scientific classification of organisms into groups based on similarities of structure or origin.

technology failure   Occurs when the ability of a company to operate is impaired because of a hardware, software, or data outage.

technology recovery strategies   Focus specifically on prioritizing the order for restoring hardware, software, and data across the organization that best meets business recovery requirements.

teergrubing   Anti-spamming approach where the receiving computer launches a return attack against the spammer, sending email messages back to the computer that originated the suspected spam.

telecommunication system   Enables the transmission of data over public or private networks.

telecommuting (virtual workforce)   Allows users to work from remote locations such as a home or hotel, using high-speed Internet to access business applications and data.

terabyte (TB)   Roughly 1 trillion bytes.

test condition   Details the steps the system must perform along with the expected result of each step.

testing phase   Brings all the project pieces together into a special testing environment to eliminate errors and bugs and verify that the system meets all the business requirements defined in the analysis phase.

text mining   Analyzes unstructured data to find trends and patterns in words and sentences.

threat   An act or object that poses a danger to assets.

threat of new entrants   One of Porter's five forces, high when it is easy for new competitors to enter a market and low when there are significant entry barriers to joining a market.

threat of substitute products or services   One of Porter's five forces, high when there are many alternatives to a product or service and low when there are few alternatives from which to choose.

time bombs   Computer viruses that wait for a specific date before executing instructions.

time-series information   Time-stamped information collected at a particular frequency.

To-Be process model   Shows the results of applying change improvement opportunities to the current (As-Is) process model.

tokens   Small electronic devices that change user passwords automatically.

traceroute   A utility application that monitors the network path of packet data sent to a remote computer.

transaction processing system (TPS)   The basic business system that serves the operational level (analysts) and assists in making structured decisions.

transactional information   Encompasses all of the information contained within a single business process or unit of work, and its primary purpose is to support the performing of daily operational or structured decisions.

transmission control protocol/Internet protocol (TCP/IP)   Provides the technical foundation for the public Internet as well as for large numbers of private networks.

twisted-pair cable   Refers to a type of cable composed of four (or more) copper wires twisted around each other within a plastic sheath.

typosquatting   A problem that occurs when someone registers purposely misspelled variations of well-known domain names.

U

unavailable   When a system is not operating or cannot be used.

unified communications (UC)   The integration of communication channels into a single service.

unit testing   Testing individual units or pieces of code for a system.

universal resource locator (URL)   The address of a file or resource on the web such as www.apple.com.

unstructured data   Data that do not exist in a fixed location and can include text documents, PDFs, voice messages, emails, etc.

unstructured decision   Occurs in situations in which no procedures or rules exist to guide decision makers toward the correct choice.

up-selling   Increasing the value of the sale.

usability   The degree to which a system is easy to learn and efficient and satisfying to use.

user acceptance testing (UAT)   Determines if the system satisfies the user and business requirements.

user-contributed content (also referred to as user-generated content)   Content created and updated by many users for many users.

user documentation   Highlights how to use the system and how to troubleshoot issues or problems.

utility computing   Offers a pay-per-use revenue model similar to a metered service such as gas or electricity.

utility software   Provides additional functionality to the operating system.

V

value chain analysis   Views a firm as a series of business processes that each add value to the product or service.

variable   A data characteristic that stands for a value that changes or varies over time.

videoconference Allows people at two or more locations to interact via two-way video and audio transmissions simultaneously as well as share documents, data, computer displays, and whiteboards.

virtual private network (VPN) Companies can establish direct private network links among themselves or create private, secure Internet access, in effect a "private tunnel" within the Internet.

virtual reality A computer-simulated environment that can be a simulation of the real world or an imaginary world.

virtualization Creates multiple "virtual" machines on a single computing device.

vishing (or voice phishing) A phone scam that attempts to defraud people by asking them to call a bogus telephone number to "confirm" their account information.

visualization Produces graphical displays of patterns and complex relationships in large amounts of data.

virus Software written with malicious intent to cause annoyance or damage.

voice over IP (VoIP) Uses IP technology to transmit telephone calls.

volatile Must have constant power to function; contents are lost when the computer's electric supply fails.

volatility Refers to a device's ability to function with or without power.

vulnerability A system weakness that can be exploited by a threat; for example, a password that is never changed or a system left on while an employee goes to lunch.

W

war chalking The practice of tagging pavement with codes displaying where Wi-Fi access is available.

war driving Deliberately searching for Wi-Fi signals from a vehicle.

warm site A separate facility with computer equipment that requires installation and configuration.

waterfall methodology A sequence of phases in which the output of each phase becomes the input for the next.

Web 1.0 (or Business 1.0) Refers to the World Wide Web during its first few years of operation between 1991 and 2003.

Web 2.0 (or Business 2.0) The next generation of Internet use—a more mature, distinctive communications platform characterized by new qualities such as collaboration, sharing, and free.

web accessibility Means that people with disabilities—including visual, auditory, physical, speech, cognitive, and neurological disabilities—can use the web.

web accessibility initiative (WAI) Brings together people from industry, disability organizations, government, and research labs from around the world to develop guidelines and resources to help make the web accessible to people with disabilities, including auditory, cognitive, neurological, physical, speech, and visual disabilities.

web browser Allows users to access the WWW.

web conferencing (webinar) Blends videoconferencing with document-sharing and allows the user to deliver a presentation over the web to a group of geographically dispersed participants.

web mining Analyzes unstructured data associated with websites to identify consumer behavior and website navigation.

web-based self-service system Allows customers to use the web to find answers to their questions or solutions to their problems.

website bookmark A locally stored URL or the address of a file or Internet page saved as a shortcut.

website name stealing The theft of a website's name that occurs when someone, posing as a site's administrator, changes the ownership of the domain name assigned to the website to another website owner.

website personalization Occurs when a website has stored enough data about a person's likes and dislikes to fashion offers more likely to appeal to that person.

what-if analysis Checks the impact of a change in a variable or assumption on the model.

white-hat hackers Work at the request of the system owners to find system vulnerabilities and plug the holes.

wide area network (WAN) Spans a large geographic area such as a state, province, or country.

Wi-Fi infrastructure Includes the inner workings of a Wi-Fi service or utility, including the signal transmitters, towers, or poles, along with additional equipment required to send a Wi-Fi signal.

Wi-Fi protected access (WPA) A wireless security protocol to protect Wi-Fi networks.

wiki A type of collaborative web page that allows users to add, remove, and change content, which can be easily organized and reorganized as required.

wire media Transmission material manufactured so that signals will be confined to a narrow path and will behave predictably.

wired equivalent privacy (WEP) An encryption algorithm designed to protect wireless transmission data.

wireless access point (WAP) Enables devices to connect to a wireless network to communicate with each other.

wireless fidelity (Wi-Fi) A means by which portable devices can connect wirelessly to a local area network, using access points that send and receive data via radio waves.

wireless LAN (WLAN) A local area network that uses radio signals to transmit and receive data over distances of a few hundred feet.

wireless MAN (WMAN) A metropolitan area network that uses radio signals to transmit and receive data.

wireless media Natural parts of the Earth's environment that can be used as physical paths to carry electrical signals.

wireless WAN (WWAN) A wide area network that uses radio signals to transmit and receive data.

workflow Includes the tasks, activities, and responsibilities required to execute each step in a business process.

workplace MIS monitoring Tracks people's activities by such measures as number of keystrokes, error rate, and number of transactions processed.

workshop training Held in a classroom environment and led by an instructor.

World Wide Web (WWW) Provides access to Internet information through documents including text, graphics, audio, and video files that use a special formatting language called HTML.

Worldwide Interoperability for Microwave Access (WiMAX) A communications technology aimed at providing high-speed wireless data over metropolitan area networks.

Z

zombie A program that secretly takes over another computer for the purpose of launching attacks on other computers.

zombie farm A group of computers on which a hacker has planted zombie programs.